FAST

FAST: FACETED APPLICATION OF SUBJECT TERMINOLOGY

Principles and Applications

LOIS MAI CHAN AND EDWARD T. O'NEILL

LIBRARIES UNLIMITED

AN IMPRINT OF ABC-CLIO, LLC
Santa Barbara, California • Denver, Colorado • Oxford, England

Library of Congress Cataloging-in-Publication Data

Chan, Lois Mai.
    FAST, Faceted Application of Subject Terminology : principles and applications / Lois Mai Chan and Edward T. O'Neill.
        p. cm.
    Includes bibliographical references and index.
    ISBN 978-1-59158-722-4 (acid-free paper)
    1. FAST subject headings   2. World Wide Web—Subject access.
3. Metadata. I. O'Neill, Edward T.   II. Title.
    Z695.Z8F373   2010
    025.4'9—dc22   2010015675

ISBN: 978-1-59158-722-4

14 13 12 11 10   1 2 3 4 5

This book is also available on the World Wide Web as an eBook.
Visit www.abc-clio.com for details.

Libraries Unlimited
An Imprint of ABC-CLIO, LLC

ABC-CLIO, LLC
130 Cremona Drive, P.O. Box 1911
Santa Barbara, California 93116-1911

This book is printed on acid-free paper ∞

Manufactured in the United States of America

CONTENTS

Preface   xv

Part I: Introduction

1   Information Organization: Approaches and Principles   3

Introduction   3
Information Searching Environments   3
   The Internet   3
   Online Databases   4
   Library Catalogs and Bibliographies   4
Subject Access to Information   4
   Keyword Searching   5
   Controlled Vocabulary Access   5
   Keyword and Controlled Vocabulary Search Results   6
   Classification   7
Principles of Controlled Vocabulary   7
   Uniform and Unique Headings   8
   Consistent and Current Terminology   9
   Specific Entry   9
Terminological Control and Term Relationships   9
Representation of Complex Subjects   10
Characteristics of Indexing Languages   11
   Subdivision Practice   11
   Enumerative versus Synthetic Languages   11
   Faceting   13
   Precoordination versus Postcoordination   14

From Cards to Computers   15
   Card Catalogs   15
   Online Catalogs and Databases   17
Controlled Vocabulary Systems   17
   Library of Congress Subject Headings (LCSH)   19
   Medical Subject Headings (MeSH)   20
   FAST (Faceted Application of Subject Terminology)   21
Selecting an Indexing/Classification Schema   22
   Compatibility with Existing Metadata   22
   Ease of Assignment   22
   Retrieval Effectiveness   22
   Cost of Maintenance   22
Conclusion   23

2   Metadata Encoding   25

Bibliographic Data   25
   Print Representation   25
      Book Catalogs   25
      Card Catalogs   26
   Digital Representation   26
      The MARC Bibliographic Formats   28
         MARC 21   28
         MARC Record Structure   29
         UNIMARC   36
      XML (Extensible Markup Language)   36
         MARCXML   38
         MODS   38
      Dublin Core   39
Authority Data   44
   Print Representation   44
   Digital Representation   44
      MARC 21   44
      Other MARC Authority Formats   46
      SKOS   46
Conclusion   48

Part II: FAST Headings

3   Introduction to FAST   53

Impact of the Internet and the World Wide Web   53
The History of FAST   55
Sources of FAST Headings   56
Principles   56
   Semantics   56
      Common and Current Usage   57
      Literary Warrant   57

Uniform Heading 57
Unique Heading 58
Syntax of Headings 59
Faceting 59
Enumeration versus Synthesis 60
Precoordination versus Postcoordination 60
Precoordination 61
Postcoordination 62
Heading Structure 62
Main Headings 62
Subdivisions 63
Qualifiers 63
Modular Approach 64
Conclusion 64

4   Topical Headings 67

Introduction 67
Functions of Topical Headings 67
Forms of Topical Headings 67
Single-Concept Headings 68
Single-Word Headings 68
Multiple-Word Headings 69
Adjectival Phrase Headings 69
Prepositional Phrase Headings 70
Multiple-Concept Headings 71
Compound Phrase Headings 71
Prepositional Phrase Headings 72
Headings with Subdivisions 72
Types of Topical Headings 73
Headings Representing Concepts and Objects 73
Form/Genre as Subjects 73
Fictitious, Legendary, and Mythological Characters 73
Named Animals 75
Imaginary Places and Organizations 75
Geologic Periods 75
Other Entities Bearing Proper Names 76
Inverted Headings 76

5   Geographic Headings 77

Introduction 77
Types of Geographic Headings 77
Jurisdictional Headings 77
Nonjurisdictional Headings 78

Changes of Name   78
    Linear Name Changes   79
    Mergers or Splits   79
        Mergers   79
        Splits   79
Language and Form of Geographic Headings   80
    Language   80
    Abbreviations   81
    Grammatical Form   81
Qualifiers   81
    Place Qualifiers   82
    Type Qualifiers   82
    Place and Type Qualifiers   83
Levels of Geographic Headings   84
    First-Level Geographic Headings   84
    Second-Level Geographic Headings   85
    Third-Level Geographic Headings   86
        City Sections and Neighborhoods   86
        New York City Boroughs   87
        London Boroughs   87
        Areas Associated with Cities   89
        Entities within Cities   89
        Bridges and Tunnels   90
Special Cases   90
    Extinct Cities and Ancient Kingdoms   90
    Archaeological Sites   91
    Bodies of Water   92
    Islands   93
    Interstates/Highways/Freeway Interchanges   94
    Disputed Territories   94
    Language-Based Territories   94
    Parks, Reserves, and so Forth   94
    *Other Man-Made Structures Associated with
        Places Larger Than a City*   95
    Extraterrestrial Bodies   95
Latitude, Longitude, and Feature Type   96

6   Chronological Headings   99

Introduction   99
Forms of Chronological Headings   99
    B.C./A.D.   100
    Geologic Periods   101
    Headings for Named Historical Periods   101
Chronological Headings Containing Dates Only   101

7	Headings for Events	103
	Introduction	103
	Forms of Event Headings	103
	Language	103
	Qualifiers	104
	Types of Event Headings	105
	Headings for Military Conflicts	105
	Headings for Meetings	106
	Headings for Sporting Events	107
	Headings for Other Events	108
	Chronological and Geographic Headings for Events	109
8	Proper Names as Subject Headings	111
	Headings for Persons	111
	Principles	111
	Names of Individual Persons	111
	Names of Families	112
	Names of Dynasties, Royal Houses, and so Forth	113
	Headings for Corporate Bodies	114
	Principles	114
	Forms of Headings for Corporate Bodies	114
	Language	114
	Qualifiers	115
	Headings for Main Corporate Bodies	116
	Governments	116
	Nongovernment Bodies	116
	Headings for Subordinate Bodies	117
	Corporate Name Changes	118
	Headings for Titles	119
	Principles	119
	Forms of Headings for Titles	119
	Language	119
	Qualifiers	120
	Types of Headings for Titles	121
	Anonymous Works	121
	Works of Known Authorship	121
	Works from Corporate Bodies, Conferences, Meetings, Etc.	122
9	Form and Genre Headings	123
	Introduction	123
	Principles	123
	Forms of Form and Genre Headings	124
	Main Heading	124
	Subdivision	124

Examples of FAST Form and Genre Headings   125
   General Form Headings   125
   Audiovisual Materials   126
   Art   126
   Cartography   126
   Law   127
   Literature   127
   Music   127
   Religion   128

10   Cross-References   129

Introduction   129
Equivalence Relationship   130
   Synonymous Terms   130
   Variant Spellings   131
   Abbreviations, Acronyms, Initials, and so Forth   131
   Different Language Terms   132
   Popular and Scientific Terms   133
   Alternative Forms   133
   Different Entry Elements   133
   Narrow Terms Not Used as Headings   134
   Ambiguous Relationships   134
Hierarchical Relationships   135
   Genus/Species (or Class/Class Member) Relationship 136
   Instance Relationship   136
   Whole/Part Relationship   136
   Compound and Complex Relationship   136
Associative Relationships   137
Cross-References for Proper Name Headings   138
   Personal Names   138
      Names of Individual Persons   138
      Family Names   139
      Names of Fictitious and Mythological Characters 139
      Dynasties   139
      Houses of Dukes, Counts, or Earls   140
   Corporate Names   140
   Geographic Names   140
      Jurisdictional Names   140
      Nonjurisdictional Names   141
      Changes in Geographic Names   141
   Headings for Other Named Entities   142
   Headings for Events   143
   Headings for Titles   144
Conclusion   144

Part III: Application of FAST

11   The FAST Database   147

Indexing Overview   147
Queries   149
Searching   150
   Keywords in Headings   150
   Advanced Searching   152
      Phrase Searching   152
      Keyword Searching   154
      Geographic Indexes   156
      Other Indexes   159
   Index View   159

12   Application of FAST Headings   161

Introduction   161
Coding for FAST Headings in Bibliographic Records   162
   MARC Records   162
   Dublin Core Records   162
Exhaustivity in Cataloging or Indexing   164
Assigning FAST Headings   172
   Identifying Concepts and Facets within the Topic   172
      Selecting Form/Genre Headings   173
      Selecting Subject Headings   173
         Topical Headings   173
            Works on a Single Topic   173
            Works on Multiple Topics   173
            Works on Complex Topics   174
            Topics with Multiple Concepts   174
         Geographic Headings   175
         Chronological Headings   176
         Name Headings   176
         Title Headings   177
   Topics with Multiple Facets   177
   Subject Relations   179
FAST Application Examples   179
   Example 1: People and Predators: from
      Conflict to Coexistence   180
   Example 2: Daily Life in Colonial New England   183
   Example 3: Style and the Nineteenth-century British Critic:
      Sincere Mannerisms   186
   Example 4: Fife and Tayside   189
   Example 5: Anne Frank: Reflections on Her Life
      and Legacy   191

Example 6: 2005 Hydrographic Survey of
    South San Francisco Bay, California [Web site]   195
Example 7: Shakespeare in the Victorian Periodicals   198
Example 8: Portrait of an Unknown Woman   200
Example 9: The Pretender   203
Example 10: First Emperor of China [DVD]   206
Example 11: Japan: Economic, Political and Social Issues   209
Example 12: Detours [Audio CD]   211

Part IV: Authority Control and Implementation

13   Derivation of FAST Headings   217

     Background   217
     Topical Headings   217
       Enumeration of Assigned Headings   217
       Validation   218
         Recoding of Forms   218
         Normalization   219
         LCSH Authority File   220
         Subdivisions   221
     Geographic Headings   222
     Event Headings   226
       Event Headings Derived from Topical Headings   226
       Event Headings Derived from Period Subdivisions   227
       Event Headings Derived from LCSH Conferences
         and Meetings Names   229
     Headings for Names of Persons and Families   229
     Headings for Names of Corporate Bodies   230
     Headings for Titles   230
       Works of Anonymous Authorship   230
       Works of Personal Authorship   231
       Works of Corporate Bodies   231
       Works from Conferences and Meetings   232
     Chronological Headings   232
     Form Headings   232

14   FAST Authority Records   235

     Introduction   235
     Authority Data   235
     Authority Records   235
       MARC Record Structure for Authorities   236
     Creation of FAST Authority Records   236
       Example 1. Vestischer Künstlerbund Recklinghausen   238
       Example 2. David D. Smyers   239
       Example 3. Battle of Agincourt   240
       Example 4. Ferryboat Captains   241

Example 5. Columbus Dispatch   242

Example 6. McConnelsville   243

Example 7. Infants—Diseases—Patients   244

Additional Examples of FAST Authority Records   246

  Topical Headings   246

  Geographic Headings   247

  Chronological Headings   248

  Personal Name Headings   249

  Corporate Headings   250

  Event Headings   251

  Title Headings   253

  Form/Genre Headings   254

Normalization   254

Conflicts   256

Additional Validation   257

Obsolete Authority Records   257

15 Authority Control   261

Definition   261

Need for Authority Control   262

Validation   262

Correction   264

  Stylistic   264

  Tagging and Subfield Coding   264

  Cross-References   264

  Typographical Errors   265

  Obsolete Headings   265

Conclusion   266

16 Faceting LCSH into FAST   267

Introduction   267

Identification and Recoding of Form Subdivisions   267

Algorithmic Faceting of LCSH to FAST   269

  Faceting of Forms   270

  Faceting of Titles   270

    Titles of Anonymous Works   270

    Titles for Works of Known Authorship   271

  Faceting of Events   271

  Faceting of Geographic Names   272

    Main Headings   272

    Subdivisions   272

  Faceting of Personal Names   273

  Faceting of Corporate Names   273

  Faceting of Chronologicals   273

  Faceting of Topicals   273

Reference Records   274
Validation   276
Conclusion   279

Appendixes

Appendix A: FAST Authority Records Structure   281
Appendix B: Geologic Periods   291
Appendix C: Geographic Names   293
Appendix D: Musical Instruments   331

Glossary   337

Bibliography   341

Index   345

About the Authors   355

PREFACE

Late in the 1990s, those interested in information retrieval began to recognize that, with the continuing rapid growth of digital resources and the emergence of numerous metadata schemes for their description, there was a strong need for subject access methods that could handle a large volume of resources with less effort and at lower cost than is the case with traditional subject cataloging. The need for such a system was also recognized within the library community, and in 1999 a subcommittee of the American Library Association recommended developing a simplified schema that could be applied by indexers not trained in subject cataloging.[1]

In 1999, while searching for a subject access system that would be compatible with Dublin Core metadata records, OCLC, a large organization that has figured prominently in the library-oriented sector of the information world and has been responsible for many innovations in information storage and retrieval for almost half a century, began exploring a new approach to subject analysis and representation that could optimize the use of technology in information retrieval. The result was the development of FAST (Faceted Application of Subject Terminology). The Library of Congress also recognized the need for subject headings that could be easily applied beyond traditional library catalogs. In particular, the Library of Congress sought to extend the use of Library of Congress Subject Headings (LCSH), the most widely used indexing vocabulary, to the metadata being created for online digital information. The Library of Congress's expertise with controlled vocabularies and OCLC's experience in applying computer technology led to an obvious partnership. The two organizations agreed to jointly develop, maintain, and test FAST. Almost 10 years after work began, the initial development of FAST is complete.

Today an enormous store of information is easily available through a few keystrokes to anyone with a computer and access to the Internet. In quantity, today's information is perhaps greater by a power of 10 than what was available to the public 50 years ago. The significance of this fact becomes obvious upon realizing that, in the information world of the 1960s, specific items of information could usually be garnered only laboriously, through libraries and through other sources of written texts such as encyclopedias, dictionaries, newspapers, magazines, books, bibliographies, serial indexes, or abstracting and indexing services. Now, in the first decade of the 21st century, people encounter enormous stores of information that challenge their ability to retrieve and manage it. FAST has been devised as a system to help manage the huge amount of information and retrieve any specific information when needed.

This book introduces and explains FAST. It addresses the following aspects of FAST: background and rationale, sources of vocabulary, facets and encoding, application guidelines, authority control, user access and interface, and recent developments. The book is intended for readers who are interested in learning about or applying FAST as an indexing vocabulary. It is also aimed at systems managers in a wide variety of information environments, managers who may eventually find FAST an economical means of attaining considerably improved search results. The authors believe FAST to be of interest to managers in a wide range of information retrieval environments, from Internet and Web operations to more or less traditional library settings, plus for almost all text-based metadata systems.

The scope of this book is the development of FAST, including its beginning in 1999, the principles underlying the system, and the structure governing the vocabulary as a whole and the individual facets in particular. The book reports on the structure of the vocabulary and its application, as well as the mechanism used in controlling and maintaining that vocabulary.

The book is divided into four parts. In each part, the historical development and underlying principles of the retrieval mechanism at issue are addressed first, because these are considered essential to an understanding of the system. Discussion on and examples of each facet are then presented in order to illustrate its application in the representation of the subject content and form/genre of information resources.

The first part consists of chapters 1 and 2 and provides a brief overview of the general approaches and principles of information organization in the current age as well as different methods used in providing subject access to information within the context of the information environment in general, followed by a review of the principles and a brief account of some of the current systems of controlled vocabulary. Chapter 1 concludes with an account of application environments and general criteria for selecting an indexing or subject cataloging schema. Chapter 2 introduces and explains the systems for encoding both bibliographic and authority data.

The second part consists of chapters 3 through 10 and presents a detailed description of FAST. Chapter 3 discusses the history, sources, principles, and structure of FAST. Chapters 4 through 9 present the eight facets in the FAST schema: topic, place, event, time, names of persons, corporate bodies, titles of works, and form/genre. The structure and form of each facet are explained in detail with ample examples. Chapter 10 explains the semantic relationships among FAST headings: relationships commonly found in controlled vocabularies, including equivalence, hierarchical, and associative relationships.

The third part consists of chapters 11 and 12. Chapter 11 describes the FAST database, including the available search options. Chapter 12 presents general guidelines and examples regarding the assignment of FAST headings to represent the subject content of information resources. It explains and illustrates the use of FAST headings in the two major types of metadata records—MARC records and

Dublin Core records—with numerous examples showing FAST headings in metadata records.

The fourth part consists of chapters 13 through 16 and presents the technical aspects of FAST. Discussion in these chapters focuses on the derivation of FAST headings from LCSH. Chapter 13 explains the process of identifying and establishing the FAST headings. Chapter 14 covers the function and structure of FAST authority records. Chapter 15 explains the operation of authority control and the creation and maintenance of the authority database and records. Chapter 16 explains how LCSH are faceted into FAST headings.

The appendixes contain tables and additional details about FAST.

The authors are indebted to many individuals for their contributions to the FAST project in general and to the contents of this book in particular. Lynn El-Hoshy, former Senior Cataloging Policy Specialist in the Cataloging Policy and Support Office of the Library of Congress, provided invaluable information regarding the LCSH system and the Library of Congress policies for its application. The OCLC team that developed the FAST schema (Anya Arnold, Rick Bennett, Eric Childress, Kay Clopton, Becky Dean, Kerre Kammerer, Chris Stanton, and Diane Vizine-Goetz) has made invaluable contributions to the existence of the schema as well as to the contents of this book.

We would also like to acknowledge the support of both the Library of Congress and OCLC for their continuing backing and assistance in the development of FAST. In addition, we wish to acknowledge the generous help of the following: Dr. Theodora L. Hodges for her assistance in proofreading the entire manuscript and making numerous editorial suggestions, Chris Stanton for proofreading and formatting the manuscript for publication, and Mary K. Hall and Jennifer Nicole Green for proofreading. We are also grateful for the counsel and support of the Subcommittee on FAST (a part of the Subject Analysis Committee of the Association of Library Collections and Technical Services) and particularly its previous chair, Qiang Jin.

To all those already mentioned, we wish to express our deepest gratitude and appreciation.

Lois Mai Chan
University of Kentucky

Edward T. O'Neill
OCLC

NOTE

1. Association for Library Collections and Technical Services, Cataloging and Classification Section, Subject Analysis Committee, Subcommittee on Metadata and Subject Analysis. *Subject Data in the Metadata Record: A Report from the ALCTS/CCS/SAC/Subcommittee on Metadata and Subject Analysis Working Draft, July 1999,* http://www.ala.org/ala/mgrps/divs/alcts/mgrps/ccs/cmtes/subjectanalysis/metadataandsubje/subjectdata.cfm (accessed April 15, 2010).

Part I

—◆·▪·◆—

INTRODUCTION

1

INFORMATION ORGANIZATION: APPROACHES AND PRINCIPLES

INTRODUCTION

An enormous store of information is easily available with a few keystrokes to anyone who has access to the Internet. The amount of information available today is not only enormously greater than what was available to the public 50 years ago but is also still growing at an unimaginable pace. The significance of this fact becomes obvious upon realizing that, in the information world of the 1960s, specific information could usually be retrieved only laboriously, through libraries and through other sources such as encyclopedias, dictionaries, newspapers, magazines, books, bibliographies, serial indexes, or abstracting and indexing services.

INFORMATION SEARCHING ENVIRONMENTS

The information world of the early 21st century is complex, with many independent agencies and factors contributing to the overall picture. The situation is perhaps made more easily understandable through the realization that information resources and activities can be grouped into three major sectors. One is represented by the Internet, another by the online information database industry, and the third by libraries, archives, museums, and so forth. At the base of the current rich store of available information are huge general-content databases of digitized materials ranging from Google's very large stock of materials to catalogs showing coded descriptive records of the contents of major libraries. There are also many special-content databases. Each of these sectors is constantly searching for improved and more cost-effective means of making information available to those who seek it.

The Internet

The Internet holds an enormous store of digital information from different sources and created by different communities, including government agencies, public and private organizations and corporations, academic institutions, and individuals.

Some sources provide universal access; others are privately owned and are restricted in access.

In recent years, the Internet has become a key player in the information world. The first appearance of the term *Internet* was during the mid-1970s. In 1989, a new system was in development at the European Organization for Nuclear Research (CERN) in Switzerland; it combined hypertext and Internet technologies and was called the *World Wide Web*. CERN released the Web in 1991 to enthusiastic popular acclaim. The Web has become a dominant force in information seeking and retrieval ever since.

Online Databases

Many databases are privately held, accessible only by subscription or at a cost to the users. But many others are available to the public directly through the Web or indirectly through library portals. Many serve academic, professional, or business communities. Typical online information databases are of the A&I (abstracting and indexing) nature.

Library Catalogs and Bibliographies

Access to materials and resources in libraries, archives, museums, and so forth, is provided through catalogs (library catalogs are now called Online Public Access Catalogs, or OPACs). Before the online age, catalogs and bibliographies represented the major means of access to organized information.

SUBJECT ACCESS TO INFORMATION

In terms of information retrieval, there are primarily two types of databases: full-text and surrogates. *Full-text* databases, as the term implies, contain all the words in whatever items they hold. For instance, Google, in addition to its enormous store of electronic resources, has digitized a significant fraction of the holdings of many academic and research libraries. Full-text searching became a reality only after the advent of computer technology and online databases. In full-text keyword searching, users submit query terms that are matched against an index of the full text of the items in the database of the system offering the search service.

Still other information databases hold brief descriptions, called *surrogates*, of each held resource. A surrogate is a record (variously called an index record, a cataloging record, a bibliographic record, or a metadata record), that contains a brief description of the information item, usually including terms representing document content. In OPACs and abstracting and indexing databases, for example, surrogates of books, articles, Web sites and many other types of materials are coded in records that carry information on what the item is *about*. They also contain other bibliographical data such as title or name, author or other creator, and other facts such as where the item can be found. Subject information (i.e., what the content is *about*) is usually conveyed by *controlled vocabulary*—that is, standardized words or phrases called *descriptors* or *subject headings*. Topical information is also carried in classification numbers; furthermore, some surrogate records include tables of contents, summaries, or abstracts.

Information databases are also organized in different ways; in fact, some hardly seem organized at all. Because many are proprietary, details on database management are not always available. Library materials are typically arranged by classification, using systems such as the Dewey Decimal Classification and the Library of Congress Classification. Many search engines also provide classificatory or hierarchical approaches through directories with different degrees of elaboration. One of the earliest and most sophisticated is Yahoo! The base of its name, which is an acronym for "yet another hierarchical officious oracle," reflects the organizing principle of the very popular search engine.[1]

In information retrieval, there are two main ways to bridge the gap between databases and searchers sitting at their keyboards. The most common access method is keyword searching; the other is controlled vocabulary searching. A third method, used less often now than the others, is through classification.

Keyword Searching

Keyword searching, also called free-text searching, refers to information retrieval by means of words from natural language. In this approach, any word or word combination, with the exception of a number of the most commonly occurring words in a particular language, may be used as search terms. Logical operators (also called Boolean operators) such as "and," "or," and "and not" are an added option in most systems. Once keywords are entered, systems respond with lists of items that match the terms submitted. (Users who also submit synonyms of their original keywords often increase their relevant search output significantly.) Keyword or natural language searching is the prevalent mode of information retrieval on the Internet and in online databases.

One advantage of keyword searching is that information may be retrieved using authors' own words, which often reflect the most current terminology in a particular subject field. A second advantage is that keyword searching is fast and easy, and many users are satisfied with its search results. A major drawback, however, is that if searchers wish to retrieve all information, or as much information as possible, on a given subject, they must search on all the synonyms for that subject. A second problem is that most keyword searches result in many irrelevant items because many words or phrases have multiple meanings.

Controlled Vocabulary Access

Before the advent of the online age, when full-text searching became a reality, information retrieval was typically done with surrogate records or indexes through controlled vocabulary terms—that is, words or phrases designated or assigned to represent the content of information items. The assigned terms (words or phrases) are typically stored in a subject heading list or thesaurus and are assigned to surrogates as content indicators. When these subject terms are assigned from a standardized list of preferred terms—that is, terms chosen specifically for the purpose of indexing—the process is called controlled vocabulary indexing and access.

Controlled vocabularies are term lists in which there are no synonyms in the main list. Rather, one term from a set of synonyms is chosen as the preferred term. Its synonyms (called "cross-references," "see references," "lead-in" terms, or "nonpreferred terms") are included in the list as a means of directing users to the preferred term. Thus, if **Teenagers** is a preferred term, a controlled vocabulary list will include synonyms as lead-in terms. *Teens* and *Adolescents*, for instance, would appear in the same list with a note to those who tried to use one of them to "see" or "use" (in other words, search) **Teenagers** instead. In an increasing number of access systems, such "use" or "see" references are hidden from searchers in the sense that if searchers submit "Adolescents," the system switches the search to "Teenagers" without alerting users to the switch.

Another aspect of controlled vocabularies is that homographs are distinguished from each other—for example, **Rings (Algebra)** and **Rings (Gymnastics).** Furthermore, almost all terms in the list are provided with a rich and generous array of cross-references. Since most systems are hierarchical, the references (which include the already described references from lead-in terms to the preferred term) lead searchers to broader terms and to narrower terms as well as to related terms at the same level of specificity. The process of authorizing or establishing selected words and phrases as valid index terms and providing cross-references is called *authority control* in the library field. The tool for maintaining authority control is called an *authority file,* a list or database consisting of *authority records,* each containing an authorized index term and its cross-references.

Library of Congress Subject Headings (LCSH) is the largest and most widely used of all extant subject heading lists. As used here, LCSH refers to the LCSH schema broadly and encompasses both the syntax rules and the list of headings including headings for names in the LC/NAF authority file that can be used as subjects. It is widely used and adapted and translated into numerous languages because of its carefully designed and well-executed authority control system. It is maintained rigorously by the Library of Congress.

Controlled vocabulary searches are usually applied to library catalogs and journal indexes consisting of document surrogates. In a controlled vocabulary search, the user's search term is matched against controlled vocabulary terms assigned by indexers to document surrogates. Such terms have been specifically chosen to reflect full document content. They may or may not be the exact words used by the author.

Controlled vocabulary access depends on two circumstances:

1. The existence of a controlled vocabulary such as LCSH.
2. The assignment of terms from that vocabulary list to represent the contents of documents in a collection or database. (Assigning subject terms to documents is called *subject indexing* or *subject cataloging.*)

Keyword and Controlled Vocabulary Search Results

Search results using keywords on full texts and using controlled vocabularies in surrogate-based systems are quite different. Keyword searching is quick and easy, and very popular. But the search results contain only items matching submitted terms. Because many topics are known by many terms—for example, *chaff, waste, garbage, refuse, rubbish, trash, discards, remains, wastrel, dross*—a keyword search of one of them will deliver only those items whose authors used that particular term in their works. In other words, if a searcher uses words not chosen by the author to represent the same object or concept, many relevant items will not be retrieved.

Another aspect of keyword searching is that output lists can be very long: a recent Google search on "cancer" retrieved over 24 million items. Keyword searches may also, and often do, contain many items that are not only poor matches but also useless for the topic the searcher had in mind.

The situation with controlled vocabulary searching is quite different. In the library world, controlled vocabulary searching—used in card or book catalogs early on—has been the norm for over 200 years; after all, it is only since the advent of digitized databases and easy access to them that keyword searching has even been a possibility. The purpose of using a controlled vocabulary is to enable a search to deliver a high proportion of material in the database searched that pertains to the topic indicated by a user's query term and to minimize irrelevant results. In information retrieval, there have long been two opposing goals:

Recall: The proportion of all relevant items in the database that are retrieved. (A good search delivers a high proportion of the items in the database that are a fair match for the query term submitted.)

Precision: The proportion of items retrieved that are relevant. (A high proportion of the items retrieved should be relevant, with few false hits.)

Controlled vocabulary searches usually rank high on the first count; that is, they do not miss much relevant material that is in the database because all material that might reasonably be listed under one or another of a set of synonyms has been gathered under the controlled term. Furthermore, possible ambiguity is limited because terms that have different meanings in different contexts—such as **Expansion (Game)** and **Expansion (Heat)**—are put in context by the addition of parenthetical terms called *qualifiers*. For the same reasons that controlled vocabulary searches score high on recall, they also perform well on precision by minimizing irrelevant material.

Classification

The third method for subject access, one that is less frequently used now than in the past, is through classification numbers or codes. Browsing library shelves was once a very popular retrieval approach. With books on a target topic in hand, or with just their class numbers, searchers browsed shelves for books with numbers before and after the starting number. This approach was satisfactory because the classification systems that govern the order of books on library shelves group similar topics together, from the more general to the more specific. Class-number browsing is still possible in libraries with their full collections on open shelves. Class-number searching is also possible, without the ambience, in OPACs that offer searching in the class-number fields of their surrogates.

PRINCIPLES OF CONTROLLED VOCABULARY

As has been noted, in a system employing controlled vocabulary, specific words or phrases designated as subject index terms are assigned to a document surrogate to represent the content of the resource. Such terms are stored; that is, they remain in the surrogate. Each term normally represents only one concept or object, and a given concept or object is normally represented by only one term.

As mentioned earlier, a controlled vocabulary system depends on a master list of predetermined terms that can be assigned to documents. For most library catalogs, manual or online, these are called *subject headings*; for many abstracting and indexing systems, they are called *descriptors* or perhaps simply *preferred* or *authorized* terms. Preferred terms are maintained in a *subject heading list* or *thesaurus*, which lists the subject access terms to be used in the cataloging or indexing operation at hand. (In some writings on information retrieval, the terms "subject heading list" and "thesaurus" are used interchangeably. In others, the term "thesaurus" is typically reserved for lists of single-concept terms called *descriptors*.) A subject heading list may contain both single-concept terms for single topics and multiple-concept strings, or main topics with subdivisions, for complex subjects. These terms are called *subject headings*.

When one term among synonyms is chosen as the preferred term (called *subject heading* or *descriptor*), the rest are included in the list as lead-in terms with *see* or *use* references that direct searchers to the preferred term. Authorized terms that are related in meaning are also linked by references: while the links from lead-in terms are called *use* or *see* references, the links to related terms are called broader term (BT), narrower term (NT), and related term (RT) references as appropriate. Further details regarding controlled vocabulary will be given later in this chapter.

Over the years, theorists and practitioners in the library field realized that retrieval effectiveness would be increased if certain principles were followed in designing their controlled vocabulary systems and so moved toward standardization. The general principles governing controlled vocabularies are summarized in the following sections.

Uniform and Unique Headings

In order to show what a collection or a database has on a given subject, a controlled vocabulary must adopt a principle of *uniform headings* (in library usage "heading" denotes an authorized term). That is, the vocabulary must bring under one index term all the material dealing principally or exclusively with that particular subject. In other words, only one preferred term should be used for a given concept or object, and no term should be used for more than one concept or object. If a concept or object has more than one name ("ascorbic acid" and "Vitamin C," for instance), one must be chosen as the valid or authorized term. In general, it is hoped that the term chosen is unambiguous and familiar to all users of the catalog or index. Similarly, if there are variant spellings of the same term (e.g., "archaeology" and "archeology") or different possible forms for the same concept or object (e.g., "snow boarding" versus "snowboarding") only one is used as the authorized term, with the others listed as cross-reference terms.

The converse of the principle of uniform headings is the principle of *unique headings*; that is, the same term should not be used to represent more than one concept or object. If the same term must be used in more than one sense, as is often the case when different disciplines or fields of knowledge are involved, some qualification or clarification must be added so that it will be clear to the user which meaning is intended—for example, **Mercury (Roman deity)** and **Mercury (Planet),** or **Rings (Mathematics)** and **Rings (Astronomy)**.

Consistent and Current Terminology

Preferred terms should be current and should conform to general usage in the context in which the controlled vocabulary list will be used. Because usage changes, a well-maintained subject heading list must be continuously updated to remove obsolete headings and replace them with current terms. Furthermore, a term selected as the "preferred term" from a set of synonyms should be consistent in level with other preferred terms; in other words, decisions to use popular terms instead of scientific terms or vice versa should be consistent, not random. Of course, the more specialized a particular collection and clientele are, the more specialized its indexing terminology should be; therefore, different disciplines or communities, such as health sciences, art, and education, often develop their own controlled vocabularies in the form of subject heading lists or thesauri.

Specific Entry

Preferred terms included in a controlled vocabulary should be as specific as (that is, no narrower or broader than) the topics they are intended to cover. The same principle holds for assigning topical terms to a document surrogate. Thus, the principle of *specific entry* governs both how controlled vocabulary terms are formed (thesaurus construction and maintenance) as well as how they are assigned to documents (indexing or subject cataloging).

TERMINOLOGICAL CONTROL AND TERM RELATIONSHIPS

As mentioned earlier, in a particular controlled vocabulary, each concept or object is represented by only one authorized term, regardless of how many other terms (synonyms) also represent the same concept or object. In order to enable a searcher to retrieve all resources about a particular concept or object, synonyms, which of course may be used as search queries, must be brought under control. Conversely, the same word or term may have multiple meanings, which is another problem for searchers. Furthermore, searchers often use a search term that is either too broad or too restrictive with regard to the subject sought; sometimes, also, the search term chosen by the searcher may not be the best for representing the subject being sought. A controlled vocabulary attempts to minimize the adverse effects of these conditions through controlling synonyms and homographs and through providing related terms.

National and international standards such, as NISO (National Information Standards Organization) and ISO (International Organization for Standardization), for constructing controlled vocabularies typically stress two different types of term relationships (commonly called *cross-references*): (1) those represented by synonyms and homographs, and (2) those related by either hierarchy (broader or narrower topics) or by proximity (overlapping topics at the same hierarchical level in the same or a different hierarchy).

In a catalog or an index using subject terms from a controlled vocabulary list, cross-references used to connect semantically related terms are essential. Three common types of term relationships (equivalent, hierarchical, and associative) are expressed in *cross-references* in a controlled vocabulary structure:

1. Equivalent (synonyms)—*see from* (or *UF*) references from lead-in terms to preferred term
2. Hierarchical (broader terms or narrower terms)—*see also* (or *BT* or *NT*) references
3. Associative (related terms)—*see also* (or *RT*) references

REPRESENTATION OF COMPLEX SUBJECTS

The subject content of an information resource or a document may consist of:

1. A single topic or concept, or multiple topics or concepts treated separately in a work (e.g., *Women; Women and children*)
2. An aspect or aspects of a topic or concept (e.g., *Self-defense for women; Social work with women*)
3. Two or more topics or concepts treated in relation to each other (e.g., *Television and women; Technology and women; Effects of violence on women*)

From this list, it is clear that except for single topics or concepts, the subject content of a work cannot always or even often be represented by a single word or a simple adjectival phrase. When this is the case, other means must be used in order to be as specific as possible.

In many cases, a phrase is used to combine two or more general terms, either of which is broader than the resulting heading (e.g., *Church and state; Intelligence testing for children; Fertilization of flowers*). Another way to represent complexity is to use two or more separate terms without indicating the nature of their relationship; for example, a document might be assigned the two separate terms, *Flowers* and *Fertilization*. Such an approach leaves it to searchers or end users to infer document content from the sum of separately assigned terms without indication of interrelationship. There may be ambiguity at this stage of the retrieval process: the two terms *Fertilization* and *Flowers* may suggest either a work on pollination by bees or one on commercial fertilizers for flowers.

When document content is multitopical, as it is in a book on, say, available psychotherapeutic treatments for traumatized war veterans, a suitable heading or set of headings may need to include more than simple words and word phrases. The term used by both grammarians and librarians for combining words to reflect wanted meaning is *syntax*, which in essence means the way in which words are put together to form phrases or clauses. (*Syn-* is a Greek prefix meaning "together with"; *taxo-* is a Greek stem meaning "arrangement.")

At the heart of the *syntax* concept is the representation of complex subjects through combination, or coordination, of terms representing different topics or different aspects or facets (defined as families of concepts that share a common characteristic) of a topic.[2] In subject representation, while a single topic may be expressed with a single word or a phrase, a complex topic is almost always expressed in the English language with multiple words. When and how to combine individual words to represent multiple or complex topics in a document is a central issue in both the design of a vocabulary and in its application.

For complex topics, term combination can occur at various stages in the process of information storage and retrieval:

1. During vocabulary construction
2. At the stage of cataloging or indexing
3. At the point of retrieval (where it is the searcher who infers content)

CHARACTERISTICS OF INDEXING LANGUAGES

Subdivision Practice

In some controlled vocabularies, a main heading may be subdivided by one or more elements called *subdivisions*. Languages that allow subdivision usually have a list of standard subdivisions that have broad application, and most such languages have additional lists of terms that may be used for subdivision under specific situations. Subdivisions are delineated from other parts of the heading by a special character or code such as the long or em (—) dash.

Subdivisions can bring out specialized aspects of a topic and thus increase the specificity of an index term. For example, if there is a heading for **Librarians** but the focus is on librarians' unions, the subdivision **Labor unions** could be appended to form **Librarians—Labor unions.** An alternate to the subdivision practice is simply to create a more specific main heading such as *Librarians' unions*. In either case, the scope of the resulting heading is similar. In this case, the advantages of subdividing are that occupational groups and types of employees receive similar treatment, a hierarchal relationship is established, and retrieval is enhanced.

Enumerative versus Synthetic Languages

Vocabularies for a fully *enumerative language* contain exhaustive lists of all permitted terms. These authoritative lists of permitted terms are generally referred to as *authority files*. For a *synthetic language*, some of the terms are created as needed, following the syntax rules (i.e., rules for combining individual terms to form complex expressions). Elaine Svenonius states, "The enumerative-synthetic distinction is between languages whose allowable expressions are listed in an authority file and languages whose expressions can be created from a basic core vocabulary using the syntax rules of the language."[3] In an enumerative system, the vocabulary builder, rather than the indexer or the user, is responsible for establishing the term.

In a fully enumerative system, all index terms authorized for use are established and included in the authority file. Svenonius states that a language is enumerative if "all expressions in it that can be used for indexing or searching are listed in the vocabulary tool such as a thesaurus" and that all of its "expressions are editorially established—that is, established by the designer of the language rather than by the indexers who apply it."[4]

By contrast, for synthetic languages, only a set of core terms is established, but those terms can be combined or extended following the synthetic languages rules. LCSH is an example of a synthetic language in the sense that there is no comprehensive list of terms or headings. LCSH, six volumes in its most recent print edition, contains a set of core headings as well as many precombined complex headings, called *subject heading strings*. LCSH is accompanied by a four-volume manual of rules detailing the policies and requirements for creating headings that are not explicitly established in the list and for the further subdivision of many of the core headings.

The LCSH heading **Burns and scalds—Patients—Family relationships** is an example of how a heading can be formed from the core set of terms. **Burns and scalds** is a core term that can be combined with other terms to create a more complex heading. The synthetic rules allow certain subdivisions to be added to the core set of established headings. Such rules often limit the types of headings to which a particular subdivision can be added. The combination **Burns and scalds—Patients—Family relationships** is formed by adding two subdivisions to the established core term **Burns and scalds.** The subdivision **Patients** is one of several hundred subdivisions that can be combined with headings for diseases and other medical conditions, so it can be used to subdivide **Burns and scalds.** Since the subdivision **Family relationships** may be added to headings representing classes of people only, it could not have been added directly to **Burns and scalds,** which is not a class of people. However, the addition of **Patients** after **Burns and scalds** changes the meaning of the heading from that of a medical condition to a class of people, and therefore **Family relationships** can be added.

In an enumerative language, the complete heading **Burns and scalds—Patients—Family relationships** would be established and included in an authority file. This shifts the editorial burden from the indexers who apply the language to the editors who design and control the language. The advantage of enumerative languages is that they are much easier to use by both indexers and searchers. The assignment of terms from synthetic languages is generally more complex since, in addition to determining what heading best describes the work, the heading itself must be formed following a complex set of synthetic rules. Complex rules, such as those for LCSH, can be very difficult to apply correctly and consistently. Enumerative languages also tend to result in more consistent and higher quality indexes because the misinterpretation or application of complex rules is a primary cause of erroneous headings.

Early controlled vocabularies were enumerative and consisted of exhaustive lists of valid terms. However, as the volume of material to be covered increased and the subject matter treated became more complicated, vocabulary size grew to the point that lists became difficult to manage. For most of the 20th century and before, size mattered. Print was the primary means of distributing vocabularies, and the size of the printed lists for enumerative languages became unmanageable. As of the end of 2007, the Library of Congress had used nearly 3.5 million different subject headings in its bibliographic records. In print form, over 50 large volumes would be required to list all of these headings. Thus, as vocabularies grew, it became impractical to print every heading, and many languages began the practice of only enumerating a core set of terms and creating the other headings in accordance with instructions.

In the 20th century, in what Svenonius called the "the most significant trend in subject-language development in the twentieth century,"[5] we saw a shift from enumerative to synthetic languages. Today only about 8% of the LCSH headings are enumerated in the subject authority file; the remaining 92% of the LCSH headings that have been assigned were formed by subject catalogers following the synthetic rules.

However, by the late 20th century and certainly by the 21st century, the importance of print files for either access or distribution faded, fundamentally altering what we think of as large. Massive vocabularies that would have required numerous printed volumes can easily be stored on a DVD or loaded onto smartphones, iPods, and laptops; we can now say, "What was large is now small." Furthermore, ubiquitous high-speed wireless communications, such as Wi-Fi and third generation cellular (3G), have eliminated much of the need to distribute vocabularies—they are only a keystroke away.

If size is no longer a major factor, synthetic languages offer few advantages in the online environment. As indexing languages become more widely available and are being applied in more environments, ease of application has overtaken vocabulary size in importance. While synthetic languages have served libraries and their patrons well for over a century, their complexity greatly restricts their use beyond the traditional cataloging environment. Because of the complexity of the synthetic rules, their successful application requires extensive experience and domain knowledge. This shift in focus from keeping the size of the vocabulary manageable to making the language easier to apply is likely to result in a shift back to the earlier enumerative language patterns.

Faceting

When individual terms in the controlled vocabulary are divided into distinctive categories or facets, such as thing/object, place, time, and form, the list is called *faceted*. Svenonius states, "Facets are groupings of terms obtained by the first division of a subject discipline into homogeneous or semantically cohesive categories."[6] In a faceted system, terms are listed in separate groups, each group representing a facet that contains terms that share the same characteristic, such as concept, object, time, place, language, genre, and so on.

Most indexing languages group terms into several broad categories. LCSH uses six distinct categories: personal names, corporate names, conference and meeting names, uniform titles, geographic names, and topics. The report on the Functional Requirements for Bibliographic Records (FRBR) proposed similar categories but replaced topic with three facets: concept, object, and event.[7]

Simply grouping the indexing terms is not sufficient to produce a faceted indexing language—the terms within categories must also be semantically cohesive. Svenonius further explains that for a language to be semantically cohesive, "terms in it [i.e., a facet] are related by paradigmatic relationships of synonymy and hierarchy, and the totality of facets used in the subject language are mutually exclusive."[8] Faceted languages can be hierarchical, but the terms can only be subdivided by other terms within the same category or facet. Using the FRBR categories, the following headings would meet the requirements of a faceted language:

Ohio—Columbus *[Place—Place]*
Operations research—Mathematical models *[Concept—Concept]*
World War II—Battle of the Bulge *[Event—Event]*

While LCSH headings are grouped into six categories based on their main heading, headings such as the following would not be considered faceted since they include subdivisions from different facets than the main heading:

Minorities—Education—Brazil—Congresses *[Topic—Topic—Place—Form]*
Library use studies—Sweden—Göteborg *[Topic—Place—Place]*
Slovenia—History—1945–1990 *[Place—Topic—Period]*

Across different indexing languages, there are no uniform definitions for facets and there is considerable variation in how specific terms are categorized. For example, one indexing language may consider the *Battle of the Bulge* to be a topic, while another language may treat it as an event.

Precoordination versus Postcoordination

Two more terms are often encountered in works on controlled vocabularies and their application. While enumeration and synthesis describe the nature of the vocabulary list, *precoordination* and *postcoordination* refer to how and when the index terms are combined. In a precoordinated system, it may be the list constructors who precombine terms from the core list. It may also be catalogers or indexers who work under system guidelines to produce complex terms at the indexing stage when no adequate term can be found in the term list. By contrast, in a postcoordinated system, single-facet headings or terms are listed separately both in the vocabulary list and in the metadata record. Consequently, the searchers must combine the terms at the point of retrieval.

The following examples show the different approaches to subject representation in cataloging and metadata records. The index terms assigned to represent the topic "church and state in Austria in the 18th century from the Catholic perspective" may be stored in the cataloging or metadata records, either as a single precoordinated heading:

Church and state—Catholic Church—Austria—18th century

or as three faceted (postcoordinated) headings:

Church and state—Catholic Church *[Topic]*
Austria *[Place]*
18th century *[Period]*

In the first example, all aspects of the subject are combined, either when constructing the vocabulary list or when the document is indexed, to create a single precoordinated subject heading. The second example illustrates the faceted approach in which terms are assigned as separate headings that are intended to be postcoordinated by the searcher at the time of retrieval.

Postcoordinated systems are more flexible than precoordinated systems for several reasons, the most cogent being that computer searching enables Boolean and other sophisticated operations to perform the combination of search terms. Precoordinated headings such as those included in LCSH were originally designed for and used in card and book catalogs. Postcoordination was impossible in the print environment, so early indexing and cataloging practice relied heavily on precoordination. In today's online environment, the advantages of postcoordination can be realized.

Although in principle the paired concepts enumerative/synthetic, faceted/ nonfaceted, and precoordination/postcoordination are independent, in practice they are closely linked. Most precoordinated languages are unfaceted and synthetic. For precoordinated languages, the number of possible headings is nearly infinite. If a language has 100,000 topics and 100,000 geographic names, there are 10 billion possible combinations using just these two facets. Combining additional facets—time, genre, and so forth—would result in nearly an infinite number of possible headings. For precoordinated headings, the only practical approach is to establish a core set of headings and create additional headings as needed following the synthetic rules of the language.

Precoordinated headings can be single-entry specific in order to, as Svenonius states, "produce subject headings conceptually coextensive with the documents they describe."[9] In principle, a single precoordinated heading is sufficient to index a document. However, in practice, it is common to use more than a single heading. Almost by definition, faceting and precoordination are incompatible since a single precoordinated heading must include elements from different facets. Faceting represents the alternate approach—it calls for assigning terms from different facets as separate headings. Since faceted headings are less complex, more headings may be required to index the document at the same level of specificity.

FROM CARDS TO COMPUTERS

Indexing and subject cataloging are used for a variety of reasons and in a number of different environments. Most subject heading schema and thesauri in common use today were originally designed to function in a print environment, either in the form of card catalogs or printed book indexes. Today these print indexes have largely been replaced by machine-readable indexes. However, to appreciate the features of the various schemas, it is helpful to understand the environments for which they were originally designed.

Card Catalogs

Card catalogs were almost universally used in libraries until the latter part of the 20th century. A typical card describing the book *Cataloging and Classification: An Introduction* is shown in Figure 1.1. Catalog cards have strict formatting requirements. The upper left portion contains the call number, in this example, the Library of Congress classification number Z693.5 U6C48. The top line is used for the author's name (i.e., the *main entry*). The body is used to describe the book and includes information such as the title, publisher, edition, and so forth. The last two lines on the card are for *added entries* (i.e., additional terms used to index the book).

Each term required that a separate card be printed and filed in the catalog. Complete cataloging for this book would require five cards, each of which would be filed separately in the catalog. Two copies of the card as shown would be required; one would be filed by the call number in the *shelflist*, a separatecatalog arranged by class number order, and the second would be filed by the main entry (the author's name) in the public catalog. Separate cards would also be produced for each of the three added entries, the two subject headings and the title shown at the bottom of the card. For the two subject heading cards, the subject headings would be typed at the top, often in red to identify them as subject headings. Examples of the two subject cards are also shown in Figure 1.2.

While this approach served libraries very well for many years, it imposed some significant limitations on subject heading schemas. Most significantly, since each heading required its own card, the number of subject headings that could be assigned was greatly restricted—usually one to three. Since only a few headings could be assigned, it was desirable to make each heading as explicit as possible.

```
Z693.5   Chan, Lois Mai.
U6C48      Cataloging and classification: an
         introduction / Lois Mai Chan. -- 2nd ed.
         New York : McCraw-Hill, c1994.
           xxii, 519 p. : ill. ; 24 cm.

           Includes bibliographical references (p.
         493-502) and index.
           ISBN 0-07-010506-5

           1.  Cataloging--United States.   2.  Class-
         ification--Books.   I.   Title.
```

Figure 1.1. Typical Catalog Card

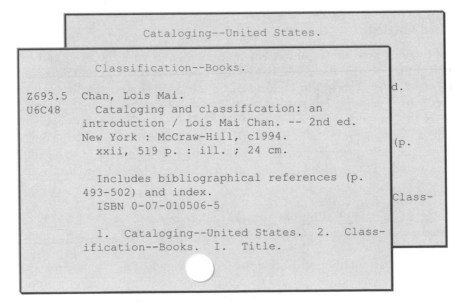

```
         Cataloging--United States.

           Classification--Books.
                                                    d.
Z693.5   Chan, Lois Mai.
U6C48      Cataloging and classification: an
         introduction / Lois Mai Chan. -- 2nd ed.
         New York : McCraw-Hill, c1994.
           xxii, 519 p. : ill. ; 24 cm.              (p.

           Includes bibliographical references (p.
         493-502) and index.
           ISBN 0-07-010506-5                        Class-

           1.  Cataloging--United States.   2.  Class-
         ification--Books.   I.   Title.
```

Figure 1.2. Cards for Subject Headings

The single precoordinated heading **Cataloging—United States** was preferred to the two postcoordinated subjects headings **Cataloging** and **United States**. In addition to limiting the number of cards required, complex headings improved the collocation. Simple headings are likely to be created for frequent assignment, resulting in a large number of clusters of cards with the same heading that can be difficult to browse. In card catalogs, precoordinated headings were far more suitable than postcoordinated headings.

Synthetic languages also offered significant advantages during the card catalog era, particularly for precoordinated headings. By precoordinating the various elements, an almost infinite number of distinct headings can be constructed, although most would never be assigned. Establishing a core set of headings and relying on application rules to form additional headings as needed was more practical than listing every possible heading.

Online Catalogs and Databases

The 1960s saw the initial application of computers in libraries, particularly for library catalogs. The MARC (MAchine-Readable Cataloging) format was developed at the Library of Congress and became the standard for the use and exchange of cataloging records in machine-readable form. In addition to its distribution of bibliographic records in print form, the Library of Congress began distributing machine-readable bibliographic records using the MARC format. OCLC was also founded in the 1960s to distribute the Library of Congress MARC records and to support the sharing of machine-readable bibliographic records created by its member libraries.

The shift away from card catalogs began in earnest in the 1970s, and the OPAC quickly replaced the card catalog in most libraries. At its peak, OCLC was printing 131 million catalog cards a year; by 2008, card production had dropped to 1.8 million. Today, the use of card catalogs is limited to a few specialized applications and a few very small libraries. Limitations imposed by the card catalog are, therefore, no longer a significant consideration when designing or evaluating subject heading schemes.

Information retrieval in an online environment presents a very different set of challenges, opportunities, and limitations than that encountered with card catalogs. With many desktop computers having a terabyte (one trillion characters) or more of memory, vocabulary size is no longer a significant restraint. Even OCLC's WorldCat, the world's largest bibliographic database, is only about a 10th of a terabyte in size.

CONTROLLED VOCABULARY SYSTEMS

As mentioned earlier, there are two types of controlled vocabulary lists: *subject headings* and *thesauri*. Although subject heading lists and thesauri are often portrayed as distinct systems, they are really just two flavors of controlled vocabulary, differing primarily in their complexity and areas of application. Subject heading lists typically include both single-concept headings and complex headings, while thesauri comprise single-concept terms, often called *descriptors*. Subject vocabularies used in cataloging records are typically precoordinated subject heading strings, while descriptors used in online databases are mostly single-concept terms. They also differ in their origins: subject heading lists have been created and employed primarily by the library community, while thesauri were developed by the abstracting and indexing community and employed, at least initially, to index journal literature.

Taylor and Joudrey list four differences between subject headings and thesauri worth noting[10]:

- Thesauri are made up of single terms and bound terms representing single concepts (often called descriptors). Bound terms occur when some concepts can only be represented by two or more words (e.g., Type A Personality; the words *type, a,* and *Personality* cannot be separated without losing the meaning. The entire phrase is necessary for expressing the concept.). Subject heading lists tend to have phrases and other precoordinated terms in addition to single terms. [The bound terms Taylor and Joudrey refer to here are phrases such as *library science, operations research, foreign relations,* and *artificial intelligence,* where multiple word phrases are used to describe single concepts and where the individual words cannot be separated without losing the meaning of the phrase.]

- Thesauri are more strictly hierarchical. Because they are made up of single terms, each term usually has only one broader term. The rules in the NISO *Guidelines for the Construction, Format, and Management of Monolingual Thesauri* that have to do with identifying broader, narrower, and related terms are much easier to follow when working with a single-term system than when working with a system that includes phrases and compound headings.[11]

- Thesauri are narrower in scope. They are usually made up of terms from one specific subject area. Subject heading lists tend to be more general in scope, covering a broad subject area or, indeed, the entire scope of knowledge.

- Thesauri are more likely to be multilingual than subject heading lists. Again, because single terms are used, equivalent terms in other languages are easier to find and maintain.

Examples of thesauri include *Art and Architecture Thesaurus,*[12] *Thesaurus of ERIC Descriptors,*[13] and *Thesaurus of Psychological Index Terms.*[14]

Early library catalogs were primarily finding-lists providing both author entries and title catchwords for each item along with a symbol or number indicating its location in the collection. A catchword was the leading word in a title if it expressed subject content; in cases like *An Introduction to Physics,* "Physics" would be used as the catchword.

Before there was a standard list for subject headings, catalogers in individual libraries assigned subject headings as they saw fit. The advantages of having a standard list had become apparent by the early 1890s, probably due to the increase in interlibrary loan operations and the introduction of centralized cataloging and later cooperative cataloging.

In 1895, the first standard list for subject headings appeared: the *List of Subject Headings for Use in Dictionary Catalogs*[15] (commonly called the ALA List), produced by an American Library Association (ALA) committee. It was discontinued after 1914 when the Library of Congress began publishing its own list, *Subject Headings Used in the Dictionary Catalogues of the Library of Congress,* now titled *Library of Congress Subject Headings* and referred to as LCSH.[16]

After Library of Congress started distributing printed catalog cards at the beginning of the 20th century, its descriptive and subject cataloging practices gradually became the de facto standard for American libraries. However, LCSH and its predecessors were designed for, and reflect the practice of, large research collections. They have never been ideally suitable for medium-sized or small collections. Early on, the gap was filled by a list compiled by Minnie Earl Sears and first published in 1923 under the title *List of Subject Headings for Small Libraries*. In syntax, this list was modeled on LCSH, and so is compatible with it. It was later renamed *Sears List of Subject Headings*, with the 19th edition appearing in 2007.[17]

Over the years, many lists of subject headings were developed for special fields and applications. Probably the best known among these is Medical Subject Headings (MeSH). Recently, FAST (Faceted Application of Subject Terminology), a new controlled vocabulary system has been developed based on LCSH vocabulary but applied under highly simplified application rules.

Library of Congress Subject Headings (LCSH)

LCSH is the most widely used system of its kind in the world and offers many advantages as a means for subject access. It is a rich vocabulary of very wide scope, with synonym and homograph control and generous cross-references. It is a dependable scheme, continuously updated, with the support of the Library of Congress. LCSH reflects the general principles of controlled vocabulary construction already detailed. It not only fills the need for which it was first undertaken but has gone beyond its early warrant to cooperate with the whole library community, in the United States and abroad.

LCSH is a very large vocabulary: the latest (31st) print edition of the *Library of Congress Subject Headings*[18] includes approximately 308,000 headings. By 2008, the machine-readable LCSH authority file had grown to nearly 300,000 records. In addition to the headings established in the subject authority file, most of the proper names established in the LC/NAF (Library of Congress/NACO Authority File) authority file can also be used as subjects, and these headings are considered to be part of LCSH. The number of headings established in each of the authority files and their use in the corresponding Library of Congress catalog is shown in Table 1.1.

Table 1.1
Established Headings and Their Use by the Library of Congress

Source of Heading	Headings Valid as Subjects	Unique Headings Assigned in the Library of Congress's Catalog
Headings in the subjects file	293,812	164,509
Headings in the names file	6,659,527	274,522
Synthetically established headings	—	3,696,930
Totals:	6,953,339	4,135,961

Upon examining Table 1.1, it is obvious that most LCSH headings are synthetically derived. Only about 10 percent of the headings found in Library of Congress's bibliographic file have been explicitly established; the vast majority of the headings assigned were formed as part of the cataloging process following the rules described in the *Subject Headings Manual*.[19] The fact that only a small percentage of the headings in the names file have been used as subjects should not be too surprising. Most name headings can be, but rarely are, used as subjects, and their subject use is secondary. The people who have authored a publication far outnumber the people who have been the subject of a publication.

At first glance, it may seem surprising that almost half of the headings established in the subject authority file have not been assigned to any records in Library of Congress's bibliographic file. However, many LCSH headings were established to enable them to be used as part of a precoordinated heading. A few examples of established LCSH headings that were assigned—but not in their established form—in the bibliographic file are shown below:

Reef fishing *geographically subdivided in* Reef fishing—Atlantic Coast (U.S.)

Tonkin, Gulf of *used as a geographic subdivision in* Pilot guides—Tonkin, Gulf of

Georgian literature—19th century—*topically subdivided in*
Georgian literature—19th century—History and criticism

Athletics—Religious aspects *used with a topical subdivision in*
Athletics—Religious aspects—Christianity

Almost 90 percent of the headings used in Library of Congress's bibliographic file were formed, primarily by precoordination, during the cataloging process. A few examples of headings that were created by catalogers include:

Roosevelt, Eleanor, 1884–1962—Fiction

Celebrities—Interviews

Landlord and tenant—Fiction

Orphans—Juvenile fiction

American literature—19th century—Bio-bibliography—Dictionaries

Spanish language—Provincialisms—Mexico

Women—Finance, Personal

Eureka (Calif.)—Newspapers

Cotton trade—England—Lancashire

LCSH is unquestionably the most widely used subject heading schema in libraries, and translated versions of LCSH have served as the basis of several non-English subject heading lists. However, the system has seen few significant applications outside of library catalogs. While there are a variety of reasons for the lack of nonlibrary applications, the complexity of its synthetic rules has been the major limitation. The successful application of LCSH requires trained and experienced subject catalogers and indexers, with skills rarely found outside of libraries.

Medical Subject Headings (MeSH)

MeSH is an example of a specialized controlled vocabulary. MeSH is the system designed and used by the National Library of Medicine (NLM) for assigning medical subject headings or indexing terms to books and journal articles in the biomedical sciences. It has gained considerable acceptance outside of NLM and is now widely used by biomedical and health sciences libraries and by the abstracting and indexing services for biomedical and health sciences. MeSH began in the mid-20th century as a subject heading list, but over the years, it has adopted many of the features common to thesauri.

FAST (Faceted Application of Subject Terminology)

FAST, the focus of this book, is a controlled vocabulary based on LCSH. In 1998, the OCLC began exploring a new approach to subject vocabulary while it was in the process of searching for a subject access system that would optimize the use of technology for Dublin Core metadata records, a newly developed metadata scheme at the time. The scope of the project has since expanded, but it is still focused on applications beyond traditional library catalogs. In keeping with the original Dublin Core premises, it was determined that a subject vocabulary suitable for the Web environment should be:

1. Simple,
2. Easy for catalogers and indexers to assign and maintain,
3. Easy for searchers to understand and search, and
4. Flexible enough for use across disciplines and in various knowledge discovery and access environments, not the least of which is the OPAC.

In creating any new subject indexing scheme, decisions must be made both on vocabulary (semantics) and on whether the system will be enumerative or faceted. Regarding semantics, OCLC decided to retain the vocabulary of LCSH for the following reasons. First, it is a comprehensive list, well-supplied with cross-references. Second, a system based on it would be compatible with LCSH proper and with library catalog records coded with the MARC 21 format, so that automatic conversion of LCSH headings would be possible. Third, there would be cost benefits from the fact that many of the changes to LCSH could be incorporated into the new schema, thus minimizing maintenance. The result of these considerations was the design of the FAST schema.

A drawback to the use of LCSH as it stands was found to be its complex set of application rules, so complex that only professionally trained catalogers can apply LCSH effectively. For this reason, OCLC decided that, although its planned new system would use LCSH vocabulary, it would be used with a simplified, faceted syntax governing how subject headings would be applied. A faceted scheme would not only simplify the assignment process, but would also allow computer technology to be used to greater advantage in vocabulary maintenance and subject authority control. The same concern with LCSH was pointed out in a penetrating study of subject access by the American Library Association Committee on Technical Services.[20] This committee carried on its work during the same period that OCLC started the deliberations that led to FAST, and it concluded with the recommendation that LCSH remain in force but with much simplified application rules.

SELECTING AN INDEXING/
CLASSIFICATION SCHEMA

In selecting a controlled vocabulary, many criteria need to be considered. In addition to the most obvious ones relating to the language of the vocabulary and the subject and scope of the collection that is to be indexed, other criteria include compatibility with existing metadata, ease of assignment, retrieval effectiveness, and cost of maintenance; these are discussed in the following sections.

Compatibility with Existing Metadata

Indexing is very expensive, and changing subject heading schemas can be a major expense. It is critical to select a schema that not only satisfies current requirements but will also meet future needs. Collections, even those that started as isolated collections, often become part of larger collections later. The Web has accelerated this trend by making it easy to form virtual collections of physically dispersed materials. Indexing schemas that are limited to particular subjects may function very well within a particular domain but may be difficult to integrate with other collections.

Ease of Assignment

Manual indexing is a slow and costly process. Most projects are limited by cost. Even in the rare cases where cost is not the constraining factor, it is often difficult to find the skilled subject catalogers or indexers required. Simpler schemas can boost productivity of less skilled and less experienced staff. Schemas designed for online environments have the potential to improve productivity greatly by effectively combining the power of the computer with the intelligence of the indexer or cataloger.

Retrieval Effectiveness

The effect of a schema on retrieval is very similar to its effect on assignment. Complex schema can be very powerful when employed by skilled searchers, but effective searching is not a trivial task. One of the more significant impacts of OPACs and other Web-accessible systems is that most searches are undertaken directly by the end user with minimal, if any, involvement by skilled intermediaries—the reference librarian or professional searcher. These end users have been heavily influenced by search engines such as Google that produce very satisfactory results without requiring experienced searchers. Today, it is more relevant to evaluate a schema based on the quality of the retrievals for end-user searches than those of the professionals.

Cost of Maintenance

Controlled vocabularies require maintenance, that is, *authority control*—the use of an authoritative list of terms to control the headings. The list of headings must be continuously revised with the inclusion of new subjects and updated to reflect current usage. A variety of errors can occur when headings are assigned—typographical errors, obsolete headings, incorrect abbreviations, and so forth—which can creep into the database in spite of the best efforts of the indexers. High-quality databases require continuous authority control. In concept, authority control functions much as spell-checkers do in other environments, detecting and correcting errors.

The characteristics of the schemas affect the difficulty and cost of authority control. It can be very difficult to apply the rules associated with synthetic languages in computerized environments, particularly when the rules are context-dependent and require extensive domain knowledge to apply. Since enumerative languages rely far less on synthetic rules, they are generally much easier to maintain.

CONCLUSION

The FAST schema, the focus of this book, is compatible with MARC, Dublin Core, and other popular metadata data structures. It may be the only general purpose English language schema created in the postprint era without the limitations associated with print. It retains the rich vocabulary of LCSH but with a faceted, enumerated, postcoordinated syntax that is easy to apply.

NOTES

1. "The History of Yahoo!—How It All Started ..." http://docs.yahoo.com/info/misc/history.html (accessed April 13, 2010).

2. David Batty, "WWW—Wealth, Weariness or Waste: Controlled Vocabulary and Thesauri in Support of Online Information Access. *D-Lib Magazine* (November 1998), http://www.dlib.org/dlib/november98/11batty.html (accessed April 9, 2010).

3. Elaine Svenonius, *The Intellectual Foundation of Information Organization* (Cambridge, MA: MIT Press, 2000), 173.

4. Ibid., 178.

5. Ibid., 173.

6. Ibid., 139.

7. International Federation of Library Associations (IFLA) Study Group on the Functional Requirements of Bibliographic Records, *Functional Requirements of Bibliographic Records: Final Report* (München, Germany: K. G. Saur, 1998).

8. Svenonius, 139.

9. Ibid., 187.

10. Arlene G. Taylor and Daniel N. Joudrey, *The Organization of Information*, 3rd ed. (Westport, CT: Libraries Unlimited, 2009), 335.

11. National Information Standards Organization (NISO), *Guidelines for the Construction, Format, and Management of Monolingual Thesauri* (Bethesda, Md.: NISO Press, 1994).

12. *Art and Architecture Thesaurus Online*, The J. Paul Getty Trust, http://www.getty.edu/research/conducting_research/vocabularies/aat/ (accessed April 13, 2010).

13. *Thesaurus of ERIC Descriptors* (Washington, DC: U.S. Department of Education, Institute of Education Sciences), http://www.eric.ed.gov/ (accessed April 9, 2010).

14. Lisa Gallagher Tuleya, ed., *Thesaurus of Psychological Index Terms*, 11th ed. (Washington, DC: American Psychological Association, 2007).

15. American Library Association, *List of Subject Headings for Use in Dictionary Catalogs* (Boston: American Library Association, 1985).

16. Library of Congress, Subject Cataloging Division, *Subject Headings Used in the Dictionary Catalogues of the Library of Congress* (Washington, DC: Government Printing Office, Library Branch, 1910–1914).

17. Joseph Miller and Joan Goodsell, eds. *Sears List of Subject Headings*, 19th ed. (New York: H. E. Wilson, 2007).

18. Library of Congress, Cataloging Policy and Support Office, *Library of Congress Subject Headings* (Washington, DC: Library of Congress, Cataloging Distribution Service, 2007).

19. Ibid.

20. ALCTS/CCS/SAC/Subcommitte on Metadata and Subject Access. *Subject Data in the Metadata Record: Recommendations and Rationale: A Report from the ALCTS/CCS/SAC/ Subcommittee on Metadata and Subject Analysis Working Draft, 1999,* http://www.ala.org/ ala/mgrps/divs/alcts/mgrps/ccs/cmtes/subjectanalysis/metadataandsubje/subjectdata. cfm (accessed April 14, 2010).

2

METADATA ENCODING

BIBLIOGRAPHIC DATA

Library catalogs are nearly as old as libraries themselves. The catalogs serve two primary purposes: they provide an inventory of the materials held by the library and they serve as an index to the library's collection. The catalog, which includes an entry describing each resource the library holds, consists of a set of bibliographic records that provide data about the library's collection. The data included in each bibliographic record, at a minimum, includes a description of the characteristics (title, author, publisher, physical properties, etc.) of the resource and the location of the resource or the information necessary to access the resource. Most entries will also include subject terms or classification numbers to provide subject access to the collection. Almost all library catalogs have multiple indexes to provide multiple ways, or access points, to retrieve the resources.

Print Representation

When catalog records were manually produced—handwritten, typed, or typeset—there were only a few options for the catalog; most catalogs took the form of either book or card catalogs. Consideration of cost and bulk placed a severe limit on the amount of information that could be included in a given record and on the number of access points that could be provided.

Book Catalogs

The book catalog lists the holdings of a particular library or group of libraries. This is the oldest form of library catalog. Entries may be handwritten as in a manuscript catalog, typed, or printed. The oldest manuscript or library catalog goes back as far as the Pinakes, compiled by Callimachus for the ancient Alexandrian library. It was the predominant form of library catalog until the late 19th century, and the use of book catalogs continued in specialized applications into the 20th century.

Book catalogs are relatively easy to reproduce and therefore were popular in library systems with branches where it was necessary to have multiple copies of the catalog. Book catalogs are difficult to update and generally rely on supplements to add new resources to the catalog between complete updates. Reproducing the catalog in microform extended the use of book catalogs. Computer output microform (COM) catalogs eliminated some of the problems associated with book catalogs. Since they were relatively inexpensive to produce, they could be reproduced more frequently, eliminating the need for supplements. However, microform catalogs were never popular with users.

Card Catalogs

Card catalogs began replacing book catalogs in the early 1900s and for almost a century were the predominant form of catalogs in the United States. In card catalogs, the entries are recorded on 3 × 5 cards, one entry per card or card set. Taylor and Joudrey report that "Card catalogs were popularized in the United States by the Library of Congress cards, first made available for sale in 1901 ..."[1] Card catalogs offered a huge advantage over book catalogs since they were easy to update— the cards for new resources could simply be inserted into the catalog. Each entry could be revised or deleted without affecting the other entries.

The fact that the Library of Congress began distributing ready-made sets of catalog cards to libraries contributed to the card catalog's widespread use and was probably the start of shared cataloging. Prior to the availability of the Library of Congress cards, cataloging was primarily a local operation with considerable variation in application. The availability of the Library of Congress cataloging information accelerated the standardization of cataloging practice, particularly in the English-speaking countries.

Continuing with the example from Chapter 1, the card set for *Cataloging and Classification* is shown in Figure 2.1.

The card set consists of five separate cards:

1. A card for the call number,
2. A card for the author (referred to as the main entry),
3. A card for the title,
4. A card for the first subject heading, and
5. Another card for the second subject heading.

If this work had had multiple authors, there would be a separate card for each author. As a result, the number of cards in a set varies depending on the number of authors and the number of subject headings. With the widespread adoption of the *Anglo-American cataloguing rules* in 1967, the requirements for the formatting of the cards were standardized. The required elements were specified, as was their position on the card. The rules even specified how the entries should be indented and capitalized.

Digital Representation

As library automation began to develop in the late 1950s, it became clear that bibliographic data would have to evolve from cards to machine-readable formats. Work on a format for machine-readable bibliographic data started in the late 1950s,

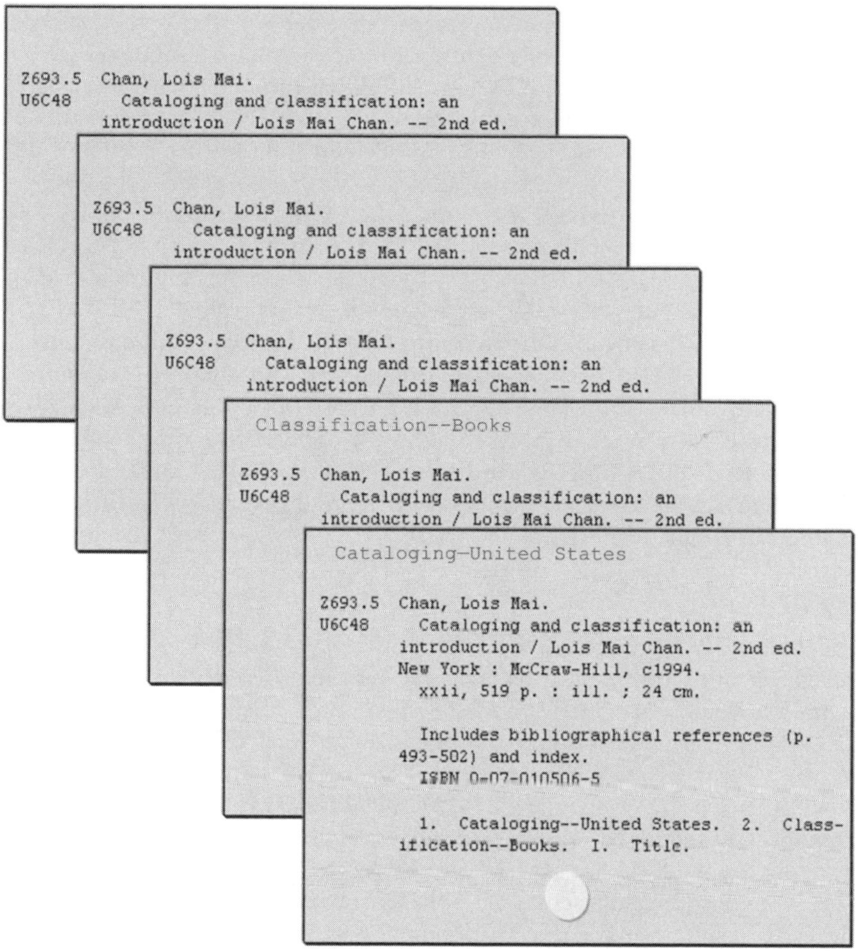

Figure 2.1. Typical Card Set

when the Library of Congress began investigating the possibility of automating its internal operations. In the early 1960s, the Council on Library Resources provided financial support for two exploratory studies. One examined the feasibility of applying automated techniques to the Library of Congress's internal operations. The other considered possible methods for converting the bibliographic data from cards to a machine-readable form in order to automate the printing of bibliographic products. These studies generated a great deal of interest and enthusiasm. As a result, a pilot project, called MARC (MAchine Readable Cataloging), was initiated in January 1966 to test the feasibility and utility of having Library of Congress distribute machine-readable cataloging data on magnetic tape to user libraries. For the pilot project, 16 libraries of different types and geographic locations were chosen to receive MARC tapes. Trial distribution began in October 1966, and by June 1968 approximately 50,000 cataloging records for English-language books had been converted to machine-readable form and distributed to the participating libraries. The results of the MARC pilot project were sufficiently encouraging for the Library of Congress to proceed on a full-scale basis.

The MARC Bibliographic Formats

The MARC formats are standards used to encode bibliographic and authority records in Online Public Access Catalogs (OPACs), though other formats are also used, particularly for nonlibrary applications. The MARC format contains codes for labeling individual areas, elements, sub-elements, and other pertinent data in bibliographic records.

Initially, individual countries developed their own formats; examples include USMARC for American libraries, UKMARC for British libraries, and CANMARC for Canadian libraries. Not long after, the International Federation of Library Associations (IFLA) developed an international scheme called UNIMARC. The MARC 21 format has been translated into various degrees of fullness into many different languages. In the interest of exchanging and sharing cataloging data internationally, and also because of the high cost of maintaining such formats, many countries have since decided to adopt or convert to either UNIMARC or USMARC. In 1999, USMARC and CANMARC were harmonized to become MARC 21. Many libraries worldwide use the English versions and their equivalents in other languages.

MARC 21

The MARC 21 formats are a set of standards developed for the purpose of representing and communicating machine-readable descriptive metadata about information items, particularly, but not solely, bibliographic items. The original MARC book format was refined and became *The MARC II Format: A Communications Format for Bibliographic Data*. The MARC structure was adopted as a national standard (ANSI standard Z39.2) in 1971 and as an international standard (International Organization for Standardization [ISO] Standard 2709) in 1973. Library of Congress MARC evolved into USMARC and then to MARC 21.

The Network Development and MARC Standards Office of the Library of Congress is responsible for the development and maintenance of the MARC 21 formats. The MARC Distribution Services, a part of Library of Congress's Cataloging Distribution Service, was established in March 1969 to disseminate MARC records to subscribing libraries and institutions. It has been doing so, in increasing volume, ever since. Initially, the cataloging data being distributed was limited to records for currently cataloged English-language books,[2] but over the years coverage has been broadened to include a full range of material types and languages.

Also in 1973, the American Library Association (ALA) committee working on machine-readable forms of bibliographic information became a MARC advisory committee working with the Library of Congress on changes and refinements in MARC formats. (The committee is best known by its acronym, MARBI). Other representatives from the American library and bibliographic community and other national libraries also participate in the continuing development of MARC. In 1982, a set of principles was prepared and published.[3] The Library of Congress continues to hold principal responsibility for the maintenance and publication of the MARC 21 formats, but all proposed changes are discussed and approved at MARBI meetings.

There are five MARC 21 formats for different types of data: (1) bibliographic data, (2) authority data, (3) classification data, (4) holdings data, and (5) community information. The bibliographic format is used to encode cataloging data and is discussed in this chapter. The authority format is used to encode authority records and will also be discussed later in this chapter. The other three MARC formats do not have direct relationship to FAST and are beyond of the scope of this book.

The *MARC 21 Format for Bibliographic Data*[4] is designed to cover bibliographic information for various types of materials, including books, maps, music, sound recordings, visual materials, continuing resources, electronic resources, and mixed materials. Initially, separate formats were prepared for different materials—books, serials, sound recordings, and so forth—and there were differences in the provisions for each medium, differences that were soon seen to cause problems in application.[5] For example, bibliographic items that fall into more than one category, such as nonprint materials in serial form, could not fit adequately into one format. Although bibliographic items in many media may be issued in serial form, provisions for serial publications or products were inconsistent among the various formats. Furthermore, comparable elements in different formats were not always handled consistently. In practice, the multiplicity of formats made maintenance and systems support difficult and cumbersome. As a result, in the early 1990s, the various medium-specific formats were rationalized and integrated into a single format.

Information about the bibliographic format is available in various forms and is included in many cataloging tool packages. The full version and the concise version are both available online and as loose-leaf publications. There are also a variety of other MARC-related documents, code lists, and tools available on the Library of Congress's Web site.[6] Details about the format are also available through OCLC's Connexion cataloging service and are included in the Cataloger's Desktop, which is available by subscription from the Library of Congress. The brief information about the bibliographic format in this book is included only as an illustration intended to assist in understanding the format. The reader should consult one of the preceding sources for current and detailed information on the format.

MARC Record Structure

Unlike the card image, the MARC record was designed primarily for machine processing and, without reformatting, is very difficult for people to interpret. The general MARC architecture is similar for all formats. The MARC format, which includes instructions on application as well as the format definitions, is complex and very detailed. It is helpful to consider the basic structure of the MARC 21 formats from three perspectives: what is the overall structure, what is included, and how is the content organized? It should be borne in mind that a MARC record consists of a sequential string of characters, with a blank space counting as a character. For example, the string "MARC format" contains 11 characters. A typical coded bibliographic record consists of hundreds of such sequences.

All of the MARC formats contain three basic structures: the leader, the directory, and the variable fields. The MARC record for the book *Cataloging and Classification* is shown here:

```
00559cam  2200169 a 450000500170000000080041000017
02000150005805000190007310000200009224500710011 2
25000120018326000370019530000350023250400640026 7
65000310033165000270036 2@20091120174046.0@930430
```

```
s1994      nyua      b     001 0 eng  @  $a007010506
5@00$aZ693.5.U6$bC48@1 $aChan, Lois Mai.@10$aCat
aloging and classification :$ban introduction /$
cLois Mai Chan.@  $a2nd ed.@  $aNew York :$bMcGr
aw-Hill,$cc1994.@  $axxii, 519 p. :$bill. ;$c24
cm.@  $aIncludes bibliographical references (p.
493-502) and index.@  0$aCataloging$zUnited State
s.@  0$aClassification$xBooks. @%
```

To assist in identifying the three parts of the record, the entries in the directory have been underlined. Certain control characters used in the MARC record are given arbitrary graphic representation in various displays of MARC records. For example, in different contexts or systems, the subfield limiting character may be represented by the dollar sign ($), the vertical bar (|) or by the double dagger (‡). The field and record terminators are often omitted from record displays, but never from the actual record. In this book, the following graphics will be used:

$ = subfield delimiter (used to separate subfields)
@ = field terminator (used to indicate the end of the field)
% = record terminator (used to indicate the end of the record)

In some limited instances in which blanks are shown as spaces, a pound sign (#) will be used to represent a blank.

1. The *leader,* fixed at 24 characters (positions 0–23), is the first field in a MARC record. It provides particular information for processing the ensuing record, including data such as total length, status (e.g., new, deleted, or corrected), type (e.g., books, maps, sound recordings, or name authority or subject authority), base address of data, and encoding level (full, minimal, complete, incomplete, etc.). Each particular element is entered at a prescribed position in the leader. Since its length is fixed, the leader does not require a field terminator.

The leader of the bibliographic record for *Cataloging and Classification* is shown in detail in Figure 2.2. Most of the information in the leader is structural (the record length, indicator count, base address of data, etc.) and is provided primarily to facilitate machine processing. However, the elements with bold labels provide information about the type or contents of the record.

Record status: Used to indicate the status of the record. The "c" status indicates that this record has been corrected or revised. The other common status code is "n" indicating that the record is new.

Type of record: Used to indicate either the type of record or, for bibliographic records, the type of resource being described. The "a" indicates that this is a record for language materials. Other codes are used to identify musical scores, cartographic materials, sound recordings, and so forth. A code of "z" indicates that the record is an authority record rather than a bibliographic record.

Bibliographic level: Used to indicate the level of the resource. The code "m" indicates that the resource is a monograph. Other common codes are used to identify collections and serials.

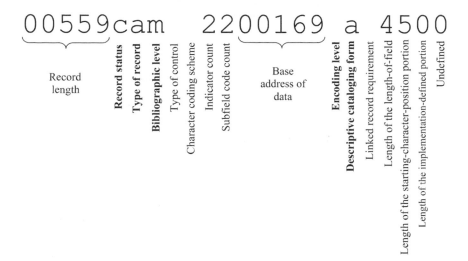

Figure 2.2. Leader from *Cataloging and Classification*

Encoding level: Used to indicate the level or completeness of the cataloging. The blank shows that this is full-level cataloging. Other common codes are used to identify Cataloging in Publication (CIP) level and core level cataloging.

Descriptive cataloging form: Used to identify the cataloging rules used. The "a" shows that the record is formulated according to the *Anglo-American Cataloguing Rules* (2nd ed.). Presumably, a new code will be added for RDA (Resource Description and Access).

This is only a very brief summary of the various codes used in the leader. Again, the complete description of the leader and the codes used is provided in the *MARC 21 Format for Bibliographic Data*.

2. The *directory* is an index to the locations of the variable fields within a record. It is similar to the table of contents in a book. It begins at record position 24 and lists the various data fields in the record, giving the relative locations of each variable field by starting character position. Directory data is automatically generated after a record is entered—the cataloger does not have to supply them. The directory consists of a series of 12 character entries, one for each of the variable fields. The elements in each directory entry are (1) the tag, (2) the field length (the total number of characters—letters, numbers, punctuation marks, subfield codes, and blanks—in the field), and (3) the field's relative starting character position in the record. A record's directory has as many of these 12-character entries as there are fields in the record. It ends with a field terminator.

The directory entry shown in Figure 2.3 indicates that it is for a field with the tag of 650 and that the field contains 31 characters. The last element, the starting character position, indicates where within the variable fields the field starts. To determine the actual starting position relative to the start of the record, the starting character position must be added to the base address of the data given in the leader. For this example, since the base address of the data is 169 and the starting character position is 331, this field starts at the 500th character of the record.

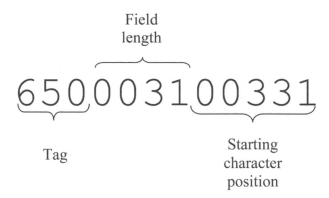

Figure 2.3. Example of Directory Entry

3. The *variable fields* contain the essence of the record (i.e., the bibliographic data). Each field is identified by the three-character numeric tag stored in the directory. The tag determines the nature of each field in the record: personal name main entry, corporate name main entry, title, subject, and so on. Each field ends with a field terminator. There are two types of fields: *control fields* and *data fields*.

Control fields are numbered 001–009; they contain either a single data element or a series of fixed-length data elements identified by relative character position.

Data fields are numbered 010–899; most of the fields in the range of 010–099 are for various numbers or codes (e.g., 020 for International Standard Book Number [ISBN], 050 for the Library of Congress call number, 082 for the Dewey Decimal Classification) while the ones in the range of 100–899 are for bibliographic, subject, and linking information, in other words, what is usually considered cataloging information. The 900–999 fields are not defined and are reserved for local use.

The data fields contain what we think of as metadata. This is the information that previously appeared on cards to describe the item being cataloged. To a large extent, the information in the leader, the directory, and the control fields either duplicates, usually in a coded form, the information in the data fields or provides information on the structure of the record in order to facilitate machine processing.

The data fields contain the following elements:

Tag: A three-digit code is used to specify the type of information in the field. Although the tag is stored in the directory, it is logically associated with the variable field.

Indicators: Two single-character indicators provide information about the field. The meaning of the indicators varies by field and depends on the tag.

Field text: The field consists of one or more subfields. Each subfield is prefixed with two characters: a subfield delimiter and a subfield code. The subfield code can be either a lowercase alphabetic character or a digit.

The indicators are two one-character positions containing values that interpret or supplement the data found in the field. The control fields do not have indicators. The indicators are not defined for all data fields; those that have not been defined are assigned the value of space (blank). The subfield codes identify the data elements within the field that require separate manipulation. Each subfield code begins with a code (represented by $ in this book) called a *subfield delimiter*—for example, $d or $2. Each subfield code is followed by the appropriate data, defined independently for each field—for example, $2fast.

Some fields, such as the 100 (main entry) or 250 (edition) fields, can occur no more than once in each record. Others, such as those for subject headings or index terms, may be repeated. Similarly, some subfields are also repeatable. The repeatability (R) or nonrepeatability (NR) of each field and subfield is indicated in the MARC 21 formats. Fields in the *bibliographic* record are grouped into blocks identified by the first character of the tag, which normally indicates the function of the data within the record.

001 – 009 Control fields
010 – 099 Control information, identification and classification numbers, etc.
100 – 199 Main entry fields
200 – 299 Titles and title-related fields (title, edition, imprint)
300 – 399 Physical description fields
400 – 499 Series statement fields
500 – 599 Note fields
600 – 699 Subject access fields
700 – 799 Added entry fields other than subject or series; linking fields
800 – 899 Series added entry fields, holdings, location, etc. fields
900 – 999 Reserved for local use

Within the 100, 400, 600, 700, and 800 blocks, the type of information (e.g., personal name, corporate name, uniform title, and geographic name) is identified by the second and third characters of the tag.

X00	Personal names
X10	Corporate names
X11	Meeting names
X30	Uniform titles
X48	Chronological terms
X50	Topical terms
X51	Geographic names
X55	Genres/forms

Indicators and subfield codes are defined individually for each field. For example, the field for topical subject headings (tag 650) in a bibliographic record uses the first indicator position to specify the level of the subject with the following codes:

Blank	No information provided
0	No level specified
1	Primary
2	Secondary

Library of Congress cataloging does not routinely provide information of the level of the heading, so the first indicator is normally blank. The second indicator is used to identify the thesaurus or subject heading system used in constructing the subject heading. The valid values for the second indicator of the subject fields are:

0 – Library of Congress Subject Headings
1 – LC subject headings for children's literature
2 – Medical Subject Headings
3 – National Agricultural Library subject authority file
4 – Source not specified
5 – Canadian Subject Headings
6 – Répertoire de vedettes-matière
7 – Source specified in subfield $2

Seven different thesaurus or subject heading systems can be identified directly. An indicator value of "7" combined with a subfield $2 can be used to identify additional schema. FAST headings are identified with the indicator "7" combined with the subfield $2fast.

The most commonly used subfield codes in topical subject heading fields are:

Code	Subfield
$a	Topical term
$v	Form subdivision
$x	General (topical) subdivision
$y	Chronological subdivision
$z	Geographic subdivision

When displaying examples of MARC fields in this book, subfield delimiters and codes will be explicitly shown and the field will appear as shown in Figure 2.4. There are no standards for displaying the content of MARC fields, but this display is representative, although it may include more detail than is typical.

When FAST subject headings are shown outside of the MARC context, the subfield delimiter and the subfield code will be replaced by a long (em) dash. For example, an individual FAST heading would be shown as:

Cataloging—Books

To make it easy to distinguish between LCSH headings and FAST headings, LCSH headings will be shown with subfield codes in bold italics. For example, if the preceding heading was an LCSH heading, it would be displayed as:

$aCataloging $xBooks

Wherever feasible, parallel content designation is used in the various formats. For example, the same subfield codes shown in the preceding example are used in fields containing topical headings in both the bibliographic and authority formats.

The MARC coding allows the record to be processed by the computer for various uses and to create various types of displays. Most of the MARC coding is

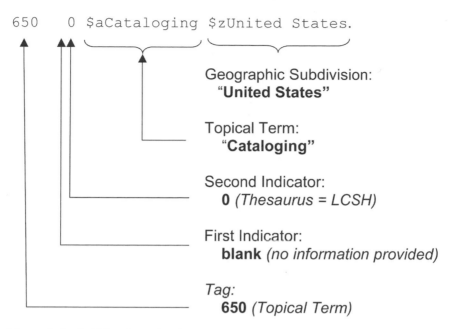

650   0 $aCataloging $zUnited States.

Geographic Subdivision:
"United States"

Topical Term:
"Cataloging"

Second Indicator:
0 *(Thesaurus = LCSH)*

First Indicator:
blank *(no information provided)*

Tag:
650 *(Topical Term)*

Figure 2.4. Field for Topical Subject Heading

omitted in the display intended for general use. However, there are circumstances in which library personnel need to see and work with fully coded records. Catalog maintenance is one, but other sectors of the library often need them too. OPAC records can be displayed in various formats and levels of detail but may not show the actual MARC coding. However, these codes enable many of the sophisticated search options available in today's OPACs. Thus, it can be seen that the same cataloging information, once coded, can be tailored for use in different environments and for different purposes—online catalogs, acquisitions lists, circulation records, and so forth. The flexibility is great: the design of each online catalog system determines what can be done with the coded catalog data.

The MARC records used as examples in this book frequently will be abridged and reformatted to improve readability and to focus on the subject aspects. The individual fields will be formatted following the pattern shown in Figure 2.4, and the fields will be combined in the display of the complete record as shown here:

```
LDR     00559cam  2200169 a 4500
005     20091120174046.0
008     930430s1994 nyua b 001 0 eng
020     $a0070105065
050 00 $aZ693.5.U6 $bC48
100 1  $aChan, Lois Mai.
245 10 $aCataloging and classification : $ban introduction /
       $cLois Mai Chan.
```

```
250      $a2nd ed.

260      $aNew York : $bMcGraw-Hill, $cc1994.

300      $axxii, 519 p. : $bill. ; $c24 cm.

504      $aIncludes bibliographical references (p. 493-502) and
         index.

650   0  $aCataloging $zUnited States.

650   0  $aClassification $xBooks.
```

In addition to the 12 fields, the leader is also displayed as the first line and identified as *LDR*. Although much of the structural details are omitted, this display includes the complete contents of the record and all of the coding related to the contents.

UNIMARC

UNIMARC was developed in the late 1970s with a similar purpose to that of USMARC: to facilitate the exchange of bibliographic data. UNIMARC is maintained by the International Federation of Library Associations (IFLA) through its Permanent UNIMARC Committee (PUC). While MARC 21 evolved from USMARC and is closely associated with Anglo-American cataloging, UNIMARC is the result of the harmonization of various, primarily European, national standards.

UNIMARC is similar in structure to MARC 21; it continues the use of the leader, directory, and variable fields. However, the content of the individual fields differs greatly between the two standards. Tags and subfield codes have completely different meanings in MARC 21 and UNIMARC. For example, topical subject headings are tagged as 650 in MARC 21 but as 606 in UNIMARC. While UNIMARC uses subfields in a similar way structurally to MARC 21, the meaning of the codes is not the same. The detailed specifications for the UNIMARC format are given in the UNIMARC Manual.[7]

XML (Extensible Markup Language)

In addition to MARC 21 bibliographic format, there are a number of other formats that have been developed by the Library of Congress to facilitate the use of MARC records in different environments. All of these standards have been developed and are maintained by the Network Development and MARC Standards Office of the Library of Congress with input from MARBI and from users.

Two of these standards—MARCXML and MODS (Metadata Object Description Schema)—are discussed in the following sections. Because these standards are encoded in XML, a brief introduction to the markup languages used to process electronic data is in order.

A markup language is used to indicate how a document or text is to be structured and presented. The term has its origin in the publishing field. Before a book or journal is published, a copyeditor or markup person goes through the manuscript and writes instructions on the margins regarding the font, type, size, and so forth for the typesetter. SGML (Standard Generalized Markup Language) was developed to process digital data. SGML is derived from IBM's Generalized Markup Language (GML). By 1986, GML had been adopted by the ISO and was promulgated as

"ISO 8879:1986 Information Processing—Text and Office Systems—Standard Generalized Markup Language (SGML)." The standard, which is rather complex, was adopted by agencies that require tremendous amounts of data to be processed from text files, notably the U. S. Department of Defense and the Association of American Publishers.

SGML is not a markup language itself but is a meta-language that is used to define markup languages. By 1992, experiences in using markup had led researchers at the Centre Européen Pour la Recherche Nucléaire (or European Organization for Nuclear Research, or just CERN), to create the HTML (Hypertext Markup Language), an application of SGML. HTML is a markup language designed for displaying documents on Web browsers.

SGML also serves as a meta-meta-language, which means that meta-languages can be created based on SGML. XML is an example of such an implementation of SGML.

XML, an instantiation or implementation of a part of SGML, was developed and is maintained by the World Wide Web Consortium (W3C).[8] An important feature of XML is that it allows documents to contain data about themselves *within* the document, much the same way that many print publications include CIP. This means that the documents can carry the metadata describing themselves. XML was initiated mainly to serve as a simpler and easier-to-implement meta-markup language than SGML with all needed concepts embodied within it. The first version of XML specification was published in 1996. The current version of XML specification is the fifth edition of the 1.0 version, as of November 26, 2008. The XML Schema[9] contains a set of specifications that guide the creation of XML-tagged records of information resources

Today, XML has grown into an all-purpose and all-pervasive way to insert structure into full-text documents and to create flexible surrogates, or metadata, for other objects. The use of XML has become so pervasive that it led Catherine Ebenezer to declare: "Every serious web technology is now expected to define its relationship to XML."[10]

The characteristics of XML can be summarized briefly as follows:

1. XML is a simplified implementation of SGML.
2. XML consists of a subset of SGML specifications.
3. Like SGML, XML is a meta-markup language for text documents.
4. Unlike HTML, XML is not a markup language for indicating display options.

In other words, XML tags assign meaning to the data (e.g., <Title>**Paradise lost**</Title>; indicates that *Paradise lost* is a title), while HTML tags indicate how the data is to be displayed (e.g., **Paradise lost**; indicates that *Paradise lost* is to be displayed in a bold font).

Elliotte Rusty Harold and W. Scott Means summarize the purposes and benefits of XML as follows:[11]

1. Flexibility: XML allows users to invent elements based on their needs.
2. Syntax: The XML Recommendation defines a grammar for XML documents that indicates where tags may be placed, what they must look like, which element names are legal, how attributes are attached to elements, etc.

3. Semantics: The markup in an XML document describes the structure of the document, i.e., the document's semantics. That is, XML supports a structural and semantic markup language.

4. Extensibility: XML can be extended and adapted to meet many different needs.

5. Interoperability: Individuals or organizations may agree to use only certain tags, forming tag sets called XML applications. As a result, XML documents based on the same XML application are interoperable.

6. Portability: XML is a simple, well-documented, straightforward data format, offering the possibility of cross-platform, long-term data formats. XML documents are text-based and can be read with any tool that can read a text file.

Similar to HTML tags, XML tags are indicated by angled brackets "<" and ">." Tags are case sensitive (e.g., <Title> is not the same as <title>), and each starting tag (e.g., <Title>) must have a corresponding ending tag (e.g., </Title>).

MARCXML

XML, originally designed to meet the challenges of large-scale electronic publishing, is now also playing an important role in the exchange of a wide variety of cataloging data and metadata on the Web. To enable MARC users to work with MARC data in the Web environment and in ways specific to their needs, the Network Development and MARC Standards Office of the Library of Congress has developed a framework called MARCXML which casts MARC data into an XML framework. Based on XML, MARCXML enables the representation of MARC 21 data in an XML environment. It allows users to work with MARC data in ways specific to their needs. The framework itself includes many components such as schemas, style sheets, and software tools. Along with the MARCXML schema, the Library of Congress also provides a variety of XML tools, including style sheets, for transforming and displaying the data.[12] The tools the Library of Congress provides also permit libraries to convert their old MARC records to MARCXML, MODS, Dublin Core, or other metadata records.

The MARCXML schema retains the semantics of MARC 21. However, some structural elements in MARC 21, such as the length of the field and starting position of field data in directory entries, are not needed in an XML record. MARC's leader and the control fields are treated as data strings, and its fields are treated as sub-elements. Nevertheless, all of the essential data in a MARC record can be converted and expressed in XML.

MODS

MODS[13] is a metadata schema for creating original resource description records that consist of selected data from the MARC bibliographic format. For encoding, it uses XML.

MODS consists of a subset of 20 bibliographic elements based on the MARC bibliographic format and selected specifically for supporting the description of electronic resources and objects. As such, it is a rich, library-oriented XML metadata schema. Yet, although it is a simpler schema than the MARC 21 Bibliographic Format, it retains compatibility with MARC 21. It also provides multiple linking functions.

For encoding, MODS uses language-based tags rather than numeric ones. The top level MODS elements are:

titleInfo
name
typeOfResource
genre
originInfo
language
physicalDescription
abstract
tableOfContents
targetAudience
note
subject
classification
relatedItem
identifier
location
accessCondition
part
extension
recordInfo

There are a great number of sub-elements and attributes for MODS listed on the Library of Congress Web site (http://www.loc.gov/standards/mods/).

The following example, based on the title field (MARC tag 245) only, shows how a title would be represented using MARC, MARCXML and MODS:

MARC
245 14 $a**The heart of Midlothian /**$c**Sir Walter Scott**

MARCXML
<datafield tag="245" ind1="1" ind2="4">
  <subfield code="a">**The heart of Midlothian**</subfield>
  <subfield code="c">**Sir Walter Scott**</subfield>
</datafield>

MODS
<titleInfo><nonSort>**The**</nonSort><title>**heart of Midlothian**</title></titleInfo>
<note type="statementOfResponsibility">**Sir Walter Scott**</note>

Dublin Core

MARC records and cataloging codes, with their extensive and detailed rules and their focus on material traditionally held by libraries, are not a good vehicle for characterizing the content of Internet and Web resources. While MARC has been successfully used for library applications since the 1960s, it has not found significant acceptance outside of the library environment. By contrast, XML has been widely adapted and is extensively used for the organization and management of information on the Web. Although MARCXML uses the XML structure, it is a hybrid that retains the basic MARC tagging and coding structure. Outside of the library environment, MARC and its associated cataloging rules are viewed as being much more complex than is needed to describe Web resources.

Accordingly, a group of information professionals met in 1995 at OCLC in Dublin, Ohio, to consider the matter. This meeting led to a new metadata schema aimed particularly at electronic resources such as those on the Web. This new schema became known as Dublin Core: the core elements identified at the Dublin meeting. Another offshoot of the initial and subsequent Dublin meetings was the Dublin Core Metadata Initiative (DCMI), an open forum that oversees the continuing development of the Dublin Core and promotes other interoperable metadata standards. DCMI's activities include not only annual global conferences, workshops, and working groups organized around specific problem domains, but also both standards liaison and educational efforts to promote widespread acceptance of metadata standards and practices. Since the first Dublin Core meeting, which was sponsored by OCLC and the National Center for Supercomputing Applications (NCSA), was held in Ohio, there have been annual workshops held in different countries around the world, including Australia, Canada, China, Finland, Germany, Japan, Mexico, Spain, the United Kingdom, and the United States.

The original objective of the 1995 Metadata Workshop was to define a set of descriptive elements simple enough for noncatalogers, including authors themselves, to describe Web resources. It began with 13 elements and later, with the addition of the elements **Description** and **Rights**, was expanded to 15.

Since its inception, Dublin Core has been well received by many different information communities worldwide. In 2001, the Dublin Core Metadata Element Set was approved by the National Information Standards Organization (NISO) as ANSI/NISO Standard Z39.85-2001. In 2003, it was approved as an international standard, ISO Standard 15836-2003 (February 2003).

The Dublin Core contains a set of 15 elements:[14]

Element Name: **Title**

Label: Title

Definition: A name given to the resource.

Comment: Typically, a Title will be a name by which the resource is formally known.

Element Name: **Creator**

Label: Creator

Definition: An entity primarily responsible for making the content of the resource.

Comment: Examples of a Creator include a person, an organization, or a service. Typically, the name of a Creator should be used to indicate the entity.

Element Name: **Subject**

Label: Subject and Keywords

Definition: A topic of the content of the resource.

Comment: Typically, Subject will be expressed as keywords, key phrases or classification codes that describe a topic of the resource. Recommended best practice is to select a value from a controlled vocabulary or formal classification schema.

Element Name: **Description**

Label: Description

Definition: An account of the content of the resource.

Comment: Examples of Description include but are not limited to, an abstract, table of contents, reference to a graphical representation of content, or a free-text account of the content.

Element Name: **Publisher**

Label: Publisher

Definition: An entity responsible for making the resource available

Comment: Examples of a Publisher include a person, an organization, or a service. Typically, the name of a Publisher should be used to indicate the entity.

Element Name: **Contributor**

Label: Contributor

Definition: An entity responsible for making contributions to the content of the resource.

Comment: Examples of a Contributor include a person, an organization, or a service. Typically, the name of a Contributor should be used to indicate the entity.

Element Name: **Date**

Label: Date

Definition: A date of an event in the life cycle of the resource.

Comment: Typically, Date will be associated with the creation or availability of the resource. Recommended best practice for encoding the date value is defined in a profile of ISO 8601 [W3CDTF] and includes (among others) dates of the form YYYY-MM-DD.

Element Name: **Type**

Label: Resource Type

Definition: The nature or genre of the content of the resource.

Comment: Type includes terms describing general categories, functions, genres, or aggregation levels for content. Recommended best practice is to select a value from a controlled vocabulary (for example, the DCMI Type Vocabulary [DCT1]). To describe the physical or digital manifestation of the resource, use the Format element.

Element Name: **Format**

Label: Format

Definition: The physical or digital manifestation of the resource.

Comment: Typically, Format will include the media-type or dimensions of the resource. Format may be used to identify the software, hardware or other equipment needed to display or operate the resource. Examples of dimensions include size and duration. Recommended best practice is to select a value from a controlled vocabulary (for example, the list of Internet Media Types [MIME] defining computer media formats).

Element Name: **Identifier**

Label: Resource Identifier

Definition: An unambiguous reference to the resource within a given context.

Comment: Recommended best practice is to identify the resource by means of a string or number conforming to a formal identification system. Formal identification systems include but are not limited to the Uniform Resource Identifier (URI) (including the Uniform Resource Locator (URL)), the Digital Object Identifier (DOI), and the International Standard Book Number (ISBN).

Element Name: **Source**

Label: Source

Definition: A reference to a resource from which the present resource is derived.

Comment: The present resource may be derived from the Source resource in whole or in part. Recommended best practice is to reference the resource by means of a string or number conforming to a formal identification system.

Element Name: **Language**

Label: Language

Definition: A language of the intellectual content of the resource.

Comment: Recommended best practice is to use RFC 3066, which, in conjunction with ISO 639), defines two- and three-letter primary language tags with optional subtags. Examples include "en" or "eng" for English, "akk" for Akkadian, and "en-GB" for English used in the United Kingdom.

Element Name: **Relation**

Label: Relation

Definition: A reference to a related resource.

Comment: Recommended best practice is to identify the referenced resource by means of a string or number conforming to a formal identification system.

Element Name: **Coverage**

Label: Coverage

Definition: The extent or scope of the content of the resource.

Comment: Typically, Coverage will include spatial location (a place name or geographic coordinates), temporal period (a period label, date, or date range), or jurisdiction (such as a named administrative entity). Recommended best practice is to select a value from a controlled vocabulary (for example, the Thesaurus of Geographic Names [TGN]) and to use, where appropriate, named places or time periods in preference to numeric identifiers such as sets of coordinates or date ranges.

Element Name: **Rights**

Label: Rights

Definition: Information about rights held in and over the resource.

Comment: Typically, Rights will contain a rights management statement for the resource, or reference a service providing such information. Rights information often encompasses Intellectual Property Rights (IPR), Copyright, and various Property Rights. If the Rights element is absent, no assumptions may be made about any rights held in or over the resource.

The simple Dublin Core record for *Cataloging and Classification* is:

```
<dc:Title>Cataloging and classification: an introduction

<dc:Identifier>0070105065

<dc:Creator>Chan, Lois Mai

<dc:Date>1994

<dc:Description>2nd ed.

<dc:Format>519 p.

<dc:Language>eng

<dc:Publisher>McGraw-Hill

<dc:Subject>Z693.5.U6 C48 1994

<dc:Subject>Cataloging—United States

<dc:Subject>Classification—Books
```

For simplicity, the ending tags are not shown in the preceding example. However, every element must have both a starting tag and an ending tag. The title element, for example, must be terminated with the ending tag </dc:Title>.

Although the original intention was to develop a simple and concise schema for describing Web resources, the Dublin Core has been used to describe other types of resources as well. In different applications, some users require more descriptive details than in other situations. Thus, there are two different views with regard to the implementation of Dublin Core: the minimalist view, supporting a minimum of elements and with simple semantics and syntax; and the structuralist view, supporting greater extensibility through finer semantic distinctions. These different views have led to two approaches to the implementation of Dublin Core: the simple (unqualified) Dublin Core and the qualified Dublin Core, with finer details allowed within each element. Simple Dublin Core consists of the original 15 elements; qualified Dublin Core includes 3 additional elements (Audience, Provenance and RightsHolder), as well as a group of terms that refine the basic elements.[15] For example, the element Date may be refined to indicate the type of date (i.e., date created, date copyrighted, date issued, etc.). Qualified Dublin Core also provides for the explicit identification of the encoding schema (MeSH, LCSH, FAST, DDC, LCC, etc.) of the value.

Element Refinement. The refinement makes the meaning of an element narrower or more specific. A refined element shares the meaning of the unqualified element, but with a more restricted scope. A client that does not understand a specific element refinement term should be able to ignore the qualifier and treat the metadata value as if it were an unqualified (broader) element. The definitions of element refinement terms for qualifiers must be publicly available.

Encoding Scheme. These qualifiers identify schemes that aid in the interpretation of an element value. These schemes include controlled vocabularies and formal notations or parsing rules. A value expressed using an encoding scheme will thus be a token selected from a controlled vocabulary (e.g., a term from a classification system or set of subject headings) or a string formatted in accordance with a formal notation (e.g., "2000-01-01" as the standard expression of a date). If an encoding scheme is not understood by a client or agent, the value may still be useful to a human reader. The definitive description of an encoding scheme for qualifiers must be clearly identified and available for public use.

AUTHORITY DATA

As discussed in the first chapter, most thesauri and subject heading schemas maintain a list of authorized or established terms. These lists are often used in conjunction with schema-specific syntactic rules that control how the authorized terms are constructed and assigned. Initially, these lists of valid terms were informally maintained. For many local collections, the assigned terms formed the index to the collection and also serve as the list of authorized terms. When new materials were cataloged, the catalog was checked to see if an appropriate term had previously been used. If so, that term would be assigned; if not, a new term would be *established*. For local collections, this was an easy way to minimize the use of different terms to describe the same concept.

Print Representation

As the use of subject heading schema began to be standardized, using an index as the authority was impractical, and it was necessary to separate the index from the authoritative list of terms or headings. As the subject headings used by the Library of Congress were adapted by other libraries, many librarians asked that the list of subject headings be published. In 1914, this list was published as *Subject Headings Used in the Dictionary Catalogues of the Library of Congress.* There has been a continuing series of print editions ever since. The 31st edition, published in 2009, titled *Library of Congress Subject Headings,* includes over 308,000 headings and references published in six volumes.

A typical entry from the *Library of Congress Subject Headings* (31st edition) is shown in Figure 2.5.

Digital Representation

While the print editions are valuable and are still widely used, there was a clear need to also provide authority information in machine readable form. In support of that effort, the Library of Congress developed a MARC format for authorities that was first published as a preliminary edition in 1976 with the title of *Authorities, a MARC Format.* The authorities format has been expanded and refined considerably since 1976, and now is titled *MARC 21 Format for Authority Data.*

MARC 21

MARC 21 Format for Authority Data[16] is intended for use by people who create and maintain authority records. It contains specifications for encoding and

Earthquake engineering *(May Subd Geog)*
  [TA654.6]
  BT Civil engineering
        Engineering geology
  RT Shear walls
  NT Earthquake hazard analysis
        Earthquake resistant design
        Lifeline earthquake engineering
  —Research *(May Subd Geog)*
Earthquake engineering laboratories
  (May Subd Geog)
  [TA654.6]
  BT Engineering laboratories
Earthquake hazard analysis
  (May Subd Geog)
  [QE539.2.S34]
  UF Engineering laboratories
        Earthquakes—Hazard analysis
        Hazard analysis, Earthquake
        Seismic hazard analysis
        Seismic risk assessment
        Seismic vulnerability assessment
  BT Earthquake engineering

Figure 2.5. Selection from the *Library of Congress Subject Headings*

identifying data elements in authority records, including those for name headings, name/title headings, uniform title headings, topical term headings, extended headings (i.e., headings with subdivisions), and references to headings.

The format for authority data retains the same basic structure—the leader, directory, and variable fields—as the format for bibliographic data. The elements in the leader are similar to those of the bibliographic format, but the type of record is set to "z" to indicate that the record is an authority record. What a given content designator means varies considerably between the MARC 21 bibliographic format and the authority format. However, within the tag blocks, the type of information identified by the second and third characters of the tag is consistent to the extent possible.

The authority record for **Earthquake engineering**—the heading used as an example from the print edition—is shown here:

```
LDR      00413cz  2200169n 4500
001      oca02110305
003      OCoLC
005      19990628162849.2
008      860211i| anannbabn         |b ana
010      $ash 85040490
040      $aDLC $beng $cDLC $dDLC
053    0 $aTA654.6
```

```
150        $aEarthquake engineering

550        $aCivil engineering $wg

550        $aEngineering $wg

550        $aEngineering geology $wg

550        $aShear walls
```

Although the authority file was the source of the information in the print edition of LCSH, there are some notable differences. The contents of the leader, control fields, and most of the 0XX fields are omitted from the printed list of headings. In the reference fields, the first byte of the $w control subfield is used to specify relationships between the reference and established heading. The common values used include:

a – Earlier heading (the term is an earlier form of the established heading),

d – Acronym (the term is an acronym for the established heading),

g – Broader term (the term is a broader term for the established heading), and

h – Narrower term (the term is a narrow term for the established heading).

Of particular interest here are the broader and narrower term relationships. The broader terms are identified by the value of "g" in the $w subfield, and the related terms are implied by the lack of a $w subfield. The Library of Congress does not routinely include narrower terms in the authority records. The narrower terms in the printed list are obtained by inverting broader terms. Since the authority record for **Earthquake hazard analysis** has **Earthquake engineering** as a broader term, it can be inferred that **Earthquake hazard analysis** is a narrower term for **Earthquake engineering**.

Other MARC Authority Formats

As with bibliographic records, there are other MARC-based formats for authority data. The MARCXML format for authority data closely parallels the MARCXML format for bibliographic data. Similarly, there is a UNIMARC format for authorities that parallels the bibliographic format. *UNIMARC Manual: Authorities Format*[17] provides a detailed description of the content designators for that format.

SKOS

The Simple Knowledge Organization System (SKOS) is a relatively new system for organizing the Web that has been developed by the W3C as part of its semantic Web activity. SKOS is a "new standard that builds a bridge between the world of knowledge organization systems—thesauri, classifications, subject headings, taxonomies, and folksonomies—and the linked data community, bringing benefits to both. Libraries, museums, newspapers, government portals, enterprises, social networking applications, and other communities that manage large collections of books, historical artifacts, news reports, business glossaries, blog entries, and other items can now use Simple Knowledge Organization System (SKOS) to leverage the power of linked data."[18] SKOS was developed and is maintained by the W3C Semantic Web Deployment Working Group.

Dublin Core and SKOS are similar and complementary efforts—Dublin Core for bibliographic data and SKOS for authority data including thesauri and subject headings. Both Dublin Core and SKOS are XML rather than MARC based. Although maintained by different organizations—Dublin Core is maintained by DCMI rather than the W3C—they both are focused on the semantic Web. Detailed SKOS specifications are provided in the *SKOS Simple Knowledge Organization System Reference*.[19]

The Library of Congress has made LCSH available in SKOS. The SKOS record for **Earthquake engineering** in RDF/XML (Resource Description Framework/ Extensible Markup Language) format,[20] as displayed on the Library of Congress's Web site, is:

```
<rdf:RDF>

<rdf:Description rdf:about="http://id.loc.gov/authorities/
sh85040490#concept">

<skos:prefLabel xml:lang="en">Earthquake engineering</
skos:prefLabel>

<owl:sameAs rdf:resource="info:lc/authorities/sh85040490"/>

<dcterms:created rdf:datatype="http://www.w3.org/2001/
XMLSchema#dateTime">1986-02-11T00:00:00-04:00</
dcterms:created>

<skos:closeMatch rdf:resource="http://stitch.cs.vu.nl/
vocabularies/rameau/ark:/12148/cb119796949"/>

<dcterms:modified rdf:datatype="http://www.w3.org/2001/
XMLSchema#dateTime">1999-06-28T16:28:49-04:00</
dcterms:modified>

<skos:narrower rdf:resource="http://id.loc.gov/authorities/
sh90004460#concept"/>

<skos:narrower rdf:resource="http://id.loc.gov/authorities/
sh85040493#concept"/>

<skos:narrower rdf:resource="http://id.loc.gov/authorities/
sh92003884#concept"/>

<skos:broader rdf:resource="http://id.loc.gov/authorities/
sh85026331#concept"/>

<skos:broader rdf:resource="http://id.loc.gov/authorities/
sh85043221#concept"/>

<skos:broader rdf:resource="http://id.loc.gov/authorities/
sh85043176#concept"/>

<skos:inScheme rdf:resource="http://id.loc.gov/
authorities#conceptScheme"/>

<skos:inScheme rdf:resource="http://id.loc.gov/
authorities#topicalTerms"/>

<rdf:type rdf:resource="http://www.w3.org/2004/02/skos/
core#Concept"/>
```

```
<skos:related rdf:resource="http://id.loc.gov/authorities/
sh99003936#concept"/>

</rdf:Description>

<rdf:Description rdf:about="http://id.loc.gov/authorities/
sh85026331#concept">

<skos:prefLabel xml:lang="en">Civil engineering</
skos:prefLabel>

</rdf:Description>

<rdf:Description rdf:about="http://id.loc.gov/authorities/
sh92003884#concept">

<skos:prefLabel xml:lang="en">Lifeline earthquake
engineering</skos:prefLabel>

</rdf:Description>

<rdf:Description rdf:about="http://id.loc.gov/authorities/
sh85040493#concept">

<skos:prefLabel xml:lang="en">Earthquake resistant design</
skos:prefLabel>

</rdf:Description>

<rdf:Description rdf:about="http://id.loc.gov/authorities/
sh99003936#concept">

<skos:prefLabel xml:lang="en">Shear walls</skos:prefLabel>

</rdf:Description>

<rdf:Description rdf:about="http://id.loc.gov/authorities/
sh85043176#concept">

<skos:prefLabel xml:lang="en">Engineering</skos:prefLabel>

</rdf:Description>

<rdf:Description rdf:about="http://id.loc.gov/authorities/
sh90004460#concept">

<skos:prefLabel xml:lang="en">Earthquake hazard analysis</
skos:prefLabel>

</rdf:Description>

<rdf:Description rdf:about="http://id.loc.gov/authorities/
sh85043221#concept">

<skos:prefLabel xml:lang="en">Engineering geology</
skos:prefLabel>

</rdf:Description>

</rdf:RDF>
```

CONCLUSION

There are three distinct approaches to encoding metadata. Although print representation used in book and card catalogs served the library community well, print is rarely used now and is no longer a significant factor for information access. For the library community, MARC remains the dominant format for encoding bibliographic and authority data. Billions of MARC records exist in library OPACs and related systems worldwide. The MARC formats are mature, well documented, carefully maintained, and have been successfully used for nearly half a century.

However, MARC has not been widely accepted outside of the library community and is not compatible with XML, the standard encoding language for the Web. There are a number of hybrid approaches, such as MARCXML, which put MARC content into an XML structure. While the hybrid approach unquestionably is a useful step in transitioning bibliographic data to the Web, it is unlikely to be a long-term solution. The hybrid approach used is complex—from the content perspective, MARCXML inherits MARC's complexity and adds an additional level by placing the MARC contents in the XML structure.

Dublin Core and SKOS are new XML-based systems that were designed specifically for Web resources and the needs of the semantic Web. While both systems have been influenced by MARC, their basic structure is independent from MARC. In the long term, this will probably prove to be an advantage, but in the short term that is not necessarily the case. These new systems are not yet mature—they are still evolving and lack extensive documentation and uniform application guidelines. However, as they mature and gain acceptance, it is anticipated that they will enable the smooth transition of bibliographic data from library OPACs to the semantic Web.

NOTES

1. Arlene G. Taylor and Daniel N. Joudrey, *The Organization of Information*, 3rd ed. (Westport, CT: Libraries Unlimited, 2009), p. 48.

2. Library of Congress, MARC Development Office, *Information on the MARC System*, 4th ed. (Washington, DC: Library of Congress, 1974), p. 1.

3. John Attig, "The USMARC Formats—Underlying Principles," *Information Technology and Libraries* 1, no. 2 (1982): 169–74.

4. *MARC 21 Format for Bibliographic Data: Including Guidelines for Content Designation*, prepared by Network Development and MARC Standards Office, Library of Congress, in cooperation with Standards and Support, National Library of Canada (Washington, DC: Library of Congress, Cataloging Distribution Service, 1999–; updated annually), http://www.loc.gov/marc/bibliographic/ecbdhome.html. (accessed April 13, 2010)

5. Walt Crawford, *MARC for Library Use: Understanding Integrated USMARC* (Boston: G. K. Hall & Co., 1989), 221–22.

6. Library of Congress, Network Development and MARC Standards Office, *MARC Standards* (Washington, DC), http://www.loc.gov/marc/ (accessed April 13 2010).

7. Alan Hopkinson, ed., *UNIMARC Manual: Bibliographic Format*, 3rd ed. (Munich, Germany: K. G. Saur, 2008).

8. "Extensible Markup Language (XML)," http://www.w3.org/XML/ (accessed April 13, 2010).

9. "XML Schema," http://www.w3.org/2001/XMLSchema.html (April 13, 2010).

10. Catherine Ebenezer, "Trends in Integrated Library Systems," *VINE* 32, no. 4 (2003): 19.

11. Elliotte Rusty Harold and W. Scott Means, *XML in a Nutshell*, 3rd ed. (Sebastopol, CA: O'Reilly, 2004), 4, 6.

12. Library of Congress. Network Development and MARC Standards Office, "MARCXML: MARC 21 XML Schema," March 13, 2009, http://www.loc.gov/standards/marcxml/ (accessed April 13, 2010).

13. Library of Congress. Network Development and MARC Standards Office, "MODS: Metadata Object Description Schema," September 25, 2009, http://www.loc.gov/standards/mods/ (accessed April 13, 2010).

14. Dublin Core Metadata Initiative, "*Dublin Core Metadata Element Set,*" Version 1.1. 2008. http://dublincore.org/documents/dces/index.shtml (accessed April 14, 2010)

15. Diane Hillmann, "Using Dublin Core," November 7, 2005, http://dublincore.org/documents/2005/11/07/usageguide/ (April 13, 2010).

16. *MARC 21 Format for Authority Data: Including Guidelines for Content Designation*, prepared by Network Development and MARC Standards Office, Library of Congress, in cooperation with Standards and Support, National Library of Canada (Washington, DC: Library of Congress, Cataloging Distribution Service; Ottawa, Canada: National Library of Canada, 1999–), http://www.loc.gov/marc/authority/ecadhome.html (accessed April 14, 2010).

17. Mirna Willer, ed., *UNIMARC Manual: Authorities Format* (Munich, Germany: K. G. Saur, 2009).

18. W3C, "SKOS Simple Knowledge Organization System," December 27, 2009, http://www.w3.org/2004/02/skos/ (accessed April 14, 2010).

19. W3C, "SKOS Simple Knowledge Organization System Reference," August 18, 2009, http://www.w3.org/TR/2009/REC-skos-reference-20090818/ (accessed April 14, 2010).

20. Library of Congress, *Authorities and Vocabularies, Earthquake Engineering,* http://id.loc.gov/authorities/sh85040490#concept (accessed April 14, 2010).

Part II

———◆·◆·◆———

FAST HEADINGS

3

———✦———

INTRODUCTION TO FAST

IMPACT OF THE INTERNET
AND THE WORLD WIDE WEB

The situation for subject access has changed dramatically with the emergence of the Internet and the World Wide Web as well as digital libraries and depositories. With the phenomenal growth of electronic resources and the availability of numerous metadata schemes for their description, there is a need for subject access methods that can handle a large volume of materials without incurring as much effort and cost as does the treatment of traditional library materials. In this new environment, traditional subject access systems face a major challenge, one that goes to the heart of information retrieval: can controlled vocabularies continue to play a helpful role in subject access in the digital age?

In 1997, the Association of Library Collections and Technical Services (ALCTS) established a Subcommittee on Metadata and Subject Analysis to identify and study the major issues surrounding the use of metadata in the subject analysis and classification of digital resources and to recommend courses for action.[1] Among the recommendations put forth by the subcommittee, the following pertain specifically to subject indexing vocabulary:

1. A combination of keywords and controlled vocabulary should be used to allow users the choice of simple free-text indexing as well as complex controlled vocabulary indexing.

2. In the Dublin Core metadata record, the subcommittee recommends the inclusion in the subject element of both free-text and controlled terms, where appropriate and feasible, in order to achieve optimal recall and precision in retrieval.

3. For the sake of semantic interoperability, the subcommittee recommends adopting an existing vocabulary or vocabularies with or without modification.

4. The adoption or adaptation of Library of Congress Subject Headings (LCSH) or Sears List of Subject Headings (for subject representation on

a broader level) as the basis for subject data in the Dublin Core metadata records for a general collection is recommended.

5. With regard to syntax, the use of full LCSH subject strings, if feasible (i.e., if time and trained personnel are available), particularly in the Online Public Access Catalog (OPAC) environment, should be encouraged. For Dublin Core, the subcommittee endorses the use of other elements (type, coverage) in addition to the subject element to accommodate different facets related to subject: topic, place, period, language, and so forth. Deconstructed subject strings should be so designated.

Regarding the choice of a controlled vocabulary for metadata records, the ALCTS subcommittee deliberated on three options: (1) use existing scheme(s), (2) adapt or modify existing scheme(s), or (3) develop new scheme(s). Developing a new scheme designed with the digital environment and the characteristics of metadata in mind is a tantalizing and tempting notion. However, developing a new scheme covering all subject fields is probably not practical, and most certainly not economical.

With regard to the first option, LCSH has long been one of the main staples for providing subject access not only for libraries but also for other information services. However, deliberations of the ALCTS subcommittee suggested that if LCSH and other traditional schemes are to be useful in the Web environment, they must undergo rigorous scrutiny and rethinking, particularly in terms of their structure and the way they are applied. Sophisticated technology can be used to extend the usefulness and power of traditional tools, but it cannot do all that is needed. Appropriately redesigned, however, traditional approaches to content retrieval can complement a simple keyword approach and may offer improved, or perhaps highly superior, retrieval results than are possible through the methods currently used in full-text document analysis and retrieval on the Web.

On balance, the ALCTS subcommittee recommended modifying and adapting an existing vocabulary, citing LCSH or Sears as the most viable options as the basis for an effective subject access tool in the networked environment. However, while the vocabulary, or semantics, of LCSH has much to contribute to the management of, and retrieval from, the enormous store of electronic resources, there are serious disadvantages in the way LCSH is currently applied. These disadvantages are:

1. LCSH headings must be assigned by skilled personnel because of the system's complex syntax and application rules.
2. LCSH heading strings (i.e., headings consisting of multiple elements including subdivisions of different facets) are costly to maintain in bibliographic or metadata records.
3. LCSH is not compatible in syntax with most other controlled vocabularies.
4. LCSH is not amenable to Web search engines.
5. LCSH's subfielding practice is difficult to encode in XML schemas such as Dublin Core and Simple Knowledge Organization System (SKOS).

These limitations mean that applying LCSH properly, in compliance with current policy and procedures, entails the following requirements: trained subject catalogers and indexers, systems with index browsing capability, systems with online thesaurus display, and sophisticated users.[2] In the current Web environment, such conditions rarely prevail. Thus, given LCSH as it stands—rules of application included—its acceptance as a major tool for Web retrieval seems unlikely. As suggested by the ALCTS subcommittee, in order to gain widespread acceptance in the networked environment, a subject access tool should possess the following characteristics:

1. Be simple and easy to apply and comprehend,
2. Be intuitive so that sophisticated training in subject indexing and classification, while highly desirable, is not required for implementation,
3. Be logical so that it requires the least effort to understand and implement, and
4. Be scalable for implementation from the simplest to the most sophisticated.

The question then becomes whether steps can be taken for LCSH to overcome its limitations and still remain useful in its traditional roles. In the face of these limitations, the ALCTS subcommittee recommended separating LCSH application syntax from matters relating to semantics and syndetics (i.e., cross-reference structure)—in other words, distinguishing between the vocabulary (the list of established LCSH headings) and the cataloging or indexing system (the way LCSH is applied in particular implementations).

THE HISTORY OF FAST

In 1998, at about the same time the ALCTS subcommittee was deliberating on the subject element in metadata records, OCLC was searching for a subject access system that could optimize the use of technology for Dublin Core metadata records. In pursuit of this aim, OCLC began exploring a new approach to subject vocabulary. A team was assembled with the purpose of developing a subject indexing vocabulary that would be based on the terminology of LCSH but would be applied with a simpler syntax based on facets. The team consisted of OCLC staff led by Edward T. O'Neill, Lynn El-Hoshy (who represented the Library of Congress), and Lois Mai Chan, an external consultant from the University of Kentucky. FAST is thus a joint development project between OCLC and the Library of Congress. OCLC and the Library of Congress share nonexclusive rights to implement, distribute, or provide access to FAST without restrictions, except for an agreement that neither organization can sell the FAST authority file.

At the beginning of its work, the team articulated several basic assumptions. It was determined early in the process that, in keeping with the premise of Dublin Core, a subject vocabulary suitable for the Web environment should meet the following requirements:

1. It should be simple in structure (i.e., easy to assign and use) and easy to maintain.
2. It should be usable by noncatalogers and in nonlibrary environments.
3. It should provide optimal access points.
4. It should be flexible and interoperable across disciplines and in various knowledge discovery and access environments including the OPAC.
5. It should be compatible with MARC (MAchine-Readable Cataloging), Dublin Core, and other popular metadata schemas.
6. It should be easy to maintain and amenable to machine manipulation.

In developing a subject schema that meets these requirements, two key decisions were required: (1) defining the semantics (the choice of vocabulary) and (2) formulating the syntax (enumeration vs. synthesis and precoordination vs. postcoordination). Regarding semantics, the FAST development team decided to retain LCSH vocabulary; by that move, compatibility with LCSH is retained, an important factor in the likely success of a new subject-tagging system.

As a subject vocabulary, LCSH offers several advantages:[3]

1. It is a rich vocabulary covering all subject areas.
2. It is the largest general indexing vocabulary in the English language.
3. There is synonym and homograph control.
4. It contains rich links (cross-references) among terms.
5. It is a de facto universal controlled vocabulary and has been translated or adapted as a model for developing subject heading systems by many countries around the world.
6. It is compatible with subject data in MARC records.
7. With a common vocabulary, automated conversion of LCSH to the new schema is possible.
8. The cost of maintaining the new schema is minimized since most of the changes to terminology in LCSH can be automatically incorporated into the new schema.

Work on developing the FAST schema began in earnest in 2000.

SOURCES OF FAST HEADINGS

FAST headings are derived from the following sources:

1. *Library of Congress Subject Headings*
   Most of the FAST headings are adopted or derived from established LCSH headings. LCSH headings that combine different facets are deconstructed into discrete headings, each representing a single facet.
2. *Headings Assigned to Bibliographic Records in WorldCat*
   Many complex headings (i.e., those containing more than one element in the heading string), are based on literary warrant (i.e., existing publications). They are derived from subject fields in the records in OCLC's WorldCat, which includes records created by the Library of Congress as well as those prepared by OCLC member libraries.
3. *Created Headings*
   In some cases, headings are created for FAST when no LCSH equivalents exist.

PRINCIPLES

Semantics

The general principles of controlled vocabulary were discussed in Chapter 1. In heading construction, FAST inherited some of the same principles on which LCSH is based. These principles, initially propounded by Charles A. Cutter,[4] include: common and current usage, literary warrant, uniform heading, and unique heading.[5] Uniform heading and unique heading are universal principles common to almost all controlled vocabularies.

Common and Current Usage

Choice of terms to be established as valid headings to be used in cataloging and indexing should be based on *common usage*. Synonymous terms are included as nonpreferred or lead-in terms, also referred to as "entry vocabulary." In choosing terms used as valid headings, preference is given to American practice, for example, **Elevators** rather than *Lifts* and **Organization** rather than *Organisation*. Needless to say, where there is a choice between a current term and an obsolete term, the former is chosen.

Literary Warrant

Writers on controlled vocabulary subject access systems frequently point out that there are two fundamentally different ways to build such systems: from the top down, so to speak (i.e., deciding what topics constitute the universe of discourse and what terms and interconnectors should be used to represent them), and from the bottom up (i.e., looking at what is written and selecting terms and interconnectors based on what is found in the literature). The latter approach is known as building on *literary warrant*, a concept first put forward by E. Wyndham Hulme[6] and adopted by LCSH. FAST subject headings were developed in especially close connection with OCLC's WorldCat. Since the majority of records in OCLC's WorldCat carry LCSH headings, from the beginning there was a close relationship between FAST and LCSH. As a result, FAST likewise follows the principle of literary warrant.

Uniform Heading

As discussed in Chapter 1, a controlled vocabulary term gathers all works on the same subject together, regardless of the author's choice of terminology. The English language, like most other languages, is rich in synonyms derived from different linguistic traditions. Many things are called by more than one name, and many concepts can be expressed in more than one way. Even within one country, variant names for the same object or concept often occur in different geographic areas. There are also many near-synonyms that are so close in meaning that it is impractical to establish them as separate subject headings. In all these cases, one of the several possible terms is chosen as the subject heading. If the term chosen appears in different forms or spellings, only one form is used. This practice is called *uniform heading*.

In establishing a subject heading, three choices are often required: name (term or term string for the entity or concept), form (grammatical construction), and entry element. When a subject has more than one name, one must be chosen as the heading to represent all materials on that subject, regardless of author's usage. For example, in FAST, as in LCSH, the heading **Older people** was chosen from among *Aged, Aging people, Elderly people, Old people, Older adults, Senior citizens*, and so forth. Similarly, **Parenting** was chosen in preference to *Parent behavior* or *Parental behavior in humans*. Frequently, a word may be spelled in different ways—for example, *Archaeology* or *Archaeology*, *Marihuana* or *Marijuana*. Again, only one of the spellings is used as the valid heading.

Perhaps the major choice in establishing a new heading is the choice among candidate synonyms. Choice of terms involves the following categories: synonymous terms, variant spellings, English and foreign terms, technical (or scientific) and popular terms, and obsolete and current terms. Examples are shown below.

CHOICE AMONG SYNONYMOUS TERMS

Superdense theory   *see* **Big bang theory**
Big bang cosmology   *see* **Big bang theory**
Nonlinear logic   *see* **Fuzzy logic**
Hothouses   *see* **Greenhouses**
Population explosion   *see* **Overpopulation**

CHOICE BETWEEN VARIANT SPELLINGS

Esthetics   *see* **Aesthetics**
Aeroplanes   *see* **Airplanes**
Audio books   *see* **Audiobooks**
Sea food   *see* **Seafood**

CHOICE BETWEEN INITIALS OR ACRONYMS AND SPELLED-OUT FORMS

Cardiopulmonary resuscitation   *see* **CPR (First aid)**
Machine-Readable Cataloging formats   *see* **MARC formats**
UFOs   *see* **Unidentified flying objects**

CHOICE BETWEEN DIFFERENT LANGUAGE TERMS

Mardi Gras (Festival)   *see* **Carnival**
Laissez-faire   *see* **Free enterprise**

CHOICE BETWEEN SCIENTIFIC (OR TECHNICAL) AND POPULAR TERMS

Blattaria   *see* **Cockroaches**
Elymus caput-medusae   *see* **Medusahead wildrye**
Forebrain   *see* **Prosencephalon**
Ascorbic acid   *see* **Vitamin C**

Unique Heading

A corollary to the principle of uniform heading is the principle of *unique heading*—that is, the idea that each heading should represent only one subject. This principle specifically addresses the issue of homographs. In order to minimize irrelevant documents in the retrieval process, words that are spelled the same but have different meanings must be distinguished.

The principle of unique headings requires that each heading represent only one subject or concept. The problem of polysemy or homographs is resolved in part by using *qualifiers*,[7] added for the purpose of disambiguation. A qualifier is a word or phrase enclosed within parentheses following the heading. For example:

Heliosphere (Astrophysics)
Heliosphere (Ionosphere)
Rings (Algebra)
Rings (Gymnastics)

A qualifier may also be used to provide context for obscure or technical terms, in which case it usually takes the form of the name of a discipline or of a category or kind of thing, for example:

Charge transfer devices (Electronics)
Excavations (Archaeology)
Forms (Law)
Grading and marking (Students)
Guo (The Chinese word)
Influence (Literary, artistic, etc.)
Open plan (Building)
Readers (Primary)
Relations (Canon law)
Relativity (Physics)
Spectral theory (Mathematics)
Streaming technology (Telecommunications)
Triangles (Interpersonal relations)

SYNTAX OF HEADINGS

In developing a syntax (i.e., how words are put together to represent single or complex subjects in a controlled vocabulary), several issues warrant consideration.

Faceting

FAST headings are categorized by facets, a term meaning an aspect of a subject. Eight facets are defined in FAST—seven subject facets and one form/genre facet:

Subject facets:
   Topic
   Place
   Time
   Event
   Person
   Corporate body
   Title of work
Form/Genre facet

Subject facets refer to headings that represent the contents of resources or documents being indexed or cataloged. They describe what the resources or documents are *about*. The form/genre facet, on the other hand, represents what the resources or documents *are*. For example, an almanac is assigned the heading "almanacs" from the *form/ genre* facet, and a book about almanacs is given the same heading from the *topic* facet.

Enumeration versus Synthesis

In a controlled vocabulary, as was stated in Chapter 1, *enumeration* means that the combination of multiple topics takes place before the heading enters the vocabulary. In other words, the vocabulary list contains ready-made terms for complex subjects as well as for simple subjects. For many complex subjects, phrase headings and heading/subdivision combinations representing multiple concepts are pre-established and represented as such in authority records. However, not all possible combinations are included. When precombined headings are not available, multiple single-concept headings may be assigned.

Another approach, called *synthesis*, is to list only some of the possible headings and to allow others to be formed as needed, following predescribed rules at the stage of indexing. FAST, unlike LCSH, is fully enumerative. With the exception of chronological headings, all of the possible headings are pre-established and represented by authority records. FAST headings for complex subjects may contain main heading/subdivision combinations, but each of these precombined headings is enumerated. The inclusion of enumerated headings in FAST is dependent on WorldCat usage (i.e., the terms are derived from headings that have been assigned to bibliographic records). Complex headings containing main headings and subdivisions are converted to FAST headings only if they are valid and if they have been used.

A major principle governing FAST is that elements contained in a main heading/subdivision combination do not cross facets. Within a facet, headings are precoordinated, but headings from different facets are assigned one by one, for postcoordination. For example, a work about economic conditions of women in the United States in the 19th century would be assigned the following FAST headings:

Topic: **Women—Economic conditions**
Place: **United States**
Time: **1800–1899**
Form: **History**

Precoordination versus Postcoordination

FAST headings represent a hybrid of precoordination and postcoordination. Headings that contain multiple concepts in a string with a main heading and one or more subdivisions are by nature precoordinated. Complex subjects that are not enumerated are assigned two or more single-concept headings to be postcoordinated at the point of retrieval.

In FAST, precoordination takes two forms: (1) a phrase heading containing multiple concepts and (2) a main heading/subdivision combination. Terms belonging to different facets are assigned separately to be combined (i.e., postcoordinated) at the point of retrieval.

Precoordination

Many headings contain multiple-concept terms in the same facet. FAST contains many precoordinated (i.e., precombined) headings. These are illustrated in the following examples.

Adjectival phrases:

Chuckwagon racing
Energy labeling
Plant inspection
Wildlife recovery

Phrases containing conjunctions or followed by "etc." (representing partial synonymy):

Bear deterrents and repellents
Camp sites, facilities, etc.
Decoration and ornament
Lacquer and lacquering

Phrases containing conjunctions (representing relationships):

Books and reading
Children and terrorism
Computers and college students
Libraries and the unemployed
Mass media and gays

Phrases containing prepositions:

Discrimination against people with disabilities
Internet in library reference services
Oil pollution of groundwater
Recorders (2) with plucked instrument ensemble

Headings with subdivisions:

Life skills—Testing
Mars (Planet)—Ares Vallis
Sound recordings—Remixing

Combinations of the preceding forms:

Illumination of books and manuscripts
Newly independent states—Diplomatic and consular service

Other highly complex and specific headings, for instance:

Children—Books and reading—Government policy
Ex-concentration camp inmates—Return visits to concentration camp sites
Jewish religious education of children with disabilities

Magnetic memory (Computers)—Testing—Computer programs
Universities and colleges—Employees—Labor unions—Law and legis-
    lation

Since many FAST users are not expected to be skilled subject catalogers or
indexers, automated terminological control must play a significant role to ensure the
quality of the subject terms assigned. With the exception of the time facet, all headings are fully enumerated within each facet. When dealing with complex subjects for
which there are precoordinated headings, cataloging or indexing consists simply of
finding the best match between the work being cataloged or indexed and available
precombined headings.

Postcoordination

No vocabulary can contain all possible term combinations. When a complex
heading containing all the concepts that would suit a particular subject is not pre-
established in FAST, headings reflecting different concepts are assigned separately
to be combined by the searcher at the point of retrieval (i.e., to be postcoordinated). As stated earlier, terms belonging to different facets may not be combined
in the same heading and must be postcoordinated.

HEADING STRUCTURE

Each FAST heading consists of a main heading with or without subdivisions. The
use of nonverbal symbols in conjunction with the words in a heading follows the
practice of LCSH and is relatively simple. The comma is used to separate a series
of parallel terms and to indicate an inverted heading—for example, **Law reports,
digests, etc.** and **Art, Mexican**. Parentheses are used to enclose qualifiers—for
example, **Shutouts (Sports)**. The dash is the signal for subdivision—for example,
Education—Aims and objectives.

Main Headings

A FAST main heading contains a word or phrase representing a topic, place, time,
person, corporate body, event, title of a work, or form/genre. Examples of main
headings include:

Arabian nights
Astronomy
Banks and banking
Bibliography
California
Catalogs
Chemistry, Organic
Computers and college students
Emigration and immigration

Lincoln, Abraham, 1809–1865
1939–1945
OCLC
Rare earth industry
Schools
Self-esteem
Spain

Subdivisions

A heading string contains a main heading followed by one or more subdivisions. A subdivision in a particular heading string must belong to the same facet as the main heading and is used to limit the scope of, or refine, the topic, for example:

Abortion—Law and legislation—Criminal provisions
Acid deposition—Environmental aspects—Mathematical models
Agricultural colonies—Government policy
Alcoholics—Services for—Planning
Americans—Travel—Historiography
Asians—Legal status, laws, etc.
Astronautics, Military—Equipment and supplies—Marketing
Bibliography—Union lists
Brain—Cancer—Patients—Family relationships
California—San Francisco—Chinatown
Michigan—Lake Charlevoix
Ohio—Columbus

Qualifiers

A qualifier is a word or phrase enclosed in parentheses following a main heading or subdivision. They are used for the following purposes:

Resolving ambiguity when a particular term has two or more meanings:

Rings (Algebra)
Rings (Gymnastics)

Providing context for obscure or technical terms:

Boundary layer (Meteorology)
Open plan (Building)
Spectral theory (Mathematics)

Identifying non-English terms:

Guo (The Chinese word)
Extra Hungariam non est vita (The Latin phrase)

Indicating the category or class of a proper name:

Banabans (Kiribati people)

Designating a special application of a general concept:

Cookery (Fish)

Specifying the medium of performance in music headings:

Concertos (Violin)

Identifying local places when the unqualified name is not unique:

California—Clear Lake (Lake County)
California—Clear Lake (Modoc County : Reservoir)
California—Clear Lake (Township)

MODULAR APPROACH

FAST adopts a modular approach in that each facet forms a distinct and discrete group of headings in a separate file. These lists may be used together or separately. In a particular application, all facets may not be required. For example, in indexing a collection of naturally occurring objects, the chronological and personal name headings may not be applicable.

Furthermore, one or more of the facets may be used with other standard lists; for instance, topical headings from FAST may be used with geographic headings from the Getty Thesaurus of Geographic Names (TGN).[8]

CONCLUSION

In summary, the FAST schema is:

1. Based on the vocabulary of the LCSH.
2. Designed for the digital environment.
3. A faceted vocabulary.
4. Usable by people with minimal training and experience in cataloging and indexing.

Advantages of FAST include:

1. It uses simple syntax.
2. It is enumerated (except for chronological headings consisting of dates only) for easy application.
3. It provides a tiered approach to allow different levels of subject representation.
4. It accommodates different retrieval models.
5. It is able to accommodate both precoordinated and postcoordinated indexing and retrieval.
6. It is amenable to computer-assisted indexing.
7. It facilitates computer-assisted authority control.
8. It facilitates mapping of subject data and cross-domain searching.

NOTES

1. Association for Library Collections and Technical Services, Cataloging and Classification Section, Subject Analysis Committee, Subcommittee on Metadata and Subject Analysis, *Subject Data in the Metadata Record: Recommendations and Rationale: A Report from the ALCTS/CCS/SAC/Subcommittee on Metadata and Subject Analysis* (1999), http://www.ala.org/ala/mgrps/divs/alcts/mgrps/ccs/cmtes/subjectanalysis/metadataandsubje/subjectdata.cfm (accessed April 14, 2010).

2. Karen M. Drabenstott, Schelle Simcox, and Marie Williams, "Do Librarians Understand the Subject Headings in Library Catalogs?" *Reference and Users Services Quarterly* 38, no. 4 (1999): 369–87.

3. Association for Library Collections and Technical Services, *Subject Data in the Metadata Record*.

4. Charles Ammi Cutter, *Rules for a Dictionary Catalog*, 4th ed. (London: The Library Association, 1953).

5. Lois Mai Chan, *Library of Congress Subject Headings: Principles and Application*, 4th ed. (Westport, CT: Libraries Unlimited, 2005), pp. 21–26.

6. E. Wyndham Hulme, "Principles of Book Classification." *Library Association Record* 13 (1911): 445–47.

7. Library of Congress, Cataloging Policy and Support Office, *Subject Headings Manual* (Washington, DC: Library of Congress, Cataloging Distribution Service, 2008), H357.

8. *Getty Thesaurus of Geographic Names* (Los Angeles, CA: J. Paul Getty Trust, 1999–), http://www.getty.edu/research/tools/vocabulary/tgn/index.html (accessed April 14, 2010).

4

TOPICAL HEADINGS

INTRODUCTION

This chapter discusses headings belonging to the FAST topical facet. Topical headings represent objects or concepts. In addition, they also include headings representing fictitious or mythological persons (including gods and goddesses), named animals, imaginary places, and organizations. For works about geologic periods, headings representing names of geologic periods have been established as topical headings, with the dates assigned separately as chronological headings.

Topical headings may be extended by topical subdivisions.

FUNCTIONS OF TOPICAL HEADINGS

The overwhelming majority of subject headings used in indexing or cataloging are topical headings, for example, **Clinical chemistry, Decision making**, and **Motion pictures**.

In contrast, some headings, such as **Encyclopedias and dictionaries, Periodicals**, and **Biography** represent the bibliographic form or genre of a work and belong in the form and genre facet. Because there may also be works written about compiling almanacs or evaluating periodicals in general, these headings may function as topical headings also. There are relatively few headings of the genre-as-subject type.

FORMS OF TOPICAL HEADINGS

FAST topical headings represent a mixture of natural and artificial forms of the English language. All main headings consist of nouns or noun-equivalents that display a variety of grammatical forms or "syntax," a term defined by Elaine Svenonius as "the order in which individual vocabulary elements of the language are concatenated to form larger expressions."[1] Single nouns, noun compounds (a and b), adjectival phrases, and prepositional phrases are based on natural forms and word order. In contrast, headings with qualifiers—such as **Iris (Eye)**—headings with subdivisions (**Sound recordings—Remixing**), and inverted headings (**Squares, Tables of**) are special formations that are not used in everyday speech.

In terms of grammatical forms, FAST inherited the structural features of the Library of Congress Subject Headings (LCSH). Topical headings appear in the following forms:[2]

  noun headings
  adjectival headings
  inverted adjectival headings
  phrase headings
  inverted phrase headings
  compound headings
  composite forms (combination of two or more of the preceding forms)

Most topical headings represent single concepts or objects. Compound and complex headings contain more than one concept or object, some expressing an additive relationship, others representing relationships (such as cause and effect, influence, bias) between concepts or objects. Still other headings represent a particular aspect of a subject, such as a process, for example, **Geography—Network Analysis**, or a property, for example, **French language—Grammar**.

Single-Concept Headings

Single-concept headings appear in the form of single-word terms or multiple-word terms.

Single-Word Headings

The simplest form of a main heading is a noun or substantive, which represents a single object or concept, for example:

  Catalogs
  Bioinformatics
  Chemistry
  Democracy
  Moneylenders
  Pleasure
  Urbanization
  Women

When adjectives and participles are chosen, they are used as substantives or noun equivalents:

  Advertising
  Poor
  Sick

With few exceptions, initial articles are eliminated from topical headings even when grammatical usage would require it, for example:

Arts [*not* The arts]
Many (Philosophy) [*not* The Many (Philosophy)]
One (The One in philosophy) [*not* The One (Philosophy)]

In the rare cases where the definite article is retained for semantic or grammatical reasons, the heading is inverted, for example: **State, The**; **Comic, The**.

In general, the plural form of a noun is used for denoting a concrete object or a class of people, for example, **Airplanes; Apples; Castles; Teachers**. This is not a rigid rule, and there are exceptions. For example, headings that represent biological species are generally in the singular, for instance, **Coconut palm**; **Japanese macaque**; **Rhesus monkey**; headings for higher levels are almost always in the plural, for example, **Palms; Macaques; Monkeys**. However, headings for domestic animals that are raised as livestock or kept as pets, as well as cultivated plants, are often in the plural form, for example, **Cats** and **Sweet potatoes**.[3]

In cases where both the singular and the plural forms of a noun have been established as headings, they have traditionally represented different subjects: usually the singular form represents a concept or abstract idea and the plural a concrete object, for example, **Essay** (as a literary form); **Essays** (for a collection of specimens of this literary form). However, in current practice, this distinction is no longer made. Another way of distinguishing between the concept and the specimens is to use the phrase form in one of the headings, for example, **Biography** (for collective biographies); **Biography as a literary form**.

In headings for art, the singular noun—for example, **Painting**; **Watercolor painting**—is used to represent both the activity and the object.[4]

Multiple-Word Headings

When a single object or concept cannot be properly expressed by a single noun, a phrase is used. Multiword terms appear in the form of adjectival or prepositional phrases.

Adjectival Phrase Headings

The most common phrase headings consist of a noun or noun phrase with an adjectival modifier. The modifier takes one of the following forms:

COMMON ADJECTIVE

Civil procedure
Digital art
Economic policy
International cooperation
Secret service

ETHNIC, NATIONAL, OR GEOGRAPHICAL ADJECTIVE

American poetry
Roman law

OTHER PROPER ADJECTIVE

Brownian movements
Christian sociology
Newtonian telescopes

PRESENT OR PAST PARTICIPLE

Laminated plastics
Self-organizing maps

COMMON NOUN

Computer software developers
Church architecture
Corporation law
Currency question
Information literacy
Race relations
Web portals

COMMON NOUN IN THE POSSESSIVE CASE

Carpenters' squares
Women's music festivals

PROPER NOUN

New Age movement
Toyota automobiles

COMBINATIONS

Veteran-owned business enterprises
Pressure-sensitive adhesives
Rapid eye movement sleep
Uninhabited combat aerial vehicles

Prepositional Phrase Headings

Prepositional phrases are used in single-concept headings when the concept is generally expressed in the English language in the form of a prepositional phrase, for example:

Balance of power
Boards of trade
Figures of speech
Right to housing
Spheres of influence
Stories without words
Willingness to pay

Multiple-Concept Headings

Multiple-concept headings appear as compound phrases, prepositional phrases, or subject heading strings consisting of a main heading with one or more subdivisions.

Compound Phrase Headings

Compound phrase headings, consisting of two or more nouns, noun phrases, or both, with or without modifiers, connected by the word *and*, the word *or*, or the word *etc.*, serve various purposes:

1. To express a reciprocal relationship between two general topics discussed at a broad level from the perspectives of both topics,[5] for example:

   Church and state

   Frontier and pioneer life

   Literature and society

   Religion and science

   Television advertising and children

   Women and literature

2. To connect subjects that are often treated together in works because they are similar, opposite, or closely associated, for example:

   Bolts and nuts

   Cities and towns

   Courts and courtiers

   Emigration and immigration

   Forests and forestry

   Frontier and pioneer life

   Good and evil

   Kings and rulers

   Labor laws and legislation

   Lamp-chimneys, globes, etc.

   Language and languages

   Mines and mineral resources

   Open and closed shelves

   Physical education and training

   School management and organization

   Universities and colleges

   Voyages and travels

3. To connect two nouns when one serves to define the other, more general noun, for example:

   Forces and couples

   Force and energy

Prepositional Phrase Headings

Prepositional phrase headings consisting of nouns, noun phrases, or both, with or without modifiers, and connected by one or more prepositions, are used to express complex relationships between topics, for example:

Child sexual abuse by clergy
Counseling in elementary education
Federal aid to adult education
Fertilization of plants by insects
Illumination of books and manuscripts
Teacher participation in curriculum planning
Voyages around the world

Headings with Subdivisions

A FAST heading may contain one or more subdivisions. Based on the principle that only elements belonging to the same facet may appear in a particular heading, topical headings may be subdivided by topical elements only, for example:

Automatic indexing—Research
Biology—Abstracting and indexing
Cataloging—Analytical entry
French language—Grammar
Hospitals—Administration—Data processing
Photoconductivity—Measurement
Sailing—Safety measures
Snowboarding—Equipment and supplies
Women—Employment—Research—Methodology

Topical subdivisions serve several functions:

1. To limit the meaning of the main heading, for example:

   English language—Grammar
   Cataloging—Analytical entry

2. To express a different aspect of the main heading, for example:

   Automatic indexing—Research
   Carnival—Social aspects
   Children—Books and reading
   Sailing—Safety measures
   Video games—Taxation
   Women—Legal status, laws, etc.

3. To express a multiple-concept topic, for example:

   Corn—Diseases and pests—Control—Environmental aspects
   Hospitals—Administration—Data processing

TYPES OF TOPICAL HEADINGS

Headings Representing Concepts and Objects

The majority of topical headings represent concepts or objects, for example:

Biology—Abstracting and indexing
Cataloging—Analytical entry
Children—Books and reading
Constitutional history
Corn—Diseases and pests—Control—Environmental aspects
Discoveries in geography
Excavations (Archaeology)
Hospitals—Administration—Data processing
Illumination of books and manuscripts
Photoconductivity—Measurement
Pilgrims (New Plymouth Colony)
Relations (Canon law)
Sailing—Safety measures
Secret service
Snowboarding—Equipment and supplies
Urbanization
Women—Legal status, laws, etc.

Form / Genre as Subjects

Form/genre headings such as **Almanacs**; **Archives**; **Periodicals**; and **Sources** are used in two ways. They represent what the work *is*, in either physical or intellectual form. (Chapter 9 explains this approach in more detail.) They may also be used as topical headings, representing what the work is *about*. For example, a book titled *Nonsubscription Side of Periodicals: Changes in Library Operations and Costs between Print and Electronic Formats* would be assigned the headings **Periodicals** and **Electronic journals** as topical headings in addition to whatever other topical headings are deemed appropriate. In contrast, a particular periodical or electronic journal would be given the corresponding heading as a genre heading along with subject headings, if appropriate.

Fictitious, Legendary, and Mythological Characters

Headings for fictitious, legendary, and mythological characters are established as topical headings, for example:

Bunyan, Paul (Legendary character)
Donald Duck (Fictitious character)

The qualifier ("Fictitious character") is used with names of characters of literary or artistic invention. Examples of headings for fictitious characters include:

Bond, James (Fictitious character)
Brown, Charlie (Fictitious character)

Holmes, Sherlock (Fictitious character)
Potter, Harry (Fictitious character)
Tarzan (Fictitious character)

Names of comic characters are also established in the form of **[Name of character]** **(Fictitious character)**, for example:

Felix the Cat (Fictitious character)
Superman (Fictitious character)

When the name of the character consists of a forename without any other distinguishing term, the creator's surname is added to the qualifier.

Elmo (Fictitious character : Henson)
Alice (Fictitious character : Carroll)

The qualifier **(Legendary character)** is used with headings for characters originating from legends, myths, or folklore:

Aeneas (Legendary character)
Don Juan (Legendary character)
Galahad (Legendary character)
Hua, Mulan (Legendary character)
Pecos Bill (Legendary character)
Robin Hood (Legendary character)
Tristan (Legendary character)

Names of gods and goddesses are also established as topical headings in the form of **[Name of god or goddess]** (**[Ethnic adjective] deity**), for example:

Amon (Egyptian deity)
Apollo (Greek deity)
Cacus (Roman deity)
God
God (Greek religion)
God (Hinduism)
Xuantian Shangdi (Chinese deity)
Pattini (Buddhist deity)
Pattini (Hindu deity)

For gods and goddesses of classical mythology who have names in both the Greek and the Latin forms, both are established as valid headings with appropriate qualifiers. When equivalencies can be determined between Greek and Roman gods and goddesses, reciprocal RT (related term) references are made between them.

Poseidon (Greek deity)
  RT **Neptune (Roman deity)**
Neptune (Roman deity)
  RT **Poseidon (Greek deity)**
Minerva (Roman deity)
  RT **Athena (Greek deity)**

Athena (Greek deity)
    RT **Minerva (Roman deity)**

Headings for mythological characters that are not gods or goddesses are established in the form of **[Name of character] ([Ethnic adjective] mythology)**, for example:

Bali (Hindu mythology)
Lilith (Semitic mythology)
Odysseus (Greek mythology)

Biblical characters, on the other hand, are established as headings for persons (see Chapter 8).

Named Animals

Topical headings are established for works about individual animals.[6] The heading consists of the name of the animal qualified by type of animal, with a cross-reference from the broader, generic term (BT), for example:

Man o' War (Race horse)
    BT **Horses**
Princess (Cat)
    BT **Cats**
Squirt (Dolphin)
    BT **Dolphins**
Lassie (Dog)
    BT **Dogs**

Imaginary Places and Organizations

Headings for imaginary places and organizations are established as topical headings, for example:

Dune (Imaginary place)
Oz (Imaginary place)
Avalon (Legendary place)
Hogwarts School of Witchcraft and Wizardry (Imaginary organization)
Kindle County (Imaginary place)
Animal Stars (Imaginary organization)
S.T.A.R.S. (Imaginary organization)

Geologic Periods

Headings for geologic periods consist of the name of the period without the dates, for example:

Holocene Geologic Period
Jurassic Geologic Period
Mississippian Geologic Period

In application, a work about a geologic period is assigned two separate headings: the name of the period as a topical heading and the dates alone as a chronological heading. For a list of geologic periods and their corresponding times, see Appendix Table A-1 (in Appendix B).

Other Entities Bearing Proper Names

Specific topical headings are also established for objects bearing proper names, for example:

Bury Saint Edmunds Cross
Congressional Award
International Simón Bolívar Prize
Nobel Prizes

Inverted Headings

As a legacy of LCSH, FAST inherited LCSH headings that reflect past practices that have yet to be updated by the Library of Congress. In the past, many LCSH topical headings were established in the inverted form in order to bring a significant word into a prominent position as the entry element, with the purpose of achieving better collocation of related topics in a manual catalog, for example:

Calendar, Celtic
Chemistry, Analytic
Chemistry, Organic
Education, Higher
Education, Preschool
Philosophy, Modern
Quotations, American

The Library of Congress has abandoned this practice when creating new headings, but many inverted headings remain and have been carried over into FAST.

NOTES

1. Elaine Svenonius, *The Intellectual Foundation of Information Organization* (Cambridge, MA: MIT Press, 2000), p. 58.
2. David Judson Haykin, *Subject Headings: A Practical Guide* (Washington, DC: Government Printing Office, 1951), pp. 21, 25.
3. Library of Congress, Cataloging Policy and Support Office, *Subject Headings Manual* (Washington, DC: Library of Congress, Cataloging Distribution Service, 2008), H1332.
4. Ibid., H1250.
5. Ibid., H1250.
6. Ibid., H1332.

5

---◆◆◆◆---

GEOGRAPHIC HEADINGS

INTRODUCTION

The FAST geographic facet contains place names that are common subjects of works. A place may represent the main focus of a work, a location that pertains to the main topic, or the origin of an object or activity.

Names of countries, and of political or administrative divisions within countries such as provinces, states, cities, and towns, are generally referred to as jurisdictional names. Other geographic names, such as those for natural features and man-made structures associated with places, are referred to as nonjurisdictional names.

This chapter discusses the general aspects of geographic heading formation and usage.

TYPES OF GEOGRAPHIC HEADINGS

Because the distinction between jurisdictional and nonjurisdictional names comes into discussion at many points, the first two sections extend, and give examples for, the brief definitions already presented. Later sections treat language, qualifiers, levels of geographic headings, and changes of name. The section after those deals with categories of geographic headings that require special treatment. A final section discusses the role and use of latitude, longitude, and feature type.

Jurisdictional Headings

Jurisdictional headings represent the names of political jurisdictions such as individual countries, principalities, territories, states, provinces, administrative districts, counties, cities, and so on. The choice of form and language used in FAST geographic headings is based on Library of Congress Subject Headings (LCSH), which, in turn, are formulated according to *Anglo-American*

Cataloguing Rules, second edition revised (AACR2R) and established in the LC/NAF authority file.

The following are examples of jurisdictional names:

China
Great Britain
Michigan
Monaco
Ontario
Puerto Rico
Slovenia

Nonjurisdictional Headings

Many geographic areas or entities are not jurisdictional units.[1] Nonjurisdictional headings are derived primarily from LCSH. Nonjurisdictional headings include the following types:

1. Geographic features, such as continents, regions, oceans, caves, lakes, mountains, rivers, valleys, and so forth
2. Archaeological sites, historic cities, and so forth
3. Canals
4. Dams
5. Parks, reserves, and so forth
6. Roads, streets, trails
7. Other man-made structures

For example:

Africa, Southern
Alps
Amazon River
Atlantic Ocean
Central America
East Asia
Himalaya Mountains
Mississippi River Valley
Ohio River Valley
United States—Oregon National Historic Trail
South China Sea
United States—Great Smoky Mountains National Park

CHANGES OF NAME

There are two types of changes, linear name changes and mergers or splits. These are discussed in the following sections.

Linear Name Changes

Examples of linear name changes include:[2]

FORMER NAME	LATEST NAME
Gold Coast	**Ghana**
British Honduras	**Belize**
Ceylon	**Sri Lanka**
Northern Rhodesia	**Zambia**
Southern Rhodesia	**Zimbabwe**
Belgian Congo	**Congo (Democratic Republic)**

When a place changes its name but retains the same territory, only the latest name is used as the geographic heading—with *USE* reference(s) from earlier name(s)—regardless of the period covered by the work being cataloged. All subject entries entered under the old name are changed to the new name.

Mergers or Splits

When the change of name involves substantial changes as a result of mergers or splits,[3] various headings are assigned depending on the area and the time period covered in the item. The general policy is to assign headings corresponding to the physical extent of the area discussed in the work being cataloged.

Mergers

When two or more jurisdictions merge, headings for both the premerger jurisdictions and the postmerger jurisdiction may be used as subject headings. The subject headings assigned to works involving places that have undergone mergers depend on the time period covered (i.e., prior to or after the merger) and whether the area discussed in the work corresponds to the pre- or postmerger jurisdiction.

An example of a merger is the joining of the Territory of Papua and the Territory of New Guinea, in 1945, to form the administrative unit of the Territory of Papua-New Guinea, which became self-governing in 1973 under the name Papua-New Guinea. The following headings are assigned to works about this place as appropriate:

Papua
New Guinea
Papua New Guinea

Splits

When a jurisdiction undergoes a split, headings for both the pre-split jurisdiction and the post-split jurisdiction may be used as subject headings. The subject headings assigned to works involving places that have undergone a split depend on the area and time period covered in the work being cataloged, and on whether the name of the earlier jurisdiction is retained by the later jurisdiction.

In the cases of Germany and Korea, the following headings are established:

Germany *[before 1945 and after 1990]*
Germany (East)

Germany (West)
Korea *[before the division or for the Korean Peninsula as a whole]*
Korea (North)
Korea (South)

LANGUAGE AND FORM OF GEOGRAPHIC HEADINGS

Language

A FAST heading takes the English form of the place name if there is one in general use, for example:

Austria—Vienna [not *Wien*]
Germany [not *Deutschland*]
Germany—Bavaria [not *Bayern*]
Italy—Florence [not *Firenze*]
South America [not *Sudamerica* or *America del sud*]
Spain [not *España*]

Some of the preceding examples contain two levels. Multilevel FAST geographic headings are discussed later in this chapter.

For nonjurisdictional headings, FAST also follows LCSH practice in preferring the English form of the name if there is one in common use. Examples of nonjurisdictional headings include:

China—West Lake [not *Xi-hu*]
Japan—Japanese Alps [not *Nihon arupusu*]
Rhine River [not *Rhein River*]

If there is no English form in general use, the name in the official language of the country is used, for example:

Brazil—Rio de Janeiro
Spain—Costa del Sol
Switzerland—Maderanertal [not *Maderaner Valley*]

When the vernacular (non-English) name is chosen as the heading for a nonjurisdictional entity, any generic term in the name is translated into English, unless the generic term in vernacular form is better known in the English-speaking world or is an integral part of the conventional name:

France—Forest of Fontainebleau [not *Forêt de Fontainebleau*]
Germany—Steinhuder Lake [not *Steinhuder Meer*]

But,

South America—Rio de la Plata [not *Plate River*]
Switzerland—Maderanertal [not *Maderaner Valley*]
Tien Shan [not *Tien Mountains*]

Vernacular names in non-Roman scripts are transliterated according to Library of Congress transliteration tables. For example, for names in the Chinese script, the Pinyin system is used:

China—Beijing
China—Qinling Mountains

Abbreviations

Geographic names are not abbreviated in FAST, with the exception of the District of Columbia. Since the abbreviation "D.C." is so common, it is used in preference to "District of Columbia." Some examples include:

Washington (D.C.) [not Washington (District of Columbia)]
Michigan [not Mich. or MI]
New York—New York [not *New York—NYC*]

Grammatical Form

Natural order is preferred over inverted order, for example:

Gulf of Mexico [not *Mexico, Gulf of*]
Lake Michigan [not *Michigan, Lake*]

Initial articles in nonjurisdictional foreign geographic names for places located in English-speaking countries are retained. The heading is inverted, however, if the initial article is the English *the*.[4] Examples include:

Kansas—El Dorado Lake
Montana—El Rancho Gumbo
Washington (D.C.)—Mall, The

Initial articles in nonjurisdictional geographic names for places located in non-English-speaking countries are omitted unless the initial article is *the* and is an integral part of the name. In such cases, the heading is inverted:

Spain—Bierzo [not *Spain—El Bierzo*]
Atlantic Ocean—Sound, The (Denmark and Sweden)

QUALIFIERS

When two or more places have the same name, qualifiers are used to distinguish among them.[5] Two types of qualifiers—place and type—are used with geographic names. In special cases, both place and type qualifiers in the form of (*Place qualifier : Type of place qualifier*) [note the special punctuation, space-colon-space, separating the two types of qualifier] may be used.

Examples of qualified headings include:

Russia (Federation)
Indiana—Center (Delaware County : Township)

The second heading above designates the township named Center, which is located in Delaware County, Indiana, as a township.

Place Qualifiers

When two or more places with the same name exist within the same first-level geographic area, place qualifiers are used to distinguish among them. For example, there are two Mill Rivers in Massachusetts, one in Berkshire County and the other in Hampshire County. To distinguish between the two, the county name is added as a place qualifier:

Massachusetts—Mill River (Berkshire County)
Massachusetts—Mill River (Hampshire County)

Only names that have been established in FAST are used as place qualifiers. In the preceding cases, the counties may be used as qualifiers because both **Massachusetts—Berkshire County** and **Massachusetts—Hampshire County** are valid headings.

The use of place qualifiers is not necessarily limited to resolving actual conflicts. For example, there is only one established heading for Michigan's Round Lake:

Michigan—Round Lake (Lenawee County)

However, Michigan's Round Lake is qualified in LCSH and the qualifier is retained in FAST. Although there are no headings established for other Round Lakes in Michigan, there are several other lakes with that name in the state. It is likely that the name was qualified to prevent future conflicts should a heading for one of the other Round Lakes in Michigan be established in the future. All place qualifiers from LCSH are retained in FAST.

Some headings contain compound qualifiers. There are at least four different White Mountains in the United States:

Alaska—White Mountains
Arizona—White Mountains
United States—White Mountains (California and Nevada)
United States—White Mountains (New Hampshire and Maine)

Two of the White Mountains are contained entirely within a single state and thus do not require qualification. However, since two of the White Mountains cross states boundaries, they are entered under **United States** and therefore must be qualified with multiple state names.

In some cases, a geographic qualifier indicates that the place is in the proximity of, rather than within, another area. In rare cases when no other suitable qualifier is available, the word *near* is added to the qualifier to clarify that it is near, but not part of, the qualifying geographic area, for example:

England—Wootton (near Woodstock (Oxfordshire))
Mexico—Villa Presidente Adolfo López Mateos (near Culiacá (Sinaloa))

Type Qualifiers

A type or a generic qualifier is used to distinguish between two or more places that have the same name and exist in the same general region but represent different types of geographic entities. Examples include:

Florida—Indian River (Lagoon)
Florida—Indian River (River)

Mexico—Baja California (Peninsula)
Mexico—Baja California (State)
New York (State)—Grand Island (Island)
New York (State)—Grand Island (Town)

When a name is not qualified, it is assumed to be the name of the city or other populated place.

Michigan—Mackinac Island [*the city on Mackinac Island*]
Michigan—Mackinac Island (Island)
Alberta—Cold Lake
Alberta—Cold Lake (Lake)
Italy—Naples
Italy—Naples (Province)
Italy—Piedmont
Italy—Piedmont (Principality)
Middle East—Jerusalem
Middle East—Jerusalem (Latin Kingdom)
South Africa—Cape of Good Hope
South Africa—Cape of Good Hope (Cape)
Wisconsin—Pine River
Wisconsin—Pine River (Waushara County : River)

When two or more places belonging to different types of jurisdictions bear the same name, a qualifier indicating the type of jurisdiction is added in accordance with AACR2R. The type-of-jurisdiction qualifier is usually an English term, if available. The vernacular term is used when there is no equivalent in English. Examples include:

Québec [*the province*]
Québec—Québec [*the city*]
Québec—Québec (Administrative region)
Québec—Québec (County)
Poland—Poznán [*the city*]
Poland—Poznán (Voivodeship)

Appendix Table A-3 contains a list of all type qualifiers that are used with FAST.

Place and Type Qualifiers

In special cases, both place and type qualifiers in the form of (*Place qualifier : Type qualifier*) are combined to form the qualifier. In this case, the type qualifier follows the geographic qualifier and is separated by the colon. Examples of combined qualifiers include:

California—Big Bear Lake (San Bernardino County : Lake)
California—Lake Valley (El Dorado County : Valley)
Illinois—Grant (Lake County : Township)
Pennsylvania—Union (Berks County : Township)
Pennsylvania—Union (Erie County : Township)

LEVELS OF GEOGRAPHIC HEADINGS

Geographic names for local places are established and applied in indirect order. The term *indirect order* refers to the practice of inserting the name of one or two larger places before the name of the local place in a heading; that is, the larger area is listed first. In other words, the structure of geographic headings is hierarchical: it begins with a first-level name that may contain up to two additional levels and can be qualified. The hierarchical structure of FAST geographic headings is based on the Geographic Area Codes (GAC).[6] In this book, levels of headings are separated by the long or em dash (—), for example, **Germany—Bavaria**.

First-Level Geographic Headings

All geographic headings begin with a first-level name as the main heading. The first-level name represents one of the following:

1. Natural features (continents, mountains, large bodies of water, etc.)
2. Countries or other first-level geographic names such as states and provinces
3. Extraterrestrial bodies
4. Geographic regions
5. Groups or types of countries

First-level geographic names are normally names of countries or larger areas. By way of exception, for the United States, Great Britain, Australia, and Canada, second-level entities such as states and provinces are treated as first-level names and entered directly (**Ohio** rather than *United States—Ohio*).

The following are examples of first-level geographic headings:

Albania
Antarctic Ocean
Asia
Baltic States
Bangladesh
British Columbia
California
Central America
Danube River
Great Lakes
Marshall Islands
Mediterranean Sea
Mississippi River
North America
Queensland
Russia (Federation)
Scotland
Trinidad and Tobago

Washington (D.C.)
Western Hemisphere

The complete list of established top-level names is given in Appendix Table A-2. First-level names fall into two classes: those that may be subdivided and those that may not be subdivided. Where multiple first-level names overlap in geographic coverage, usually only one of the names may be subdivided. For each of the names that are not subdivisible, there is always an alternate entity with similar geographic coverage that may be subdivided, for example:

Caribbean Sea [*subdivisible*]
Caribbean Area [not *subdivisible*]

In Appendix Table A-2, the subdivisible headings are shown in boldface.

Middle East is also treated as a first-level heading for geographic entities or features that are contained in two or more of the following countries: Iran, Iraq, Saudi Arabia, Syria, Turkey, Oman, Yemen, United Arab Emirates, Qatar, Kuwait, Jordan, Lebanon, and Israel. For example:

Middle East—Alexander River
Middle East—Jerusalem
Middle East—Persian Gulf States

Second-Level Geographic Headings

Geographic entities that lie within, or are part of, a first-level geographic entity are entered as second-level headings. Second-level headings include the following:

1. Provinces, states, and so forth, other than those located in Australia, Canada, Great Britain, and the United States
2. Districts, counties, cities
3. Sites (outside of cities)
4. Bridges and tunnels that lie outside of a city and are not closely associated with a specific city
5. Man-made structures that lie outside of a city, including camps, conservation districts, fairgrounds, golf courses, parks, recreation districts, utility districts, and water districts
6. Bays and similar bodies of water associated with first-level bodies of water

Examples of two-level headings:

Alaska—Lake Clark
Arizona—Glen Canyon Dam
Atlantic Ocean—Baltic Sea
China—Grand Canal
England—Cow Common Cemetery Site
England—London
England—Thames River
Europe—European Union countries
France—Forest of Fontainebleau

France—Provence
Germany—Steinhuder Lake
Illinois—Chicago
Iran—Tehran
Japan—Japanese Alps
Jordan—Amman
Kentucky—Bourbon County
Mediterranean Sea—Bay of Naples
Michigan—Lake Charlevoix
New Hampshire—Mount Washington
New York (State)—New York
Pacific Ocean—Jervis Bay
Russia (Federation)—Siberia
South Africa—Kruger National Park
South America—Rio de la Plata
Switzerland—Maderanertal
United States—Interstate 75
United States—Yellowstone National Park

Third-Level Geographic Headings

Third-level headings represent the following:

1. City sections
2. Neighborhoods
3. Highway interchanges
4. Sites within a city
5. Geographic features within a city
6. Bays and similar bodies of water associated with second-level bodies of water
7. Bridges and tunnels within a city or closely associated with a city
8. Other man-made structures within cities

Examples include the following:

China—Beijing—Western Hills
Czech Republic—Prague—Charles Bridge
British Columbia—Victoria—Point Ellice Bridge
Illinois—Chicago—Beltway
Ontario—Lake Rosseau—Portage Bay

City Sections and Neighborhoods

City sections are usually entered as third-level headings, for example:

Ohio—Columbus—German Village
California—San Francisco—Chinatown
Massachusetts—Boston—North End

It is sometimes necessary to add a qualifier to a city section when there is ambiguity.

New York City Boroughs

For sections of the boroughs in New York City, there may be four levels in reality: the state, the city, the borough, and the city section. Because FAST only allows up to three levels in a heading, the borough is omitted from these headings unless it is necessary for differentiation. In the latter case, the name of the borough is added as a qualifier.

New York (State)—New York—Greenwich Village
New York (State)—New York—Chelsea (Manhattan)
New York (State)—New York—Bay Terrace (Queens)

The LCSH heading for Chelsea was qualified by Manhattan because there is also a Chelsea in Staten Island. Even though no heading has been established for the Staten Island Chelsea, "Manhattan" was retained as a qualifier. For Bay Terrace, "Queens" was retained as a qualifier because there is another Bay Terrace in the borough of Staten Island. For New York city sections, if the LCSH heading is qualified, the qualifier is generally retained in FAST even when it is not necessary to prevent a conflict.

London Boroughs

London boroughs require special treatment, because London has two types of boroughs: inner boroughs and outer boroughs. Inner boroughs are treated in the same manner as the New York City boroughs, and the name of the borough is retained as a qualifier only when it is necessary for differentiation. The 12 inner boroughs in London are:

Camden
Greenwich
Hackney
Hammersmith and Fulham
Islington
Kensington and Chelsea
Lambeth
Lewisham
Southwark
Tower Hamlets
Wandsworth
Westminster

Outer boroughs of London are retained as subdivisions, and the term *London* is not included in the heading. Outer boroughs are treated as suburbs; they are thus second-level headings and are not treated as parts of London. The 20 outer boroughs in London are:

Barking and Dagenham
Barnet
Bexley
Brent
Bromley
Croydon
Ealing
Enfield
Haringey
Harrow
Havering
Hillingdon
Hounslow
Kingston upon Thames
Merton
Newham
Redbridge
Richmond upon Thames
Sutton
Waltham Forest

Examples of headings for boroughs in London:

England—London—Westminster
  [London is included since Westminster is an inner borough]
England—Harrow
  [London is not included since Harrow is an outer borough]
England—Bromley—Crofton Site
  [Site in an outer borough]
England—London—Bankside (Southwark)
  [The borough is used as a qualifier since there is another Bankside in London]
England—Richmond upon Thames—Richmond Bridge
  [Bridge in an outer borough]
England—Barking and Dagenham—Barking
  [Barking is a section of Barking and Dagenham]

English county names are not subdivided in FAST headings, although they may be used as qualifiers if needed for differentiation. For example, although Frampton on Severn is in Gloucestershire County, Gloucestershire is not included in the following heading: **England—Frampton on Severn**.

Areas Associated with Cities

There are four kinds of headings that designate the various areas associated with an individual city as defined by the Library of Congress.[7] In terms of territory, these four types of headings have been defined as follows:

[**City name**]: the city jurisdiction itself.

[**City**] **Suburban Area:** the territory associated with the city, including neighboring residential areas lying outside the city and nearby smaller satellite jurisdictions, but not the city itself.

[**City**] **Metropolitan Area:** a designated area consisting of the city itself and those densely populated territories immediately surrounding it that are socially and economically integrated with it.

[**City**] **Region:** an area including the city itself and its surrounding territory, the exact size and boundaries of which are indefinite and may vary according to the work being cataloged.

For example:

Italy—Naples
Italy—Naples Metropolitan Area
Italy—Naples Region
Massachusetts—Boston
Massachusetts—Boston Metropolitan Area
Massachusetts—Boston Suburban Area
Massachusetts—Boston Region
Middle East—Jerusalem
Middle East—Jerusalem Metropolitan Area
Middle East—Jerusalem Region
New York (State)—New York Metropolitan Area
Washington (D.C.) Suburban Area

A metropolitan area, a suburban area, or a region involving two cities, is represented by two separate headings, for example:

Texas—Dallas Metropolitan Area
Texas—Fort Worth Metropolitan Area
    [*not Texas—Dallas-Fort Worth Metropolitan Area*]

Entities within Cities

Headings for districts, quarters, sections, and man-made structures located within a city, such as streets, plazas, parks, bridges, monuments, and so forth, consist of the heading for the city subdivided by the name of the entity.[8] The name for the entity is normally in the vernacular form of the country in which it is located, except for pre-1500 buildings and for structures that have well-established English names. Examples include:

> Italy—Naples—Piazza del Mercato
> Italy—Naples—Quartiere San Lorenzo
> Italy—Naples—Via del Marzano
> California—San Diego—Balboa Park
> China—Beijing—Tian'an Men
> England—London—London Bridge
> New York (State)—New York—Brooklyn Bridge
> France—Marne-la-Vallée—Disneyland Paris
> Italy—Rome—Roman Forum
> California—Los Angeles—Sunset Boulevard
> England—London—Roman Forum Site
> New York (State)—New York—Times Square
> China—Beijing—Yihe Yuan
> Missouri—Saint Louis—Jefferson National Expansion Memorial

Bridges and Tunnels

Bridges and tunnels fall under the rules for city sections. If they are contained entirely within a city or are primarily associated with a city, they appear as third-level headings. Otherwise they are entered as second-level headings.

> California—San Francisco—Golden Gate Bridge
> Europe—Mária Valéria Híd
> Pennsylvania—Staple Bend Tunnel

SPECIAL CASES

Some types of geographic headings are given special treatment because of their unique nature. These include names of ancient or early cities and of archaeological sites; the same is true for parks, reserves, and other man-made structures associated with places.

Extinct Cities and Ancient Kingdoms

Extinct cities and ancient kingdoms are subordinated to the appropriate continent or region, for example:

> Africa—Hippo (Extinct city)
> Asia—Angkor (Extinct city)
> Europe—Albania (Ancient kingdom)
> Europe—Knossos (Extinct city)
> Middle East—Petra (Extinct city)

The Middle East is treated as equivalent to a continent in headings for ancient places that were located in one of the following present-day countries: Iran, Iraq, Saudi Arabia, Syria, Turkey, Oman, Yemen, United Arab Emirates, Qatar,

Kuwait, Jordan, Lebanon, and Israel. They are treated as second-level headings under Middle East:

Middle East—Terqa (Extinct city)
Middle East—Memphis (Extinct city)
Middle East—Asia (Roman province)

If there is evidence that the exact original site of the ancient or early city has been continuously or recurrently occupied up until modern times, the heading established for the modern city is used, with references from the ancient name, for example:

England—London [used for *England—Londinium*]
Austria—Vienna [used for *Austria—Vindobona*]

General guidelines based on Library of Congress policy[9] (modified by FAST rules) for establishing ancient or early cities that no longer exist are described below:

1. Use the form of the name most commonly found in standard reference sources (encyclopedias, gazetteers, etc.).
2. Add the qualifier *Extinct city* to a city in Europe, Africa, or Asia if it existed only before medieval times. Examples include:

Europe—Pompeii (Extinct city)
Middle East—Troy (Extinct city)

The name of the larger jurisdiction in which the city would be located today is added as a qualifier if there are two or more cities by the same name, for example:

Middle East—Philadelphia (Extinct city)
Pennsylvania—Philadelphia
Greece—Thebes
Middle East—Thebes (Egypt : Extinct city)
Middle East—Abila (Extinct city)
[*The larger jurisdiction is not added because there is no other city by the same name.*]

3. Cities of the Americas that ceased to exist by 1500 are treated as archaeological sites, for example:

Mexico—Chichén Itzá Site

Archaeological Sites

Headings for archaeological sites are entered under appropriate first- or second-level headings, and the term *Site* is added to the name. Examples include:

Mexico—Cobá Site
Colorado—Fourth of July Valley Site
Israel—Masada Site
England—London—Roman Forum Site
Arizona—Tucson—Lewis-Weber Site

If the site is a named cave or mound, the name of the cave or mound is used as the site name, for example:

Mexico—Texcal Cave
Iraq—Shanidar Cave

Bodies of Water

Bodies of water can be subdivided. Gulfs, straits, bays, and so forth are associated with, and therefore are used to subdivide, the larger body rather than the surrounding land area:

Atlantic Ocean—Aland Sea
Atlantic Ocean—Dingle Bay
    [not *Ireland—Dingle Bay*]
Atlantic Ocean—Gulf of Paria
    [not *Gulf of Paria (Venezuela and Trinidad and Tobago)*]
Hudson Bay—James Bay
    [not *James Bay (Nunavut)*]
Indian Ocean—Mermaid Sound
    [not *Mermaid Sound (Western Australia)*]
Lake Michigan—Grand Traverse Bay
    [not *Grand Traverse Bay (Michigan)*]
Pacific Ocean—Bering Sea
Pacific Ocean—Jervis Bay
    [not *Jervis Bay (New South Wales and Australian Capital Territory)*]
Pacific Ocean—Puget Sound
    [not *Washington (State)—Puget Sound*]

A strait is entered under the smaller of the two bodies of water to which it is connected.

Arctic Ocean—Nares Strait
Atlantic Ocean—Davis Strait
Black Sea—Kerch Strait

Rivers and canals, however, are associated with the surrounding land and are entered as a subdivision under the smallest geographic entity in which they are fully contained.

China—Grand Canal
China—Yangtze River
England—Oxford Canal
North America—Fortymile River

Rivers that are not wholly contained within first-level headings are entered under their own names. These rivers usually have their own GACs. Examples include:

Amazon River
Congo River

Danube River
Mekong River
Mississippi River
Ohio River
Rhine River

Inland channels are treated like rivers or canals and associated with land while larger channels are treated like straits and associated with bodies of water.

Atlantic Ocean—English Channel
Europe—Neretva Channel
Greece—Oreos Channel

Lakes, except for the North American Great Lakes, are subordinated to the surrounding land.

Alaska—Lake Clark
Wisconsin—Lake Geneva

The Great Lakes, either collectively or individually, are first-level names and as such are entered directly:

Great Lakes
Lake Michigan—Grand Traverse Bay
Lake Erie

Islands

An island or group of islands that is a part of a jurisdictional entity is entered subordinately to the smallest jurisdictional entity in which it is included:

Hawaii—Hawaii Island
Hawaii—Leeward Islands
Italy—Capri Island
Spain—Balearic Islands

Specific islands or cities on islands are also treated as second level headings, for example:

Greece—Andros Island
New York (State)—Long Island
Spain—Alaró

Areas associated with bodies of water are established as individual headings, for example:

China—Yangtze River
China—Yangtze River Delta
China—Yangtze River Estuary
China—Yangtze River Gorges
China—Yangtze River Gorges Region

China—Yangtze River Region
China—Yangtze River, South Channel
China—Yangtze River Valley
China—Yangtze River Watershed

Interstates/Highways/Freeway Interchanges

Interstates and highways follow the same rules as rivers, and freeway interchanges are treated the same way as a neighborhood or city section, for example:

Arizona—Phoenix—Hohokam Freeway
Jordan—King's Highway
Kentucky—Kentucky Highway 80
United States—Interstate 5—179th Street Interchange

Disputed Territories

Disputed territories are associated with the smallest nonjurisdictional areas in which they are fully contained.

Middle East—Tunb Islands
Middle East—Jerusalem

Language-Based Territories

Geographic territories based on language are treated as a subdivision of the general geographic area and may be combined with directional limitations:

Africa, French-speaking Western
Africa, Portuguese-speaking
Caribbean Area, English-speaking
Switzerland, Italian-speaking

Parks, Reserves, and so Forth

The following types of entities are also established as geographic headings:

1. Public and private parks of all kinds
2. Nature conservation areas, natural areas, natural history reservations, nature reserves
3. Wild areas, wilderness areas, roadless areas
4. Forests, forest reserves and preserves
5. Seashores, marine parks and reserves, wild and scenic rivers
6. Wildlife refuges, bird reservations and sanctuaries, game ranges and preserves, wildlife management areas
7. National monuments and so forth
8. Trails

Headings for individual parks, reserves, and so forth, including those located within cities, are established as second- or third-level headings under appropriate higher-level headings. Examples of headings for individual parks, reserves, and so forth, include:

Arizona—Grand Canyon
California—Big Sur Coast National Scenic Area
California—Hearst-San Simeon State Historical Monument
England—London—Hyde Park
England—North York Moors National Park
England—Oxford—University of Oxford Gardens
Germany—Naturpark Hohe Mark
Kentucky—Mammoth Cave National Park
Michigan—Hiawatha National Forest
New Mexico—Bandelier National Monument
New York (State)—New York—Central Park
United States—Yellowstone National Park
Washington (State)—Mount Saint Helens National Volcanic Monument
Wisconsin—Ice Age National Scientific Reserve

Other Man-Made Structures Associated with Places Larger Than a City

Structures such as reservoirs, dams, roads, bridges, and other man-made structures not located within a city are entered under the appropriate first-level headings. Examples include:

Asia—Silk Road
Canada—Confederation Bridge
England—Great Bridge
Europe—Strada di Francia
Massachusetts—Battle Road
Florida—EPCOT Center
Missouri—Harry S. Truman Reservoir
United States—Hoover Dam
Virginia—Mount Vernon (Estate)
Saskatchewan—Sturgeon Fort

Extraterrestrial Bodies

For extraterrestrial bodies in the solar system, first-level headings are established for individual planets and the moon, for example:

Mars (Planet)
Jupiter (Planet)
Moon

In addition, there are three other categories of first-level headings:

1. **Outer space:** Anything, including man-made objects, that orbits the earth.
2. **Solar system:** Anything that orbits the sun, other than planets, which have their own GAC.
3. **Deep space:** Anything that does not orbit the Sun or the Earth. Stars are in this category.

Planets, satellites, and comets are established as second-level headings. Examples of extraterrestrial headings include:

Outer space—Hubble Deep Field
Solar system—Amphitrite (Asteroid)
Solar system—Bennett comet
Solar system—Ceres (Dwarf Planet)
Solar system—Shoemaker-Levy 9 comet
Jupiter (Planet)—Ganymede (Satellite)
Deep space—Andromeda (Constellation)
Deep space—Andromeda Galaxy
Deep space—Magellanic Clouds
Deep space—Milky Way

LATITUDE, LONGITUDE, AND FEATURE TYPE

Latitude, longitude, and feature type are extremely useful attributes of geographic places. Latitude and longitude can greatly improve searching effectiveness. Using latitude and longitude, all of the geographic names in a given region can easily be identified. Graphical user interfaces built on maps can be used to simplify searching and can link to a wide variety of external databases such as Google Maps (http://maps.google.com/) and other similar databases.

Whenever possible, the latitude, longitude, and the geographic feature type are included in the FAST authority records for geographic names. While a variety of sources are used to determine the latitude, longitude, and feature type, the primary sources, in order of preference, are:

1. LCSH authority file,
2. LC/NAF authority file,
3. GeoNames geographical database,
4. Other sources, and
5. User-contributed data.

FAST authorities are derived from and linked to both Library of Congress subject and name authority records. If the Library of Congress authority record from which the FAST authority record is derived includes the latitude, longitude, or feature type in an identifiable form, that information is retained in the FAST authority file.

If the latitude, longitude, and feature type are not available from a Library of Congress source, the GeoNames geographical database is used (http://www.

geonames.org/). GeoNames contains over eight million geographical names and integrates geographical data such as names of places in various languages, elevation, population, latitude, longitude, and other similar information from various sources. As part of the FAST development, specialized software was created to match the FAST geographic names to entries in the GeoNames database. Although some names may have been mismatched, because the matching was very conservative, the information from GeoNames was not used unless it was extremely likely that the matched name represented the same geographic entity.

Based on the Library of Congress sources and GeoNames, the latitude and longitude were added to approximately two-thirds of the FAST geographic names. However, that still leaves thousands of geographic names lacking latitude, longitude, and feature type. To rectify this, the FAST development team, by searching a variety of sources, including several authoritative atlases, was able to identify the most frequently assigned names lacking latitude and longitude. Provisions were also made to allow users of the FAST database to add latitude, longitude, and feature type to FAST authority records. The procedures for adding this information to the FAST authority records are described in Chapter 11.

NOTES

1. Library of Congress, Cataloging Policy and Support Office, *Subject Headings Manual* (Washington, DC: Library of Congress, Cataloging Distribution Service, 2008), H690.

2. Ibid., H708.

3. Ibid., H710.

4. Ibid., H690.

5. Ibid., H810.

6. Library of Congress, Network Development and MARC Standard Office, *MARC Code List for Geographic Areas,* http://www.loc.gov/marc/geoareas/gacshome.html (accessed April 13, 2010).

7. Library of Congress, *Subject Headings Manual*, H790.

8. Ibid., H720, H1334.

9. Ibid., H715.

6

CHRONOLOGICAL HEADINGS

INTRODUCTION

Chronological headings represent the time period treated or covered in the document or resource at hand. Chronological headings are assigned to reflect the actual time coverage in the resources and are not necessarily limited to specific periods associated with particular events. Authority records for chronological headings are established only when needed for references or linkages.

FORMS OF CHRONOLOGICAL HEADINGS

Each FAST chronological heading contains either a single date or a date range consisting of a beginning and an ending date, and either the beginning or the ending date can be open. The only general restriction on FAST chronological headings is that when a date range is used, the second date must be later than the first.

The following format is used for FAST chronological headings:

[{**Since, To**}] *Date1* [-[*Date2*]]

> Where *Date1* and *Date2* are defined as: *year* [(([*month* [*day*]])]
>
> *Date1* is the only required value
>
> (*In the display above, square brackets* [ ] *indicate optional parameters, while braces* { } *indicate alternatives.*)

An individual date usually consists of only a year. However, a month or day and month can also be included in the form of:

2001 (September 11)
1841 (January)
2002 (February 8–24)

1774 (September 5–October 26)
1989 (December 1)–1990 (January 20)

Hours or smaller time units are not used in FAST.

Headings representing centuries are presented in the form of **xx00–xx99**, for example, **1800–1899** for the 19th century.

In order to improve readability, open date ranges are displayed with either "**Since**" or "**To.**" If the beginning date in a range is unknown, it is replaced by the phrase "**To xxxx**," for example, **To 1905**. If the ending date is indeterminate, it is expressed as "**Since xxxx**," for example, **Since 1905**.

In summary, there are five different forms of FAST chronological headings:

1. A single date:

   1945
   2001 (September 11)

2. A beginning date:

   Since 1775
   Since 1987

3. An ending date:

   To 1500
   To 1900

4. A date range:

   221 B.C.–220 A.D.
   1032–1499
   1931 (March)–1931 (October)

5. Geologic period:

   From 140 to 190 million years ago

B.C. / A.D.

All dates are based on the Gregorian calendar. Dates before the Common Era are designated as B.C.—for example, 221 B.C. Dates after the Common Era are represented by positive Arabic numerals, for example, 1914–1918.

All dates are considered to be after the Common Era (designated by A.D.) unless "B.C." is explicitly added. The only case where A.D. is added is when a date range starts with a B.C. date but ends with an A.D. date. For date ranges that are entirely B.C., "B.C." is added only to the ending date. Some examples of chronological headings involving B.C. dates include:

510–30 B.C.
146 B.C.–323 A.D.
To 146 B.C.
586 B.C.
48–47 B.C.

Geologic Periods

Geologic periods are a special case of a date range. Names of geologic periods are treated as topical headings, with the date ranges assigned separately as chronological headings. The time periods corresponding to the geological eras are expressed as a date range without including the name of the period.

Since the geologic date ranges comprise very large values, instead of using "B.C.," geologic periods are expressed in the form of "**From x million years ago**" or "**From x to x million years ago.**" When the year range is of the same magnitude, the magnitude is not repeated.

Quaternary Geologic Period:	**From 2 million years ago**
Pleistocene Geologic Epoch:	**From 10 thousand to 2 million years ago**
Oligocene Geologic Epoch:	**From 25 to 40 million years ago**

Headings for Named Historical Periods

Authority records for chronological headings are only created when necessary to provide a cross-reference. Historical periods with distinctive names are established in the form of the date(s) with the name of the period as a *see* reference. For example:

Early Period (Buddhism) *see* **To 250 B.C.**
Medieval Period (Great Britain) *see* **1066–1485**
Colonial Period (United States) *see* **1600–1775**
World War II Period *see* **1939–1945**
Elizabeth II, Reign of (Great Britain) *see* **Since 1952**

Qualifiers are frequently added to the name of the period to provide context. Establishing authority records with cross-references from the name of the period associates a default set of dates with the historical periods. When only the historical period is known, the default dates can be used as the chronological heading. However, the use of more specific dates is preferred when they are available.

CHRONOLOGICAL HEADINGS CONTAINING DATES ONLY

The following chronological headings contain dates only:

1812 (July 17)
   [Surrender of Fort Mackinac to the British during the War of 1812]
1939–1945
   [World War II]
1958 (November 18–19)
   [Sinking of SS Carl D. Bradley in Lake Michigan]

2002 (February 8–24)

[2002 Winter Olympics in Salt Lake City]

1981

[Air Traffic Controllers' Strike]

Among these headings, **1939–1945** is the only heading with an established authority record, since chronological headings are only established when needed for cross-references.

7

HEADINGS FOR EVENTS

INTRODUCTION

In FAST, an event is defined as something that happens or occurs during a particular time period. The definition covers both recurring events and single-occurrence events. FAST event headings are derived from: (1) Library of Congress Subject Headings (LCSH) topical headings, (2) LCSH conference and meeting names, and (3) LCSH period subdivisions that are identified by name (in applying headings to documents, for each nonrecurring event heading, the dates alone are also assigned separately as a chronological heading). As defined in *Functional Requirements for Bibliographic Records* (FRBR), an event "encompasses a comprehensive range of actions and occurrences that may be the subject of a work."[1] However, only event names that have been used at least once as a subject heading in a WorldCat bibliographic record are established as FAST headings.

All significant words in event headings are capitalized; and, as is the general practice, all geographic names are spelled out.

FORMS OF EVENT HEADINGS

Language

English language names are used unless the vernacular name is in common use. For example:

China Relief Expedition
Paris Peace Conference (1946)
Sino-American Conference on Mainland China
Tour de Suisse (Bicycle race)

Qualifiers

Recurring events and world events typically do not require date qualifiers. For example:

American Checker Federation World Championship Title Match
American International Toy Fair
Asian International Trade Fair
Baptist World Congress
Conference on the Law of the World
Congrès de droit international
Greek Independence Day Parade
Frederic Chopin International Competition
Intel World Chess
International Ballet Competition
ISCM World Music Days
Miss Universe Pageant
Shanghai World Expo

In the FAST vocabulary list, qualifiers are frequently added to event headings when required for identification, disambiguation, or differentiation. Three types of qualifiers are used: event type, place of event, and event date. Recurring events do not have date qualifiers and have place qualifiers only if the events take place at a single location.

Qualifiers are used in event headings to indicate the nature of the event or to resolve conflicts.

1. Event type qualifiers

   Around the World in 80 Days Motor Challenge (Automobile race)
   COMLA (Conference)
   Tour de France (Bicycle race)
   Trafalgar 200 (Anniversary celebration)
   World Series (Baseball)

2. Date qualifiers

   Abyssinian Expedition (1867–1868)
   Conquest of Peru (1522–1548)
   Partition of India (1947)
   Hurricane Andrew (1992)

3. Place qualifier

   War of 1859 (Italy)

Many headings contain multiple qualifiers in the form of *Event name (Place of event : date of event)*. For example:

Agricultural Laborers' Strike (Parma, Italy : 1908)
Burning of New London by the British (Connecticut : 1781)

Central Park Jogger Rape Trial (New York, New York : 1990)
Declaration of Independence (Brazil : 1822)
Siege of Acre (Israel : 1291)
Siege of Acre (Israel : 1799)
Siege of Antwerp (Belgium : 1584–1585)

Historical events can be local, national, or global in scope. For example, wars may be global or regional. Events, such as revolutions, coups, invasions, revolts, occupations, conquests, and so forth, are usually national in scope. Bombardments, captures, raids, uprisings, and other similar events are generally treated as local events. The place qualifier consists of the name of place at the appropriate level.

Unless the event name already contains the name of the place, a local event is qualified by the local place name, further qualified by the country or first-order political division:

American Revolution Bicentennial (1976)
John Brown's Raid (Harpers Ferry, West Virginia : 1859)
New Sweden Tercentenary Celebration (1938)
War of Independence (Scotland : 1285–1371)

TYPES OF EVENT HEADINGS

There are four main categories of event headings:

1. Headings for military conflicts
2. Headings for conferences, meeting, congresses, and so forth
3. Headings for sporting events
4. Headings for other types of events

Headings for Military Conflicts

Headings for wars, battles, sieges, and so forth are formatted with the place and date as the qualifier, unless it is redundant.

Bombardment of Alexandria (Egypt : 1882)
Burning of Columbia (South Carolina : 1865)
Concord, Battle of (Massachusetts : 1775)
Corinthian War (Greece : 395–386 B.C.)
Hanover, Battle of (York County, Pennsylvania : 1863)
Nazi Putsch (Austria : 1934)
Persian Gulf War (1991)
Siege of Baton Rouge (Louisiana : 1862)
Soviet occupation of Afghanistan (1979–1989)
The Count's War (Denmark : 1534–1536)
War of 1859 (Italy)

Headings for world wars are not qualified by place, for example, **World War (1914–1918); World War (1939–1945)**.

If the name of the event already contains the name of the local place, the local place name is not repeated in the qualifier:

Siege of Acre (Israel : 1291)
Siege of Acre (Israel : 1799)
Siege of Jerusalem (701 B.C.)
Siege of Paris (France : 885–887)
Siege of Rhodes (Greece : 1480)
Warsaw, Battle of (Poland : 1920)

Revolutions, coups, revolts, and so forth are generally on the national level. Headings for such events are qualified by the name of the country and the date, unless the information is already apparent in the name of the event.

Acarnanian Revolt (Greece : 1836)
An Lushan Rebellion (China : 755–763)
Insurrection (Crete : 1866–1868)
Movement for the Restoration of Democracy (Nepal : 1990)
Revolution (Colombia : 1840–1841)
Revolution (Colombia : 1899–1903)
Revolution (France : 1789–1799)
Revolution (Russia : 1905–1907)

Dates as well as place names are added to differentiate revolutions, wars, etc., that have the same name.

Civil War (Greece : 1944–1949)
Civil War (Congo : 1960–1965)
Civil War (Congo : 1997)
Coup d'état (Greece : April 21, 1967)
Coup d'état (Greece : December 13, 1967)

The American Civil War is considered to be a single event and is represented by the single heading:

American Civil War (1861–1865)

In addition, the following revolutions are also given similar treatment:

American Revolution (1775–1783)
Bolshevik Revolution (1917–1921)
European Revolutions of 1848
War of 1812

Headings for Meetings

Named conferences, meetings, congresses, and so forth are treated as events. They are similar to historical events in nature and structure in that both categories include occurrences identified by specific names and are generally associated with specific places or dates. FAST headings for names of conferences, congresses, etc.

are derived from the Name Authority File and the subject fields in the MARC records in WorldCat, including records prepared by the Library of Congress and by OCLC member libraries. Except for the qualifiers, such headings conform to the rules for corporate bodies set forth in Chapter 24 of *Anglo-American Cataloguing Rules*, second edition revised (AACR2R).[2]

The heading for a conference, meeting, congress, and so forth consists of its name without qualifiers unless there is a conflict or the name does not convey the meaning of the conference.

China War Reporting Conference

Commonwealth Conference

Conference on Disarmament in Europe

International Labour Conference

Potsdam Conference

Richmond Friends Conference

United Nations Conference on Contracts for the International Sale of Goods

United Nations Conference on the Human Environment

Vatican Council

White House Conference on Library and Information Services

Badger Boys State (Conference)

COMLA (Conference)

Commonwealth Conference

Commonwealth Conference (Oregon)

Conference on Disarmament in Europe

Conference on Disarmament (United Nations)

A number of headings for organizations contain the word "conference." These are treated as corporate headings (see discussions in Chapter 8) and should not be confused with event headings. Examples are shown here:

Administrative Conference of the United States

Conference on Security and Cooperation in Europe (Organization)

World Conference on Religion and Peace (Organization)

Headings for Sporting Events

Headings for sporting events, like other recurring events, are not qualified by either place or time. When necessary, they may be qualified by the event type.

Headings for sporting events are qualified by the type of event if it is not clear from the name of the event.

Olympic Games

Special Olympics World Summer Games

U.S. Invitational Chess Championship

Giro di Sicilia (Automobile race)

Gold Cup (Motorboat race)

Little League World Series (Baseball)
Rose Bowl (Football game)
Tour de Suisse (Bicycle race)
World Cup (Soccer)

Headings for Other Events

Other event headings include those for strikes, trials, expeditions, exhibits, festivals, natural disasters, etc.

Cannes Film Festival
Child Welfare Exhibit
China Relief Expedition
Colonial and Indian Exhibition
Edinburgh International Book Festival
Hong Kong International Film Festival
International Book Fair
Miss USA Pageant
New York Shakespeare Festival
Sundance Film Festival

Qualifiers are added to identify the type of event or to resolve conflicting headings:

SoHo Dances (Concert series)
World War (1914–1918)
World War (1939–1945)

Hurricanes and storms are qualified by date only:

Hurricane Andrew (1992)
Hurricane Georges (1998)
Tropical Storm Allison (2001)
Tropical Storm Grace (1997)

Headings for exhibitions, strikes, trials, earthquakes, volcanic eruptions, and other events of a local scope are qualified by place and date, for example,

Communist Trial (New York, New York : 1949)
Corn Scandal (Greece : 1986–1989)
Demonstration (Shanghai, China : 1947)
Ford Motor Company Strike (Windsor, Ontario : 1943)
Kent State Shootings (Kent, Ohio : 1970)
Minas Expedition (Nova Scotia : 1747)
Nuremberg Trial of Major German War Criminals (Germany : 1945–1946)
Earthquake (Whittier, Alaska : 1964)
Eruption of Vesuvius (Italy : 79)
San Francisco Earthquake and fire (California : 1906)

CHRONOLOGICAL AND GEOGRAPHIC
HEADINGS FOR EVENTS

Events are often closely associated with particular dates. Although many event headings include the date(s) as the qualifier(s), the qualifiers are not considered substitutes for the chronological headings, which are assigned in addition. The date(s) in a chronological heading need not correspond to the date(s) in the qualifier(s). For example, in the heading **Bolshevik Revolution (1917–1921)**, the dates in the qualifier are used to specify the revolution or to provide context, while the dates in the chronological heading reflect the actual time period covered by the resource being cataloged. The chronological heading **1917–1919** could be assigned to a book on the Bolshevik Revolution if the book covers only the first few years of the revolution. However, if the actual dates covered are not known, the dates of the event as a whole (e.g., **1917–1921**) can be used as the default date for the chronological heading.

Also, some events are closely associated with particular places, and many of these events will have the place of the event as a qualifier. As with dates, the place qualifiers are not substitutes for a geographic heading. For example, a book about Grant's Vicksburg campaign should be assigned the following headings to adequately describe the resource:

Geographic heading: **Mississippi**

Chronological heading: **1862–1863**

Event heading: **American Civil War (1861–1865)**

NOTES

1. IFLA Study Group on the Functional Requirements for Bibliographic Records, *Functional Requirements for Bibliographic Records: Final Report* (Munich, Germany: K. G. Saur, 1998), p. 27.

2. *Anglo-American Cataloguing Rules*, 2nd ed., prepared under the direction of the Joint Steering Committee for Revision of AACR, a committee of: the American Library Association, the Australian Committee on Cataloguing, the British Library, the Canadian Committee on Cataloguing, Chartered Institute of Library and Information Professionals, the Library of Congress (Chicago: American Library Association, 2005).

8

———◦•◦———

PROPER NAMES AS
SUBJECT HEADINGS

This chapter discusses three groups of proper names: names of persons, names of corporate bodies, and names of titles of works. Each of these three types of names is treated as a separate facet in FAST.

HEADINGS FOR PERSONS

FAST headings for persons include names of individuals and names of families. Headings for individual persons are based on headings in the LC/NAF authority file and therefore conform to the rules set forth in chapter 22 of *Anglo-American Cataloguing Rules*, second edition revised (AACR2R).[1] Headings for families are derived from *Library of Congress Subject Headings* (LCSH). Only names that have been used at least once as a subject in a WorldCat bibliographic record are established as FAST headings.

Name-title headings, consisting of the name of the author and the title of a work, are part of the title facet rather than the personal name facet.

Principles

Headings containing personal and family names are assigned as subject headings to works discussing individual persons or families. FAST headings for persons are generally limited to real persons. Headings for fictitious, legendary, and mythological persons are treated as topical headings (see discussion in Chapter 4).

Names of Individual Persons

Names of individual persons are used as subject headings for biographies, eulogies, Festschriften, criticisms, bibliographies, and literary works in which the persons figure. To ensure that the same form of a name is used for a person both as an author heading and a subject heading, headings consisting of names of persons are established according to the same rules.

The heading for an individual person contains one or more of the following elements:

Surname, Forename(s), Numeration, Person's title, Qualifier, Date(s)

The qualifier "Jr." and any qualifier consisting of numerals are omitted from the heading; dates and other qualifiers are added to differentiate persons with the same name.

Headings for names of persons are not subdivided. The following are examples of headings for individual persons:

Alexander, the Great, 356–323 B.C.

Alexandra, Queen, consort of Edward VII, King of Great Britain, 1844–1925

Bonaventure, Saint, Cardinal, ca. 1217–1274

Byron, George Gordon Byron, Baron, 1788–1824

Clinton, Bill, 1946–

Columbus, Christopher

Disraeli, Benjamin, Earl of Beaconsfield, 1804–1881

Ebbo, Archbishop of Reims, ca. 775–851

Jesus Christ

John XXIII, Pope, 1881–1963

Kennedy, John F. (John Fitzgerald), 1917–1963

Kilgour, Frederick G.

Lafayette, Marie Joseph Paul Yves Roch Gilbert Du Motier, marquis de, 1757–1834

Lindbergh, Charles A. (Charles Augustus), 1902–1974

Madonna, 1958–

Peter I, Emperor of Russia, 1672–1725

Plato

Solomon, King of Israel

Windsor, Edward, Duke of, 1894–1972

Names of biblical characters are established as headings for persons with appropriate qualifiers, for example:

Abraham (Biblical patriarch)

Adam (Biblical figure)

Aaron (Biblical priest)

Moses (Biblical leader)

Names of gods and goddesses are established as topical headings (see chapter 4).

Names of Families

The heading for a family appears in the form of [*Surname*] **family**, for example:

Adams family

Cook family

Koch family

Windsor family

No effort is made to distinguish between families with the same surname. The heading **Kennedy family,** for example, is used for works about any family with the surname Kennedy. If the same family has been known by different names, the most common form of the name is chosen as the heading, with *see* references from other forms. For example, *see* references are made from the following names to the heading **Smith family**:

Shmit family

Smidth family

Smithe family

Smitt family

Smitz family

Smyth family

Smythe family

Variants are usually determined from the work being cataloged and from standard reference works. Another source of variants is references to surnames already used as headings.

Names of Dynasties, Royal Houses, and so Forth

Headings containing names of dynasties, royal houses, and so forth that represent the people or families rather than historical periods during which they ruled are treated as personal names. They appear in the following forms:

[Surname] **dynasty,** *[dates if known]*

[Surname], **House of**

Examples include:

Ptolemaic dynasty, 305–30 B.C.

Sayyid dynasty, 1414–1451

Herodian dynasty, 37 B.C.–ca. 100 A.D.

Nala dynasty

Habsburg, House of

Lancaster, House of

Medici, House of

Windsor, House of

See references are made from variant forms of the name, for example, *Hapsburg, House of see* **Habsburg, House of**.

Headings for individually named houses of dukes, counts, or earls are established in the form of [*Name*], [*Title of rank in English*] of. For example:

Barcelona, Counts of

Elgin, Earls of

Mecklenburg, Dukes of

Headings for other aristocratic or noble families are established in the form of [*Name*] **family**. For example, **Tokugawa family.**

HEADINGS FOR CORPORATE BODIES

FAST headings for names of corporate bodies are derived from the names in the LC/NAF authority file. Headings for names of corporate bodies conform to the rules set forth in chapters 23 and 24 of AACR2R. Some of the corporate headings are derived from those assigned to bibliographic records in WorldCat. However, only names that have been used at least once as a subject in a WorldCat bibliographic record are established as FAST headings.

Headings for imaginary organizations are treated as topical headings and as such are discussed in Chapter 4.

Principles

A corporate body, as defined in AACR2R, is: "An organization or group of persons that is identified by a particular name and that acts, or may act, as an entity. Typical examples of corporate bodies are associations, institutions, business firms, nonprofit enterprises, governments, government agencies, religious bodies, local churches, and conferences."[2]

In FAST, corporate bodies include all those named in the preceding definition, except for conferences, meetings, and so forth, which are treated as event headings (see discussion in Chapter 7). Also excluded are headings for family names, which, even when they appear to fit the definition of corporate headings, are categorized as personal headings (see previous discussion). Name-title headings are treated as a separate facet and are not included in the corporate name facet. Corporate bodies include public and private organizations, societies, groups, associations, institutions, government agencies, archdioceses and dioceses, commercial firms, churches, and many types of man-made structures such as buildings.

Corporate names used as subject headings are discussed in the following sections. Some of the headings are qualified by generic terms or names of places, as required by *AACR2R* and Library of Congress descriptive cataloging policies.[3]

Forms of Headings for Corporate Bodies

The heading for a corporate body contains the main heading and may contain one or more subheadings or qualifiers.

Language

The heading for a corporate body contains its name in the official language of the body, based on items issued by the body in its language or in references sources.[4]

Académie de Paris
American Carpatho-Russian Orthodox Greek Catholic Diocese in U.S.A.
Colonial Williamsburg Foundation
Landesmuseum Hannover

Massachusetts Institute of Technology

Rand Corporation

Société des musées québécois

Syrian Antiochian Orthodox Archdiocese of New York and All North America

If the name appears in multiple languages, the official language of the body is used. For example:

Cinémathèque canadienne

[*not* Canadian Film Museum]

Schweizerische Landesbibliothek

[*not* Bibliothèque nationale suisse or Swiss National Library]

If the name is in a non-Roman script, it is Romanized according to the system used by the Library of Congress. Examples include:

Beijing tu shu guan

Dai Nihon Suisankai

Rossiĭsko-niderlandskoc nauchnoe obshchestvo

Zhongguo wen hua xue yuan

For international bodies, the English form of the name is chosen.

International Atomic Energy Agency

North Atlantic Treaty Organization

World Health Organization

Qualifiers

A qualifier is added to a corporate heading when the name does not convey the nature of the body or when there are two or more bodies with the same name.

Four types of qualifiers are used:

1. Generic qualifier indicating type of corporate body

   Dallas Cowboys (Football team)

   Golden State Warriors (Basketball team)

   Lloyd's (Firm)

   Queen Elizabeth 2 (Ship)

   Teens (Musical group)

   World Conference on Religion and Peace (Organization)

2. Name of place

   Balmoral Castle (Scotland)

   Blenheim Palace (England)

   Casa rotonda (Stabio, Switzerland)

   First Baptist Church (Brooklyn, New York, N.Y.)

   First Baptist Church (Georgetown, Washington, D.C.)

   Grand Hôtel (Stockholm, Sweden)

Grand Hotel (Yokohama-shi, Japan)
Labour Party (Great Britain)
Labour Party (Ireland)
Narodna biblioteka (Serbia)

3. Name of institution

Arthur M. Sackler Gallery (Smithsonian Institution)
Center for the American Woman and Politics (Eagleton Institute of Politics)
Institute of 1770 (Harvard University)

4. Date

New York Peace Society (1844–18??)

Some headings contain more than one qualifier. For example, after the 1995 season, the Cleveland Browns moved to Baltimore and became the Baltimore Ravens. In 1999, a new franchise was granted in Cleveland that retained the Browns name. As a result, a date qualifier was used to distinguish between the two Browns teams:

Cleveland Browns (Football team : 1946–1995)
Cleveland Browns (Football team : 1999–)

Headings for Main Corporate Bodies

The heading for a main corporate body consists of its name with or without qualifiers. There are two types of corporate bodies: government and nongovernment bodies.

Governments

The heading for a government consists of the name of the place over which the government has jurisdiction. For example:

Brazil
Iceland
India
British Columbia
Michigan

The conventional name of the government,[5] if there is one, is used as the heading, unless the official name is in common use:

Germany [*not* Bundesrepublik Deutschland]
Kentucky [*not* Commonwealth of Kentucky]
United States [*not* United States of America]

Nongovernment Bodies

The heading for a nongovernment body consists of the name of the body with or without qualifiers.

ACCEDC (Organization)
Alcatel Telecommunications Cable (Firm)
America Reads Challenge (Program)
Biblioteca apostolica vaticana
Catholic Church
International Business Machines Corporation
Microsoft Corporation
University of Oxford

Headings for Subordinate Bodies

In accordance with AACR2R, headings for subordinate or affiliated bodies may appear in one of the forms below:

1. The name of the subordinate body alone as the main heading. For example:

   Bodleian Library
   [a subordinate body of the University of Oxford]
   Catholic Charities of the Archdiocese of New York
   [a subordinate body of the Archdiocese of New York, which is a subordinate body of the Catholic Church]
   Library of Congress
   [a subordinate body of the U.S. Congress]
   Unesco
   [a subordinate body of the United Nations]
   United States Sanitary Commission
   [a U.S. government agency]

The heading is qualified when the name conflicts with that of another body, for example:

Cappella Sistina (Vatican Palace, Vatican City)
Cappella Sistina (Santa Maria Maggiore (Church : Rome, Italy))
United Nations Development Programme (Viangchan, Laos)
United Nations Development Programme (Zambia)
National Science Council (Ireland)
National Science Council (U.S.)

The name of the country as a qualifier is abbreviated in accordance with AACR2R, as shown in the preceding example.

2. The name of the parent body as the main heading, and the subordinate body as a subheading (separated by a period and two spaces as shown in the examples below), for example:

   Anglican Church of Australia. Diocese of Melbourne
   Bet ha-ḥolim "Hadasah" (Jerusalem). Synagogue
   Biblioteca apostolica vaticana. Museo sacro

Catholic Church. Diocese of Avila (Spain)

Catholic Church. Archdiocese of Fermo (Italy)

Catholic Church. Archdiocese of Toronto

Colonial Williamsburg Foundation. Library

Episcopal Church. Diocese of Newark

Episcopal Church. Diocese of Puerto Rico

Library of Congress. Cataloging Policy and Support Office

Massachusetts Institute of Technology. Energy Laboratory

Unesco. Division of the Unesco Library, Archives and Documentation Services

United Nations. Division of Human Rights

United States. Marine Corps

University of Oxford. Indian Institute

Worcester College (University of Oxford). Library

A corporate heading may contain multiple layers of subordinate bodies. For example:

California. Legislature. Assembly. Committee on Agriculture

Harvard University. Faculty of Arts and Sciences. Committee on Educational Policy

Library of Congress. Cataloging Distribution Service. Customer Services Section

North Atlantic Treaty Organization. Advisory Group for Aerospace Research and Development. Flight Mechanics Panel

United States. Congress. Senate

Virginia Polytechnic Institute and State University. University Libraries. Advisory Committee on Preservation

United States. Marine Corps. Division, 3rd. Battalion, 3rd. Kilo Company. Platoon, 2nd

Headings for corporate bodies do not carry subdivisions, although they may contain subordinate units shown as subheadings separated from the main heading or other subunits by the period and two spaces as illustrated in the preceding examples.

Corporate Name Changes

When the name of a corporate body is changed, only the latest name of the body is used. For example, Virginia Polytechnic Institute and State University has used the following names since it was established in 1872:

Virginia Agricultural and Mechanical College *[1872–1895]*

Virginia Agricultural and Mechanical College and Polytechnic Institute *[1895–1944]*

Virginia Polytechnic Institute *[1944–1970]*

Virginia Polytechnic Institute and State University *[1970–]*

However, only the current name, **Virginia Polytechnic Institute and State University,** is used as the subject, and anything about the university would be assigned that heading regardless of the particular period that was covered. A work covering the founding of the Virginia Agricultural and Mechanical College would be assigned the heading **Virginia Polytechnic Institute and State University.** The authority record would include the three earlier names as cross-references.

HEADINGS FOR TITLES

FAST headings for titles of works as subjects are derived from headings in the LC/NAF authority file and therefore conform to the rules set forth in Chapter 25 of *AACR2R.*[6] However, only titles that have been used as a subject in a WorldCat bibliographic record are established as FAST headings.

Principles

The title of a work used as an access point is called a *uniform title* and defined in AACR2R as: "A title of a work chosen from multiple titles by which the work has been known for the purpose of collocating and identifying works with different titles."[7] When the title of a work is used as a subject heading, the requirement of having multiple titles does not apply. A FAST uniform title is simply the subject heading for a work about another work in the form of the title by which the work being discussed is known.

Forms of Headings for Titles

Except for the order of the elements and the beginning element, headings for titles conform to the rules set forth in Chapter 25 ("Uniform Titles") of *AACR2R.* In contrast to the rules specified in *AACR2R,* FAST headings for titles begin with the title rather than the author of the work. In FAST headings, authors' names are used as qualifiers. Furthermore, FAST headings for titles do not include language, version, or date.

For a work of known authorship, the heading for the uniform title consists of the title of the work qualified by the name of the person or corporate body responsible for the intellectual content of the work as defined in AACR2R:

Title of work (Name of creator)

Dates of authors are not added after their names unless necessary to avoid conflicts, for example, **Hamlet (Shakespeare, William).**

For an anonymous work, the heading for the uniform title consists of the title of the work alone, for example, **Chanson de Roland.**

Language

Except for classical and Byzantine Greek works, the title of the work in the original language, transliterated if the original is in a non-Roman script, is used in the title heading. for example:

Etranger (Camus, Albert)
Exil et le royaume (Camus, Albert)

Hong lou meng (Cao, Xueqin)
Romeo and Juliet (Shakespeare, William)

Following AACR2R, for a work originally written in classical or Byzantine Greek, a well-established English title is used if there is one,[8] for example:

Iliad (Homer)
  [*not* Ilias (Homer)]
Apology (Plato)
  [*not* Apologia (Plato)]
Trojan women (Euripides)
  [*not* Troades (Euripides)
Children of Heracles (Euripides)
  [*not* Heraclidae (Euripides)]

If there is no English title, the Latin title is used, for example:

Timaeus (Plato)
  [*not* Timaios (Plato)]

If there is neither a well-established English title nor a Latin title, then the Greek title is used.

For a work created before 1501 that is written neither in Greek nor in Roman script, an established title in English is used if there is one.[9] For example:

Arabian nights

Qualifiers

Titles are qualified by creators' names for identification as shown in the preceding examples. Qualifiers are also added to the title to clarify the nature of the work or to distinguish between two or more works with the same title or two or more headings consisting of the same words:

1. to clarify the nature of the work:

   Hong lou meng (Television program)
   Microsoft Excel (Computer file)
   2001, a space odyssey (Motion picture)
   Dream of the red chamber (Choreographic work : Lin, Hwai-min)

2. to distinguish two or more works with the same title:

   Genesis (Anglo-Saxon poem)
   Genesis (Old Saxon poem)
   Star trek (Television program)
   Star trek (Computer file)
   Star trek (Motion picture : 1979)
   Star trek (Sound recording)

Foundation directory
Foundation directory (Online)

3. to distinguish two or more headings consisting of the same words but representing different facets:

Ali Baba (Folk tale) [a title heading]
Ali Baba (Legendary character) [a topical heading]

Types of Headings for Titles

Headings for titles fall into three general classes based on type of authorship: anonymous works, works of known authorship, and works from corporate bodies or conferences, meetings, and so forth. These are discussed in the following sections.

Anonymous Works

The heading for a work of unknown authorship consists of the title alone.

Beowulf
Bible
Koran
Sindbad the sailor
Talmud

Works that are in essence part of another work occur primarily when the parent work is a sacred scripture—of which the Bible is one. Titles of parts of anonymous works are not established as FAST headings unless they already exist in the LC/NAF authority file.

For a part of an anonymous work, the title portion consists of the uniform title and the name of the part or section of the work:

Bible. N.T. Mark
Bible. O.T. Deuteronomy
Koran. Surat Yusuf
Talmud. Avodah zarah

Works of Known Authorship

For a work of known authorship, the heading consists of the uniform title qualified by the name of the creator. The name of the creator is that of a personal author or a corporate body that is responsible for its intellectual content as defined by AACR2R. For example:

Inferno (Dante Alighieri)
Odyssey (Homer)
Paradise lost (Milton, John)
Sun also rises (Hemingway, Ernest)
Symphonies (Ives, Charles)

Symposium (Plato)

Symposium (Xenophon)

1996 Farm Act (United States)

Articuli sive errores 219 condemnati Parisiis a domino Stephano Parisiensi episcopo A.D. 1277 (Catholic Church. Diocese of Paris (France:. Bishop 1268–1279: Tempier))

Divine Liturgy of Saint John Chrysostom (Greek Orthodox Archdiocese of North and South America)

Education Act 1981 (Great Britain)

Job Training Partnership Act (United States)

Tracts for the times (University of Oxford)

The heading for a part or section of a work consists of the uniform title of the work and the name of the part or section:

United Nations Convention on the Law of the Sea. Rights of Access of Land-locked States to and from the Sea and Freedom of Transit

Works from Corporate Bodies, Conferences, Meetings, Etc.

For works resulting from the collective responsibility of a corporate body or conference, meeting, and so forth, the heading consists of the title of the work qualified by the name of the corporate body or conference, meeting, and so forth.

Annual Symposium proceedings (Society of Flight Test Engineers. National Symposium)

Catalogue of sale (London, England: Sotheby's (Firm))

Constitutio de sacra liturgia (Vatican Council)

Final Act (Conference on Security and Cooperation in Europe)

Proceedings of the Conference of Latin Americanist Geographers (Conference of Latin Americanist Geographers)

Symposia (Society for General Microbiology. Symposium)

NOTES

1. *Anglo-American Cataloguing Rules*, 2nd ed., prepared under the direction of the Joint Steering Committee for Revision of AACR, a committee of: the American Library Association, the Australian Committee on Cataloguing, the British Library, the Canadian Committee on Cataloguing, Chartered Institute of Library and Information Professionals, the Library of Congress (Chicago: American Library Association, 2005).

2. Ibid., Appendix D-2.

3. *Library of Congress Rule Interpretations* (Washington, DC: Cataloging Distribution Service, Library of Congress, 1989–).

4. *Anglo-American Cataloguing Rules,* 24 3/5, 24 7.

5. Ibid., 24 3C.

6. Ibid., chapter 25.

7. Ibid., Appendix D-9.

8. Ibid., 8 1.

9. Ibid., 25 10.

9

FORM AND GENRE HEADINGS

INTRODUCTION

FAST form and genre headings are derived from form subdivisions in Library of Congress Subject Headings (LCSH). Following the current practice of the Library of Congress, LCSH main headings derived from LCSH topical headings representing literary and artistic genres are also treated as topical headings in FAST. On the other hand, headings converted from LCSH subdivisions representing form or other genres are treated as form headings and so belong in the FAST form facet.

Principles

Form and genre headings represent what a work *is* rather than what it is *about*. Form headings include those indicating the form of presentation or arrangement of contents (such as bibliography, biography, catalog, dictionary, directory), intended audiences or intellectual level such as juvenile works, and physical medium such as fiction films, interactive multimedia sound recordings, and video recordings.

Genre headings indicate the genres specific to works in a particular discipline or area. They are applicable to works in specific disciplines such as art, law, literature, music, and religion. In these fields, the form of the works are often considered of greater importance than their subject content.

It should be noted that many of the same form headings are also used to represent works *about* the form, and when this is the case, they are topical headings; for example, the heading **Almanacs** is established both as a topical heading for a work *about* almanacs as well as a form heading for a work that *is* an almanac. In other words, the same term is used for both purposes. Thus, in treating a work that seems to be an almanac, the indexer must answer the question, "*Is* this work in essence an almanac, or is it *about* almanacs?" If it *is* an almanac, it is a *form* heading and any subdivisions must also belong to the form facet, but if the work is *about* almanacs, it is a *topical* heading and any subdivisions must also represent the topical facet.

When the same term can be used both as a topical heading and a form heading, separate authority records are established. As a result, in FAST, conflicts are permitted between form headings and topical headings—that is, the same term can be established as both a topical and a form heading.

In some cases, different headings are used for works of a particular genre and for works about that genre—for example, **Short stories** [form heading for a collection of short stories] and **Short story** [topical heading about the literary genre]. In FAST, the former belongs in the form facet and the latter in the topical facet.

Forms of Form and Genre Headings

Main Heading

A FAST form/genre heading consists of either a word or a phrase. For example:

Abstracts
Bibliography
Catalogs and collections
Computer games
Conference proceedings
Databases
Guidebooks
Notebooks, sketchbooks, etc.
Periodicals
Rules
Software
Sources

Subdivision

A form heading may carry a subdivision representing another form. For example:

Bibliography—Microform catalogs
Bibliography—Graded Lists
Bio-bibliography—Dictionaries
Biography—Anecdotes
Biography—Dictionaries
Biography—Pictorial works
Conversation and phrase books—for Computer industry employees
Maps—Bibliography
Maps—Manuscript
Music—Texts
Personal narratives—French
Sources—Periodicals
Textbooks—for foreign speakers

In some cases, the subdivision represents a more specific form than the main heading. As a result, the main heading-subdivision combination is hierarchical, for example, **Catalogs—Exhibition catalogs**; **Catalogs—Video catalogs**; and so forth.

One of the advantages of the hierarchical structure is *granularity*, that is, allowing different levels of application. For example, for a small collection or a collection where the different types of catalogs need not be distinguished, application may stop at the broad level by using the main heading **Catalogs** only.

EXAMPLES OF FAST FORM AND GENRE HEADINGS

Some of the more commonly used form and genre headings as well as those used in specific subject areas are shown here:

General Form Headings

Aerial Photography
Archives
Audiotape catalogs
Bio-bibliography—Dictionaries
Bibliography of bibliographies
Biography
Biography—Dictionaries
Blogs
Case studies
Catalogs
Catalogs—Video catalogs
Charts, diagrams, etc.
Chronology—Charts, diagrams, etc.
Conference proceedings
Data dictionaries
Data tape catalogs
Dictionaries
Directories
Discography
Facsimiles
Genealogy
Guidebooks
Handbooks, manuals, etc.
Indexes
Interactive multimedia
Interviews
Library use studies
Literary collections

Microform catalogs
Miscellanea
Newspapers
Online chat groups
Outlines, syllabi, etc.
Pictorial works
Posters
Quotations
Software
Sound recordings—for Arabic speakers
Sources—Periodicals
Speeches in Congress
Statistics
Study guides
Style manuals
Tables
Telephone directories—Yellow pages
Television interviews
Terminology
Textbooks—for foreign speakers
Trademarks
Translations
Union lists (Library catalogs)
Video catalogs

Audiovisual Materials

Fiction films
Fiction radio programs
Fiction television programs
Science fiction films
Science fiction radio programs
Science fiction television programs

Art

Art
Photographs
Exhibition catalogs

Cartography

Atlases
Bathymetric maps
Comparative maps

Index maps
Maps
Maps for people with visual disabilities
Maps for the blind
Maps—Manuscript
Mental maps
Outline and base maps
Pictorial maps
Physical maps
Relief models
Remote-sensing maps
Topographic maps
Tourist maps

Law

Constitution
By-laws
Trials, litigation, etc.

Literature

Drama
Fiction
Literary collections
Poetry
Science fiction
Short stories
Stories, plots, etc.

Music

3-piano scores
Chord diagrams
Chorus scores with organ
Chorus scores without accompaniment
Excerpts, Arranged—Scores and parts
Excerpts, Arranged—Vocal scores with organ
Excerpts, Arranged—Piano scores (4 hands)
Excerpts—Chorus scores with organ
Excerpts—Vocal scores with organ
Lead sheets
Librettos
Organ scores
Orchestral excerpts

Scores
Scores and parts
Vocal scores with organ
Vocal scores with organ and piano
Chord diagrams
Chorus scores with piano
Excerpts
Methods
Methods—Alternative rock
Methods—Alternative rock—Group instruction
Methods—Alternative rock—Self-instruction
Methods—Barrelhouse
Methods—Big band
Methods—Big band—Group instruction
Methods—Western swing
Methods—Western swing—Self-instruction
Parts (Solo)
Simplified editions
Studies and exercises
Studies and exercises—Big band
Studies and exercises—Right hand
Studies and exercises—Swing
Thematic catalogs
Vocal scores with organ
Vocal scores without accompaniment

Religion

Apologetic works
Biography—Sermons
Catechisms
Devotional literature
Harmonies
Hymns
Hymns—Texts
Pastoral letters and charges
Prayers
Radio sermons
Sermons

10

—◦◦•◦◦—

CROSS-REFERENCES

INTRODUCTION

In most controlled vocabularies that adhere to the principle of uniform heading, each person or corporate body is represented in a uniform way by a single established heading regardless of how many names the person has had or has used in his or her works. Likewise, a given place, concept, or object is represented by only one valid term or heading. However, everyday language is full of synonyms and terms that overlap in meaning, and users cannot always be expected to know which of several synonyms or near-synonymous terms, or which of several possible forms, has been chosen as the authorized term for a particular concept or object. Furthermore, users benefit from being made aware of other valid terms that are related to the subject they are seeking. Therefore, it is in the best interest of users if the system provides linkages between related terms as well as between authorized and unauthorized terms. Both objectives are achieved by means of cross-references. In retrieval, cross-references carry a great deal of the burden of leading users to desired information.

When there are synonymous terms for a given subject, one is chosen as the authorized or preferred term to be used in indexing, and the rest are included in the list as references directing the searcher to the authorized or preferred term for the subject. Authorized terms that are related in meaning are also linked by references: the links from lead-in terms are called USE references, and the links to related terms are, depending on the type of relationship, called broader term (BT) and related term (RT) references. Narrower term (NT) references are not explicitly included in the FAST authority record but can be inferred by reversing the BT references.

As a vocabulary based on the Library of Congress Subject Headings (LCSH) system, FAST also inherited the LCSH cross-reference structure. Three types of relationships are represented in FAST:

1. Equivalence (from an unestablished term to a valid term), expressed in terms of USE and UF (used for) and AUF (also used for) references;

2. Hierarchical (from one valid term to one or more broader terms), expressed as BT (broader term); and

3. Associative (from one valid term to one or more terms related on the same level), expressed as RT (related term) references.

Without these references, all the burden of refining searches would fall on the end-user. The examples in this chapter show the gathering of different types of cross-references relating to a particular concept or object under the authorized term followed by the references.

EQUIVALENCE RELATIONSHIP

As explained in Chapter 3, references based on the equivalence relationship serve to link synonymous terms to the valid heading.[1] Most controlled-vocabulary systems include not only terms established as valid but also other terms that are synonyms for those terms. Thus, a searcher submitting a search term that is not valid is told, through a USE reference under the term he or she submitted, what the valid term is for the subject of interest. The terms from which such references are made are often referred to as "lead-in terms." They allow the user to access material on a particular subject by searching with any term that is synonymous with the valid heading under which all materials on the subject are found. In FAST, a USE reference, also called a *see* reference in some controlled vocabularies, guides both indexer and user from a term that is not used as a heading to the term that is. USE references are made from synonymous terms, variant spellings, alternative forms, different entry elements, opposite terms, and overly narrow terms. Thus, USE references provide an entry (or lead-in) vocabulary for the system. While only valid subject headings are assigned as indexing terms to documents or resources, the control of synonyms enables retrieval of all materials on a particular topic regardless of the terms used by the author or indexer and those used by searchers. Without USE references, documents or resources would be retrieved only when the author or indexer and the searchers use the same term.

In many online systems, such referencing is automatic, so searchers inputting any one of a number of equivalent terms can retrieve all of the material the system has on the topic to which the term refers. In transparent cross-referencing, users are not aware of the fact that the term they have submitted is different from the one by which the system has tagged documents on the desired subject. However, no matter how sophisticated the system, this can only happen if equivalent terms are linked at both the thesaurus construction and system design stages.

In FAST, the following types of USE references are made.

Synonymous Terms

Examples of USE references from synonymous, but invalid, terms to the valid heading in FAST are shown in the following examples:

Biochemistry
>   UF Biological chemistry
>   Physiological chemistry
>   [For the user, this means:
>   Biological chemistry *USE* **Biochemistry**
>   Physiological chemistry *USE* **Biochemistry**]

Online journalism
> UF Internet journalism
>> Electronic journalism

Software architecture
> UF Computer software architecture
>> Computer software—Design
>> Computer software—Architecture
>> Architecture, Software

Older people
> UF Seniors (Older people)
>> Senior citizens
>> Older persons
>> Older adults
>> Old people
>> Elderly people
>> Aging people
>> Aged

Variant Spellings

USE references are made from different spellings and different word forms:

Archaeology
> UF Archeology

Audiobooks
> UF Audio books

Dogs
> UF Dog

Color
> UF Colour

Mosquitoes
> UF Mosquitos

Popular music
> UF Pop music

Seafood
> UF Sea food

Abbreviations, Acronyms, Initials, and so Forth

If the heading has been established in the spelled-out form, USE references from abbreviated forms are not generally made, unless such forms are well-known to the general public:

Adenylic acid
> UF AMP (Biochemistry)

Ammonium nitrate fuel oil
> UF AN-FO
>
> ANFO

Electronic mail systems
> UF E-mail systems
>
> Email systems

Conversely, if the heading has been established in the form of an abbreviation, acronym, or initials, a USE reference is regularly made from the spelled-out form:

CPR (First aid)
> UF Cardiopulmonary resuscitation

MARC formats
> UF Machine-Readable Cataloging formats

Different Language Terms

USE references are generally not made from equivalent terms in foreign languages to topical headings that are established in English, unless the foreign terms are well known to English-speaking users:

Alps
> UF Alpe
>
> Alpen
>
> Alpes
>
> Alpi

Carnival
> UF Fasnacht
>
> Fastnacht
>
> Mardi Gras (Festival)

Free enterprise
> UF Laissez-faire

UF references from vernacular names are made to English-language headings. For example:

China—Yellow River
> UF China—Hoang Ho
>
> China—Huang He
>
> China—Huang Ho
>
> China—Huanghe
>
> China—Hwang Ho

UF references are also made from English translations to headings established in the vernacular. For example:

China—Yangtze River
> UF China—Long River

Popular and Scientific Terms

UF references are made from popular terms to the scientific term chosen as the heading, and from scientific terms to the popular term chosen as the heading:

Mosquitoes
> UF Culicidae

Prosencephalon
> UF Forebrain

Vitamin C
> UF Ascorbic acid

Alternative Forms

Because of the principle of uniform heading, which requires that a heading appear in only one form in the catalog, references are made to an established heading from other syntactic forms likely to be consulted by users.

Aerobic exercises
> UF Aerobics

Older people—Education
> UF Education of the aged

Different Entry Elements

When a heading is inverted, a UF reference is generally provided from the direct form:

Chemistry, Organic
> UF Organic chemistry

Education, Higher
> UF Higher education

Painting, French
> UF French painting

Education, Elementary
> UF Elementary education

When a compound heading expresses a relationship between two objects or concepts, a UF reference is made from the form with the terms in reverse order:[2]

Architecture and state
> UF State and architecture

Computers and college students
> UF College students and computers

If the heading is in the form of a topic subdivided by other topic(s), a UF reference is made from the reversed form. For example:

Advertising—Newspapers
> UF Newspapers—Advertising

Narrow Terms Not Used as Headings

When a term is considered too narrow to be useful as a separate heading, a UF reference is sometimes made from the narrower term to a broader established heading:

Liberty
UF Civil liberty
Personal liberty
Pollution
UF Chemical pollution
Pollution—Control
Popular music
UF Popular songs
Popular vocal music
Schools—Accounting
UF High schools—Accounting
Public schools—Accounting

Ambiguous Relationships

Most equivalence relationships, including those described in the preceding examples, link an unestablished lead-in term to an equivalent established term. The use of the term in a UF reference implies that the term is invalid and should not be assigned. In fact, when a term appears as a UF it implies that (1) the term is invalid and (2) that there is an equivalent term that should be used instead. For example, Kampgrounds of America is commonly known simply as KOA, but the form of the name established by the Library of Congress is **Kampgrounds of America, Inc**. It would therefore be reasonable to expect a UF reference such as:

Kampgrounds of America, Inc.
UF KOA

However, while the term *KOA* meets the second equivalence condition, there is an equivalent term that should be used instead, it is an established heading and, as such, it does not meet the first condition. **Koa** is a valid heading—it is established as the heading for the Hawaiian acacia plant, a species of flowering tree. Therefore it is not appropriate to create a UF reference for KOA.

The common approach to dealing with references of this type has been to exclude the reference. For LCSH, no UF references are added unless the reference meets both conditions. However, that approach results in the loss of valuable information. Someone searching for the campground would only find materials about the flowering tree. Terms used to identify names and topics are rarely unique and unambiguous. Although the problem is not limited to acronyms, it is more common with acronyms.

In FAST, equivalence references from one valid term to another valid term are permitted and are identified as a AUF relationship. Some examples of FAST headings with AUF relationships include:

Kampgrounds of America, Inc.
AUF KOA

Queensland. Land Administration Commission

AUF LAC *[LAC is commonly used as an abbreviation for the Land Administration Commission. Lac is established as a topical heading for the resinous insect secretion.]*

Cobra (Association)

AUF COBRA *[Cobra is established as a personal name]*

Colombia. Ministerio de Educación Nacional

AUF MEN *[the heading* Men *is established for the topic]*

Association of European Operational Research Societies

AUF EURO *[Euro is established for the European currency]*

Association for Institutional Research

AUF AIR *[Air is established for the topic]*

AUF references are appropriate when (1) there is an equivalence relationship and (2) the lead-in term is valid but also represents a different concept or entity. While the AUF reference is similar to the RT references in that both terms are valid, it represents a distinct type of relationship. RT references link two terms with similar meanings, such as **Entomology** and **Insects**. It is likely that someone who is interested in insects might also be interested in entomology and vice versa.

HIERARCHICAL RELATIONSHIPS

Hierarchical references and related-term references connect two or more terms that are both (or all) valid subject headings.[3] Headings related hierarchically are connected by BT references. Under each valid heading, other headings representing concepts on a level immediately above that heading in the hierarchy are listed as BT, except when the heading in question represents the *top term* in the hierarchy or when the BT cannot be readily identified. The reciprocal NT (narrower term) relationship is implicit; headings representing concepts on a level immediately below that heading in the hierarchy are implied from the BT for the listed heading.

The following chain of references illustrates the hierarchical principle reflected in the BT references. Although the hierarchical structure is not always as rigorous as might be expected, each term in a chain of subjects from a hierarchy is usually connected to the one immediately above it by a BT reference. For example:

Chordata

BT **Animals**

Vertebrates

BT **Chordata**

Mammals

BT **Vertebrates**

Primates

BT **Mammals**

Hierarchical references like the preceding examples are made between headings having the relationships delineated as follows.

Genus/Species (or Class/Class Member) Relationship

Apes
    BT **Primates**
Rodents
    BT **Mammals**

Instance Relationship

Dogs
    BT **Domestic animals**
Togo (Dog)
    BT **Dogs**
Jupiter (Roman deity)
    BT **Gods, Roman**
Mars (Roman deity)
    BT **Gods, Roman**

Whole/Part Relationship

Hand
    BT **Arm**
Fingers
    BT **Hand**
Fingernails
    BT **Fingers**
Prosencephalon
    BT **Brain**

Compound and Complex Relationship

For headings containing multiple topics or concepts, additional BT references are made from those topics or concepts not used as the entry element (i.e., the initial word). Such topics, which often represent generic concepts with regard to the compound or complex headings, are presented in their established heading form:

Music and anthropology
    BT **Anthropology**
Education and crime
    BT **Crime**
Hydrogen as fuel
    BT **Fuel**
Internet in library reference services
    BT **Reference services (Libraries)**
Domestic relations (Canon law)
    BT **Canon law**

In polyhierarchical relationships, a heading belongs to more than one hierarchy. In these cases, a reference is made from the next broader heading in each hierarchy:

Biochemistry
    BT **Biology**
        Chemistry
        Medical sciences
Causeways
    BT **Bridges**
        Roads
Children
    BT **Age groups**
        Family
        Life cycle, Human
Ecogeomorphology
    BT **Geomorphology**
        Ecology
Gospel singers
    BT **Singers**
        Gospel musicians
Motor vehicles
    BT **Transportation, Automotive**
        Vehicles
Sheep dogs
    BT **Herding dogs**
        Livestock protection dogs

BT references are also made from headings that correspond to subdivisions. For example:

Cataloging—Contracting out
    BT **Contracting out**
Presidents—Election
    BT **Elections**

However, references of this type are not made if the terms are too broad or general, such as **[Topic]—Application** and **[Topic]—Utilization**.

ASSOCIATIVE RELATIONSHIPS

Associative or RT references are made between valid terms that are related other than hierarchically (i.e., related topics that are on the same hierarchical level or from different hierarchical trees). These references appear under both headings involved.

Religion   **Theology**
    RT **Theology**   RT **Religion**

Comprehension	Memory
RT **Memory**	RT **Comprehension**

RT references are made in the following cases, unless they share a common BT or begin with the same word or word stem.

1. To link two terms with overlapping meanings.

Ships	**Boats and boating**
RT **Boats and boating**	RT **Ships**
Longevity	**Old age**
RT **Old age**	RT **Longevity**
Drugs—Overdose	**Medication errors**
RT **Medication errors**	RT **Drugs—Overdose**
Online journalism	**Digital media**
RT **Digital media**	RT **Online journalism**

2. To link a discipline and the object studied.

Seismology	**Earthquakes**
RT **Earthquakes**	RT **Seismology**
Entomology	**Insects**
RT **Insects**	RT **Entomology**
Exfoliative cytology	**Epithelial cells**
RT **Epithelial cells**	RT **Exfoliative cytology**

3. To link a class of persons and their fields of endeavor, provided that the two headings do not begin with the same word stem.

Physicians	**Medicine**
RT **Medicine**	RT **Physicians**
Teachers	**Education**
RT **Education**	RT **Teachers**

CROSS-REFERENCES FOR PROPER NAME HEADINGS

Certain types of proper name headings require special cross-references. These are discussed in the following sections.

Personal Names

Names of Individual Persons

Cross-references for headings of individual persons are made according to *AACR2R*. Generally references are added for variant forms of the valid heading and for other names that the person is or was previously identified by. Examples include:

Onassis, Jacqueline Kennedy, 1929–1994
UF Kennedy, Jacqueline Bouvier, 1929–1994

   Kennedy, Jackie, 1929–1994

   Onassis, Jackie, 1929–1994

   Bouvier, Jacqueline, 1929–1994

   Jiaquilin, 1929–1994

   Jackie, 1929–1994

Roosevelt, Eleanor, 1884–1962

  UF Roosevelt, Eleanor Roosevelt, 1884–1962

   Roosevelt, Franklin D., Mrs., 1884–1962

   Roosevelt, Anna Eleanor Roosevelt, 1884–1962

Family Names

For headings of family names, UF references are made for different spellings not used as valid headings:

Adams family

  UF Adam family

   Adamson family

   Addams family

   Adems family

   Adom family

Cook family

  UF Cooke family

   Cooks family

Names of Fictitious and Mythological Characters

For headings of fictitious and mythological characters, treated as topical headings, UF and RT references are made from variant names and different entry elements. Examples include:

Randolph, Snooky (Fictitious character)

  UF Snooks (Fictitious character)

  UF Snooky (Fictitious character)

Zeus (Greek deity)

  BT Gods, Greek

  RT Jupiter (Roman deity)

Potter, Harry (Fictitious character)

  UF Harry Potter (Fictitious character)

Dynasties

For royal houses, UF references are made from variant forms of the name to the valid heading.[4] Examples include:

Habsburg, House of

  UF Austria, House of

   Hapsburg, House of

House of Austria

House of Habsburg

House of Hapsburg

Saxe-Coburg-Gotha, House of

UF Coburg, House of

Houses of Dukes, Counts, or Earls

For names of houses of dukes, counts, or earls, UF references from variant names, forms, and entry elements are made. Examples include:

Leinster, Dukes of

UF Dukes of Leinster

Masino, Counts of

UF Counts of Masino

Derby, Earls of

UF Earls of Derby

Corporate Names

For headings of individual corporate bodies, references are made from variant forms of the name and from different entry elements, for example,

Catholic Charities of the Archdiocese of New York

UF Catholic Charities of New York

Catholic Church. Archdiocese of New York (N.Y.). Catholic Charities

Library and Information Technology Association (U.S.)

UF American Library Association. Library and Information Technology Association

LITA

L.I.T.A.

If the name of a nonjurisdictional corporate body changes, both the earlier and the later names are used as valid headings. For example, the "Ohio College Library Center" changed its name to "OCLC." Both of these are established as valid headings with *see also* references connecting the two.

Geographic Names

Jurisdictional Names

Jurisdictional headings and cross-references are made according to the provisions of AACR2R and maintained as name headings in the authority file. Examples include:

Austria

UF Ao-ti-li

Ostmark

Alpen-unde Donau-Reichsgaue

al-Nimsā

Ausztria

Østrig

Avusturya

Österreich

Autriche

Malaysia—George Town (Pinang)

UF Malaysia—Georgetown (Pinang)

Malaysia—Pinang (Pinang)

Malaysia—Penang (Pinang)

Malaysia—George Town

Nonjurisdictional Names

Nonjurisdictional headings and cross-references are established and recorded in authority records.[5] UF references are made from variant names (including former names), different language forms, and different entry elements. For example:

England—Vale of Berkeley

UF England—Berkeley, Vale of

Spain—Costa del Sol

UF Spain—Sol, Costa del

Montana—El Rancho Gumbo

UF Montana—Rancho Gumbo

Turkey—Gallipoli Peninsula

UF Turkey—Gelibolu Peninsula

California—Geysers, The

UF California—Big Geysers

California—The Geysers

Europe—Pompeii (Extinct city)

UF Pompei (Extinct city)

Alps

UF Alpe

Alpen

Alpes

Alpi

Changes in Geographic Names

When the name of a place is changed in a linear fashion, only the latest name is used as a subject heading. For example, **Sri Lanka** is used as the valid geographic heading instead of the earlier name *Ceylon*. Examples where a UF reference is made from former names to the latest names include:

Sri Lanka

UF Ceylon

Belize

UF British Honduras

Ghana
  UF Gold Coast

In the case of name changes from mergers or splits in which different names of the same place are used as headings for works covering different periods, UF references are made from earlier names and variant forms of the name.
  Following are examples of changes in jurisdictional names:

Germany
  UF Bundesrepublik Deutschland
    Deutschland
    Federal Republic of Germany
    Weimar Republic
    Etc.
Germany (East)
  UF Democratic German Republic
    East German Democratic Republic
    East Germany
    Eastern Germany
    Ostdeutschland
    Etc.
Germany (West)
  UF Federal Republic of Germany
    Bundesrepublik Deutschland
    German Federal Republic
    Western Germany
    Etc.

No RT references are made among related headings such as **Germany**, **Germany (East)** and **Germany (West)**.

Headings for Other Named Entities

Appropriate cross-references are made for headings of other types of named entities and events. Examples include:

Princess (Cat)
  BT **Cats**
Squirt (Dolphin)
  BT **Dolphins**
Lassie (Dog)
  BT **Dogs**
London and Port Stanley Railway company
  BT **Railroads**
London Bridge (London, England)
  BT **Bridges**

Headings for Events

Appropriate cross-references are made for headings of events. Examples include:

Persian Gulf War (1991)
>UF Desert Storm, Operation (1991)
>>Gulf War (1991)
>>Operation Desert Storm (1991)
>>War in the Gulf (1991)
>RT **Iraq-Kuwait Crisis (1990–1991)**

World War (1914–1918)
>UF European War (1914–1918)
>>First World War (1914–1918)
>>Great War (1914–1918)
>>World War 1 (1914–1918)
>>World War I (1914–1918)
>>World War One (1914–1918)
>>WW I (World War, 1914–1918)
>>WWI (World War, 1914–1918)

World Cup (Soccer)
>UF FIFA World Cup
>>Copa Mundial de la FIFA
>>Coupe du monde de la FIFA
>>FIFA-Weltpokal
>>Football World Cup
>>Soccer World Cup

Tour de France (Bicycle race)
>UF Grande boucle (Bicycle race)
>>Tur de Frans (Bicycle race)

Vietnam War (1961–1975)
>UF Vietnamese Conflict (1961–1975)
>>Vietnam Conflict (1961–1975)
>>Vietnamese War (1961–1975)

February Revolution (1917)
>UF February Revolution (Russia : 1917)

Commonwealth Conference (Oregon)
>UF Oregon Commonwealth Conference

Potsdam Conference
>UF Tripartite Conference
>>Potsdamer Konferenz
>>Konferenz von Potsdam
>>Conference of Berlin
>>Berlin Conference
>>*Etc.*

Headings for Titles

Hamlet (Shakespeare, William)

UF Tragedy of Hamlet, Prince of Denmarke (Shakespeare, William)

Hamlet, Prince of Denmark (Shakespeare, William)

Shakespeare's Hamlet (Shakespeare, William)

Shakespeare's tragedy of Hamlet (Shakespeare, William)

Three-text Hamlet (Shakespeare, William)

Etc.

Arabian nights

UF Thousand nights and one night

Thousand and one nights

Alif laila

Mille et une nuits

Tales of the Arabian nights

Etc.

Constitution (New York (State) : 1894)

UF New York State Constitution (1894 : New York (State))

Constitution of the State of New York (1894 : New York (State))

Treaties, etc. (Allied and Associated Powers (1914–1920))

UF Treaty of Versailles and related treaties (Allied and Associated Powers (1914–1920))

CONCLUSION

Cross-references provide a useful structure of relationships among indexing terms. The principle of uniform heading relies heavily on cross-references for subject collocation. Synonyms connect users' search terms to the appropriate valid headings, thereby enhancing access points. Furthermore, hierarchical and associative references help users navigate their searches through related terms. The importance of cross-references cannot be overemphasized. Cross-references are important in any controlled vocabulary; indeed, such vocabularies would be much less effective without them.

NOTES

1. Library of Congress, Cataloging Policy and Support Office, *Subject Headings Manual* (Washington, DC: Library of Congress, Cataloging Distribution Service, 2008), H373.
2. Ibid., H310.
3. Ibid., H370, H375.
4. Ibid., H1574.
5. Ibid., H690.

Part III

APPLICATION OF FAST

11

THE FAST DATABASE

The form, structure, and principles underlying FAST were covered in Chapters 3–10 of this book. Chapters 11 and 12 treat the practical aspects of using FAST. This chapter deals with searching the FAST database to identify appropriate subject headings. Chapter 12 will look at the process of assigning FAST subject headings.

There are a variety of ways to access the FAST authority file. For heavy users, the authority file can be loaded into a local database or OPAC. OCLC also maintains a Web-accessible FAST database that is freely available for searching at http://fast. oclc.org/. It is the use of the OCLC FAST database that is described here.

Upon entering the FAST database, the following screen will appear (Figure 11.1):

A Project of OCLC Research   *Powered by OCLC SiteSearch*

OCLC FAST

Select an individual database to search:

FAST Forms   FAST Subjects

Figure 11.1. FAST Home Page

Selecting the *FAST subjects* link will allow for searching subject facets. The form facet is searched using the *FAST Forms* link.

INDEXING OVERVIEW

Three different types of indexes are provided: keyword indexes, phrase indexes, and other indexes. The keyword indexes store the individual words extracted from the specified fields. Phrase indexes provide access to complete fields, and the other indexes provide support access to particular data elements. The full list of FAST indexes is as follows:

Keyword Indexes	Fields Indexed
Keywords in all headings	1xx & 4xx fields
Keywords in topical headings	150 & 450 fields
Keywords in geographic headings	151 & 451 fields
Keywords in event headings	111 & 411 fields
Keywords in personal name headings	100 & 400 fields
Keywords in corporate name headings	110 & 410 fields
Keywords in uniform title headings	130 & 430 fields
Keywords in period headings	148 & 448 fields
Keywords in LCSH source heading	7xx fields (ind2 = 0)

Phrase Indexes	
Full headings	1xx & 4xx fields
Subfields	1xx & 4xx fields
Full *see also* headings	5xx fields
LCSH source heading	7xx fields (ind2 = 0)

Other Indexes	
FAST authority record number (ARN)	001 field, number only
Record status	Leader, byte 05
Level of establishment	008 field, byte 33

Level of Establishment	
Geographic area code (GAC)	043 field
Geographic feature	670 field, subfield $b
Geographic coordinates	034 field
LCCN for LCSH source heading	7xx; subfield $0 (numeric portion only)

Unless otherwise specified, all subfields, except the $w and $0–$9 subfields, are indexed.

For consistency and ease of searching, the keyword and phrase indexes are normalized using FAST normalization rules. These rules are a modified version of the North Authority Cooperative Program (NACO) normalization rules.[1] Diacritics and most punctuation are stripped, and all letters are converted to lower case. The five words, *and, or, not, near,* and *within,* are stop words and are dropped as part of the indexing process.

```
LDR     00572cz 2200181n 4500
001     fst00848727
003     OCoLC
005     20090914163117.0
008     041024nn anznnbabn    || ana d
016  7  $afst00848727 $2OCoLC
```

```
040      $aOCoLC $beng $cOCoLC $ffast
053    0 $aZ695.72
150      $aCataloging of books for the blind
450      $aCataloging of books in raised characters
550      $aBlind $xBooks and reading $0(OCoLC)fst00834295
688      $aLC (2008) Subject Usage: 0
688      $aWC (2008) Subject Usage: 2
750    0 $aCataloging of books for the blind $0(DLC)sh 85020832
```

The index entries for this authority record are shown in the following table:

Keyword Indexes	Index Entries
All keywords	cataloging, characters, blind, books, for, in, of, raised, reading, the
Keywords in headings	cataloging, characters, blind, books, for, in, of, raised, the
Keywords in topical headings	cataloging, characters, blind, books, for, in, of, raised, the
Keywords in LCSH source heading	cataloging, blind, books, for, of, the

Phrase Indexes	
Full headings	cataloging of books for the blind; cataloging of books in raised characters
Subfield	cataloging of books for the blind; cataloging of books in raised characters
Full See Also reference	books, blind, reading
LCSH source heading	cataloging of books for the blind

Other Indexes	
FAST authority record number (ARN)	fst00848727
Record status	n [New]
LCCN for LCSH source heading	sh 85020832

QUERIES

When searching, the same normalization rules are applied to the query so it is unnecessary for the end user to be familiar with the rules. The wildcards "#", "?", and "*" can be used to return patterns of results. The pound sign (#) substitutes for a single character, the question mark (?) for multiple characters, and the asterisk (*) is used for truncation. For example, to search for either woman or women, use *wom#n* as the search term. The term *river** matches to all words starting with "river," including river, rivera, rivers, riverbend, riverweed, and so forth. The query keyword "his?ogy" will match to both histology and histopathology. None of the wildcard characters are permitted in the first three character positions of the query.

Searching produces an ordered list of the FAST authorized headings. Each heading is also a link to a display of that full record. All results are ordered primarily by facet (that is, by the MARC tag used for the facet). The headings within the facet are then ordered alphabetically. To allow movement to a new portion of the result list, a "Jumpto ##" list appears both above and below the result list. For very long lists, ellipses replace some of the numbers, and inserting a desired location into the "Goto" box allows movement directly to that section of the list.

SEARCHING

The type of search being performed is indicated by blue highlighting of the three-entry bar above the search box. The default search is a simple keyword search of the words in the FAST headings, labeled *Keywords in All Headings*. The *Advanced* option supports Boolean searches, and the *Index View* allows for the viewing and selecting of index entries directly. These three approaches to searching will be addressed separately in the following sections.

Keywords in Headings

A search using the *Keywords in All Headings* box will return all authorized headings that contain the words entered in the query. The specific subfields indexed vary by facet and are listed in the index list given earlier in this chapter. This option assumes a Boolean AND relationship between all the words in the query and will retrieve all authorized headings or cross-references containing those words. However, only the words in the authorized heading and cross-references are matched; words from other fields in the authority record are not searched.

When in doubt about the type of search to use, this is often a good choice. It is simple and works well if the words in the query are very explicit and result in a limited number of hits. If the search is less explicit, it can be difficult to identify the desired heading from a long result list. For example, the keyword "Cancer" generates almost a thousand hits containing the word "cancer," and the entry for the full heading **Cancer** is deep in the results list.

However this approach works well for most searches. A search for "Sailboats" can be entered as in Figure 11.2:

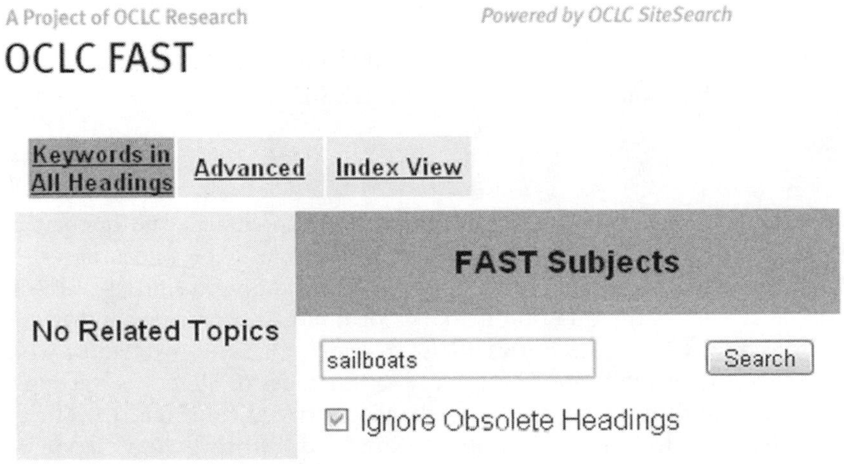

Figure 11.2. Default Query Screen

This search will result in the following display (Figure 11.3):

Figure 11.3. Search Results for "Sailboats"

Individual authority records can be displayed by clicking on the heading. If the heading sought is not in the initial display, either "Goto" or "Jump to" can be used to display the other headings retrieved. Clicking on **Photography of sailing ships** produces the following display (Figure 11.4):

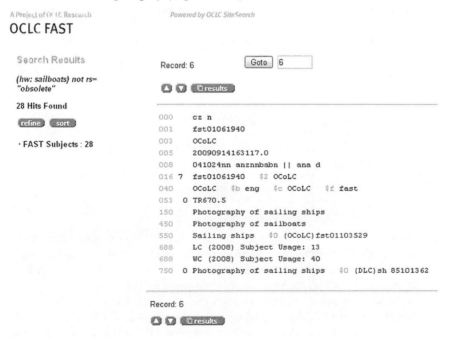

Figure 11.4. FAST Authority Record for **Photography of sailing ships**

Advanced Searching

The *Advanced* search option allows explicit Boolean searching and the specification of individual indexes. There is an index for each individual facet covering both the authorized heading and any cross-references or *see also* references. The links to the Library of Congress Subject Headings (LCSH) are indexed separately. See the complete list of indexes described in the "Indexing Overview" section of this chapter. Boolean searches are performed using the drop-down box preceding the search entry box. The Boolean operators *and, or,* and *not* are available.

Phrase Searching

There are four phrase indexes: the full headings index, the subfield index, the *see also* reference index, and the LCSH source heading index. When searching for a known heading, one method to find and view the record is to use the *Advanced Search* page to take advantage of the "Full Headings" index. For the heading **Education—Abstracting and Indexing**, the search query "education abstracting and indexing" is shown in Figure 11.5:

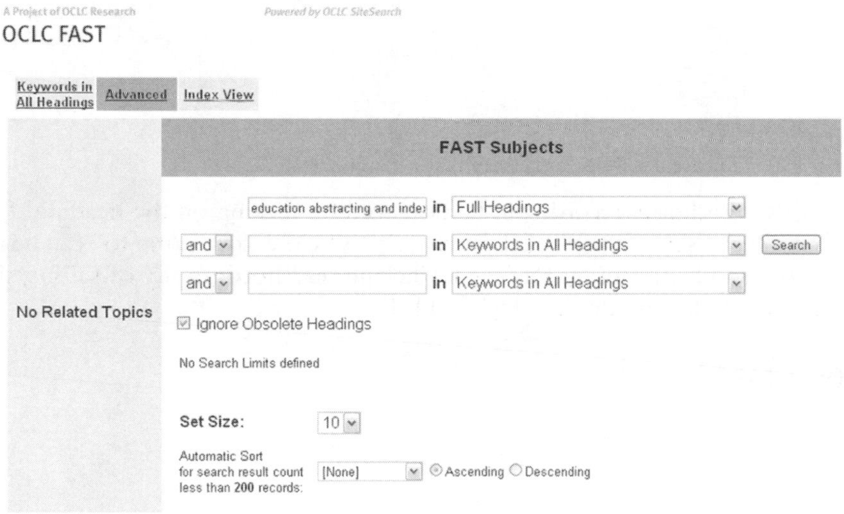

Figure 11.5. Query Screen for Advanced Searches

This search results in a single hit for the heading. Since the query is normalized, the following queries are equivalent since neither capitalization nor punctuation is significant:

```
education abstracting and indexing

Education-Abstracting and Indexing
```

Subfield delimiters and subfield codes can be entered either as a space or dash.

When looking for the heading **Education, Higher** including any subdivisions, search for "education, higher*" with the query terminated with the asterisk (*) to indicate truncation. This query produces the screen in Figure 11.6.

The first heading retrieved does not appear to match the query. Because both authorized headings (1xx fields) and cross-references (4xx fields) are indexed, the authority record for **Collective labor agreements—Education, Higher** includes *Education, Higher—Collective labor agreements* as a cross-reference.

Figure 11.6. Search Results for "Education, Higher"

A similar search can be performed by searching "education, higher" against the subfield index. Since the query is normalized, it will retrieve all headings with either **Education, Higher** as a main heading or **Education (Higher)** as a subdivision. The initial screen resulting from this search is as appears in Figure 11.7:

Figure 11.7. Search Results Using the Subfield Index for "Education, Higher"

The LCSH source heading index is used to retrieve a FAST heading using the LCSH heading from which it was derived. Among other uses, this index is very helpful for finding the equivalent FAST heading for an LCSH heading. The FAST heading corresponding to the LCSH heading **Little Traverse Bay (Mich.)** can be found by searching the LCSH source heading index for "little traverse bay (mich.)". The search produces the following screen (Figure 11.8) since two FAST headings were derived from the same LCSH headings:

A Project of OCLC Research   *Powered by OCLC SiteSearch*

OCLC FAST

Search Results   Records: 1 - 2

(lp= "little traverse bay mich")
not rs= "obsolete"   1. **151** Lake Michigan--Little Traverse Bay
                                                 Database: FAST Subjects
2 Hits Found
                                             2. **151** Michigan--Little Traverse Bay Region
(refine) (sort)   **Database:** FAST Subjects

· FAST Subjects : 2
                                             Records: 1 - 2

Figure 11.8. Search Results for LCSH Source Heading Search

Keyword Searching

Keyword searching allows Boolean searches of individual words. For example, to search for FAST headings for Little Traverse Bay, the following search (Figure 11.9) can be employed:

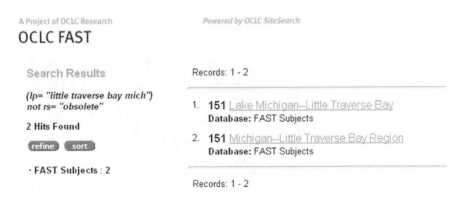

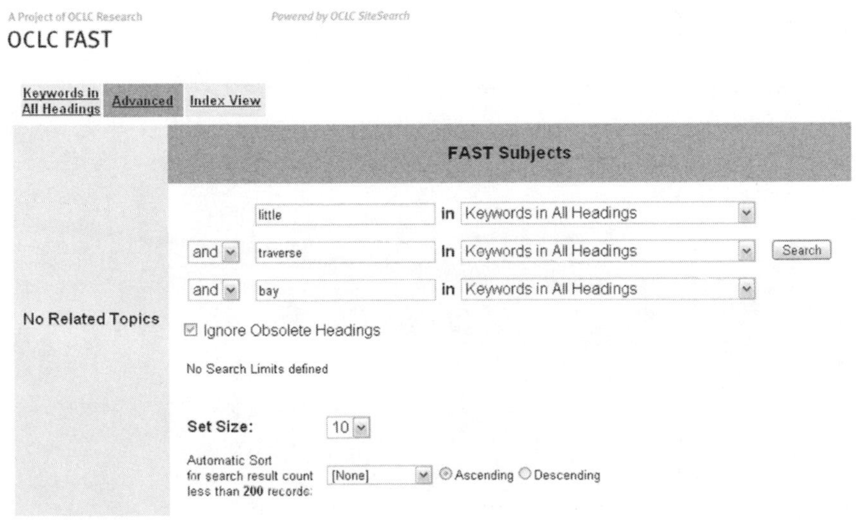

Figure 11.9. Keyword Query Screen

This search will result in the following (Figure 11.10):

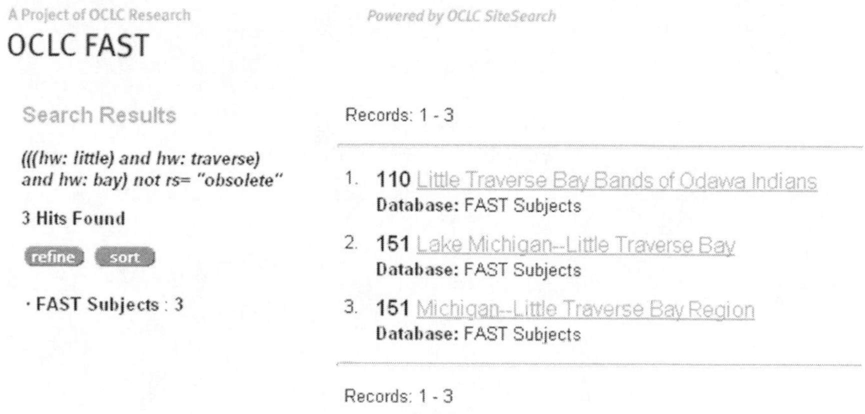

Figure 11.10. Keyword Search Results for "Little Traverse Bay"

As a convenience, multiple words can be entered in the search box. For keyword searching, an *and* relationship between the words is assumed. The single entry "little traverse bay" is equivalent to explicitly joining the three words with *and*. Since the relationship between the words is *and*, the order of the words is not significant—the query "traverse bay, little" is equivalent to "little traverse bay".

It is possible to search for either Grand Traverse Bay or Little Traverse Bay by entering the following (Figure 11.11):

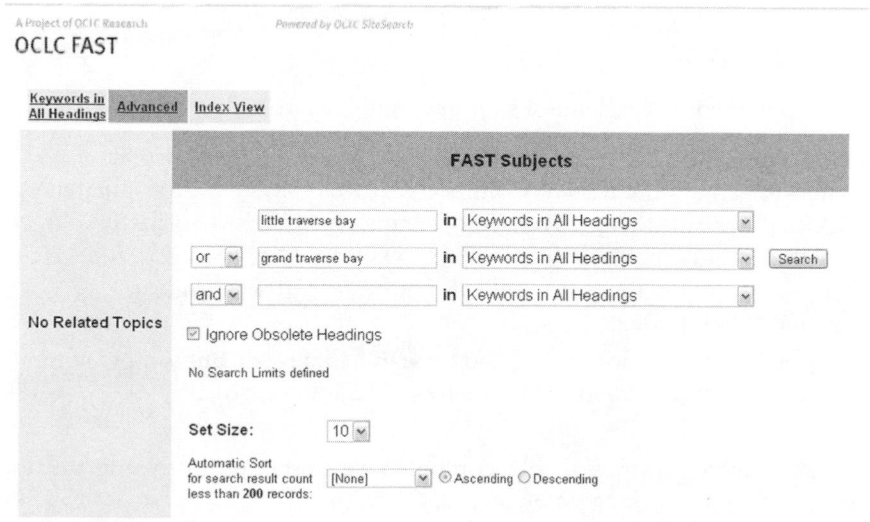

Figure 11.11. Boolean Search Query

This search retrieves the following result (Figure 11.12):

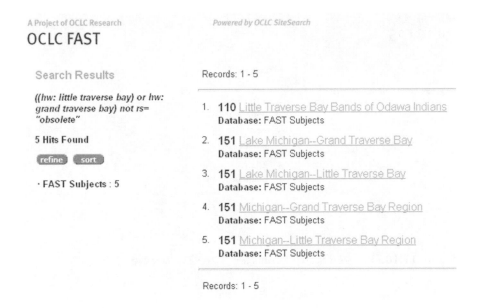

Figure 11.12. Search results for the Boolean Query

In addition to searching across all facets, searches can be limited to a single facet by searching a facet-specific index. For example, if only geographic names were the target of the search in Figure 11.11, the *Keywords in Geographic Headings* could have been selected instead of *Keywords in All Headings*. If that had been done, only the last four headings would have been retrieved.

Geographic Indexes

There are three specialized indexes for geographic searches:

Geographic Feature identifies the type of geographic feature; its use is limited to geographic names. Common feature types include populated places (cities), oceans, lakes, rivers, mountains, valleys, and so forth. The complete list of geographic features is shown in Appendix Table A-4.

Geographic Coordinates specify the latitude and longitude for geographic names.

Geographic Area Code (GAC) can be searched directly but is more commonly used to limit geographic searches to a specified region.

The geographic feature is usually combined with other terms to limit the results to records for a particular type of geographic feature. Limiting searches to a single geographic feature can greatly improve the precision. For example, if one was interested in lakes in Michigan, the query could combine the GAC "n-us-mi" (the GAC code for Michigan) with the geographic feature "Lake" as follows (Figure 11.13):

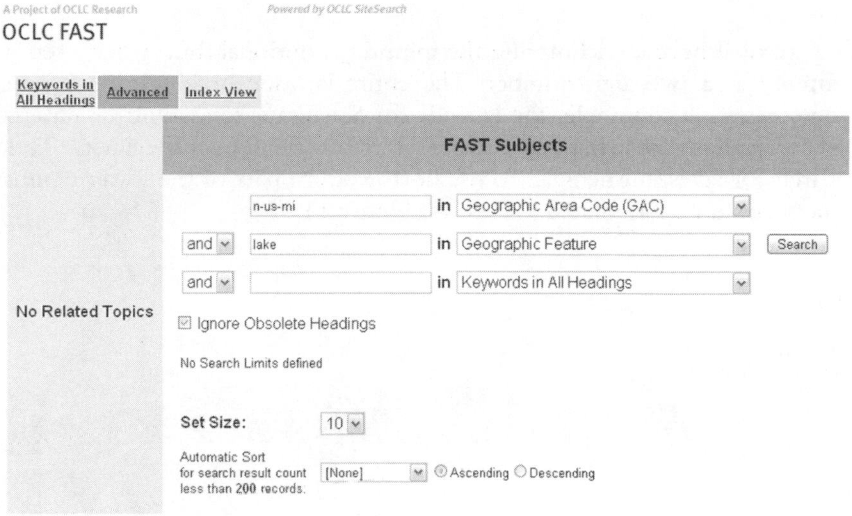

Figure 11.13. Geographic GAC Query

This would generate the following screen (Figure 11.14):

Figure 11.14. Search Results for the GAC Geographic Query

The search could have also been done using the latitude and longitude rather than the GAC. The latitude and longitude are entered in the form:

Direction: Degrees: Minutes.

The direction is either N (north) or S (south) for the latitude and E (east) or W (west) for the longitude. The degrees are entered as a three-digit number with leading zeros if necessary. Entering the minutes is optional, but, when used, they are entered as a two-digit number. The entire latitude or longitude is entered without spaces. For example, the latitude for San Francisco would be entered as n03746. Generally, only the degrees are entered to avoid over specificity. To limit the search for lakes in Michigan to the northwestern part of the lower peninsula, the query could be formulated as follows (Figure 11.15):

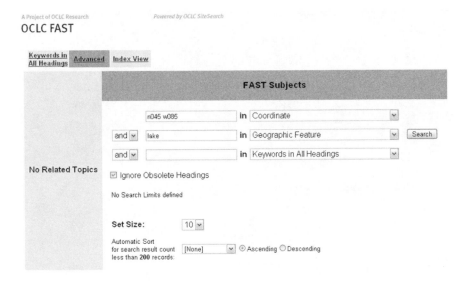

Figure 11.15. Query Using Geographic Coordinates

This query would retrieve two records for Lake Charlevoix and Walloon Lake. The authority record for Lake Charlevoix is shown in Figure 11.16:

A Project of OCLC Research   *Powered by OCLC SiteSearch*
OCLC FAST

Search Results   Record: 1

((co: "n045" "w085") and fe=   Record: 1
"lake") not rs="obsolete"

1 Hits Found   000   cs n
                                  001   fst01335204
refine   003   OCoLC
                                  005   20091211104203.0
· FAST Subjects : 1   008   060620nn anznnbabn || ana d
                                  016 7 fst01335204 $2 OCoLC
                                  034       $d W0850800 $e W0850800 $f N0451600 $g N0451600 $2 geonames
                                  040   OCoLC $b eng $c OCoLC $f fast
                                  043   n-us-mi
                                  151   Michigan $z Lake Charlevoix
                                  451   Michigan $z Charlevoix, Lake
                                  550   Lakes $0 (OCoLC)fst00990901
                                  551   Michigan $z Charlevoix County $0 (OCoLC)fst01211332 $w g
                                  670   GeoNames [algorithmically matched] $b lake;45°16'00"N 085°08'00"W MauIt
                                  670   GNIS, MI $b (Lake Charlevoix)
                                  688   LC (2008) Subject Usage: 3
                                  688   WC (2008) Subject Usage: 23
                                  751 0 Charlevoix, Lake (Mich.) $0 (DLC)sh 91001125
                                  751 7 Lake Charlevoix $0 (GeoNames)4988581 $2 geonames $w nnna

Record: 1

Figure 11.16. FAST Authority Record for **Lake Charlevoix**

FAST geographic authority records with the latitude and longitude will also include a *MapIt* link as in the record in Figure 11.16. MapIt links to Google Maps, and clicking on it will bring up the map of the region covered in the authority record as well as provide access to a variety of other information provided by Google Maps.

While most FAST geographic authority records include the latitude and longitude, there are still many records lacking the latitude, longitude, and feature type information. All geographic authority records without this information will allow the searcher the option of adding this information. Clicking on the *Add Coordinate Page* link will bring up the following template (Figure 11.17). The geographic feature types are listed in a drop-down menu. While this is the first case where users are encouraged to contribute to the development of FAST, it is expected that other options for users to enrich FAST will follow.

Add Coordinates for this Geographic Location

Please enter the coordinates and place type

Latitude [## #### in deg or deg, min, sec using all boxes]⎵⎵⎵⎵ Deg⎵⎵⎵ Min 00⎵⎵ Sec ○N ○S

Longitude [## #### in deg or deg, min, sec using all boxes]⎵⎵⎵⎵ Deg⎵⎵⎵ Min 00⎵⎵ Sec ○E ○W

Geographic Feature Type ⎵⎵⎵⎵⎵⎵⎵⎵⎵ ▾

Coordinate Source Reference ⎵⎵⎵⎵⎵⎵⎵

[Add Coord]

Figure 11.17. Adding Geographic Coordinates to Authority Records

Other Indexes

In addition to the preceding indexes, there are other specialized indexes:

FAST authority record number is used to retrieve records and their authority record numbers. Either the full number including the prefix (fst00012345) or just the numeric portion (12345) can be entered.

Record status has limited use. It is normally combined with another query to limit the results to records with the specified record status.

Library of Congress Control Number for LCSH source heading index is used to retrieve a FAST heading using the LCCN for the LCSH heading from which it was derived.

Index View

Index View supports the browsing of any of the indexes by providing a look at its actual entries and is similar to the listing of words in a dictionary. This can be useful when the actual spelling or form is not certain. For example, entering "orthopaedic" with the index *Keywords in Headings* selected shows several variations on the term that may be of interest, including the more common spellings or forms such as "orthopedics" and "orthopedic," as well as the related terms used in the field such as "orthopedist" and "orthophotography." Clicking on the entry is equivalent to searching using that entry, and a result set will be produced (Figure 11.18).

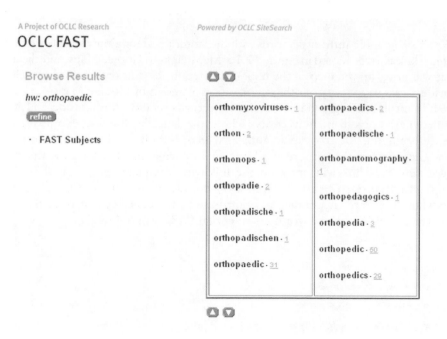

Figure 11.18. Browsing the Indexes

When using the *Full Heading* or *Subfield* index, the *Index View* allows examination of similar headings. Using the "smith robert" example in Figure 11.19, the search of the full personal name headings shows that there is also a "smith rob," a "smith robb," and many additional "smith robert" entries with middle names or initials.

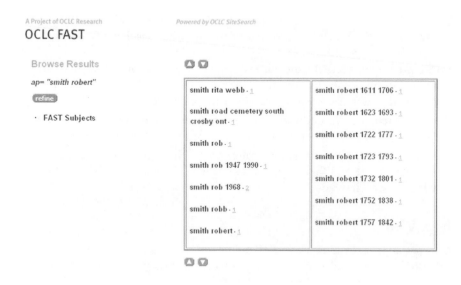

Figure 11.19. Browsing Personal Names

NOTE

1. Thomas B. Hickey, Jenny Toves, and Edward T. O'Neill, "NACO Normalization," *Library Resources and Technical Services* 50, no. 3 (2001): 166–72.

12

---·•◆•·---

APPLICATION OF FAST HEADINGS

INTRODUCTION

The quality and effectiveness of subject indexing depend in large part on the individuals who assign index terms or subject headings. Their understanding of and familiarity with the nature and the structure of the subject vocabulary, their interpretation of a given work, and their ability to coordinate available subject terms with the content of the work all affect the quality of subject representation and the effectiveness of subject access and retrieval.

The use of controlled vocabularies and the establishment of policies and rules are practices designed to attain consistency in indexing or cataloging. Nevertheless, while subject vocabulary can be formalized, it is extremely difficult to codify the procedures for assigning subject terms to specific works because the subjective judgments of individual indexers and catalogers inevitably enter into the process. Differences from person to person in their interpretation of content are to be expected, and even the same individual reading the same work at different times may not make the same indexing judgment. However, while perfect consistency is unreachable, a high degree of consistency is desirable.

Inconsistency in subject treatment may also creep into a file because some works may have been indexed or cataloged under different guidelines or assumptions about the appropriate depth of subject indexing or cataloging. The depth of indexing or cataloging of a document may vary from *summarization*, which aims to express only its overall subject content, to *exhaustive* or *in-depth indexing*, which aims to enumerate all its significant concepts or aspects or to represent individual component parts of the work. Summarization is a common practice in comprehensive bibliographic tools such as library catalogs or general bibliographies, while exhaustive or in-depth indexing is more prevalent in subject representation of journal articles and technical reports.

In this book, the term *subject* refers to the overall content of a work (e.g., "the impact of television violence on children in the United States"), the term *topic* or *topics* refers to a particular theme or themes that make up the subject (e.g., "impact," "television violence," "children in the United States"), and the term *concept* or *concepts* refers to the basic unit or units of a topic, including different aspects or facets of the topic (e.g., "impact," "television," "violence," "children," and "United States").

CODING FOR FAST HEADINGS IN BIBLIOGRAPHIC RECORDS

MARC21 and Dublin Core are the two most common formats for bibliographic data. FAST subject headings are fully compatible with both formats. As discussed in Chapter 2, MARC itself has several different forms of representation, with the MARC communications format and MARCXML being the most common. For simplicity, all MARC records discussed in this chapter will be displayed in a "screen image" type format that is independent of the particular underlying MARC data structure. Likewise, displays used for the Dublin Core records omit much of the coding that is not necessary to interpret the content. The MARC records shown in this chapter are intended to illustrate subject indexing in general and the use of FAST in particular. The examples of bibliographic records used in the examples generally will be brief, with many significant fields omitted. The fields included are limited to the subject related fields and the fields necessary for minimal descriptive cataloging.

MARC Records

Details about MARC coding are given in Chapter 2 of this book. When FAST headings are assigned to MARC records, the codes specified for subject fields in the MARC 21 Format for Bibliographic Records are used. The following tags and their associated fields are used for subject-related and form/genre fields:

> 600 Personal name
> 610 Corporate name
> 611 Event name
> 630 Title
> 648 Chronological term
> 650 Topical term
> 651 Geographic name
> 655 Form/Genre

Each of these fields may be repeated, as there are often multiple FAST headings in a given facet in a particular record.

The first indicator is defined individually for each type of heading. The second indicator, showing the source of the subject vocabulary or index terms, with the value "7" and the subfield "*$2fast*", identifies a FAST heading in each 6xx field.

Dublin Core Records

The contents of Dublin Core records are formulated according to the *Dublin Core Data Element Set*[1] and typically encoded in XML. The Dublin Core Element Set was discussed in Chapter 2. The three Dublin Core elements used with FAST headings are:

COVERAGE

Definition: The spatial or temporal topic of the resource, the spatial applicability of the resource, or the jurisdiction under which the resource is relevant.

Comment: Spatial topic and spatial applicability may be a named place or a location specified by its geographic coordinates. Temporal topic may be a named period, date, or date range. A jurisdiction may be a named administrative entity or a geographic place to which the resource applies. Recommended best practice is to use a controlled vocabulary such as the Thesaurus of Geographic Names (TGN). Where appropriate, named places or time periods can be used in preference to numeric identifiers such as sets of coordinates or date ranges.

FAST facets: Geographic, chronological.

Qualification: Templates for entering FAST headings from these facets into qualified Dublin Core are:

```
<dcterms:spatial xsi:type='http://registry.loc.gov/
vocabulary/sources/fast'>

    Geographic heading</dcterms:spatial>
<dcterms:temporal xsi:type='http://registry.loc.gov/
vocabulary/sources/fast'>

    Chronological heading</dcterms:temporal>
```

SUBJECT

Definition: The topic of the resource.

Comment: Typically, the subject will be represented using keywords, key phrases, or classification codes. Recommended best practice is to use a controlled vocabulary. To describe the spatial or temporal topic of the resource, use the coverage element.

FAST facets: Topical, person, corporate body, event, title.

Qualification: No differentiation is made between FAST topical, person, corporate body, events, and title headings. Headings from those five facets are identified simply as subjects. The template for entering FAST headings from these facets into qualified Dublin Core is:

```
<dcterms:subject xsi:type='http://registry.loc.gov/
vocabulary/sources/fast'>

  topical, person, corporate body, event, or title heading

</dc:subject>
```

TYPE

Definition: The nature or genre of the resource.

Comment: Recommended best practice is to use a controlled vocabulary such as the DCMI Type Vocabulary [DCMITYPE]. To describe the file format, physical medium, or dimensions of the resource, use the format element.

FAST facet: Form/genre.

Qualification: The template for entering FAST headings from the form/genre facet into qualified Dublin Core is:

```
<dc:type xsi:type='http://registry.loc.gov/vocabulary/
sources/fast'>

  form/genre

</dc:type>
```

EXHAUSTIVITY IN CATALOGING OR INDEXING

Another aspect relating to the level of subject representation is the exhaustivity[2] or depth of indexing or subject cataloging. When subject terms are assigned based primarily on the content of the entire work, the result is referred to as *summarization*. Another approach, *in-depth indexing*, attempts to bring out the contents of individual units, such as chapters or component parts within the work, in addition to using heading or headings that summarize the overall content. In other words, subject terms may be assigned to the work as a whole or to its individual component parts as well. It is the indexing or cataloging policy of a given library or information agency that governs primarily both the depth and exhaustiveness and the level of representation. Furthermore, individual judgments may vary considerably even under a given policy.

The following examples demonstrate summarization and in-depth cataloging/indexing.

1. Examples of summarization:

   Title: *Elementary education for the poorest and other deprived groups: the real challenge of universalisation*

   FAST heading:

   Topical: **Education, Elementary**

   Title: *Modern methods of middle school teaching: reaching special education students*

   FAST heading:

   Topical: **Special education**

In each case, the one heading summarizes the overall content of the work. The various aspects of the subject are not represented individually.

2. Examples of exhaustive indexing or cataloging:

   Title: *Teaching to change the world*

Publisher's description:[3]

In 1998, the first edition of Teaching To Change The World broke new ground in teacher education by positioning the foundations and practices of American schooling in the context of the struggle for social justice, democratic communities, and a better world. Indeed, "teaching to change the world" has become more than a book title; for thousands of individuals and for entire teacher education programs it is an everyday expression that embodies rigorous preparation and the highest professional aspirations for becoming a teacher.

Author Jeannie Oakes was the founding director of UCLA's Center X—the institutional home of the university's teacher education program—a program based on the research and principles that Teaching To Change The World represents. Oakes draws from her distinguished research career as a sociologist of education to integrate the components of educational foundations into a thematic and ideological whole. The result is a sustainable theory of education that positions new teachers to be highly competent in the classroom, lifelong education reformers, and education leaders and partners with students and families. Co-author Martin Lipton brings to this book 31 years of classroom experience and a parallel career as education writer and consultant. His photographs of the book's featured teachers and their students reveal that social justice classrooms are both ordinary and inspired.

Table of contents:

1. Schooling: Wrestling with History and Tradition
2. Traditional Learning Theories: Transmission, Training, and IQ
3. Contemporary Learning Theories: Problem Solving, Understanding, and Participation
4. Curriculum: Philosophy, History, and Politics: What Should Students Learn?
5. Curriculum Content: The Subject Matters
6. Instruction and Assessment: Classrooms as Learning Communities
7. Classroom Management: Caring and Democratic Communities
8. Grouping and Categorical Programs: Can Schools Teach All Students Well?
9. The School Culture: Where Good Teaching Makes Sense
10. Connections with Families and Communities
11. Teaching to Change the World: A Profession and a Hopeful Struggle

FAST headings:

Topical: **Educational change**

Effective teaching

Public schools

Education–Aims and objectives

Curriculum planning

Classroom management

Geographic: **United States**

In the preceding example, various themes treated in the collection or work are brought out by individual headings in addition to the heading or headings that summarize the overall content.

Title: *$700 billion bailout : the Emergency Economic Stabilization Act and what it means to you, your money, your mortgage, and your taxes*

Table of Contents:

Introduction: The Emergency Economic Stabilization Act of 2008: The Patriot Act Meets the World of Finance.

1. The Big Hoist: Will the $700 Billion Bailout of the Mortgage and Credit Markets Work? (It Had Better).
2. The Three Most Important Things You Need to Know Now—Mortgages, Rates, and Housing.
3. Where to Put Your Money Now (Hint: Not in a Vacation Home).
4. Taxes and Politics: EESA Digs a Deeper Money Hole for All of Us.

Epilogue: The Last Word: If I Ran the Regulatory Zoo.
Excerpts from the Emergency Economic Stabilization Act of 2008.

FAST headings:

Topical: **Economic stabilization**
        Government lending—Law and legislation
        Federal aid
        Mortgage banks—Law and legislation
        Foreclosure
        Banking law
        Deposit insurance
        Alternative minimum tax
Geographic: **United States**

For electronic resources, the in-depth approach is particularly helpful in bringing out the depth of the content and providing ample access points. An example based on the digital library *American Memory* is shown below:

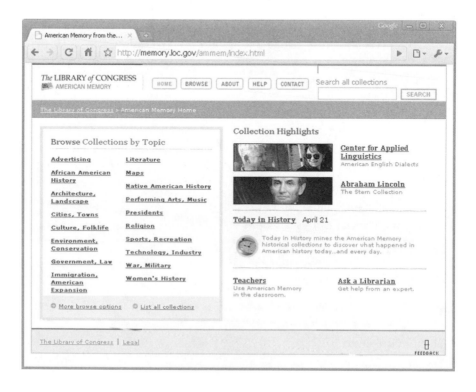

American Memory [Electronic Resource]

American Memory is available on the Library of Congress's Web site at http://www.loc.gov/index.html. The following description of *American Memory* is provided in the "About" section of the Web site:

Mission

American Memory provides free and open access through the Internet to written and spoken words, sound recordings, still and moving images, prints, maps, and sheet music that document the American experience. It is a digital record of American history and creativity. These materials, from the collections of the Library of Congress and other institutions, chronicle historical events, people, places, and ideas that continue to shape America, serving the public as a resource for education and lifelong learning.

History

The seed that grew into the American Memory historical collections was planted in a pilot program that ran from 1990 through 1994. The pilot experimented with digitizing some of the Library of Congress's unparalleled collections of historical documents, moving images, sound recordings, and print and photographic media—the "nation's memory." It identified audiences for digital collections, established technical procedures, wrestled with intellectual-property issues, explored options for distribution such as CD-ROM, and began institutionalizing a digital effort at the Library. Forty-four schools and libraries across the country received CD-ROMs with these materials as part of the pilot. As the American Memory pilot drew to a close, the Library surveyed the 44 selected schools and libraries that had participated. The response was enthusiastic, especially from teachers and students in middle and high schools who wanted more digitized resources. But distributing these materials in CD-ROM format was both inefficient and prohibitively expensive.

Fortunately, by 1994, the Internet and its World Wide Web were beginning to transform the presentation and communication of human knowledge. The Library took advantage of the opportunity and, on Oct. 13, 1994, announced that it had received $13 million in private sector donations to establish the National Digital Library Program. That day, building on the concepts the pilot had demonstrated, the Library of Congress launched the American Memory historical collections as the flagship of the National Digital Library Program—a pioneering systematic effort to digitize some of the foremost historical treasures in the Library and other major research archives and make them readily available on the Web to Congress, scholars, educators, students, the general public, and the global Internet community.

From the outset, the National Digital Library was truly a collaborative national endeavor. Bipartisan support from Congress for $15 million over five years and a unique public-private partnership involving entrepreneurial and philanthropic leadership led to more than $45 million in private sponsorship from 1994 through 2000.

Beginning in 1996, the Library of Congress sponsored a three-year competition with a $2 million gift from the Ameritech Corporation to enable public,

*research, and academic libraries, museums, historical societies, and archival in-
stitutions (with the exception of federal institutions) to digitize American history collections and make them available on the Library's American Memory
site. The competition produced 23 digital collections that complement American
Memory, which now features more than 100 thematic collections.*

*The National Digital Library exceeded its goal of making 5 million items
available online by 2000. American Memory will continue to expand online historical content as an integral component of the Library of Congress's
commitment to harnessing new technology as it fulfills its mission "to sustain
and preserve a universal collection of knowledge and creativity for future
generations."*

About the Collections

*American Memory is a gateway to the Library of Congress's vast resources of
digitized American historical materials. Comprising more than 9 million
items that document U.S. history and culture, American Memory is organized into more than 100 thematic collections based on their original format,
their subject matter, or who first created, assembled, or donated them to the
Library.*

*The original formats include manuscripts, prints, photographs, posters,
maps, sound recordings, motion pictures, books, pamphlets, and sheet music.
Each online collection is accompanied by a set of explanatory features designed to make the materials easy to find, use, and understand. Collections
may be browsed individually, searched individually (including full-text
searching for many written items), or searched across multiple collections.
The Library's expert research and reference staff is available online to assist patrons in accessing American Memory materials through the Ask a
Librarian service.*

*American Memory also reflects the success of a visionary national collabora-
tion involving many different institutions and both public and private initia-
tives. In particular, a three-year competition sponsored by the Library between
1996 and 1999 with a $2 million gift from the Ameritech Corporation enabled
a select group of non-federal public, research, and academic libraries; museums;
historical societies; and archival institutions to digitize 23 collections of historical materials and make them available as part of the American Memory site
(http://memory.loc.gov), complementing and enhancing the Library's own
online resources.*

The following example illustrates FAST headings assigned to this work shown
in both the MARC record format and the Dublin Core record display based on
summarization indexing:

MARC RECORD FOR *AMERICAN MEMORY:*

```
LDR    00724cmm 22002054a 4500
005    20091016141326.0
007    cr |||||||||||
008    060822m19949999dcu m f eng
```

```
010      $a 2006586290

043      $an-us---

050 00 $aE173

245 00 $aAmerican memory $h[electronic resource] :
         $bhistorical collections for the National Digital
         Library.

246 1   $iTitle in HTML header: $aAmerican memory from the
         Library of Congress

260      $aWashington, DC : $bLibrary of Congress, $c[1994]-

538      $aMode of access: World Wide Web.

651   7 $aUnited States. $2fast

655   7 $aHistory. $2fast

655   7 $aSources. $2fast

710 2   $aLibrary of Congress. $bNational Digital Library
         Program. 856 40 $uhttp://memory.loc.gov
```

THE SIMPLE DUBLIN CORE RECORD FOR *AMERICAN MEMORY*:

```
<dc:contributor>Library of Congress. National Digital
Library Program.</dc:contributor>

<dc:coverage>United States</dc:coverage>

<dcterms:date>[1994]-</dcterms:date>

<dc:description>Title from Web page (viewed on June 27,
2002).</dc:description>

<dc:description>Compiled by the National Digital Library
Program, Library of Congress</dc:description>

<dc:description>Derived from the collections of the
Library of Congress, presents digital versions of source
materials relating to the history and culture of the
the United States. Includes manuscripts, photographs,
sound recordings, motion pictures, music, and maps.
</dc:description>

<dc:identifier>http://memory.loc.gov</dc:identifier>

<dc:language>eng</dc:language>

<dc:publisher>Library of Congress</dc:publisher>

<dc:relation> Mode of access: World Wide Web.</dc:relation>

<dc:subject>E173</dc:subject>

<dc:subject>027.073</dc:subject>

<dc:title>American memory : historical collections for
the National Digital Library</dc:title>

<dc:title>American memory from the Library of Congress
</dc:title>

<dc:type>History</dc:type>

<dc:type>Sources</dc:type>
```

The strength of simple Dublin Core record format is simplicity. It is generally adequate for small or limited collections. However, it lacks specificity and doesn't provide any means to identify a particular schema. There is no means to establish from the record itself whether the values are from FAST or some other controlled vocabulary. It is often advantageous to include subject headings from different schemas—FAST, LCSH, MeSH, and so forth—in the same record. Therefore, the qualified Dublin Core record format is usually preferred, particularly when subject headings from multiple thesauri may be used.

DUBLIN CORE QUALIFIED RECORD FOR *AMERICAN MEMORY*:

```
<dc:contributor>Library of Congress. National Digital
Library Program.</dc:contributor>

<dcterms:spatial xsi:type="http://id.loc.gov/vocabulary/
sources/subject/fast" United States</dcterms:spatial>

<dcterms:issued>[1994]-</dcterms:issued>

<dc:description>Title from Web page (viewed on June 27,
2002).</dc:description>

<dc:identifier xsi:type="http://purl.org/dc/terms/URI">
http://memory.loc.gov</dc:identifier>

<dc:language xsi:type="http://purl.org/dc/terms/
ISO639-2">eng</dc:language>

<dc:publisher>Library of Congress</dc:publisher>

<dcterms:requires>Mode of access: World Wide Web.
</dcterms:requires>

<dc:subject xsi:type="http://purl.org/dc/terms/LCC">E173
</dc:subject>

<dc:title>American memory : historical collections for the
National Digital Library.</dc:title>

<dcterms:alternative>American memory from the Library of
Congress.</dcterms:alternative>

<dc:type xsi:type="http://id.loc.gov/vocabulary/sources/
subject/fast" History.</dc:type>

<dc:type xsi:type="http://id.loc.gov/vocabulary/sources/
subject/fast" Sources.</dc:type>
```

The following additional FAST headings, shown in the MARC format, could also be added to provide in-depth indexing:

```
650  7 $aArt, American. $2fast
650  7 $aArchitecture, American. $2fast
650  7 $aSocial history. $2fast
650  7 $aAmerican literature. $2fast
650  7 $aIndians of North America. $2fast
650  7 $aPresidents. $2fast
650  7 $aAmericans. $2fast
```

```
650   7   $aPolitical science $xPolitics and government. $2fast
650   7   $aAdvertising. $2fast
650   7   $aAfrican Americans. $2fast
650   7   $aCities and towns. $2fast
650   7   $aCulture. $2fast
650   7   $aConservation of natural resources. $2fast
650   7   $aLaw. $2fast
650   7   $aEmigration and immigration. $2fast
650   7   $aReligion. $2fast
650   7   $aSports. $2fast
650   7   $aRecreation. $2fast
650   7   $aIndustrial engineering. $2fast
650   7   $aWar. $2fast
650   7   $aWomen. $2fast
655   7   $aManuscripts. $2 fast
655   7   $aBiography $vPortraits. $2fast
655   7   $aMaps. $2fast
```

In-depth indexing of very large and broad resources like *American Memory* often results in a large number of general headings. As an alternative to in-depth indexing of the site as a whole, it may be preferable to separately describe the individual sections of the site. For example, *The Alfred Whital Stern Collection of Lincolniana*, which is part of *American Memory*, could be separately described. The home page for this collection is shown below:

This particular collection within *American Memory* can be described in the following MARC record:

```
LDR      00900cmm 22002534a 4500

005      20091016141326.0

008      060822m19949999dcu m f eng

007      cr ||||||||||||

043      $an-us---

050      00 $aE457.65

245 00 $aAmerican memory $h[electronic resource] : $bThe
          Alfred Whital Stern Collection of Lincolniana.

246 1    $iTitle in HTML header: $a The Alfred Whital Stern
          Collection of Lincolniana - About This Collection -
          (American Memory from the Library of Congress)

260      $aWashington, DC : $bLibrary of Congress, $c[1994]-

538      $aMode of access: World Wide Web.

600   7 $aLincoln, Abraham, $d1809-1865. $2fast

611   7 $aAmerican Civil War, 1861-1865. $2fast

648   7 $a1809-1865. $2fast

650   7 $aPresidents. $2fast

650   7 $aPopular music. $2fast

651   7 $aUnited States. $2fast

655   7 $aBibliography. $2fast

655   7 $aHistory. $2fast

655   7 $aSources. $2fast

700 1    $aStern, Alfred Whital, $d1881-1960.

710 2    $aLibrary of Congress. $bNational Digital Library
          Program.

856 40 $uhttp://memory.loc.gov/ammem/collections/
          stern-lincoln/about.html
```

ASSIGNING FAST HEADINGS

Once the policy on exhaustivity of indexing has been decided, the next step is to identify the form/genre, if any, that best describes the resource and then to categorize the subjects into their appropriate FAST facets—in other words, to determine the facet to which each particular concept belongs.

Identifying Concepts and Facets within the Topic

The first step in assigning FAST headings is to analyze the overall content of the entire work or the part of a larger work to be indexed and to identify its main topics or themes and their component concepts. The next step is to categorize the topics and concepts by their appropriate FAST facets.

The FAST database contains all of the valid main headings and main heading/ subdivision combinations. Headings in different facets are assigned separately. Within individual indexing policies, headings are assigned based on appropriateness to the content of the work. The usual practice is to select the heading that matches mostly closely the topic to be represented. For example, for the topic of oranges, the heading **Orange**, rather than the heading **Citrus** is assigned. This is called following the principle of *specificity*. If no FAST heading for a particular topic has been established, then either a broader heading or a combination of headings can be assigned for the work being cataloged or indexed.

Selecting Form/Genre Headings

Form/genre headings are assigned as appropriate, to identify the type of resource. As discussed earlier, form/genre headings are used to indicate what the resource is rather that what it is about. For example, an encyclopedia of American art would be assigned the form/genre heading **Encyclopedias.** Form/ genre headings are assigned less frequently than subjects, and no form/genre headings have been established in LCSH for many common types of resources including nonfiction books. Less than 14 percent of all bibliographic records in WorldCat contain an LCSH form/genre heading or subdivision. Since FAST form/genre headings are derived from LCSH, the indexer should not expect to find form/genre headings for all types of materials. However, when appropriate, form/genre headings will be included with the examples used for the subject headings.

Selecting Subject Headings

Topical Headings

Works on a Single Topic

A heading that matches most closely the topic to be represented, if available, is assigned to a work on a single topic:

Resource: A book on Christian doctrines
FAST heading:
   Topical: **Theology, Doctrinal**

Resource: A book on start-up companies
FAST heading:
   Topical: **New business**

Works on Multiple Topics

For a work covering two or three topics treated separately, a heading representing precisely each of the topics should be assigned.

Resource: An encyclopedia of science and engineering
FAST headings:
Topical: **Science**
       Engineering
Form/genre: **Encyclopedias**

Sometimes, there may not be a heading covering a particular concept precisely. In such cases, two headings are assigned. In the following example, two separate headings (**Finance** and **Capital market**) are assigned to represent the concept of "financial markets."

Resource: A book covering money, banking, and financial markets
FAST headings:
Topical: **Money**
       Banks and banking
       Finance
       Capital market

Resource: A book about infants, children, and adolescents
FAST headings:
Topical: **Children**
       Infants
       Teenagers

For a work on four or more topics, a general heading covering all topics or concepts treated in the work may be assigned. The general heading usually represents a broader concept covering all individual topics treated in the work. Alternatively, separate headings may be assigned for each topic or concept.

Works on Complex Topics

A complex topic is one that contains multiple related concepts in the same or different facets, such as *nutrition for the elderly* or *education of librarians in the United States*. Many FAST headings contain multiple concepts in the same facet, expressed in phrase form or in the form of main heading/subdivision combinations. When the topic consists of concepts belonging to different facets, a separate heading for each facet is assigned. Examples are shown in the following sections.

Topics with Multiple Concepts

If all concepts treated in a work belong to the same facet, the heading covering all concepts is assigned, if there is an enumerated precoordinated heading. For example:

Resource: A book on how sunlight affects plants
FAST heading:
  Topical: **Plants—Effect of light on**

If there is no precombined heading, separate headings for individual concepts are assigned. For example,

Resource: A study of the parasites of termites
FAST headings:
   Topical: **Parasites**
          Termites

Resource: A textbook about designing building structures
FAST headings:
   Topical: **Buildings**
          Structural design
          Structural analysis (Engineering)

Resource: A book on treating asthma with breathing exercises
FAST headings:
   Topical: **Asthma—Alternative treatment**
          Breathing exercises

Geographic Headings

Geographic headings are normally assigned to identify specific places. In assigning geographic headings, multiple headings can be used to identify all of the locations that are the subject of the work. However, if the set of multiple headings cover most of the larger place, assigning a single heading for the larger area would be preferred.

Resource: An Ohio road map
FAST headings:
   Topical: **Roads**
   Geographic: **Ohio**
   Form/Genre: **Maps**

Resource: A travel guide to Michigan's west coast
FAST headings:
   Topical: **Travel**
   Geographic: **Michigan**
          Lake Michigan
   Form/Genre: **Guidebooks**

Resource: A book of historical photographs of buildings in Noe Valley
FAST headings:
   Topical: **Historic buildings**
   Geographic: **California—San Francisco—Noe Valley**
   Form/Genre: **Pictorial works**
          History

Chronological Headings

FAST chronological headings normally contain exact periods. However, periods derived from LCSH are usually longer than the period covered in particular works. In application these longer periods are used when more specific dates are not available.

Resource: A book on designing small American houses in the 1930s
FAST headings:
  Topical: **Small houses—Designs and plans**
  Architecture, Modern—Designs and plans
  Geographic: **United States**
  Chronological: **1930–1939**

Resource: Proceedings of a conference on China's Christian colleges from 1900 to 1950
FAST headings:
  Topical: **Church colleges**
  Education, Higher
  Geographic: **China**
  Chronological: **1900–1950**
  Form/genre: **Conference proceedings**

In assigning chronological headings, a single heading is used for contiguous periods. Multiple chronological headings should only be assigned to works covering noncontiguous periods. For example, a work on the two world wars that excluded 1919–1938, the period between the wars, could be assigned the following headings:

1914–1918
1939–1945

However, if the intervening years were also covered, the resource would be assigned a single heading for the entire period:

1914–1945

Name Headings

Works about individual persons are assigned personal name headings, for example,

Resource: A biography of S. *Francesco de Sales*
FAST headings:
  Persons: **Francis, de Sales, Saint, 1567–1622**
  Form/genre: **Biography**

Works related to the origin, development, activities, and functions of individual corporate bodies are assigned subject headings under corporate names. Like personal name headings, headings for corporate bodies are established according to *Anglo-American Cataloguing Rules,* second edition revised[4] (AACR2R), for example,

> Resource: The annual report of Charles Stark Draper Laboratory, Inc.
> FAST headings:
>> Corporate bodies: **Charles Stark Draper Laboratory**
>> Form/genre: **Periodicals**

Title Headings

A commentary or criticism of a work is assigned the title heading for the work being discussed. For example:

> Resource: Commentaries on the *New Testament*
> FAST headings:
>> Title [as subject]: **Bible. N.T.**
>> Form/genre: **Commentaries**

> Resource: A review and criticism of *Milton's Paradise Lost*
> FAST headings:
>> Title [as subject]: **Paradise lost (Milton, John)**
>> Form/genre: **Criticism, interpretation, etc.**

Topics with Multiple Facets

If the individual concepts within a topic belong to different facets, separate headings in each facet, including the form/genre facet, are assigned.

> Resource: A catalog of piano rolls
> FAST headings:
>> Topical: **Player piano rolls**
>> Form/genre: **Catalogs**

> Resource: A history of the Mississippi Department of Archives and History
> FAST headings:
>> Geographic: **Mississippi**
>> Corporate bodies: **Mississippi. Dept. of Archives and History**
>> Form/genre: **History**

> Resource: *What do banks do?* [a book for young readers]
> FAST headings:
>> Topical: **Banks and banking**
>> Form/genre: **Juvenile works**

Resource: A Web site on the southern civil rights movements in the 20th
    century
FAST headings:
    Topical: **Race relations**
            Civil rights movements
            African Americans–Civil rights
    Geographic: **Southern States**
    Chronological: **1900–1999**

Resource: A bio-bibliography of early English literature, 12th–17th centuries
FAST headings:
    Topical: **Authors, English**
            English literature
    Chronological: **1100–1699**
    Form/genre: **Bio-bibliography**
            Biography
            Criticism, interpretation, etc.

Resource: An Italian language textbook for English speakers
FAST headings:
    Topical: **Italian language**
    Form/genre: **Textbooks—for English speakers**

Resource: A newsletter on the prevention and treatment of alcohol abuse in
    Wisconsin
FAST headings:
    Topical: **Alcoholism—Prevention**
            Alcoholics—Rehabilitation
    Geographic: **Wisconsin**
    Form/genre: **Periodicals**

Resource: A statistical analysis of South Africa's trade with Finland
FAST headings:
    Topical: **Commerce**
    Geographic: **Finland**
            South Africa
    Form/genre: **Statistics**

Resource: An encyclopedia of global warfare during the age of Louis XIV
FAST headings:
    Topical: **Military history, Modern**

Chronological: **1600–1799**

Form/genre: **Encyclopedias**

Subject Relations

Many works treat multiple topics in relation to each other. Such relationships include general relations, influence, tool or application, comparison, and bias (the target audience of the work). Where appropriate, headings representing such relations are assigned if available. For example, **Body temperature— Effect of drugs on; Fungi in agriculture; Television and politics**; and so forth. If such headings do not exist, separate headings for each topic involved are assigned.

Resource: The militia movement and the radical right in the United States

FAST headings:

Topical: **Militia movements**

Right-wing extremists

Radicalism

Geographic: **United States**

Resource: Australian social customs [a book written for children]

FAST headings:

Topical: **Manners and customs**

Geographic: **Australia**

Form/genre: **Juvenile works**

FAST APPLICATION EXAMPLES

This section discusses the use of FAST headings in MARC and Dublin Core metadata records. Although the bibliographic description in MARC records is constructed according to AACR2R, many of the descriptive fields have been omitted for brevity and to focus on the subject aspects. Contents of these records are typically encoded according to *MARC 21 Format for Bibliographic Data*.[5] Dublin Core records are based on the Dublin Core Data Element Set and typically encoded in XML.

Since FAST is derived from LCSH, and LCSH headings can be algorithmically converted to FAST, LCSH and FAST headings frequently co-occur in the same record. Qualified Dublin Core allows the use of qualifiers to refine the semantics of the elements and to specify the encoding schema. With qualified Dublin Core, a FAST event heading can be tagged as *"<dc:subject xsi:type='http://registry. loc.gov/vocabulary/sources/fast'>"* to indicate that what follows is a FAST subject heading. Although qualification adds a level of complexity, except for applications where FAST will be the only subject schema used, the use of qualified Dublin Core is recommended. Only qualified Dublin Core will be used in the following examples.

Example 1: *People and Predators: from Conflict to Coexistence*

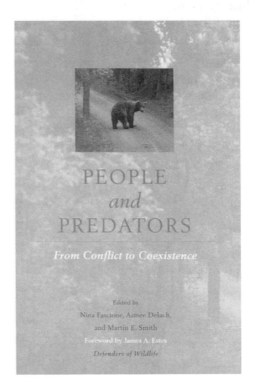

Publisher's description:[6]

> *In People and Predators, leading scientists and researchers offer case studies of human-carnivore conflicts in a variety of landscapes, including rural, urban, and political. The book covers a diverse range of taxa, geographic regions, and conflict scenarios, with each chapter dealing with a specific facet of human-carnivore interactions and offering practical, concrete approaches to resolving the conflict under consideration. Chapters provide background on particular problems and describe how challenges have been met or what research or tools are still needed to resolve the conflicts.*
>
> *People and Predators will helps [sic] readers to better understand issues of carnivore conservation in the 21st century, and provides practical tools for resolving many of the problems that stand between us and a future in which carnivores fulfill their historic ecological roles.*

Table of contents:

Minimizing Carnivore-Livestock Conflict: The Importance and Process of Research in the Search for Coexistence

Characteristics of Wolf Packs in Wisconsin: Identification of Traits Influencing Depredation

Wolves in Rural Agricultural Areas of Western North America: Conflict and Conservation

Ecology and Management of Striped Skunks, Raccoons, and Coyotes in Urban Landscapes

Birds of Prey in Urban Landscapes

Challenges in Conservation of the Endangered San Joaquin Kit Fox

Carnivore Conservation and Highways: Understanding the Relationships, Problems, and Solutions

Living with Fierce Creatures? An Overview and Models of Mammalian Carnivore Conservation

Dispersal and Colonization in the Florida Panther: Overcoming Landscape Barriers—Biological and Political

State Wildlife Governance and Carnivore Conservation

Conserving Mountain Lions in a Changing Landscape

Restoring the Gray Wolf to the Southern Rocky Mountains: Anatomy of a Campaign to Resolve a Conservation Issue

FAST headings:

Topical: **Predatory animals—Ecology**

Predatory animals—Control—Environmental aspects

Carnivora

Wildlife conservation

Geographic: **North America**

MARC record:

```
LDR    00921cam 2200253 a 4500
008    040227s2004 dcuab b 101 0 eng
010    $a 2004004597
020    $a1559630841 (pbk. : alk. paper)
043    $an------
050 00 $aQL737.C2 $bP36 2004
082 00 $a639.97/97 $222
245 00 $aPeople and predators : $bfrom conflict to
       coexistence / $cedited by Nina Fascione,
       Aimee Delach, Martin E. Smith ; foreword
       by James A. Estes.
260    $aWashington : $bIsland Press, $cc2004.
300    $axvi, 285 p. : $bill., maps ; $c24 cm.
650  7 $aPredatory animals $xEcology $2fast
650  7 $aPredatory animals $xControl $xEnvironmental
       aspects. $2fast
650  7 $aCarnivora. $2fast
650  7 $aWildlife conservation. $2fast
```

```
651  7  $aNorth America. $2fast

700 1   $aFascione, Nina.

700 1   $aDelach, Aimee.

700 1   $aSmith, Martin E. $q(Martin Edgar), $d1955-

710 2   $aDefenders of Wildlife.
```

Dublin Core record:

```
<qualifieddc>

<dctermset>

<dcterms:contributor>Fascione, Nina.
</dcterms:contributor>

<dcterms:contributor>Delach, Aimee.
</dcterms:contributor>

<dcterms:contributor>Smith, Martin E. (Martin Edgar),
1955-</dcterms:contributor>

<dcterms:contributor>Defenders of Wildlife.
</dcterms:contributor>

<dcterms:spatial xsi:type="http://id.loc.gov/vocabulary/
sources/subject/fast">North America </dcterms:spatial>

<dcterms:issued>c2004</dcterms:issued>

<dcterms:description>"Defenders of Wildlife."
</dcterms:description>

<dcterms:extent>xvi, 285 p. : ill., maps ; 24 cm.
</dcterms:extent>

<dcterms:language xsi:type="http://purl.org/dc/terms/
ISO639-2">eng</dcterms:language>

<dcterms:publisher>Island Press</dcterms:publisher>

<dcterms:subject xsi:type="http://purl.org/dc/terms/
DDC">639.97/97</dcterms:subject>

<dcterms:subject xsi:type="http://purl.org/dc/terms/
LCC">QL737.C2 P36 2004</dcterms:subject>

<dcterms:title>People and predators : from conflict to
coexistence</dcterms:title>

<dcterms:subject xsi:type="http://id.loc.gov/vocabulary/
sources/subject/fast">Predatory animals--ecology
</dcterms:subject>

<dcterms:subject xsi:type="http://id.loc.gov/vocabulary/
sources/subject/fast">Predatory animal--control--
environmental aspects</dcterms:subject>

<dcterms:subject xsi:type="http://id.loc.gov/vocabulary/
sources/subject/fast">Carnivora</dcterms:subject>
```

```
<dcterms:subject xsi:type="http://id.loc.gov/
vocabulary/sources/subject/fast">Wildlife conservation
</dcterms:subject>

</dctermset>

</qualifieddc>
```

Example 2: *Daily Life in Colonial New England*

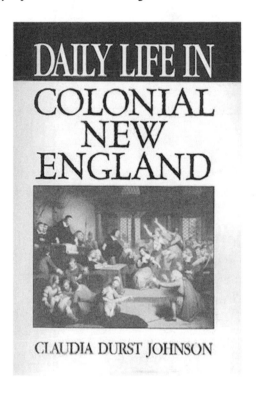

Publisher's description:[7]

> *Life for the individuals who chose to come to New England during the Colonial Period was difficult. This reference resource explores the everyday details of the colonial life in New England and exposes as myth much of what we might believe about this era, environment, and people. How exactly and why did their religious beliefs help structure their lives? What roles did women play in this society? How were people tried and punished for their crimes? Students can find thoroughly researched answers to these questions and others to help them learn exactly what everyday life was like for New Englanders during the Colonial Period.*
>
> *Students may be surprised to find what a large role the environment played in these people's lives, from the structuring of their homes to their diet and health. Religion was a driving force for most of them, in ways that may be difficult for modern-day readers to understand. Here readers will find an excellent*

description of how religion could play the role it did and how it affected the details of everyday living. Details of the lives of the Native Americans in New England during this era as well as Africans who had been brought to this location by the settlers are also provided.

Table of contents:

1. The Doctrinal Foundation of Colonial Life
2. Clergy and the Church
3. Government and Law
4. Crime and Punishment
5. Labor
6. Shelter and Attire
7. Food and Health
8. Marriage and Sex
9. Arts and Amusements
10. Native Americans
11. Africans
12. Indentured Servants
13. Education
14. Fear and Persecution in Daily Life
Conclusion

FAST headings:

Topical: **Manners and customs—Religious aspects**
        Religious life
Geographic: **New England**
Chronological: **To 1775**
Type: **History**

MARC record:

```
LDR     00649cam  2200193 a 4500
008     000728s2002 ctuab b 001 0 eng
010     $a 00061721
020     $a0313314586 (alk. paper)
043     $an-usn--
050  00 $aF7 $b.J59 2002
082  00 $a974/.02 $221
100  1  $aJohnson, Claudia Durst, $d1938-
245  10 $aDaily life in colonial New England / $cClaudia
        Durst Johnson.
260     $aWestport, Conn. : $bGreenwood Press, $c2002.
300     $axxvii, 215 p. : $bill., maps ; $c25 cm.
648   7 $aTo 1775. $2fast
```

```
650   7 $aManners and customs $xReligious aspects. $2fast

650   7 $aReligious life. $2fast

651   7 $aNew England. $2fast

655   7 $aHistory. $2fast

830   4 $aThe Greenwood Press "Daily life through history"
         series.
```

Dublin Core record:

```
<qualifieddc>

<dctermset>

<dcterms:creator>Johnson, Claudia Durst, 1938-
</dcterms:creator>

<dcterms:spatial xsi:type="http://id.loc.gov/vocabulary/
sources/subject/fast">New England
</dcterms:spatial>

<dcterms:issued>2002</dcterms:issued>

<dcterms:description>Includes bibliographical
references and index.</dcterms:description>

<dcterms:extent>xxvii, 215 p. : ill., maps ; 25 cm.
</dcterms:extent>

<dcterms:language xsi:type="http://purl.org/dc/terms/
ISO639-2">eng</dcterms:language>

<dcterms:publisher>Greenwood Press</dcterms:
publisher>

<dcterms:isPartOf>The Greenwood Press "Daily life through
history" series</dcterms:isPartOf>

<dcterms:subject xsi:type="http://purl.org/dc/terms/
DDC">974/.02</dcterms:subject>

<dcterms:subject xsi:type="http://purl.org/dc/terms/LCC">
F7 .J59 2002</dcterms:subject>

<dcterms:title>Daily life in colonial New England
</dcterms:title>

<dcterms:temporal xsi:type="http://id.loc.gov/
vocabulary/sources/subject/fast">To 1775
</dcterms:temporal>

<dcterms:subject xsi:type="http://id.loc.gov/vocabulary/
sources/subject/fast">Manners and Customs—Religious
Aspects</dcterms:subject>

<dcterms:subject xsi:type="http://id.loc.gov/
vocabulary/sources/subject/fast">Religious Life
</dcterms:subject>
```

```
<dcterms:type xsi:type="http://id.loc.gov/vocabulary/
sources/subject/fast">History</dcterms:type>

</dctermset>

</qualifieddc>
```

Example 3: *Style and the Nineteenth–century British Critic: Sincere Mannerisms*

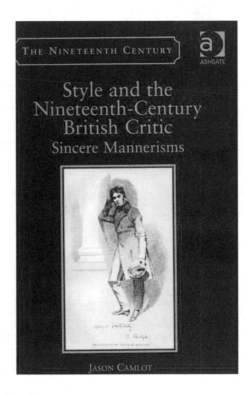

Publisher's description:[8]

In analyzing the nonfiction works of writers such as John Wilson, J.S. Mill, De Quincy, Ruskin, Arnold, Pater, and Wilde, Jason Camlot provides an important context for the nineteenth-century critic's changing ideas about style, rhetoric, and technologies of communications. In particular, Camlot contributes to our understanding of how new print media affected the Romantic and Victorian critic's sense of self, as he elaborates the ways nineteenth-century critics used their own essays on rhetoric and stylistics to speculate about the changing conditions for the production and reception of ideas and the formation of authorial character. Camlot argues that the early 1830s mark the moment when a previously coherent tradition of pragmatic rhetoric was fragmented and redistributed into diverse, localized sites of an emerging periodical market. Publishing venues for writers multiplied at midcentury, establishing a new stylistic norm for criticism—one that affirmed style as the manifestation of English discipline and objectivity. The figure of the professional critic soon subsumed the authority of the polyglot intellectual, and the later decades of the nineteenth century brought about a debate on aesthetics and criticism that set ideals on Saxon-root "virile" style against more culturally inclusive theories of expression.

Table of contents:

Introduction: Sincere Mannerisms
1. The Character of the Periodical Press
2. The Origins of Modern Earnest
3. The Downfall of Authority and the Magazine
4. Thomas De Quincey's Periodical Rhetoric
5. The Political Economy of Style: John Ruskin and Critical Truth
6. The Style Is the Man: Style Theory in the 1890's
Conclusion

FAST headings:

Topical:	**English prose literature**
	English language—Rhetoric
	Periodicals—Publishing
	English language—Style
	Mannerism (Literature)
	Style, Literary
Geographic:	**Great Britain**
Chronological:	**1800–1899**
Form:	**Criticism, interpretation, etc.**

MARC record:

```
LDR     00975cam 2200277 a 4500
008     070514s2008 enk b 001 0 eng
010     $a 2007020026
020     $a0754653110
043     $ae-uk---
050 00 $aPR778.C93 $bC36 2008
082 00 $a828/.80809 $222
100 1  $aCamlot, Jason, $d1967-
245 10 $aStyle and the nineteenth-century British critic :
        $bsincere mannerisms / $cJason Camlot.
246 3  $aStyle and the 19th-century British critic
260    $aAldershot, England ; $aBurlington, VT : $bAshgate,
        $cc2008.
300    $a194 p. ; $c25 cm.
648 7  $a1800-1899. $2fast
650 7  $aEnglish prose literature. $2fast
650 7  $aEnglish language $xRhetoric. $2fast
```

```
650   7 $aPeriodicals $xPublishing. $2fast

650   7 $aEnglish language $xStyle. $2fast

650   7 $aMannerism (Literature). $2fast

650   7 $aStyle, Literary. $2fast

651   7 $aGreat Britain. $2fast

655   7 $aCriticism, interpretation, etc. $2fast
```

Dublin Core record:

```
<qualifieddc>

<dctermset>

<dcterms:creator>Camlot, Jason, 1967-</dcterms:creator>

<dcterms:spatial xsi:type="http://id.loc.gov/vocabulary/
sources/subject/fast">Great Britain</dcterms:spatial>

<dcterms:issued>c2008</dcterms:issued>

<dcterms:description>Includes bibliographical references
(p. [171]-183) and Index.</dcterms:description>

<dcterms:language xsi:type="http://purl.org/dc/terms/
ISO639-2">eng</dcterms:language>

<dcterms:publisher>Ashgate</dcterms:publisher>

<dcterms:isPartOf>The nineteenth century</
dcterms:isPartOf>

<dcterms:isPartOf>Nineteenth century (Aldershot,
England)</dcterms:isPartOf>

<dcterms:subject xsi:type="http://purl.org/dc/terms/
DDC">828/.80809</dcterms:subject>

<dcterms:subject xsi:type="http://purl.org/dc/terms/
LCC">PR778.C93 C36 2008</dcterms:subject>

<dcterms:title>Style and the nineteenth-century British
critic : sincere mannerisms</dcterms:title>

<dcterms:alternative>Style and the 19th-century British
critic</dcterms:alternative>

<dcterms:temporal xsi:type="http://id.loc.gov/vocabulary/
sources/subject/fast">1800-1899</dcterms:temporal>

<dcterms:subject xsi:type="http://id.loc.gov/vocabulary/
sources/subject/fast">English prose literature
</dcterms:subject>

<dcterms:subject xsi:type="http://id.loc.gov/vocabulary/
sources/subject/fast">English language--rhetoric
</dcterms:subject>

<dcterms:subject xsi:type="http://id.loc.gov/vocabulary/
sources/subject/fast">Periodicals--publishing
</dcterms:subject>
```

```
<dcterms:subject xsi:type="http://id.loc.gov/vocabulary/
sources/subject/fast">English language--style
</dcterms:subject>

<dcterms:subject xsi:type="http://id.loc.gov/vocabulary/
sources/subject/fast">Mannerism (Literature)
</dcterms:subject>

<dcterms:subject xsi:type="http://id.loc.gov/vocabulary/
sources/subject/fast">Style, literary</dcterms:subject>

<dcterms:type xsi:type="http://id.loc.gov/vocabulary/
sources/subject/fast">Criticism, interpretation, etc.
</dcterms:type>

</dctermset>

</qualifieddc>
```

Example 4: *Fife and Tayside*

Publisher's description:[9]

> *A street atlas of Fife and Tayside, offering comprehensive coverage of the region from Brechin and Montrose in the north-east to Stirling in the south-west, and including Kincardine and Queensferry. It includes a route planner that shows the A and B roads.*
>
> *This fully revised street atlas of Fife and Tayside gives comprehensive and detailed coverage of the region. The route planner shows all the A and B roads, and can be used when driving to get close to the destination before turning to*

the relevant large-scale street map. The street maps show every named road, street and lane very clearly, with major roads picked out in colour. The maps are at a scale of 1.75 inches to 1 mile, with larger scale maps at a scale of 3.5 inches to 1 mile in the south and for the following towns: Arbroath, Auchterarder, Brechin, Carnoustie, Crieff, Cupar, Dunblane, Dundee, Forfar, Glenrothes, Kinross, Kirriemuir, Leven, Montrose, Perth, Rattray and St Andrews. Dundee city centre is shown at 7 inches to 1 mile. Other information on the maps includes postcode boundaries, car parks, railway and bus stations, post offices, schools, colleges, hospitals, police and fire stations, places of worship, leisure centres, footpaths and bridleways, camping and caravan sites, golf courses, and many other places of interest. New to this edition are fixed single and multiple speed-camera locations, with corresponding speed limits. The comprehensive index lists street names and postcodes, plus schools, hospitals, railway stations, shopping centres and other such features picked out in red, with other places of interest shown in blue.

FAST headings:

Topical:	**Roads**
Geographic:	**Scotland—Fife**
	Scotland—Tayside
Form:	**Maps**

MARC record:

```
LDR     00425nam 22001573 4500
008     081013s2008 xx 000 0 eng d
020     $a0540092037
043     $ae-uk-st
082 04  $a912.4128 $221
245 00  $aPhilip's Street Atlas Fife and Tayside.
260     $bPhilip's $c2008.
300     $a224 p. : $bmaps ; $c27cm.
650  7  $aRoads. $2fast
651  7  $aScotland $zFife. $2fast
651  7  $aScotland $zTayside. $2fast
655  7  $aMaps. $2fast
```

Dublin Core record:

```
<qualifieddc>
<dctermset>
<dcterms:issued>2008</dcterms:issued>
<dcterms:spatial xsi:type="http://id.loc.gov/vocabulary/
sources/subject/fast">Scotland--Fife
</dcterms:spatial>
```

```
<dcterms:spatial xsi:type="http://id.loc.gov/vocabulary/
sources/subject/fast">Scotland--Tayside
</dcterms:spatial>

<dcterms:extent>224 p. ; 27 cm.</dcterms:extent>

<dcterms:language xsi:type="http://purl.org/dc/terms/
ISO639-2">eng</dcterms:language>

<dcterms:publisher>Philip's</dcterms:publisher>

<dcterms:title>Philip's Street Atlas Fife and Tayside.
</dcterms:title>

<dcterms:subject xsi:type="http://id.loc.gov/vocabulary/
sources/subject/fast">Roads</dcterms:subject>

<dcterms:type xsi:type="http://id.loc.gov/vocabulary/
sources/subject/fast">Maps</dcterms:type>

</dctermset>

</qualifieddc>
```

Example 5: *Anne Frank: Reflections on Her Life and Legacy*

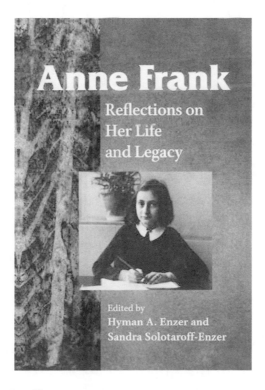

Publisher's description:[10]

Of all the memoirs that convey the human devastation of Hitler's Final Solution, Anne Frank's The Diary of a Young Girl is by far the most popular and influential. Since its publication in Holland in 1947, the diary has been translated into more than fifty languages, reprinted in millions of copies, and transformed into plays, films, teaching guides, and political tracts. These contending interpretations all serve to illuminate as well as obscure the "real" Anne Frank. This book is the most complete anthology of the disparate facts and interpretations of Anne Frank. Here in a concise, readable volume are two dozen articles and memoirs most relevant for understanding her life, death, and legacy. They assess Anne Frank's qualities as a writer and scrutinize the proliferating controversies about her reputation, especially the way the stage and film versions have altered perceptions of her life and her diary. They also consider how interpreters of Jewish experience in World War II have defined Anne Frank's significance for memorializing the Holocaust. Anne Frank's memoir of eight Jews hiding in an attic for two years continues to resonate as a haunting reminder of the promise of a generation that was almost completely snuffed out. Thrown into relief by the horrors she constantly feared and eventually suffered, the young girl's uninhibited observations and self-analysis retain their poignancy and power. Supplemented by a complete record of the diary's publishing history and an extensive bibliography and index, this book provides an intriguing glimpse at how fact, fiction, history, and legend are intertwined.

Table of contents:

Foreword by Buddy Elias

Preface and Acknowledgements

Major Identifications

The Diary Versions

Chronology

Note to the Reader

Introduction

Part I: History, Biography, and Authenticity

    1. Anne Frank

    2. The Arrest

    3. The Betrayal

    4. Visiting Hours after 9 A.M.

    5. Her Last Days

    6. Bergen-Belsen

    7. The Darkest Days

    8. Epilogue to the Diary of Anne Frank

Part 2: Writer and Rewriter

    9. The Legend and Art of Anne Frank

    10. The Development of Anne Frank

    11. Introduction to *The Tales from the House Behind*

    12. Writing Herself against History: Anne Frank's Self-Portrait as a Young Artist

    13. Death and the Maiden

    14. Anne Frank's Reading: A Retrospective

    15. Reading Anne Frank as a Woman

Part 3: Anne Frank on Stage and Screen

16. The American History of Anne Frank's Diary

17. Metamorphosis into American Adolescent

18. At the Theater: Berlin Postscript

19. This Time, Another Anne Confronts Life in the Attic

20. Don Quixote and the Star of David

21. Germany's New Flagellants

22. Anne Frank and Film

23. Review Essay: Anne Frank Remembered

Part 4: Memorializing the Holocaust

24. The Ignored Lesson of Anne Frank

25. Twisting the Truth: The Diary of Anne Frank

26. The Americanization of the Holocaust on the Stage and Screen

27. The Uses—and Misuses—of a Young Girl's Diary: "If Anne Frank Could Return from among the Murdered, She Would be Appalled"

28. Anne Frank—and Us: Finding the Right Words

29. Anne Frank and Etty Hillesum: Diarists

30. The Anne Frank House: Holland's Memorial Shrine of the Book

31. Femme Fatale

Appendixes

Bibliography

Publication Acknowledgments

Contributors

Index

FAST headings:

Personal Name:	**Frank, Anne, 1929–1945**
Uniform Title:	**Achterhuis (Frank, Anne)**
Chronological:	**1939–1945**
Topical:	**Holocaust, Jewish (1939–1945)**
	Jewish children in the Holocaust
	Holocaust memorials
Geographic:	**Netherlands—Amsterdam**

MARC record:

```
LDR    01020cam 2200253 a 4500
008    990324s2000 ilu b s001 0beng
010    $a 99006291
020    $a0252068238 (pbk. : alk. paper)
043    $ae-ne---
050 00 $aDS135.N6 $bF7318 2000
```

082 00 $a940.53/18/09492 $221

245 00 $aAnne Frank : $breflections on her life and
       legacy / $cedited by Hyman Aaron Enzer and Sandra
       Solotaroff-Enzer ; foreword by Bernd Elias.

260     $aUrbana : $bUniversity of Illinois Press, $cc2000.

300     $axxv, 285 p. ; $c24 cm.

504     $aIncludes bibliographical references (p. [251]-259)
        and index.

600 17 $aFrank, Anne, $d1929-1945. $2fast

630 07 $aAchterhuis (Frank, Anne). $2fast

648 7 $a1939-1945. $2fast

650 7 $aHolocaust, Jewish (1939-1945). $2fast

650 7 $aJewish children in the Holocaust. $2fast

651 7 $aNetherlands $zAmsterdam. $2fast

700 1 $aEnzer, Hyman Aaron, $d1916-

700 1 $aSolotaroff-Enzer, Sandra, $d1933-

Dublin Core record:

```
<qualifieddc>

<dctermset>

<dcterms:contributor>Enzer, Hyman Aaron, 1916-
</dcterms:contributor>

<dcterms:contributor>Solotaroff-Enzer, Sandra, 1933-
</dcterms:contributor>

<dcterms:spatial xsi:type="http://id.loc.gov/vocabulary/
sources/subject/fast">Netherlands--Amsterdam
</dcterms:spatial>

<dcterms:issued>c2000</dcterms:issued>

<dcterms:description>Includes bibliographical references
(p. [251]-259) and index.</dcterms:description>

<dcterms:extent>xxv, 285 p. ; 24 cm.</dcterms:extent>

<dcterms:language xsi:type="http://purl.org/dc/terms/
ISO639-2">eng</dcterms:language>

<dcterms:publisher>University of Illinois Press
</dcterms:publisher>

<dcterms:subject xsi:type="http://purl.org/dc/terms/
DDC">940.53/18/09492</dcterms:subject>

<dcterms:subject xsi:type="http://purl.org/dc/terms/
LCC">DS135.N6 F7318 2000</dcterms:subject>

<dcterms:title>Anne Frank : reflections on her life and
legacy</dcterms:title>
```

```
<dcterms:subject xsi:type="http://id.loc.gov/vocabulary/
sources/subject/fast">Jewish Children in the
Holocaust</dcterms:subject>

<dcterms:subject xsi:type="http://id.loc.gov/vocabulary/
sources/subject/fast">Holocaust, Jewish (1939-1945)
</dcterms:subject>

<dcterms:subject xsi:type="http://id.loc.gov/vocabulary/
sources/subject/fast">Frank, Anne,--1929-1945
</dcterms:subject>

<dcterms:temporal xsi:type="http://id.loc.gov/vocabulary/
sources/subject/fast">1939-1945</dcterms:temporal>

</dctermset>

</qualifieddc>
```

Example 6: *2005 Hydrographic Survey of South San Francisco Bay,
California* [Web site]

Abstract:[11]

*An acoustic hydrographic survey of South San Francisco Bay (South Bay) was
conducted in 2005. Over 20 million soundings were collected within an area of
approximately 250 sq km (97 sq mi) of the bay extending south of Coyote Point
on the west shore, to the San Leandro marina on the east, including Coyote Creek
and Ravenswood, Alviso, Artesian, and Mud Sloughs. This is the first survey of
this scale that has been conducted in South Bay since the National Oceanic and
Atmospheric Administration National Ocean Service (NOS) last surveyed the
region in the early 1980s. Data from this survey will provide insight to changes
in bay floor topography from the 1980s to 2005 and will also serve as essential*

baseline data for tracking changes that will occur as restoration of the South San Francisco Bay salt ponds progress [sic]. This report provides documentation on how the survey was conducted, an assessment of accuracy of the data, and distributes the sounding data with Federal Geographic Data Committee (FGDC) compliant metadata. Reports from NOS and Sea Surveyor, Inc., containing additional survey details are attached as appendices.

FAST headings:

Topical:	**Hydrography**
Geographic:	**Pacific Ocean—San Francisco Bay**
Form:	**Bathymetric maps**

MARC record:

```
LDR      00870cam 2200205Ia 4500

008      070612s2007 vauab sb f000 0 eng d

006      m d f

007      cr mn||||m||||

043      $an-us-ca

245 00 $a2005 hydrographic survey of south San Francisco
         Bay, California $h[electronic resource] / $cby Amy C.
         Foxgrover ... [et al.].

246 3  $aTwo thousand five hydrographic survey of south San
         Francisco Bay, California

260      $aReston, Va. : $bU.S. Geological Survey, $c2007.

300      $a1 electronic text (iii, 110 p.) : $bHTML, digital,
         PDF file.

650  7 $aHydrography. $2fast

651  7 $aPacific Ocean $zSan Francisco Bay. $2fast

655  7 $aBathymetric maps. $2fast

700 1  $aFoxgrover, Amy C.

710 2  $aWestern Coastal and Marine Geology Program
         (Geological Survey)

710 2  $aGeological Survey (U.S.)

856 40 $uhttp://purl.access.gpo.gov/GPO/LPS87502
```

Dublin Core record:

```
<qualifieddc>

<dctermset>

<dcterms:contributor>Foxgrover, Amy C.
</dcterms:contributor>
```

```
<dcterms:contributor>Western Coastal and Marine Geology
Program (Geological Survey)</dcterms:contributor>

<dcterms:contributor>Geological Survey (U.S.)
</dcterms:contributor>

<dcterms:spatial xsi:type="http://id.loc.gov/vocabulary/
sources/subject/fast">Pacific Ocean—San Francisco
Bay </dcterms:spatial>

<dcterms:issued>2007</dcterms:issued>

<dcterms:description>Title from PDF title screen
(viewed on June 12, 2007).</dcterms:description>

<dcterms:description>At head of title on HTML title
screen: Western Coastal and Marine Geology.
</dcterms:description>

<dcterms:description>Includes bibliographical references.
</dcterms:description>

<dcterms:description>Contains figures as TIFF file,
Powerpoint slide, and PDF poster.</dcterms:description>

<dcterms:extent>1 electronic text (iii, 110 p.) : HTML,
digital, PDF file.</dcterms:extent>

<dcterms:language xsi:type="http://purl.org/dc/terms/
ISO639-2">eng</dcterms:language>

<dcterms:publisher>U.S. Geological Survey
</dcterms:publisher>

<dcterms:isPartOf>Open-file report ; 2007-1169
</dcterms:isPartOf>

<dcterms:isPartOf>U.S. Geological Survey open-file report
; 2007-1169.</dcterms:isPartOf>

<dcterms:requires>Mode of access: Internet from the USGS
web site. Address as of 10/31/07: http://pubs.usgs.gov/
of/2007/1169/; current access via PURL.</dcterms:requires>

<dcterms:subject>I 19.76:2007-1169</dcterms:subject>

<dcterms:title>2005 hydrographic survey of south San
Francisco Bay, California</dcterms:title>

<dcterms:alternative>Two thousand five hydrographic
survey of south San Francisco Bay, California
</dcterms:alternative>

<dcterms:subject xsi:type="http://id.loc.gov/vocabulary/
sources/subject/fast">Hydrography</dcterms:subject>

<dcterms:type xsi:type="http://id.loc.gov/vocabulary/
sources/subject/fast">Bathymetric maps</dcterms:type>

</dctermset>

</qualifieddc>
```

Example 7: *Shakespeare in the Victorian Periodicals*

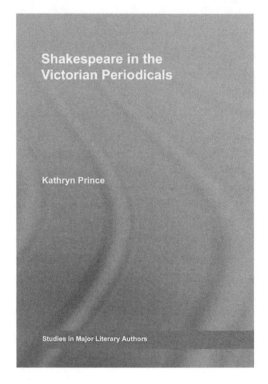

Publisher's description:[12]

> *Based on extensive archival research,* Shakespeare in the Victorian Periodicals *offers an entirely new perspective on popular Shakespeare reception by focusing on articles published in Victorian periodicals. Shakespeare had already reached the apex of British culture in the previous century, becoming the national poet of the middle and upper classes, but during the Victorian era he was embraced by more marginal groups. If Shakespeare was sometimes employed as an instrument of enculturation, imposed on these groups, he was also used by them to resist this cultural hegemony.*

Table of contents:

Introduction: The Nineteenth-Century Popular Press and Shakespeare Reception History
1. Making Shakespeare Readers in the Early Working Class Press
2. Shakespeare for Manly Boys and Marriageable Girls
3. Character Criticism and Its Discontents in Periodicals for Women
4. The Theatres Regulation Act and the Great Exhibition in the *Theatrical Journal*
5. Victorian Periodicals and England's National Theatre Debate
Notes
Bibliography

FAST headings:

Personal Name: **Shakespeare, William, 1564–1616**
Chronological: **1800–1899**

Topical:	**Periodicals—Publishing**
	Literature—Appreciation
Geographic:	**Great Britain**
Form:	**Criticism, interpretation, etc.**
	History

MARC record:

```
LDR     00711cam 22002174a 4500
020     $a0415962439 (acid-free paper)
043     $ae-uk---
050 00  $aPR2969 $b.P75 2008
082 00  $a822.3/3 $222
100 1   $aPrince, Kathryn, $d1973-
245 10  $aShakespeare in the Victorian periodicals /
        $cKathryn Prince.
260     $aNew York : $bRoutledge, $c2008.
300     $ax, 180 p. ; $c24 cm.
440 0   $aStudies in major literary authors
600 17  $aShakespeare, William, $d1564-1616. $2fast
648  7  $a1800-1899. $2fast
650  7  $aPeriodicals $xPublishing. $2fast
650 17  $aLiterature $xAppreciation. $2fast
651  7  $aGreat Britain. $2fast
655  7  $aCriticism, interpretation, etc. $2fast
655  7  $aHistory. $2fast
```

Dublin Core record:

```
<qualifieddc>
<dctermset>
<dcterms:creator>Prince, Kathryn</dcterms:creator>
<dcterms:spatial xsi:type="http://id.loc.gov/vocabulary/
sources/subject/fast">Great Britain </dcterms:spatial>
<dcterms:issued>2008</dcterms:issued>
<dcterms:description>1. publ.</dcterms:description>
<dcterms:description>Includes bibliographical references
and index</dcterms:description>
<dcterms:extent>X, 180 S.</dcterms:extent>
<dcterms:language xsi:type="http://purl.org/dc/terms/
ISO639-2">eng</dcterms:language>
<dcterms:publisher>Routledge</dcterms:publisher>
<dcterms:isPartOf>Studies in major literary authors
</dcterms:isPartOf>
<dcterms:subject xsi:type="http://purl.org/dc/terms/
LCC">PR2969</dcterms:subject>
```

```
<dcterms:title>Shakespeare in the Victorian periodicals
</dcterms:title>

<dcterms:type>Text</dcterms:type>

<dcterms:temporal xsi:type="http://id.loc.gov/vocabulary/
sources/subject/fast">1800-1899</dcterms:temporal>

<dcterms:subject xsi:type="http://id.loc.gov/
vocabulary/sources/subject/fast">Periodicals--
publishing</dcterms:subject>

<dcterms:subject xsi:type="http://id.loc.gov/
vocabulary/sources/subject/fast">Literature--
appreciation </dcterms:subject>

<dcterms:subject xsi:type="http://id.loc.gov/vocabulary/
sources/subject/fast">Shakespeare, William,--1564-1616
</dcterms:subject>

<dcterms:type xsi:type="http://id.loc.gov/vocabulary/
sources/subject/fast">Criticism, interpretation, etc.
</dcterms:type>

<dcterms:type xsi:type="http://id.loc.gov/vocabulary/
sources/subject/fast">History</dcterms:type>

</dctermset>

</qualifieddc>
```

Example 8: *Portrait of an Unknown Woman*

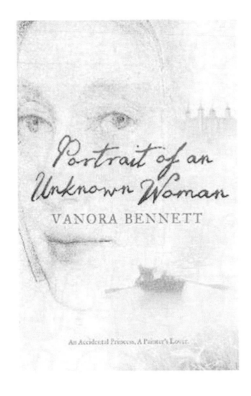

Publisher's description:[13]

> In the year 1527, the great portraitist Hans Holbein, fleeing the Protestant Reformation, comes to England under commission to Sir Thomas More. Over the course of the next six years, Holbein paints two nearly identical portraits of the More family, his dear and loyal friends. But closer examination of the second painting reveals several mysteries. . . .
>
> Set against the turmoil and tragedy of Henry VIII's court, Portrait of an Unknown Woman vividly evokes sixteenth-century England on the verge of enormous change—as viewed through the eyes of Meg Giggs, More's intelligent, tenderhearted, headstrong adopted daughter, who stands at the center of this sweeping, extraordinary epic. It is a tale of sin and religion, desire and deception—the story of a young woman on the brink of sensual awakening and a country on the edge of mayhem.

FAST headings:

Personal Name:	**Holbein, Hans, 1497–1543**
	More, Thomas, Sir, Saint, 1478–1535
Chronological:	**1485–1603**
Topical:	**Upper class**
	Portrait painting
	Foster children
	Artists
	Family
	Social history
Geographic:	**Great Britain**
Form:	**Fiction**
	History

MARC record:

LDR		01032cam 2200289Ia 4500
008		080425s2008 nyua b 000 1 eng
020		$a0061252565 (pbk.)
043		$ae-uk--- $ae-uk-en
050	14	$aPR6102.E666 $bP67 2008
082	04	$a823/.92 $222
100	1	$aBennett, Vanora, $d1962-
245	10	$aPortrait of an unknown woman / $cVanora Bennett.
260		$aNew York : $bHarper, $cc2008.
300		$a449 p. : $bill. ; $c21 cm.
520		$aBritish journalist Bennett makes her fiction debut with a sweeping reinterpretation of Sir Thomas More's family as it coped with the vicissitudes of Henry VIII's reign.

```
600 17 $aHolbein, Hans, $d1497-1543. $2fast

600 17 $aMore, Thomas, $cSir, Saint, $d1478-1535. $2fast

648  7 $a1485-1603. $2fast

650  7 $aUpper class. $2fast

650  7 $aPortrait painting. $2fast

650  7 $aFoster children. $2fast

650  7 $aArtists. $2fast

650  7 $aFamily. $2fast

650  7 $aSocial conditions. $2fast

651  7 $aGreat Britain. $2fast

655  7 $aFiction. $2fast

655  7 $aHistory. $2fast
```

Dublin Core record:

```
<qualifieddc>

<dctermset>

<dcterms:creator>Bennett, Vanora, 1962-</dcterms:creator>

<dcterms:spatial xsi:type="http://id.loc.gov/vocabulary/
sources/subject/fast">Great Britain </dcterms:spatial>

<dcterms:issued>2006</dcterms:issued>

<dcterms:description>Included bibliography (p.511-513).
</dcterms:description>

<dcterms:extent>x, 513 p. : ill., port., map ; 23 cm.
</dcterms:extent>

<dcterms:language xsi:type="http://purl.org/dc/terms/
ISO639-2">eng</dcterms:language>

<dcterms:publisher>Harper Collins</dcterms:publisher>

<dcterms:subject xsi:type="http://purl.org/dc/terms/
DDC">823/.92</dcterms:subject>

<dcterms:title>Portrait of an unknown woman</dcterms:title>

<dcterms:type>Historical fiction.</dcterms:type>

<dcterms:subject xsi:type="http://id.loc.gov/vocabulary/
sources/subject/fast">Upper class</dcterms:subject>

<dcterms:temporal xsi:type="http://id.loc.gov/vocabulary/
sources/subject/fast">1485-1603</dcterms:temporal>

<dcterms:subject xsi:type="http://id.loc.gov/
vocabulary/sources/subject/fast">Portrait Painting
</dcterms:subject>
```

```
<dcterms:subject xsi:type="http://id.loc.gov/vocabulary/
sources/subject/fast">Foster children</dcterms:subject>

<dcterms:subject xsi:type="http://id.loc.gov/vocabulary/
sources/subject/fast">Artists</dcterms:subject>

<dcterms:subject xsi:type="http://id.loc.gov/vocabulary/
sources/subject/fast">Family</dcterms:subject>

<dcterms:subject xsi:type="http://id.loc.gov/vocabulary/
sources/subject/fast">Social conditions</dcterms:subject>

<dcterms:subject xsi:type="http://id.loc.gov/vocabulary/
sources/subject/fast">Holbein, Hans,--1497-1543
</dcterms:subject>

<dcterms:subject xsi:type="http://id.loc.gov/vocabulary/
sources/subject/fast">More, Thomas,--Sir, Saint,--
1478-1535</dcterms:subject>

<dcterms:type xsi:type="http://id.loc.gov/vocabulary/
sources/subject/fast">Fiction</dcterms:type>

<dcterms:type xsi:type="http://id.loc.gov/vocabulary/
sources/subject/fast">History</dcterms:type>

</dctermset>
</qualifieddc>
```

Example 9: *The Pretender*

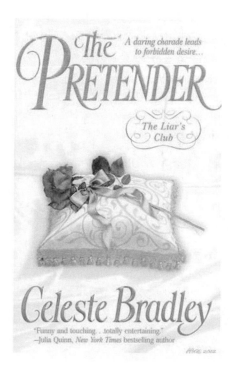

Publisher's description:[14]

> *Rule #1: Never fall in love.*
> *Celeste Bradley captivated critics and readers alike with her unforgettable novel Fallen, which was nominated for the prestigious RITA Award from Romance Writers of America for Best First Book. Now, she brings us The [Pretender], the first book in the wildly fun, exciting, and sexy new Liar's Club series both featuring irresistible heroes who are out to steal their leading ladies hearts!*
> *She had a secret she'd do anything to hide.*
> *Agatha Cunnington, a headstrong beauty from the country, has come to London in search of her missing brother James. The only clue she has is a cryptic letter signed The Griffin. Agatha decides to disguise herself as a respectable married woman so that she can go about the city unnoticed. But for her charade to work she needs a suitable "husband," preferably someone tall, elegant, and rakish—someone like Simon Montague Rain.*
> *He had a secret he'd do anything to hide.*
> *Simon Montague Rain, also known as The Magician, is a member of The Liar's Club, a renegade group of rogues and thieves in the service of the Crown. When someone begins murdering members of the undercover cabal one by one, Simon is given the mission to bring in The Griffin, one of his comrades who is suspected of betraying his brothers. Simon goes undercover and infiltrates the home of "Mrs." Agatha Applequist who he believes is the Griffin's mistress. Before Simon knows what's happened, he finds himself irresistibly drawn to Agatha's soft, feminine charms—and he is tempted beyond reason to break the first rule of The Liar's Club: never fall in love.*

FAST headings:

Chronological:	**1800–1899**
Topical:	**Missing persons**
	Secret service
	Social life and customs
Geographic:	**England**
Form:	**Fiction**

MARC record:

```
LDR     00496nam 2200169Ia 4500
008     080318r20082003nyu 000 1 eng d
020     $a0312946007
100 1   $aBradley, Celeste.
245 14  $aThe pretender / $cCeleste Bradley.
260     $aNew York : $bSt. Martin's Press, $c2003 $g(2008
        printing)
300     $a372 p. ; $c17 cm.
490 1   $aBook one in the Liar's Club
```

```
648   7  $a1800-1899. $2fast

650   7  $aMissing persons. $2fast

650   7  $aSecret service. $2fast

650   7  $aSocial life and customs. $2fast

651   7  $aEngland. $2fast

655   7  $aFiction. $2fast
```

Dublin Core record:

```
<qualifieddc>

<dctermset>

<dcterms:creator>Bradley, Celeste.</dcterms:creator>

<dcterms:spatial xsi:type="http://id.loc.gov/vocabulary/
sources/subject/fast">England</dcterms:spatial>

<dcterms:issued>c2003</dcterms:issued>

<dcterms:extent>1 v. ; 21 cm.</dcterms:extent>

<dcterms:language xsi:type="http://purl.org/dc/terms/
ISO639-2">eng</dcterms:language>

<dcterms:publisher>St. Martin's Paperbacks
</dcterms:publisher>

<dcterms:isPartOf>Book one in the Liar's Club
</dcterms:isPartOf>

<dcterms:isPartOf>Bradley, Celeste. Liar's Club ;
bk. 1.</dcterms:isPartOf>

<dcterms:title>The pretender</dcterms:title>

<dcterms:type>Historical romance.</dcterms:type>

<dcterms:temporal xsi:type="http://id.loc.gov/vocabulary/
sources/subject/fast">1800-1899</dcterms:temporal>

<dcterms:subject xsi:type="http://id.loc.gov/vocabulary/
sources/subject/fast">Missing persons</dcterms:subject>

<dcterms:subject xsi:type="http://id.loc.gov/vocabulary/
sources/subject/fast">Secret service</dcterms:subject>

<dcterms:subject xsi:type="http://id.loc.gov/vocabulary/
sources/subject/fast">Social life and customs
</dcterms:subject>

<dcterms:type xsi:type="http://id.loc.gov/vocabulary/
sources/subject/fast">Fiction</dcterms:type>

</dctermset>

</qualifieddc>
```

Example 10: *First Emperor of China* [DVD]

Netflix's description:[15]

> *Originally presented in IMAX theaters, this documentary opens a door in The Great Wall and reveals the history of the first emperor of China, an era previously unknown by much of the Western world. In addition to current video of significant historical sites, such as the Emperor's private sanctuary, re-creations are used to tell the story of how Qin Shihuang, who gave China its name, came to rule the land and create a powerful nation.*

FAST headings:

Personal Name:	**Qin shi huang, Emperor of China, 259–210 B.C.**
Chronological:	**221 B.C.–220 A.D.**
Topical:	**Death and burial of a person**
	Terra-cotta sculpture, Chinese
	Antiquities
Geographic:	**China—Shaanxi Sheng**
Form:	**Video recordings**
	Documentary films
	History

MARC record:

```
LDR     01063cgm 2200253Ka 4500
008     060110s2006 xxu042 g vleng d
```

```
007      vd cvaizq

024 1    $a690445032324

043      $aa-cc---

050 14   $aDS747.9.C47 $bF57 2006

082 04   $a931/.04 $222

245 00   $aFirst emperor of China $h[videorecording].

260      $a[United States] : $bRazor Digital Entertainment,
         $c[2006]

300      $a1 videodisc (ca. 42 min.) : $bsd., col. ; $c4 3/4 in.

520      $aChronicles the period of Qin Shihuang's rule. From
         thegrandiose inner sanctum of Emperor Qin royal
         palace, to fierce battles with feudal kings, this
         historical drama re-creates the glory and the
         terror of the Qin Dynasty.

600 07   $aQin shi huang, $cEmperor of China, $d259-210 B.C.
         $2fast

648   7  $a221 B.C.-220 A.D. $2fast

650   7  $Death and burial of a person. $2fast

650   7  $aTerra-cotta sculpture, Chinese. $2fast

650   7  $aAntiquities. $2fast

651   7  $aChina $zShaanxi Sheng. $2fast

655   7  $aVideo recordings. $2fast

655   7  $aDocumentary films. $2fast

655   7  $aHistory. $2fast
```

Dublin Core record:

```
<qualifieddc>

<dctermset>

<dcterms:contributor>Razor Digital Entertainment (Firm)
</dcterms:contributor>

<dcterms:spatial xsi:type="http://id.loc.gov/
vocabulary/sources/subject/fast">China--Shaanxi Sheng
</dcterms:spatial>

<dcterms:issued>[2006]</dcterms:issued>

<dcterms:description>Catalogue from web art.
</dcterms:description>

<dcterms:description>Originally released in 1989.
</dcterms:description>

<dcterms:abstract>Chronicles the period of Qin Shihuang's
rule. From the grandiose inner sanctum of Emperor Qin
royal palace, to fierce battles with feudal kings, this
historical drama re-creates the glory and the terror of
the Qin Dynasty.</dcterms:abstract>
```

```
<dcterms:extent>1 videodisc (ca. 42 min.) : sd., col. ;
4 3/4 in.</dcterms:extent>

<dcterms:language xsi:type="http://purl.org/dc/terms/
ISO639-2">eng</dcterms:language>

<dcterms:publisher>Razor Digital Entertainment
</dcterms:publisher>

<dcterms:isPartOf>IMAX theaters 15/70 collection
</dcterms:isPartOf>

<dcterms:requires>DVD, region 1, full screen
presentation; Dolby Digital.</dcterms:requires>

<dcterms:subject xsi:type="http://purl.org/dc/terms/
DDC">931/.04</dcterms:subject>

<dcterms:subject xsi:type="http://purl.org/dc/terms/
LCC">DS747.9.C47 F57 2006</dcterms:subject>

<dcterms:title>First emperor of China</dcterms:title>

<dcterms:subject xsi:type="http://id.loc.gov/
vocabulary/sources/subject/fast">Death and burial
of a person</dcterms:subject>

<dcterms:temporal xsi:type="http://id.loc.gov/
vocabulary/sources/subject/fast">221 B.C.-220 A.D.
</dcterms:temporal>

<dcterms:subject xsi:type="http://id.loc.gov/
vocabulary/sources/subject/fast">Terra-cotta
sculpture, Chinese</dcterms:subject>

<dcterms:subject xsi:type="http://id.loc.gov/
vocabulary/sources/subject/fast">Antiquities
</dcterms:subject>

<dcterms:subject xsi:type="http://id.loc.gov/
vocabulary/sources/subject/fast">Qin shi huang,
--Emperor of China, --259-210 B.C.</dcterms:subject>

<dcterms:type xsi:type="http://id.loc.gov/
vocabulary/sources/subject/fast">Video recordings
</dcterms:type>

<dcterms:type xsi:type="http://id.loc.gov/
vocabulary/sources/subject/fast">Documentary films
</dcterms:type>

<dcterms:type xsi:type="http://id.loc.gov/
vocabulary/sources/subject/fast">History
</dcterms:type>

</dctermset>

</qualifieddc>
```

Example 11: *Japan: Economic, Political and Social Issues*

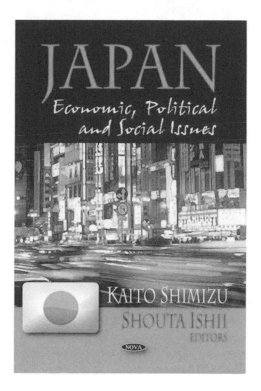

Publisher's description:[16]

> *This book elaborates leading-edge economic, political and social issues about Japan. Japan has the world's tenth largest population, with about 128 million people. The Greater Tokyo Area, which includes the capital city of Tokyo and several surrounding prefectures, is the largest metropolitan area in the world, with over 30 million residents.*
>
> *A major economic power, Japan has the world's second largest economy by nominal GDP. It is a member of the United Nations, G8, G4 and APEC, with the world's fifth largest defense budget. It is also the world's fourth largest exporter and sixth largest importer and a world leader in technology and machinery.*

Table of contents:

1. Interpersonal Relationships and Mental Health among Japanese College Students
2. Accountability and Assessment: A New Era of Japanese Higher Education
3. Ethical Views of Japanese Managers: Insight from the Rationality of Ends/Market Orientation-Grid
4. Earnings Management to Meet Earnings Benchmarks: Evidence from Japan
5. Contemporary Monetary Policy and Financial System Issues of Japan

6. International Intrafirm Transfer of Management Technology by Japanese Multinational Corporations
7. Bofutsushosan "Kampo Medicine" Use in Metabolic Syndrome: Research the Scientific Basis and Clinical Trial in Japanese Obesity
8. China's Rise in Southeast Asia After 9-11: Implications for Japan and the United States
9. Toward a Constructive Sino-Japanese Relationship in the New Millennium

FAST headings:

Chronological:	**Since 2000**
Topical:	**Economics**
	Political science
Geographic:	**Japan**

MARC record:

```
LDR     00658cam 2200205 a 4500
008     080401s2008 nyua b 001 0 eng
010     $a 2008014840
020     $a1604566752 (hardcover)
043     $aa-ja---
050 00 $aHC462.95 $b.J3555 2008
082 00 $a330.952 $222
245 00 $aJapan : $beconomic, political and social issues /
        $cKaito Shimizu and Shouta Ishii, editors.
260     $aNew York : $bNova Science Publishers, $cc2008.
300     $axi, 204 p. : $bill. (some col.) ; $c27 cm.
648  7 $aSince 2000. $2fast
650  7 $aEconomics. $2fast
650  7 $aPolitical science. $2fast
651  7 $aJapan. $2fast
700 1  $aShimizu, Kaito.
700 1  $aIshii, Shouta.
```

Dublin Core record:

```
<qualifieddc>
<dctermset>
<dcterms:contributor>Shimizu, Kaito.</dcterms:contributor>
<dcterms:contributor>Ishii, Shouta.</dcterms:contributor>
<dcterms:spatial xsi:type="http://id.loc.gov/vocabulary/
sources/subject/fast">Japan</dcterms:spatial>
<dcterms:issued>c2008</dcterms:issued>
<dcterms:description>Includes bibliographical references
and index.</dcterms:description>
```

```
<dcterms:extent>xi, 204 p. : ill. (some col.) ; 27 cm.
</dcterms:extent>

<dcterms:language xsi:type="http://purl.org/dc/terms/
ISO639-2">eng</dcterms:language>

<dcterms:publisher>Nova Science Publishers
</dcterms:publisher>

<dcterms:subject xsi:type="http://purl.org/dc/terms/
DDC">330.952</dcterms:subject>

<dcterms:subject xsi:type="http://purl.org/dc/terms/
LCC">HC462.95 .J3555 2008</dcterms:subject>

<dcterms:title>Japan : economic, political and social
issues</dcterms:title>

<dcterms:subject xsi:type="http://id.loc.gov/vocabulary/
sources/subject/fast">Economics</dcterms:subject>

<dcterms:subject xsi:type="http://id.loc.gov/vocabulary/
sources/subject/fast">Political science</dcterms:subject>

<dcterms:temporal xsi:type="http://id.loc.gov/vocabulary/
sources/subject/fast">Since 2000</dcterms:temporal>

</dctermset>

</qualifieddc>
```

Example 12: *Detours* [Audio CD]

Songs:

> God Bless This Mess
> Shine over Babylon
> Love Is Free
> Peace Be Upon Us
> Gasoline
> Out of Our Heads
> Detours
> Now That You're Gone
> Drunk with the Thought of You
> Diamond Ring
> Motivation
> Make It Go Away (Radiation Song)
> Love Is All There Is
> Lullaby For Wyatt

FAST headings:

> Chronological: **2001–2010**
> Topical: **Rock music**
>   **Alternative rock music**

MARC record:

```
LDR     00632cjm 2200205 a 4500

008     081017s2008 caurcnn d n eng

007     sd fsngnnmmned

010     $a 2008644182

024 1   $a602517570030

050 00  $aHM1630.18.C76 $bD48 2008

082 00  $a782.42166 $222

100 1   $aCrow, Sheryl. $4prf

245 10  $aDetours $h[sound recording] / $cSheryl Crow.

260     $aSanta Monica, CA : $bA & M Records, $cp2008.

300     $a1 sound disc : $bdigital ; $c4 3/4 in.

650 0   $aRock music $y2001-2010.

650 0   $aAlternative rock music.

648  7  $a2001-2010. $2fast

650  7  $aRock music. $2fast

650  7  $aAlternative rock music. $2fast
```

Note that this record contains both LCSH headings [the second indicator value of '0'] and FAST headings [the second indicator value of '7' and the subfield $2].

Dublin Core record:

```
<qualifieddc>

<dctermset>

<dcterms:creator>Crow, Sheryl.</dcterms:creator>

<dcterms:issued>p2008</dcterms:issued>

<dcterms:description>A & M Records: B0010779-00 (set);
B0010599-02 (CD); AMRR-12347-9 (DVD).
</dcterms:description>

<dcterms:description>Compact disc.</dcterms:description>

<dcterms:description>Sheryl Crow, vocals, guitar ; with
various accompanying musicians.</dcterms:description>

<dcterms:extent>1 sound disc : digital ; 4 3/4 in. + 1
videodisc (DVD : sd., col. ; 4 3/4 in.)</dcterms:extent>

<dcterms:language xsi:type="http://purl.org/dc/terms/
ISO639-2">eng</dcterms:language>

<dcterms:publisher>A & M Records</dcterms:publisher>

<dcterms:subject xsi:type="http://purl.org/dc/terms/
LCSH">Rock music--2001-2010.</dcterms:subject>

<dcterms:subject xsi:type="http://purl.org/dc/terms/
LCSH">Alternative rock music.</dcterms:subject>

<dcterms:title>Detours</dcterms:title>

<dcterms:temporal xsi:type="http://id.loc.gov/vocabulary/
sources/subject/fast">2001-2010</dcterms:temporal>

<dcterms:subject xsi:type="http://id.loc.gov/vocabulary/
sources/subject/fast">Rock music</dcterms:subject>

<dcterms:subject xsi:type="http://id.loc.gov/vocabulary/
sources/subject/fast">Alternative rock music
</dcterms:subject>

</dctermset>

</qualifieddc>
```

NOTES

1. Dublin Core Metadata Initiative, *Dublin Core Metadata Element Set*, Version 1.1, April 1, 2010, http://dublincore.org/documents/dces/index.shtml (accessed on April 12, 2010).

2. Arlene G. Taylor and Daniel N. Joudrey, *The Organization of Information*, 3rd ed. (Westport, CT: Libraries Unlimited, 2009), pp. 310–13.

3. McGraw-Hill Higher Education, *Teaching to Change the World*, 3rd ed., 2007, http://catalogs.mhhe.com/mhhe/viewProductDetails.do?isbn=0072982004 (accessed April 12, 2010).

4. *Anglo?American Cataloguing Rules*, 2nd ed., 2002 revision, prepared under the direction of the Joint Steering Committee for Revision of AACR, a committee of the American Library Association, the Australian Committee on Cataloguing, the British Library, the Canadian Committee on Cataloguing, Chartered Institute of Library and Information Professionals, the Library of Congress (Chicago: American Library Association, 2002).

5. Library of Congress, Network Development and MARC Standards Office, *MARC 21 Format for Bibliographic Data* (update No. 11, October 2009), http://www.loc.gov/marc/bibliographic/ecbdhome.html (accessed April 13, 2010).

6. Island Press, "People and Predators: from Conflict to Coexistence," http://island-press.org/bookstore/details5bae.html?prod_id=175 (accessed April 13, 2010).

7. Greenwood Publishing Group, "Daily Life in Colonial New England," http://www.greenwood.com/catalog/BGR1458.aspx (accessed April 12, 2010).

8. Ashgate, "Style and the Nineteenth-Century British Critic," http://www.ashgate.com/default.aspx?page=637&calcTitle=1&title_id=6268&edition_id=8582 (accessed April 12, 2010).

9. Octopus Publishing Group, "Philip's Street Atlas Fife and Tayside," http://www.octopusbooks.co.uk/books/general/9780540092031/philips-street-atlas-fife-and-tayside/ (accessed April 12, 2010).

10. University of Illinois Press, "Anne Frank: Reflections on Her Life and Legacy," http://www.press.uillinois.edu/books/catalog/76sga7nq9780252024726.html (accessed April 12, 2010).

11. Amy Foxgrover, et al., 2005 Hydrographic Survey of South San Francisco Bay, California, 2007, http://pubs.usgs.gov/of/2007/1169/ (accessed April 12, 2010).

12. Routledge Taylor & Francis Group, "Shakespeare in the Victorian Periodicals," http://www.routledge.com/books/Shakespeare-in-the-Victorian-Periodicals-isbn 9780415962438 (accessed April 12, 2010).

13. HarperCollins, "Portrait of an Unknown Woman," http://www.harpercollins.com/books/9780061252563/Portrait_of_an_Unknown_Woman/index.aspx (accessed April 12, 2010).

14. Macmillan, "The Pretender," http://us.macmillan.com/thepretender (accessed April 12, 2010).

15. Netflix, "First Emperor of China: IMAX," 1989, http://www.netflix.com/Movie/First_Emperor_of_China_IMAX/7774593?trkid=222336 (accessed April 12, 2010).

16. Nova Publishers, "Japan: Economic, Political and Social Issues," https://www.novapublishers.com/catalog/product_info.php?products_id=7322 (accessed April 12, 2010).

Part IV

AUTHORITY CONTROL AND IMPLEMENTATION

13

———•◦•———

DERIVATION OF FAST HEADINGS

BACKGROUND

FAST headings are derived from: (1) established headings from LCSH authority file, (2) name headings established in the LC/NAF authority file, and (3) headings assigned in OCLC's WorldCat bibliographic database. In a few rare cases, headings were created specifically for FAST if there was no equivalent LCSH heading.

The LCSH authority file is the primary source for FAST headings. Many headings—particularly topical headings—were also derived from the LCSH headings assigned in WorldCat. Literary warrant was a significant criterion for identifying FAST topical headings that had not been established in LCSH. This applies to headings assigned by the Library of Congress as well as those assigned by OCLC member libraries. Most name headings were adopted or derived from headings from the LC/NAF authority file.

TOPICAL HEADINGS

Enumeration of Assigned Headings

All headings from 650 fields with a second indicator value of "0" were extracted from WorldCat bibliographic records. The second indicator value of "0" indicates that the heading is an LCSH heading rather than a heading from one of the other subject schemas. The initial set of topical headings was generated by scanning WorldCat and extracting every LCSH topical heading with all of its subdivisions. The extracted headings were then sorted, and, after collecting the usage data, duplicate headings were removed. The resulting file contained every unique topical heading along with the number of times it had been assigned. This file of unique headings contained almost 10 million different headings. Two separate heading usage counts (shown in brackets in the following examples) were included: the total WorldCat usage and the usage in bibliographic records created or distributed by the Library of Congress.

A small section of the file of unique headings is as follows:

Oaths (Canon law) [23; 0]
Oaths (Canon law). [2; 0]
Oaths (Canon law) $xEarly works to 1800. [1; 0]
Oaths (Canon law) $xHistory. [1; 1]
Oaths (Canon law) $xStudy and teaching. [1; 0]
Oaths (Germanic law) [2; 0]
Oaths (Greek law) [6; 1]
Oaths (Greek law) in literature. [1; 0]
Oaths (Islam) [1; 0]
Oaths (Islamic law) [10; 1]
Oaths (Islamic law). [1; 0]
Oaths (Islamic law) $xEarly works to 1800. [1; 1]
Oaths (Jewish Law) [1; 0]
Oaths (Jewish law) [71; 22]
Oaths (Jewish law). [2; 0]
Oaths (Jewish law) $xEarly works to 1800. [1; 1]
Oaths (Law) $zAustralia $zVictoria. [2; 0]
Oaths (Roman law) [35; 7]
Oaths (Roman law). [6; 0]

Validation

Recoding of Forms

Many of the headings in the preceding list contain form subdivisions coded as a general ($x) subdivisions. Identifying and recoding the form subdivisions was the first step in the validation process. The form subdivisions were identified using procedures developed specifically for the FAST project by O'Neill and colleagues.[1] After recoding the form subdivisions, all subdivisions except the general ($x) subdivisions were removed. If the resulting heading exactly matched another heading in the file, the headings were combined and the usage counts were updated. As a result, the number of headings in the preceding example was reduced from 19 to 15.

Oaths (Canon law) [25; 1]
Oaths (Canon law). [2; 0]
Oaths (Canon law) $xStudy and teaching. [1; 0]
Oaths (Germanic law) [2; 0]
Oaths (Greek law) [6; 1]
Oaths (Greek law) in literature. [1; 0]
Oaths (Islam) [1; 0]
Oaths (Islamic law) [11; 2]
Oaths (Islamic law). [1; 0]
Oaths (Jewish Law) [2; 1]

Oaths (Jewish law) [71; 22]
Oaths (Jewish law). [2; 0]
Oaths (Law) [2; 0]
Oaths (Roman law) [35; 7]
Oaths (Roman law). [6; 0]

Normalization

After merging the duplicates, as just described, the file still contained many stylistic variants. To remove these variant headings, the headings were normalized using the NACO rules.[2] The normalization process eliminated most stylistic variations by dropping diacritics and parentheses, changing all alphabetic characters to lower case, eliminating most punctuation, and making other similar stylistic changes. In the following examples, the em or long dash (—) is used to represent the subfield delimiter. The normalized forms for the preceding headings are:

oaths canon law
oaths canon law
oaths canon law
oaths canon law—study and teaching
oaths germanic law
oaths greek law
oaths greek law in literature
oaths islam
oaths islamic law
oaths islamic law
oaths jewish law
oaths jewish law
oaths jewish law
oaths law
oaths roman law
oaths roman law

When multiple headings resulted in the same normalized form, only a single heading from the set was retained. The heading to be retained was selected based on its weighted usage. Headings assigned by the Library of Congress were weighted more heavily than headings from other sources. The procedure usually resulted in the retention of the preferred form of the heading. This step also included the removal of terminal periods unless they were part of an abbreviation. After this step, the headings in the preceding example, with parentheses restored, were reduced to the following:

Oaths (Canon law)
Oaths (Canon law)—Study and teaching
Oaths (Germanic law)
Oaths (Greek law)

Oaths (Greek law) in literature
Oaths (Islam)
Oaths (Islamic law)
Oaths (Jewish law)
Oaths (Law)
Oaths (Roman law)

LCSH Authority File

The process greatly reduced the number of headings, but the remaining headings still had a relatively high error rate. The LCSH authority file was used piecewise to validate the remaining headings. A process similar to that used to extract the headings from the bibliographic records was used to extract the established headings from the authority file. Only the main heading and general subdivisions were extracted. These authoritative headings or their initial portions were then used to validate the assigned headings or the initial portion of the headings. As a result, the validated portion of the heading matched an established LCSH heading. In the following example, the validated portion of the heading is shown in bold.

Infantes
Infants
Infants—Bathing
Infants—Care and hygiene
Infants—Care
Infants—Diseases
Infants—Diseases—Diagnosis
Infants—Diseases—Patients
Infants—Diseases—Patients—Contemporaries
Infants—Diseases—Psychological aspects
Infants—Disases
Infants—Health and hygiene
Infants—Health and hygiene—Study and teaching

Some headings were fully validated, some were partially validated, and others remained unvalidated. Not all of the unvalidated headings are invalid, however. As used here, the term "unvalidated" refers to headings whose status is unknown.

Since the cross-references from the LCSH authority file represent nonpreferred terms that are not valid, they were used to identify invalid headings. A list of all topical cross-references (450 fields) was compiled from the LCSH authority file. The list was then compared to the extracted headings. After normalization, any extracted heading matching a cross-reference was invalidated and removed. In the above example, "Infants—Care and hygiene" is a cross-reference to **Infants—Care** so "Infants—Care and hygiene" was invalidated and removed from the list.

The next step was to extract all unvalidated main headings along with the corresponding usage information. These included headings such as Infantes [invalid] and **Woodwind trios (English horn, oboes (2))** [a valid free-floating phrase heading]. This group of unvalidated main headings was reviewed to identify those that were valid.

Music headings constituted the largest group of valid but still unvalidated headings. The validation of the music headings itself was a major effort. The rules for constructing music headings are complex—trios require three instruments, woodwind trios can only have woodwind instruments, instruments must be listed in a particular order, and so on. A few examples of valid, but unestablished, LCSH headings for music include:

Harp and organ music, Arranged

Euphonium and horn music

Nonets (Piano, flute, guitar, violins (2), viola, violoncellos (3))

In the first instance, **Harp and organ music** is established but not with **Arranged**. In the second case, many less common combinations of instruments, for example, **Euphonium and horn music,** have not been established but are, nevertheless, valid. And in the last instance, only the more common or representative combination of instruments are established in LCSH. In FAST, all headings with valid combinations of instruments are established. The validation included checking the names and order of the instruments. A list of valid combinations of instruments is shown in Appendix Table A-5.

After most of the main headings had either been validated or invalidated, the results were used to validate many more of the headings in the main file. All headings that had not been at least partially validated were then deleted.

Subdivisions

The next step in the process was to check the subdivisions that were not previously validated. A list of all free-floating subdivisions was compiled from LCSH and used to validate the subdivisions. However, the subdivision validation included only a limited check as to whether the subdivision was used within its scope. For example, for the heading:

Infants—Diseases—Patients

The subdivision **Patients** was validated as a free-floating subdivision. According to LCSH rules, the use of the subdivision **Patients** is limited to individual diseases and types of diseases. Since the authority record for **Infants—Diseases** does not explicitly indicate that it is a disease, no checks could be performed to verify that the subdivision was used within its scope. However, checks were done to ensure that the subdivision was at least appropriate for the facet. The heading **Infants—Diseases—Patients**—Contemporaries was invalidated since the use of the subdivision "—Contemporaries" is limited to personal names.

This validation process resulted in three groups of headings: (1) fully validated headings (those that matched LCSH authority records), (2) combinations of valid headings and free-floating subdivisions, and (3) unvalidated headings. All in the first group were established as FAST headings. Infrequently used headings in the second group, particularly those that had not been used by the Library of Congress, were manually reviewed to identify any invalid headings. The frequently used headings in the last group were also reviewed to identify any valid headings. After this final review, the remaining headings were established as FAST topical headings.

GEOGRAPHIC HEADINGS

FAST geographic headings were derived from two primary sources:

1. Jurisdictional headings based on *Anglo-American Cataloguing Rules,* second edition revised (AACR2R), as established in the LC/NAF authority file.
2. Nonjurisdictional headings as established in the LCSH authority file.

The first step in establishing FAST geographic names was to identify the set of names that would comprise the FAST first-level geographic names. As discussed in Chapter 5, the FAST first-level names closely correspond to the geographic names in the Geographic Area Codes (GAC) table.[3] The major difference between the GAC table and first-level name table is the treatment of China. In FAST, China is considered a first-level name with the provinces treated as second-level names. This varies from the GAC table in which Chinese provinces are treated as first-level names with their own GAC entries. The complete list of FAST first-level names is given in Appendix Table A-2.

In LCSH, free-floating terms can be added to those already in the GAC Code List. For example, terms such as "Valley" or "Watershed" can be added to river names so that **Ohio River** and **Ohio River Valley** are both valid LCSH headings. *Ohio River* is included in the GAC Code List with the GAC of n-uso, but *Ohio River Valley* is not. To enable names with free-floating terms to be used as first-level names, common combinations of names from the GAC Code List with the following free-floating terms were added to the set of authorized first-level names:

Region
Valley
Watershed

These terms were added selectively following Library of Congress practice. In addition, **Metropolitan Area** and **Suburban Area** were added directly to **Washington (D.C.)**. The treatment of Washington is unique since no other cities are first-level entries.

A file of geographic authority records was created by extracting all geographic headings authorized for use as subjects from both sources mentioned earlier. For example, the following is the record for Charlevoix County:

```
010 $an 81002806
040 $aDLC $beng $cDLC $dWaU
043 $an-us-mi
151 $aCharlevoix County (Mich.)
451 $aCharlevoix Co., Mich. $wnnaa
670 $aHixson (W. W.) and Company. Plat book of Charlevoix Co.
    193-?
781 0 $z Michigan $zCharlevoix County
```

Only geographic headings authorized for use as subjects were extracted. Records were also extracted from LCSH for nonjurisdictional names including the following record for Lake Charlevoix:

```
010  $ash 91001125

040  $aDGPO $beng $cDLC $dDLC

151  $aCharlevoix, Lake (Mich.)

451  $aLake Charlevoix (Mich.)

550  $aLakes $zMichigan $wg

670  $aWork cat.: U.S. National Ocean Service. United States—
     Great Lakes, Lake Michigan, Lake Charlevoix, 1990: $bmap
     recto (Lake Charlevoix)

670  $aGNIS. MI $b(Lake Charlevoix)

670  $aLippincott.

675  $aWeb. geog.

781 0 $zMichigan $zCharlevoix, Lake
```

Only authority records for headings without subdivisions were included in the FAST authority file. Authority records for headings such as the following were excluded since, in each case, there always should be another authority record for the geographic name without the subdivisions.

Africa—In motion pictures
France—History—House of Valois, 1328-1589
Great Britain—Description and travel
India—History—20th century—Humor
Czechoslovakia—Literatures
Mexico—Foreign relations—1810–1821
China—Relations—Soviet Union

This file of geographic authority records was the basis of the FAST authorities. FAST geographic names differ from those of LCSH in several major aspects:

1. Geographic names are not abbreviated. Rather, abbreviations commonly used in LCSH are spelled out. This is done to minimize the uncertainty about how the name should be entered.
2. Geographic names are entered in indirect order (i.e., including the name of a larger place). For example, **Japan—Tokyo.**
3. Geographic names are not inverted.
4. Geographic names are hierarchical, with up to three levels.
5. Large bodies of water may be subdivided by smaller bodies of water.
6. There are a limited number of first-level geographic names. FAST first-level geographic headings were derived from the GAC table.
7. The use of place qualifiers is limited.

An algorithm was developed to convert the LCSH form of the name to the form of the name used for FAST. As the first step in this process, all abbreviations are spelled out and any inverted names are put in direct order. For example:

Charlevoix, Lake (Mich.) → *Lake Charlevoix (Michigan)*

For qualified LCSH headings, the next step was to treat the qualifier as the top level geographic name and the remainder of the heading as a subdivision, so that:

Lake Charlevoix (Michigan) → **Michigan—Lake Charlevoix**

which is the correct form of the name for FAST.

Many LCSH headings contain a type-of-name qualifier, for example:

Washington (State)
Bologna (Italy : Province)

where "State" and "Province" are used to indicate that the heading represents the state or province rather than the city. A table of the valid type qualifiers was developed to identify type qualifiers. The conversion algorithm relied on this table of type qualifiers to differentiate between place and type qualifiers. Any terms within parentheses that did not match a type qualifier were considered to be place names. In the following example, "Greece" was identified as the place name and "Island" as the type, and therefore the heading was converted as:

$aRhodes (Greece : Island) → **Greece—Rhodes (Island)**

One difficult problem in the mapping was identifying city sections. To assist in identifying city sections, a table of all cities that could be subdivided into city sections was created. When the qualifier was the name of a subdivisible city, the heading was assumed to be for a city section and was mapped as a three-level FAST heading. For example:

$aHamline-Midway Neighborhood (Saint Paul, Minn.)
   → **Minnesota—Saint Paul—Hamline-Midway Neighborhood**

since Saint Paul is one of the cities where city sections are permitted.

However, in the following Railroad Creek example, Chelan County is a county rather than a city. Although the syntactic structure of this heading is similar to the preceding neighborhood example, in this case the county name is used as a place qualifier.

$aRailroad Creek (Chelan County, Wash.)
   → **Washington (State)—Railroad Creek (Chelan County)**

Although the algorithm was able to map successfully the vast majority of LCSH headings to FAST headings, there were still numerous cases where the conversion failed to create the correct FAST heading.

$aInterstate 75
   → **United States—Interstate 75**
$aDarien Gap Highway (Colombia and Panama)
   → **South America—Darien Gap Highway**

$aMichigan—Grand Traverse Bay
  → **Lake Michigan—Grand Traverse Bay**

The preceding examples illustrate three of the more common cases where the algorithmic mapping frequently failed:

1. When a place, such as Interstate 75, spans multiple first-level geographic areas, LCSH permits it to be entered directly. For FAST, it must be entered under the smallest first-level geographic area in which it is fully contained.
2. In the second example, the geographic name also spans multiple first-level geographic areas but is qualified. The conversion algorithm correctly handled the more common combinations of qualifiers such as New York and Pennsylvania or Germany and Poland; however, it could not identify all possible combinations.
3. The last example is the result of the FAST policy that smaller bodies of water appear as subdivisions under the larger body of water with which they are associated, rather than being qualified by the surrounding land mass as is done in LCSH.

The result of the algorithm conversion was a file of LCSH geographic names and their FAST form as produced by the algorithm. While most of the FAST headings were correct, the error rate was high enough to require further validation. The result of the algorithmic conversion of the geographic names in the preceding example was as follows:

$aInterstate 75
  → **Interstate 75**
$aDarien Gap Highway (Colombia and Panama)
  → **Colombia and Panama—Darien Gap Highway**
$aMichigan—Grand Traverse Bay
  → **Michigan—Grand Traverse Bay**

None of these were valid.

After the algorithm mapped the LCSH names to the corresponding FAST form, the headings then underwent the following validation steps:

1. A single-level heading must match one of the geographic names in the list of FAST first-level names given in Appendix Table A-2.
2. The first-level name from two- and three-level headings must match one of the subdivisible geographic names in the list of FAST first-level names given in Appendix Table A-2.
3. The second-level of a three-level heading must correspond to one of the cities or similar second-level names that can be further subdivided.
4. The first two names from a three-level heading must be valid.
5. For headings qualified by place, the place qualifier must be a valid geographic name.
6. Type qualifiers are limited to those in the list of type qualifiers (Appendix Table A-3).
7. FAST geographic names that failed any of the preceding conditions were reviewed and manually corrected to complete the initial list of valid FAST geographic names.

EVENT HEADINGS

The event facet does not have a parallel in LCSH. FAST uses the FRBR (Functional Requirements of Bibliographic Records) definition of an event—"an action or occurrence"[4]—and includes reoccurring events such as conferences and sporting events. Events headings are derived from (1) LCSH topical headings, (2) LCSH conference and meetings names, and (3) LCSH period subdivisions. Headings for nonrecurring events take the form of:

Event name (Place of event : Date of event)

If either the place or date is part of the event name, it is not repeated in the qualifier. Recurring events do not have date qualifiers and will have place qualifiers only if the events always occur at the same location.

A stylistic difference between FAST and LCSH lies in the capitalization practices. LCSH capitalizes most significant words but, by convention, does not capitalize certain categories of events, including conquests, dynasties, interventions, occupations, and so forth. These exceptions are not retained; in FAST all significant words in event headings are capitalized.

Event Headings Derived from Topical Headings

In LCSH, many events are established as topical headings. Wars, battles, strikes, trials, and expeditions are a few of the common types of events treated as topical headings in LCSH. For FAST, these headings are reformatted with the place and date as a qualifier. As is the general practice, abbreviations for geographic names are spelled out.

LCSH topical headings for events generally include both the place and date delimited by commas. The general pattern for LCSH topical events is:

Event name, place of event, date(s) of event

The place name may have multiple levels. Examples of events that are established as LCSH events include:

> *$aLittle Bighorn, Battle of the, Mont., 1876*
> *$aSekigahara, Battle of, Japan, 1600*
> *$aFord Motor Company Strike, Windsor, Ont., 1943*

Two criteria were used to identify LCSH topical authority records for events: the heading contained an event name (strike, battle, war, expedition, etc.) or it contained a date. Since all of the LCSH event headings would have previously been included in the list of FAST topical headings, that list of headings was scanned to identify potential events. The resulting list was then parsed into its three elements; the event name, the place of the event, and the date of the event. See, for example, the following heading:

> *$aLittle Bighorn, Battle of the, Mont., 1876*
> → Little Bighorn, Battle of the *[event name]*
>   Mont. *[place of event]*
>   1876 *[date of event]*

Each of the individual elements was then validated. Once it was confirmed that the heading represented an event, it was reformatted into a FAST heading. Some examples of LCSH headings and the corresponding FAST headings are:

> $aCommunist Trial, New York, N.Y., 1949*
> → **Communist Trial (New York, New York : 1949)**
> *$aMinas (N.S.) Expedition, 1747*
> → **Minas Expedition (Nova Scotia : 1747)**
> *$aConcord, Battle of, Concord, Mass., 1775*
> → **Concord, Battle of (Massachusetts : 1775)**

The resulting authority records for event headings include the Library of Congress Control Number (LCCN) for the original LCSH headings as well as the LCSH headings themselves.

Event Headings Derived from Period Subdivisions

Other LCSH events are established as geographic headings with period subdivisions. It is common practice in LCSH to include names of events such as wars, revolutions, sieges, bombardments, and so forth as period subdivisions. For example, in LCSH, the French and Indian War is established as:

> *$aUnited States $xHistory $yFrench and Indian War, 1755–1763*

where the *French and Indian War, 1755–1763* is a period subdivision. All LCSH headings with named period subdivisions were considered as potential event headings. LCSH geographic headings representing events usually take the form:

> *Geographic heading $xHistory $yPeriod subdivision*

LCSH named period subdivisions generally fall into one of three types; geologic periods, named time periods, and events. Geologic periods were easy to identify; they are the only period subdivisions without dates. Distinguishing between named time periods and events was more problematic. Generally, named time periods represent broader periods and are not associated with particular events. Typical named time periods in LCSH are:

> *$aFrance $xHistory $yHouse of Valois, 1328–1589*
> *$aRome $xHistory $yAntoninus Pius, 138–161*
> *$aNorway $xHistory $yOscar I, 1844–1859*
> *$aChina $xHistory $yNorthern and Southern dynasties, 386–589*
> *$aAnnapolis (Md.) $xHistory $yColonial period, ca. 1600–1775*

Named time periods are not considered events and were not included in the list of FAST events. Some event names such as the *French and Indian War* are quite explicit and could be established as FAST event headings. However there are many cases where the event name itself is too generic, for example:

> *Colombia—History—Coup d'état, 1953*

The phrase *Coup d'état*, even with a date, is vague as a heading. To clarify its meaning, the event name in the FAST heading is qualified with additional information, for example, **Coup d'etat (Greece : May 22–23, 1973)**.

Events are generally considered to be local, national, or global in scope. In LCSH, many global events, such as World War II, are considered topical. Since the corresponding FAST headings for this class of events are derived from LCSH topical headings, they do not have to be considered when dealing with period subdivisions. Events, such as revolutions, coups, invasions, revolts, occupations, conquests, and so forth, are usually considered to be national in scope and, therefore, the country is used as the place element. Sieges, bombardments, captures, raids, uprisings, and other similar events are treated as local in scope. For these local events, the place element in LCSH consists of the local place name qualified by the country or first-order political divisions.

To be identified as an event, the heading had to represent an action or occurrence. Common types of events include wars, sieges, blockades, and other similar headings. While in most cases it was relatively easy to distinguish between named time periods and events, there were numerous cases that required manual review and judgment. After the review, the LCSH headings identified as events were converted to the FAST format. Some common examples of LCSH geographic headings representing events and the corresponding FAST event headings include:

> *$aSpain $xHistory $yCivil War, 1936–1939*
> → Civil War (Spain : 1936–1939)
>
> *$aRome $xHistory $yRevolt of Sertorius, 82–72 B.C.*
> → Revolt of Sertorius (Rome : 82–72 B.C.)
>
> *$aGeorgia (Republic) $xHistory $yRevolution, 1905–1907*
> → Revolution (Georgia : 1905–1907)
>
> *$aTula (Russia) $xHistory $ySiege, 1941*
> → Siege of Tula (Russia : 1941)
>
> *$aMoravia $x History $yMongol Invasion, 1242*
> → Mongol Invasion of Moravia (1242)
>
> *$aHarpers Ferry (W. Va.) $xHistory $yJohn Brown's Raid, 1859*
> → John Brown's Raid (Harpers Ferry, West Virginia : 1859)

The place element in event qualifiers serves to disambiguate the event rather than functioning as a substitute for the geographic name, and the form of the name used in the qualifier may be modified. In LCSH, a number of period subdivisions are used with different geographic headings. For example, **Civil War, 1861–1865** appears as a subdivision under a variety of different place names, such as:

> *$aTexas $xHistory $yCivil War, 1861–1865*
> *$aTallmadge (Ohio) $xHistory $yCivil War, 1861–1865*
> *$aAlabama $xHistory $yCivil War, 1861–1865*
> *$aTennessee, East $xHistory $yCivil War, 1861–1865*

In FAST, the American Civil War is considered to be a single event and is represented by a single heading. To ensure that all occurrences of **Civil War, 1861–1865** in LCSH are converted to the same heading, they are converted to the collective event heading:

American Civil War (1861–1865)

Four other events receive similar treatment:

American Revolution (1775–1783)
Bolshevik Revolution (1917–1921)
European Revolutions of 1848
War of 1812

As with the event names derived from LCSH topical headings, the list of FAST events derived from LCSH geographic headings were added to the list of FAST event headings.

Event Headings Derived from LCSH Conferences and Meetings Names

Conference and meeting names were the third source of FAST event headings. LCSH headings for conferences and meetings conform to the rules for corporate bodies set forth in Chapter 24 of AACR2R. In addition to place and date qualifiers, other qualifiers may be added to identify the event type or to resolve conflicts. Examples of LCSH headings for conferences, meetings, and events and their corresponding FAST headings are:

$aPotsdam Conference (1945)
   → **Potsdam Conference**
$aWorld Cup (Soccer)
   → **World Cup (Soccer)**
$aChild Welfare Exhibit (1911 : Chicago, Ill.)
   → **Child Welfare Exhibit**
$aTour de France (Bicycle race)
   → **Tour de France (Bicycle race)**
$aHong Kong International Film Festival
   → **Hong Kong International Film Festival**
$aMiss USA Pageant
   → **Miss USA Pageant**

All LCSH conference and meeting name headings were considered to be events when converted to FAST headings. However, since only a small proportion of conferences and meetings names are used as subjects, only those names that had been used as a subject in WorldCat were included as event headings.

HEADINGS FOR NAMES OF PERSONS AND FAMILIES

FAST headings for names of people are derived from the names in the LC/NAF authority file. Headings for names of individual persons conform to the rules set forth in chapter 22 of AACR2R. However, only names that have been used at least once as a subject (600) in a WorldCat bibliographic record were established as FAST headings. Name-title headings are not included in the personal name facet. Instead they are treated as titles and are included in that facet.

Some examples of personal names commonly used as subjects include the following:

Jesus Christ
Kennedy family
Obama, Barack
Phelps, Michael, 1985–
Winslet, Kate

HEADINGS FOR NAMES OF CORPORATE BODIES

FAST headings for names of corporate bodies are derived from the names in the LC/NAF authority file. Headings for names of corporate bodies, buildings, structures, and so forth conform to the rules set forth in Chapters 23 and 24 of AACR2R. However, only names that have been used at least once as a subject (610) in a bibliographic WorldCat record were established as FAST headings. Only those headings authorized as subjects were considered. As with personal names, name-title headings are excluded. Corporate name headings are not subdivided although they frequently include subordinate units. Examples of corporate names include:

Library of Congress. Card Distribution Section
University of Kentucky. College of Pharmacy
General Motors Company
New York (N.Y.). Fire Dept.

HEADINGS FOR TITLES

The title facet, like the event facet, does not have an exact parallel in LCSH. In LCSH, except for uniform titles in field x30 of the MARC record for anonymous works, all title headings include a $t subfield for the uniform title.

In MARC records, title headings coded x30 include only titles of unknown authorship; uniform titles of known authorship are tagged x00, x10, or x11. In FAST, the title facet includes both works of known authorship and anonymous works, and both are tagged as x30. FAST title headings are derived from the LC/NAF authority file and include uniform titles for anonymous works as well as works by personal authors and those with intellectual responsibility (i.e., main entry) under corporate bodies and conferences and meetings.

Works of Anonymous Authorship

For anonymous works, the uniform title consists of the $a (Uniform title) and $p (Name of part or section of work) subfields derived from the LC/NAF authority file. Uniform titles derived from uniform title headings are not qualified by author, although they may have other qualifiers.

$aBeowulf
→ **Beowulf**
$aBible. $pO.T. $pDeuteronomy
→ **Bible. O.T. Deuteronomy**

$aApocalypse of Paul
   → **Apocalypse of Paul**
$aTurboTax
   → **TurboTax**
$aStar trek (Television program)
   → **Star trek (Television program)**

Works of Personal Authorship

Uniform titles are also derived from personal name/title headings in the LC/NAF authority file. The qualifier (name) consists of the following subfields from the LC/NAF authority records: $a (Personal Name), $b (Numeration), and $c (Title) subfield. These subfields, without subfield codes, are enclosed in parentheses to form the FAST qualifier. The title portion of the FAST heading is derived from the $t subfield in 100 fields.

$aMilton, John, $d1608–1674. $tParadise regained. $lItalian
   → **Paradise regained (Milton, John)**
$aHemingway, Ernest, $d1899–1961. $tSun also rises
   → **Sun also rises (Hemingway, Ernest)**

Works of Corporate Bodies

For uniform titles derived from corporate name/title headings, the qualifier consists of the subfields $a (Corporate name) and $b (Subordinate unit) from the LC/NAF headings, if present. These subfields, without subfield codes, are enclosed in FAST heading.

$aUnited States. $tJob Training Partnership Act
   → **Job Training Partnership Act (United States)**
$aGreat Britain. $tChildren Act 1989
   → **Children Act 1989 (Great Britain)**

Since treaties generally involve multiple countries, they are treated as special cases of works by corporate bodies. The general form for treaty headings is:

Treaties, etc. (list of countries : date of treaty)

The names of countries in the qualifier are listed in alphabetical order.

$aJapan. $tTreaties, etc. $gUnited States, $d1971 Mar. 8
   → **Treaties, etc. (Japan and United States : 1971 Mar. 8)**

For some treaties, only a single country is identified in the authorized heading; the additional countries are included as cross-references. In these cases, the countries that are parties to the treaty are extracted from both the authorized heading and from any relevant cross-references. For example, the relevant LC/NAF headings for the North American Free Trade Agreement (NAFTA):

110 $aCanada. $tTreaties, etc. $d1992 Oct. 7
410 $aMexico. $tTreaties, etc. $d1992 Oct. 7
410 $aUnited States. $tTreaties, etc. $d1992 Oct. 7

would be converted to one FAST heading:

Treaties, etc. (Canada, Mexico, and United States : *1992 Oct. 7*)

Works from Conferences and Meetings

For uniform titles derived from conference/meeting name/title headings, the heading consists of the $t subfield (name of work) with the $a subfield (name of meeting following jurisdiction name) as a qualifier.

$aVatican Council $n(2nd : $d1962-1965). $tConstitutio de sacra liturgia
→ **Constitutio de sacra liturgia (Vatican Council)**

$aConference on Security and Cooperation in Europe $d(1972 : $cHelsinki, Finland). $tFinal Act. $lGerman.
→ **Final Act (Conference on Security and Cooperation in Europe)**

As with personal and corporate names, LC/NAF headings to be converted to FAST headings were selected on the basis of literary warrant. That is, the title had to have been used at least once as a subject in WorldCat. Furthermore, the selection criteria are based on the literary warrant of the FAST form of the heading, not the LCSH form. FAST headings are less granular than the corresponding LCSH headings since some subfields are not retained in FAST. For example, the single FAST heading **Shorter catechism (Westminster Assembly)** is derived from the following three LCSH headings:

$aWestminster Assembly $d(1643–1652). $tShorter catechism
$aWestminster Assembly $d(1643–1652). $tShorter catechism. $lGreek & Latin
$aWestminster Assembly $d(1643–1652). $tShorter catechism. $lLatin

This poses the problem of identifying the preferred heading to be used as the source for the FAST heading. The approach was to select the heading with the fewest subdivisions; the first heading in this case.

CHRONOLOGICAL HEADINGS

FAST chronological headings are limited to a single date or a range of dates. Therefore, there is no need to routinely create authority records for chronological headings. For example, no authority record is needed for the chronological heading **1900-1999** corresponding to the 20th century. Authority records for chronological headings are only created when necessary for cross-references. Examples of chronological headings established for cross-references include:

1914–1918 *for the cross-reference* World War I Period
1066–1154 *for the cross-reference* Norman Period (Great Britain)
1316–1322 *for the cross-reference* Philip V, Reign of (France)
1916–1928 *for the cross-reference* Warlord Period (China)

FORM HEADINGS

FAST form headings are derived from LCSH form subdivisions. Following the current practice of Library of Congress, main headings representing forms or genres are treated as topical headings. Headings converted from subdivisions representing genres are treated as form headings in FAST.

LCSH subdivision authority records are the preferred source of FAST form headings. Most of the form subdivision records were converted to FAST form headings.

NOTES

1. Edward T. O'Neill, Lois Mai Chan, Eric Childress, Rebecca Dean, Lynn M. El-Hoshy, and Diane Vizine-Goetz, "Form Subdivisions: Their Identification and Use in LCSH," *Library Resources and Technical Services* 45, no. 4 (2001): 187–97.

2. Ibid.; Thomas B. Hickey and Edward T. O'Neill, "NACO Normalization," *Library Resources and Technical Services* 50, no. 3 (2001): 166–72.

3. Library of Congress, Network Development and MARC Standards Office, *MARC Code List for Geographic Areas,* 2006 edition (last updated April 7, 2008), http://www.loc.gov/marc/geoareas (accessed April 14, 2010).

4. IFLA Study Group on the Functional Requirements of Bibliographic Records, *Functional Requirements of Bibliographic Records: Final Report* (Munich, Germany: K.G. Saur, 1998).

14

FAST AUTHORITY RECORDS

INTRODUCTION

This chapter discusses authority records for FAST headings encoded according to the *MARC 21 Format for Authority Data,* a standard used to encode authority data.[1] This format contains codes for labeling individual areas, elements, sub-elements, and other pertinent data included in the authority record.

AUTHORITY DATA

A controlled vocabulary system relies on a master list of predetermined terms that can be assigned to bibliographic or metadata records. For most library catalogs, manual or online, these are called *subject headings* or *established headings*; for many abstracting and indexing systems, they are called *descriptors* or simply *preferred* or *authorized* terms. Preferred terms are maintained in a *subject headings list* or *thesaurus*, which lists the subject access terms to be used in the cataloging or indexing operation at hand. As discussed in Chapter 10 of this book, when there are synonymous terms for a given subject, these terms are included in the list, with references directing the searcher to the authorized or preferred term for the subject. Authorized terms that are related in meaning are also linked by references: the links from lead-in terms are called *use* references, and the links to related terms are, depending on the types of relationship, called *broader term* (BT) and *related term* (RT) references. *Narrower term* (NT) references are not explicitly included in the FAST authority record but can be inferred by reversing the BT references.

AUTHORITY RECORDS

The FAST system maintains an authority file consisting of authority records, each of which contains information related to a particular heading, including the authorized or established form of the heading, synonyms not used as valid headings, and other headings related hierarchically or associatively to the heading in question.

The MARC format is used as the vehicle for constructing authority records. An authority record consists of fields, each of which is identified by a three-character tag. The MARC 21 format is maintained and is well-documented by the Library of Congress, and this book will focus only on the aspects where FAST's use of the format differs from standard practice. The major parts of a FAST authority record are:

MARC Record Structure for Authorities

Leader (LDR)

Control Fields (001–007)

Fixed Length Data Elements (008)

Numeric and Code Fields (01X–09X)

Established Headings (1XX)

See From References (4XX)

See Also References (5XX)

Application History Note (688)

Heading Linking Entry Fields (7XX)

Details on the fields as used in FAST authority records are provided in Appendix A.

Within each authority record there is only one 1XX field, which contains the valid heading for the person, corporate, topic, event, and so forth. Records may contain multiple 4XX and 5XX fields. In addition, each authority record may contain one or more 7XX fields that provide machine links within a system between equivalent headings in the same system or in different systems. In the case of FAST, a 7XX field is used to link the FAST heading to the corresponding heading in either the LC/NAF or the LCSH authority file.

CREATION OF FAST AUTHORITY RECORDS

The derivation phase of the FAST development resulted in a file of authorized FAST headings. Each authority record includes, among other information, the facet (indicated by the tag), the indicator values, and the Library of Congress Control Number (LCCN) for the LCSH authority record from which it was derived. A representative sample of the resulting file with blanks represented by the "#" is shown in Table 14.1:

The established heading and tag contain most of the information necessary to form the 1XX field for the authorized heading. The LCCN is used to identify the LCSH or LC/NAF authority record on which the FAST heading is based.

Initially, the FAST authority records were created in a multiple-step process. In the first step, a minimal authority record was built as shown here:

```
001     tmp00000000

003     OCoLC

008     000000nn anznnbabn    || and  d

1XX     Authorized FAST Heading

7XX     $0(DLC) LCCN
```

Table 14.1
Sample of Authorized FAST Headings

LCCN	Tag	Ind	Authorized FAST heading
n 80065009	110	2#	Vestischer Künstlerbund Recklinghausen
n 2001106568	100	1#	Smyers, David D.
sh 85002200	111	0#	Agincourt, Battle of (France : 1415)
sh 98003548	150	##	Ferryboat captains
n 82165711	130	#0	Columbus dispatch
n 91021714	151	##	Ohio $zMcConnelsville
sh 85066032	150	##	Infants $xDiseases $xChemotherapy

Most of the elements in the leader are used to define the structural nature of the record such as the record length, the number of indicators, the base address of data, and so forth. These elements conform to standard usage but for the sake of simplicity are not explicitly shown in the examples. The three elements shown are:

Record status (byte 5), default value 'n' for new record
Type of record (byte 6), default value 'z' for authority data
Encoding level (byte 17), default value 'n' for complete authority record

Initially each authority record was assigned a temporary record number in the 001 field as was required by the software used to review and edit these preliminary records. This temporary number was replaced with a valid FAST number when the record was added to the authority file. The Control Number Identifier (003) field is "OCoLC" for all FAST authority records.

The Fixed-Length Data Elements (008) field contains 40 bytes of positionally-defined data elements. The elements and their default values for FAST authority records are shown in Table 14.2. The elements shown in bold font may be updated to accurately describe the heading. No other values of the non-bolded elements are used in FAST authority records.

The next step in the creation of the authority records was to extract the relevant information from the LCSH or LC/NAF authority records and to add that information to the corresponding FAST authority records. In particular, the established heading in the 1XX field of the Library of Congress authority record was added to the 7XX field in order to link the Library of Congress authority record to the FAST record. Any relevant references, after being converted to the FAST format, were transferred from the Library of Congress authority record to the FAST authority record; for geographic headings, the GAC codes were added to complete the preliminary authority record. Examples of the process for seven different headings are shown in the following sections:

Table 14.2
Fixed-Length Data Elements and Their Default Values

Byte Position	Description	Default Setting	Interpretation
00–05	**Date entered on file**	000000	Initially undefined
06	**Direct or indirect geographic subdivision**	n	Not applicable
07	Romanization scheme	n	Not applicable
08	Language of catalog	#	No information provided
09	Kind of record	a	Established heading
10	Descriptive cataloging rules	n	Not applicable
11	Subject heading system	z	Other (FAST)
12	Type of series	n	Not applicable
13	Numbered or unnumbered series	n	Not applicable
14	Heading use—main entry	b	Not appropriate
15	Heading use—subject added entry	a	Appropriate
16	Heading use—series added entry	b	Not appropriate
17	Type of subject subdivision	n	Not applicable
18–27	Undefined character positions	#	Undefined
28	**Type of government agency**	|	No attempt to code
29	Reference evaluation	|	No attempt to code
30	Undefined character position	#	Undefined
31	Record update in process	a	Record can be used
32	**Undifferentiated personal name**	n	Not applicable
33	**Level of establishment**	d	preliminary
34–37	Undefined character positions	#	Undefined
38	Modified record	#	Not modified
39	Cataloging source	d	Other

Example 1. Vestischer Künstlerbund Recklinghausen

MINIMAL FAST AUTHORITY RECORD:

```
001     tmp00000001
003     OCoLC
008     000000nn anznnbabn   || and
040     $aOCoLC $beng $cOCoLC $ffast
110 2   $aVestischer Künstlerbund Recklinghausen
710 2   $0(DLC) n 80065009
```

LC/NAF Authority Record:

001	oca00446598	
005	19901128070947.1	
008	800708n| acannaab| |a ana |||	
010	$an 80065009	
040	$aDLC $cDLC $dDLC	
110 2	$aVestischer Künstlerbund Recklinghausen	
410 2	$aVestischer Künstlerbund	
670	$aVestischer Künstlerbund Recklinghausen und Gäste aus Douai, 1979 (a.e.) $bt.p. (Vestischer Künstlerbund Recklinghausen) p. 3 (established in 1962)	
670	$aGanz tief unten, 1989?: $bt.p. (Vestischer Künstlerbund)	
670	$aInt. dir. of arts, 1989/90 $b(Vestischer Künstlerbund, Recklinghausen)	
675	$aDomay, 1977; Kunst-Adressbuch u. Kalendarium, 1976.	

Upgraded FAST Authority Record:

001	tmp00000001
003	OCoLC
008	000000nn anznnbabn ||and d
040	$aOCoLC $beng $cOCoLC $ffast
110 2	$aVestischer Künstlerbund Recklinghausen
410 2	$aVestischer Künstlerbund
710 2	$aVestischer Künstlerbund Recklinghausen $0(DLC) n 80065009

Example 2.   David D. Smyers

Minimal FAST Authority Record:

001	tmp00000002
003	OCoLC
008	000000nn anznnbabn ||and d
040	$aOCoLC $beng $cOCoLC $ffast
100 1	$aSmyers, David D.
700 1	$0(DLC) n 2001106568

LC/NAF Authority Record:

001	oca05484389
005	20050119051844.0

```
008     010508n| acannaabn    |n aaa

010     $an 2001106568

035     $a(Uk)003800622

040     $aDLC $beng $cDLC

100 1   $aSmyers, David D.

670     $aSmyers, David D. The hustler's handbook, 1999: $bt.p.
        (David D. Smyers)

670     $aYouth offender's golden rules of guidance, c2005:
        $beCIP data sheet (David D. Smyers; DOB: Sept. 30,
        1939)
```

UPGRADED FAST AUTHORITY RECORD:

```
001     tmp00000002

003     OCoLC

008     000000nn anznnbabn     ||and  d

040     $aOCoLC $beng $cOCoLC $ffast

100 1   $aSmyers, David D.

700 1   $aSmyers, David D. $0(DLC) n 2001106568
```

Example 3.   Battle of Agincourt

MINIMAL FAST AUTHORITY RECORD:

```
001     tmp00000003

003     OCoLC

008     000000nn anznnbabn     || and  d

040     $aOCoLC $beng $cOCoLC $ffast

111 0   $aAgincourt, Battle of (France : 1415)

750 0   $0(DLC) sh 85002200
```

LCSH AUTHORITY RECORD:

```
001     oca02002560

005     20030113075926.0

008     021119|| anannbabn    |a ana

010     $ash 85002200

040     $aDLC $cDLC $dDLC

053 0   $aDC101.5.A2

150     $aAgincourt, Battle of, Agincourt, France, 1415

450     $aAgincourt, Battle of, 1415 $wnne

450     $aAgincourt (France), Battle of, 1415 $wnne
```

550	$aHundred Years' War, 1339-1453 $xCampaigns $zFrance $wg
670	$a00702931: Hibbert, C. Agincourt, 2000.

UPGRADED FAST AUTHORITY RECORD:

001	tmp00000003
003	OCoLC
008	000000nn anznnbabn || and d
040	$aOCoLC $beng $cOCoLC $ffast
111 0	$aAgincourt, Battle of (France : 1415)
411	$aAgincourt, Battle of (1415)
411	$aAgincourt, Battle of (Agincourt, France, 1415)
411	$aAgincourt (France), Battle of (1415)
511	$aHundred Years' War (1339-1453)
750 0	$aAgincourt, Battle of, Agincourt, France, 1415 $0(DLC) sh 85002200

Example 4. Ferryboat Captains

MINIMAL FAST AUTHORITY RECORD:

001	tmp00000004
003	OCoLC
008	000000nn anznnbabn || and d
040	$aOCoLC $beng $cOCoLC $ffast
150	$aFerryboat captains
750	$0(DLC) sh 98003548

LCSH AUTHORITY RECORD:

001	oca04775310
005	19980709113011.6
008	980609i| anannbab || a ana ||| c
010	$ash 98003548
040	$aMnMHCL $cDLC
150	$aFerryboat captains
450	$aFerry boat captains
550	Ship captains $wg
670	$a96-17145: Flanagan, A. Riding the ferry with Captain Cru, 1996.
670	$aHennepin $b(Ferryboat captains)
675	$aNY Times online archives, May 29, 1998

Upgraded FAST Authority Record:

```
001      tmp00000004
003      OCoLC
008      000000nn anznnbabn    || and  d
040      $aOCoLC $beng $cOCoLC $ffast
150      $aFerryboat captains
450      $aFerry boat captains
550      $aShip captains
750      $aFerryboat captains $0(DLC) sh 98003548
```

Example 5.   Columbus Dispatch

Minimal FAST Authority Record:

```
001      tmp00000005
003      OCoLC
008      000000nn anznnbabn    || and d
040      $aOCoLC $beng $cOCoLC $ffast
130 0    $aColumbus dispatch
730 0    $0(DLC) n 82165711
```

LC/NAF Authority Record:

```
001      oca00861581
005      19840322000000.0
008      830409n| acannaab      ||a ana |||
010      $an 82165711
040      $aDLC $cDLC
130 0    $aColumbus dispatch.
430 0    $aColumbus dispatch, Columbus, O. $wnnaa
430 0    $aColumbus Sunday dispatch
670      $aColumbus, Ohio city dir., 1979 $b(Columbus dispatch)
         adv. p. 59 (daily & Sunday Dispatch)
670      $aAyer, 1980 $b(Dispatch)
670      $aThe Columbus dispatch, Sun., 2/15/81: $bmasthead
         (The Columbus dispatch); OCLC #8736947 (The Columbus
         dispatch, Began 4-1-75; continues Columbus evening
         dispatch)
```

Upgraded FAST Authority Record:

```
001      tmp00000005
003      OCoLC
008      000000nn anznnbabn    || and  d
```

```
040     $aOCoLC $beng $cOCoLC $ffast

130 0   $aColumbus dispatch

430 0   $aColumbus dispatch, Columbus, O

430 0   $aColumbus Sunday dispatch

730 0   $aColumbus dispatch $0(DLC) n 82165711
```

Example 6.   McConnelsville

MINIMAL FAST AUTHORITY RECORD:

```
001     tmp00000006

003     OCoLC

008     000000nn anznnbabn    || and  d

040     $aOCoLC $beng $cOCoLC $ffast

151     $aOhio $zMcConnelsville

751 0   $0(DLC) n 91021714
```

LC/NAF AUTHORITY RECORD:

```
001     oca02905280

005     20080126072233.0

008     910302n| acannaabn    |a ana

010     $an 91021714

040     $aDLC $beng $cDLC $dDLC $dOCoLC

043     $an-us-oh

151     $aMcConnelsville (Ohio)

451     $aMcConnellsville (Ohio)

451     $aOld Town (Ohio)

451     $aMc Connelsville (Ohio)

67      $aNUCMC data from Indiana Historical Society for
        Howard, F.W. Papers, 1806-1903 $b(McConnelsville,
        Ohio)

670     $aRand McNally comm'l atlas, 1985 $b(McConnelsville,
        Ohio; in Morgan County)

670     $aGNIS, April 21, 2003 $b(McConnelsville--PPL,
        39°38'55"N 81°51'12"W, variants: McConnellsville,
        Mcconnelsville, Old Town)

670     $aOCLC #39082377: Geological Survey (U.S.).
        Mc Connelsville quadrangle, Ohio--Morgan Co.,
        1994.
```

```
670      $aEmail from OMarion, April 21, 2003 $b(the
         name appears that way [Mc Connelsville] on the
         map itself)
781 0    $zOhio $zMcConnelsville
```

UPGRADED FAST AUTHORITY RECORD:

```
001      tmp00000006
003      OCoLC
008      000000nn anznnbabn   || and  d
040      $aOCoLC $beng $cOCoLC $ffast
043      $an-us-oh
151      $aOhio $zMcConnelsville
451      $aMcConnellsville (Ohio)
451      $aOld Town (Ohio)
451      $aMc Connelsville (Ohio)
670      $aGNIS, April 21, 2003 $b(McConnelsville--PPL,
         39°38′55″N 81°51′12″W, variants: McConnellsville,
         Mcconnelsville, Old Town)
751 0    $aMcConnelsville (Ohio) $0(DLC) n 91021714
```

Example 7.   Infants—Diseases—Patients

MINIMAL FAST AUTHORITY RECORD:

```
001      tmp00000007
003      OCoLC
008      000000nn anznnbabn   || and  d
040      $aOCoLC $beng $cOCoLC $ffast
150      $aInfants $xDiseases $xChemotherapy
750      $0(DLC) sh 85066032
```

LCSH AUTHORITY RECORD:

```
001      oca02107599
005      20091109143018.0
008      860211i| anannbabn |n ana
010      $ash 85066032
040      $aDLC $beng $cDLC $dDLC
053      $aRJ
150      $aInfants $xDiseases
681      $iExample under $aDiseases
```

LCSH SUBDIVISION AUTHORITY RECORD:

```
001     oca05155885

005     20091109151912.0

008     990706i| dnannbbba     |a ann

010     $ash 99004980

040     $aIEN $beng $cDLC $dDLC

073     $aH 1150 $zlcsh

180     $xChemotherapy

580     $xTreatment $wg

680     $iUse as a topical subdivision under individual
        diseases and types of diseases.

681     $ireference under the heading $aChemotherapy
```

UPGRADED **FAST** AUTHORITY RECORD:

```
001     tmp00000007

003     OCoLC

008     041024nn anznnbabn     || ana  d

040     $aOCoLC $beng $cOCoLC $ffast

150     $aInfants $xDiseases $xChemotherapy

750  0  $aInfants $xDiseases $0(DLC) sh 85066032

700  0  $xChemotherapy $0(DLC) sh99004980
```

In some cases, there are multiple links to LCSH authority records. In Example 7, **Infants—Diseases—Chemotherapy** is the equivalent LCSH heading but that heading has not been established in FAST, at least as a single heading. It was formed by combining the established heading **Infants—Diseases** with the established subdivision **Chemotherapy**. In cases like this, multiple links will be made to the LCSH and LC/NAF authority files.

The final step in creating a FAST record was its incorporation into the FAST authority file. During this step, the FAST authority record number was assigned, the Time and Date of Latest Transaction (005) field was added to the record, the "Date enter on file" element of the Fixed-Length Data Elements (008) field was set, and the level of establishment element of the Fixed-Length Data Elements (008) field was changed from "d" (preliminary) to either "a" (fully established) or "c" (Provisional). For the heading **Ferryboat captains**, the FAST authority record was transformed to:

```
001     fst00923141

003     OCoLC

005     20041024193259.0

008     041024nn anznnbabn     || ana  d

040     $aOCoLC $beng $cOCoLC $ffast
```

```
150      $aFerryboat captains

450      $aFerry boat captains

550      $aShip captains

750 0    $aFerryboat captains $0(DLC) sh 98003548
```

In addition to the these changes to the record itself, a series of validation steps were performed before adding the authority record to the FAST authority file, including verifying that:

1. The 1XX field was unique and did not conflict with any authorized heading in other authority records.
2. No cross-references (4XX fields) conflicted with an authorized heading in another authority record.
3. No cross-references (4XX fields) matched the authorized heading or another cross-reference in the new authority record.
4. Each *see also* reference (5XX fields) matched an authorized heading.
5. The heading in the linking field (7XX) matched an established LCSH heading that was valid for subject use or matched an established LC/NAF heading.

Any authority record that could not be validated was not added to the FAST authority file until it had been manually reviewed.

ADDITIONAL EXAMPLES OF FAST AUTHORITY RECORDS

Topical Headings

Topical headings are coded as field 150 in authority records. Subdivisions are coded as subfield $x. For example:

```
001      fst00831961

003      OCoLC

005      20041024193246.0

008      041024zneanz          ||babn n ana  d

040      $aOCoLC $beng $cOCoLC $ffast

053      $aQD415 $bQD436 $cChemistry

053      $aQH345 $cBiology

053      $aQP501 $bQP801 $cPhysiology

150      $aBiochemistry

450      $aBiological chemistry

450      $aPhysiological chemistry

550      $aBiology

550      $aChemistry

550      $aMedical sciences
```

```
688      $aLC subject usage: 2,173 (2006)

688      $aWC subject usage: 7,760 (2006)

750  0   $aBiochemistry $0(DLC)sh 85014171


001      fst00798165

003      OCoLC

005      20041024193237.0

008      041024zneanz   ||babn n ana  d

040      $aOCoLC $beng $cOCoLC $ffast

053      $aRA781.15

150      $aAerobic exercises

450      $aAerobics

550      $aExercise

550      $aRespiration

688      $aLC subject usage: 157 (2006)

688      $aWC subject usage: 4,501 (2006)

750  0   $aAerobic exercises $0 (DLC)sh 85001290


001      fst00920597

003      OCoLC

005      20041024193300.0

008      041024zneanz   ||babn n ana  d

040      $aOCoLC $beng $cOCoLC $ffast

150      $aFishes $xReproduction $xEffect of light on

550      $aFishes $xEffect of light on

688      $aLC subject usage: 0 (2005)

688      $aWC subject usage: 0 (2005)

750  0   $aFishes $xReproduction $xEffect of light on
         $0 (DLC)sh2003004673
```

Geographic Headings

Geographic headings are tagged as 151 fields in authority records. Indicators, except "0" in field 751, are undefined and left blank, and second- and third-level subdivisions are coded as subfield $z. For example:

```
001      fst01316662

003      OCoLC

005      20080204104610.0

008      060620nneanz||babn n ana d

040      $aOCoLC $beng $cOCoLC $ffast
```

```
043      $aa-cc

151      $aChina $zBeijing $zYihe Yuan

451      $aChina $zBeijing $zI Ho Yüan

451      $aChina $zI Ho Yüan (Peking)

451      $aChina $zBeijing $zSummer Palace

451      $aChina $zBeijing $zYi He Yuan

         $aLC subject usage: 6 (2006)

688      $aWC subject usage: 62 (2006)

751 0    $aYihe Yuan (Beijing, China) $0(DLC)sh 85063869


001      fst01240375

003      OCoLC

005      20080204094445.0

008      060620nneanz    ||babn n ana  d

040      $aOCoLC $beng $cOCoLC $ffast

043      $azmo

151      $aMoon

450      $aSelenology

550      $aSatellites

688      $aLC subject usage: 943 (2006)

688      $aWC subject usage: 6,375 (2006)

751 0    $aMoon $0(DLC)sh 85087107


001      fst01241058

003      OCoLC

005      20080204094445.0

008      060620nneanz    ||babn n ana  d

040      $aOCoLC $beng $cOCoLC $ffast

043      $azs

151      $aSolar system $zHalley's comet

451      $aComet Halley

688      $aLC subject usage: 48 (2006)

688      $aWC subject usage: 217 (2006)

751 0    $aHalley's comet $0(DLC)sh 85058465
```

Chronological Headings

Chronological headings are coded as field 148 in authority records. Indicators are undefined and left blank. There are no subdivisions for chronological headings. For example:

```
001      fst01356021
003      OCoLC
005      20070123205420.0
008      070114n| anznnbabn    || ana  d
040      $aOCoLC $beng $cOCoLC $ffast
148      $aTo 250 B.C.
448      $aEarly Period (Buddhism)

001      fst01355747
003      OCoLC
005      20080304104931.0
008      070114n| anznnbabn    || ana  d
040      $aOCoLC $beng $cOCoLC $ffast
148      $a1775-1783
448      $aRevolutionary Period (United States)
```

Personal Name Headings

Personal name headings are coded as field 100 in authority records. The first indicator specifies the type of personal name according to the following codes:

0 - Forename
1 - Surname
3 - Family name

The second indicator is undefined and left blank.
The only authorized subfield codes are the following:

CODE	SUBFIELD
$a	Personal name
$b	Numeration
$c	Titles and other words associated with a name
$d	Dates associated with a name
$q	Fuller form of name

For example:

```
001      fst00000693
003      OCoLC
005      20080131145614.0
008      040924n| anznnbabn    |n aaa  d
040      $aOCoLC $beng $cOCoLC $ffast
100 1    $aOnassis, Jacqueline Kennedy, $d1929-1994
400 1    $aKennedy, Jacqueline Bouvier, $d1929-1994
```

```
400 1  $aKennedy, Jackie, $d1929-1994

400 1  $aOnassis, Jackie, $d1929-1994

400 1  $aBouvier, Jacqueline, $d1929-1994

400 0  $aJiaguilin, $d1929-1994

400 0  $aJackie, $d1929-1994

700 10 $aOnassis, Jacqueline Kennedy, $d1929-1994 $0(DLC)n
       50002974


001    fst00088204

003    OCoLC

005    20080131173904.0

008 0  40924n| anznnbabn  |n aaa      d

040    $aOCoLC $beng $cOCoLC $ffast

100 1  $aClinton, Bill, $d1946-

400 1  $aClinton, William J. $q(William Jefferson), $d1946-

400 1  $aBlythe, William Jefferson, $d1946-

400 1  $aKlintūn, Bīl, $d1946-

400 1  $aK̲lintţon, Bil, $d1946-

400 1  $aKlinton, Bill, $d1946-

400 1  $aKlinton, Uiĺi'a'm Dzhefferson, $d1946-

400 0  $aKelindun, $d1946-

700 10 $aClinton, Bill, $d1946- $0(DLC)n 82029644
```

Corporate Headings

Corporate headings are coded as field 110 in authority records. The first indicator identifies the type of corporate name entry element:

0 - Inverted name
1 - Jurisdiction name
2 - Name in direct order

The second indicator is undefined and left blank.

Subfield $a identifies the main heading, and subheadings are coded with $b. For example:

```
001    fst00524808

003    OCoLC

005    20080131145614.0

008    050513n| anznnbabn  |n ana d

040    $aOCoLC $beng $cOCoLC $ffast

110 2  $aOCLC

410 2  $aOCLC Online Computer Library Center
```

```
410 2    $aOnline Computer Library Center

410 2    $aO.C.L.C. (1977- )

410 2    $aOCLC, inc.

710 20   $aOCLC $0(DLC)n 78015294


001      fst00569162

003      OCoLC

005      20080131173904.0

008      20080131173904.0

040      $aOCoLC $beng $cOCoLC $ffast

110 2    $aLibrary of Congress. $bDecimal Classification Office

410 1    $aUnited States. $bLibrary of Congress. $bDecimal
         Classification Office

410 2    $aLibrary of Congress. $bProcessing Dept. $bDecimal
         Classification Office

410 2    $aLibrary of Congress. $bSubject Cataloging
         Division. $bDecimal Classification Office

410 2    $aLibrary of Congress. $bDewey Decimal Classification
         Editorial Office

710 20   $aLibrary of Congress. $bDecimal Classification Office
         $0(DLC) n 82076267


001      fst01457758

003      OCoLC

005      20080131173904.0

008      080131n| anznnbabn    |n ana  d

040      $aOCoLC $beng $cOCoLC $ffast

110 2    $aHarvard University. $bFaculty of Arts and Sciences.
         $bOffice of the Registrar.

410 2    $aHarvard University. $bFaculty of Arts and Sciences.
         $bRegistrar's Office

710 20   $aHarvard University. $bFaculty of Arts and Sciences.
         $bOffice of the Registrar. $0(DLC)n 83125660
```

Event Headings

Event headings are coded as field 111 in authority records. The first indicator identifies the type of event name used as the entry element:

0 - Inverted name
1 - Jurisdiction name
2 - Name in direct order

The second indicator is undefined and left blank.

Subfield $a is the only subfield; no other subfields are used in field 111. Examples include:

```
001    fst01409064

003    OCoLC

005    20080201012403.0

008    061009n| anznnbabn    |n ana  d

040    $aOCoLC $beng $cOCoLC $ffast

111 2  $aTour de France (Bicycle race)

411 2  $aGrande boucle (Bicycle race)

411 2  $aTur de Frans (Bicycle race)

711 20 $aTour de France (Bicycle race) $0(DLC)n 98020404


001    fst01172689

003    OCoLC

005    20070109131419.0

008    041024zneanz        ||babn n ana  d

040    $aOCoLC $beng $cOCoLC $ffast

053 0  $aDC241 $bDC244.7

111    $aWaterloo, Battle of (Belgium : 1815)

411    $aBelle-Alliance, Battle of (Belgium : 1815)

411    $aWaterloo, Battle of (1815)

450    $aWaterloo, Battle of, Waterloo, Belgium, 1815

450    $aBelle-Alliance, Battle of, Waterloo, Belgium, 1815

450    $aWaterloo (Belgium), Battle of, 1815

688    $aLC subject usage: 250 (2006)

688    $aWC subject usage: 1,188 (2006)

750 0  $aWaterloo, Battle of, Waterloo, Belgium, 1815 $0
       (DLC) sh 85145739


001    fst01405244

003    OCoLC

005    20080131145614.0

008    061009n| anznnbabn    |n ana  d

040    $aOCoLC $beng $cOCoLC $ffast

111 2  $aGeneva Conference

411 2  $aKonferencja genewska

411 2  $aZhenevskoe soveshchanie
```

```
411 2   $aGenfer Konferenz

411 1   $aGeneva.

411 2   $aGeneva Conference on Indo-China and Korea

411 2   $aGeneva Conference on the Problem of Restoring Peace in
        Indo-China

411 2   $aJih-nei-wa hui i

411 2   $aRineiwa hui ji

411 2   $aGenfer Indochinakonferenz

711 20  $aGeneva Conference $d(1954) $0(DLC)n 50068579
```

Title Headings

Title headings are tagged as Uniform Title (130) fields in authority records. The first indicator is undefined and left blank, and the second indicator records the number of nonfiling characters. Subfield $p identifies the parts. Qualifiers are treated as part of subfield $a.

```
001     fst01356294

003     OCoLC

005     20080131145614.0

008     061116n| anznnbabn     |n aaa  d

040     $aOCoLC $beng $cOCoLC $ffast

130     $aIliad (Homer)

430 0   $aHomērou Iliada (Homer)

430 0   $aIliada (Homer)

430 0   $aIlias (Homerus)

430 0   $aHomeri Ilias (Homer)

700 00  $aHomer. $tIliad $0(DLC)n 78030104
```

```
001     fst01356193

003     OCoLC

005     20080131173904.0

008     061116n| anznnbabn     |n aaa  d

040     $aOCoLC $beng $cOCoLC $ffast

130 1   $aRomeo and Juliet (Shakespeare, William)

430 1   $aTragedy of Romeo and Juliet (Shakespeare, William)

430 1   $aRomeo and Juliet for young people (Shakespeare,
        William)

430 1   $aExcellent conceited tragedie of Romeo and Juliet
        (Shakespeare, William)
```

```
430 1  $aTragedie of Romeo and Juliet (Shakespeare, William)

430 1  $aTragic time and comic time in Shakespeare's plays
       (Shakespeare, William)

430 1  $aWilliam Shakespeare's Romeo and Juliet (Shakespeare,
       William)

430 1  $aFirst quarto of Romeo and Juliet (Shakespeare,
       William)

700 10 $aShakespeare, William, $d1564-1616. $tRomeo and
       Juliet $0(DLC)n 82116107
```

Form/Genre Headings

Form/genre headings are tagged as field 155 in authority records. Indicators are undefined and are left as blanks. Subfield $a contains the main heading, and form subdivisions are coded as $v.

```
001    fst01423707

003    OCoLC

005    20070912125809.0

008    060313nneanz    ||babn n ana  d

040    $aOCoLC $beng $cOCoLC $ffast

155    $aBibliography $vExhibition catalogs

785 0  $vBibliography $vExhibitions $0(DLC)sh 99001291


001    fst01423869

003    OCoLC

005    20080303130400.0

008    060313nneanz    ||babn n ana  d

040    $aOCoLC $beng $cOCoLC $ffast

155    $aCatalogs $vVideo catalogs

755  7 $aVideo catalogs $0fst01692926 $2fast

785 0  $vVideo catalogs $0(DLC)sh 99001760
```

NORMALIZATION

FAST, like most schemas, requires every established heading to be unique. The question is exactly what is meant by *similar*, or how similar can two headings be and still be considered unique? For instance, is **Eugene O'Neill** different enough from **Eugene O'neill**? Is the capitalization sufficient to differentiate two headings?

Normalization is the transformation of a string of characters into a more generic form. It is used to create a standard form of a heading that can then be used to compare headings. Typical normalizations include reducing all alphabetic characters to a single case and eliminating diacritics and punctuation. For bibliographic data, The NACO *Authority File Comparison Rules*[2] are widely accepted. Hickey, Toves, and O'Neill found that the NACO rules "are quite good, but they lack both general applicability and repeatability" and "The fact that the rules explicitly rely on the MARC record structure limits their application."[3] To overcome these limitations, they recommended two changes to the rules. With their recommended revisions, the FAST normalization rules specify that:

1. All alphabetic characters are retained in lower case.
2. All diacritics, apostrophe, brackets, subfield delimiter, and the vertical bar are deleted (the NACO rules specify that subfield delimiter is retained).
3. All digits, pound signs, ampersands, and plus signs are retained.
4. Most other characters, including the comma, are converted to blanks (the NACO rules specify that the first comma in an $a subfield should be retained).
5. Leading and trailing blanks are deleted and multiple consecutive blanks are replaced with a single blank.

Since FAST is intended to function in environments where subfielding cannot be assumed, simplified normalization rules were adapted. Additional details on the revised normalization process are provided by Hickey, Toves, and O'Neill. Examples of headings and their normalized forms are shown in Table 14.3.

Table 14.3
Examples of Normalized Headings

Heading	Normalized Form
Germany$zGrossenlüder	germany grossenluder
La Roche-l'Abeille, Battle of (France : 1569)	la roche labeille battle of france 1569
Iraq-Kuwait Crisis (1990–1991)	iraq kuwait crisis 1990 1991
Suchasnist´ (Firm)	suchasnist firm
ABC ware (Tableware)	abc ware tableware
Florida$zCoral Gables	florida coral gables
Al'a⌐n (The Arabic word)	alan the arabic word
Johnson, J. L.	johnson j l
Paroisse Saint-Sulpice (Montréal, Québec)	paroisse saint sulpice montreal quebec
Asi⌐a⌐ (Personal Name)	asia personal name
Canada.$bGovernor General (1869–1872 : Lisgar)	canada governor general 1869 1872 lisgar
France$zLépine (Champagne-Ardenne)	france lepine champagne ardenne
Witwicki, Władysław, $d1878–1948	witwicki wladyslaw 1878 1948
Hemmingstedt, Battle of (Germany : 1500)	hemmingstedt battle of germany 1500
Querétaro (Mexico : State)	queretaro mexico state

CONFLICTS

Two headings are said to be in conflict if they are identical or so similar that they are very difficult to distinguish. To address these questions, FAST first transforms the heading into a standardized form by *normalizing* the heading. Any two headings within the same file that have the identical normalized form are considered to be in conflict.

The restriction on conflicts between established headings is logical since having two very similar headings would result in significant confusion for both indexers and end-users. However, potential conflicts arise naturally with many types of headings. When authors share the same name, for instance, additional information is required to resolve the resulting conflicts. While there are a number of ways to resolve conflicts, the three most common are:

1. Adding birth and/or death dates to personal names.
2. Adding fuller forms of personal names.
3. Adding a qualifier to the heading.

For personal names, either adding the fuller form of the name or adding birth and/or death dates is common. Conflicts between topical headings occur when the same word or phrase has different meanings depending on the context. For example, **Masks** is a topical heading used to refer to face masks that are part of a costume. However, masks can also refer to the masks used in the production of integrated circuits. To distinguish between the two meanings and to provide context, the heading for masks used in the production of integrated circuits is qualified: **Masks (Electronics)**.

If the personal name heading **Black, Jack** had been previously established, the heading for the horse named Black Jack (the riderless horse in more than 1,000 armed forces funerals including President John F. Kennedy's) could not be established simply as "Black Jack." Doing so would create a conflict since both headings would normalize to *black jack*. Even though this conflict crosses facets—the heading for the horse would be established in the topical facet—the conflict must be resolved before the new heading is established.

The conflict between the person and the horse can be resolved by adding the qualifier *Horse* and establishing the heading for the horse as **Black Jack (Horse)**. In many cases, the LCSH heading from which the FAST heading was derived was qualified and the LCSH qualifier was retained. There is also a second person with the name of Jack Black. This conflict was resolved by establishing the heading for the second person with his birth date as **Black, Jack, 1969–**. As in this example, conflicts can generally be resolved without modifying the original heading.

Conflicts between headings established in the form facet and headings established in any of the seven subject facets are permitted. In LCSH, there are many headings that can be used as either subjects or forms. **Catalogs, Bibliography, Maps,** and **Periodicals** are a few of the LCSH headings that can be used either as topical or form headings. If the resource is a map, the form heading **Maps** would be assigned. However, if rather than being a map, the resource was about maps, the topical heading **Maps** would be used. FAST continues the LCSH practice and considers the subject authorities and the form authorities to be two separate authority files. Conflicts are prohibited within either of the two authority file but not between them.

ADDITIONAL VALIDATION

FAST also prohibits conflicts between cross-references (4XX fields) and established headings. The normalized form of a cross-reference must be distinct from the normalized form of an established heading. Cross-references are not required to be unique; the same cross-reference can appear in different authority records. An additional requirement is that every *see also* reference (5XX field) must match an established heading. For example, the heading **Smoking cessation** has five cross-references:

> Smoking cessation programs
> How-to-stop-smoking programs
> Quit-smoking programs
> Smoke-ending programs
> Stop-smoking programs

None of these are valid headings—they are included as cross-references since they (1) are not valid headings and (2) are synonyms for the preferred heading **Smoking cessation.**

Cross-references serve two different purposes. For personal names, cross-references are used (1) to identify variants forms of the names that the person is known by or has published under and (2) to indicate that when the form of the name used in the cross-reference is encountered, it should be replaced with the authorized form of the name. For example, the FAST authority record for **Mech, L. David** includes cross-references from *Mech, David* and *Mech, Dave.*

Occasionally the dual purposes of the cross references present problems. If a new author uses the name *David Mech,* the author could not be established as **Mech, David** since that would conflict with the cross-reference in the authority record for **L. David Mech.** To avoid the conflict, either the cross-reference would have to be deleted from the original record or additional details (birth date, fuller form of the name, and so forth) added to the new record. The latter option is preferable.

OBSOLETE AUTHORITY RECORDS

Subject heading vocabularies are revised regularly to reflect changes in language use. FAST recognizes two levels of changes to authority records:

1. Changes to the established heading that do not affect the normalized form of the heading. For example:

   United Fruit company Strike, 1934
     → **United Fruit Company Strike, 1934**
   Eve (Biblical figure) in rabbinical literature
     → **Eve (Biblical figure)—In rabbinical literature**
   Tennessee—Thompsons Station → Tennessee—Thompson's Station

These changes are made by revising the existing authority record. There are also a variety of other changes including the addition of cross-references and notes that can be made to existing authority records.

2. Changes to the established heading that do affect the normalized form of the heading. Examples of changes that alter the normalized form include:

All terrain cycling → **Mountain biking**
Coffee habit → **Coffee drinking**
Assignments → **Assignments (Law)**
Czechoslovakia—Detva → **Slovakia—Detva**
California—Princeton → **California—Princeton (Colusa County)**

Changes affecting the normalized form require a new authority record. As an example, when the heading **Coffee habit** in the authority record below:

```
LDR      00235nz 2200097n 4500
001      fst00866357
008      041024nn anznnbabn    || ana  d
053  0   $aRC567.5
150      $aCoffee habit
550      $aCaffeine habit
750  0   $aCoffee habit $0(DLC)sh 85027711
```

is changed to **Coffee drinking**, a new authority record for **Coffee drinking** would be created:

```
LDR      00243nz 2200097n 4500
001      fst01721153
008      090330nn anznnbabn    || ana  d
053  0   $aRC567.5
150      $aCoffee drinking
450      $aCoffee habit $wnne
750  0   $aCoffee drinking $0(DLC)sh 85027711
```

The new authority record **Coffee drinking** has a new FAST authority record number. The new record includes a *used for* (UF) reference from **Coffee habit** with the $w subfield value of "nne" indicating not only that **Coffee drinking** should be used instead of **Coffee habit** but also that previously **Coffee habit** was a valid heading.

Authority records for all headings that were previously valid are retained in the FAST authority file, but they are revised to reflect that they are now obsolete. The key change is that the record status (byte 5 of the leader) is changed from "n" (new) to "x," indicating that it is not a valid heading. The status of "x" indicates that the record is obsolete and has been logically, but not physically, deleted from the FAST authority file. In the FAST database, these obsolete authority records are normally excluded from the search results. However, if "Ignore Obsolete Headings" is unchecked, such headings will be included in the result set.

A new 7XX linking entry is also added to the original authority record that links to the replacement heading. This linking entry is normally the last field of the record and can be used to navigate from an obsolete heading to its replacement. The updated authority record for the now obsolete heading **Coffee habit** is:

```
LDR     00297xz 2200109n 4500

001     fst00866357

008     041024nn anznnbabn    || ana  d

053   0 $aRC567.5

150     $aCoffee habit

550     $aCaffeine habit

750   0 $aCoffee habit $0(DLC)sh 85027711

750   7 $aCoffee drinking $wna $0(OCoLC)fst01721153 $2fast
```

In addition to the obsolete status "x", the status "s" can be used to indicate that the heading is obsolete but replacement is not a simple one-to-one. Typically the status value of "s" indicates that the obsolete heading was split into two or more headings. An example of such a split was when the LCSH heading **Nurses and nursing** was split into the two separate headings **Nurses** and **Nursing**. Although this change occurred prior to the completion of FAST, a similar change today would require the status of the original authority be changed to "s" and links provided to both **Nurses** and **Nursing**.

NOTES

1. Library of Congress, *MARC 21 Format for Authority Data*, 1999 edition, last updated February 2010, http://www.loc.gov/marc/authority/ecadhome.html (accessed April 14, 2010).

2. NACO, *Authority File Comparison Rules (NOCO Normalization)*, September 16, 1998, revised February 9, 2001, http://www.loc.gov/catdir/pcc/naco/normrule.html (accessed April 13, 2010).

3. Thomas B. Hickey, Jenny Toves, and Edward T. O'Neill, "NACO Normalization: A Detailed Examination of the Authority File Comparison Rules," *Library Resources and Technical Services* 50, no. 3 (2006): 169.

15

AUTHORITY CONTROL

DEFINITION

In order to ensure the consistency and currency of authorized terms in any subject headings list or thesaurus, ongoing maintenance is required. The mechanism for ensuring consistency is *authority control*, the process of making sure the headings or descriptors assigned to metadata records conform to those authorized for the particular schema in use. Headings are explicitly authorized if the heading is established in an authority file. Headings can also be implicitly authorized if the rules for creating headings in a particular schema are followed. In many languages a minimum set of headings are established, with the proviso that those terms can be combined or extended following the rules for the language in question.

The purpose of authority control is similar to that of the now ubiquitous spell checkers; authority control should detect incorrect headings and, when possible, correct or suggest corrections. Just as spell checkers use dictionaries to determine the correct spelling of a word, authority control relies on an authority file to determine the correct form of a heading. When rigorously applied, authority control results in consistent and valid headings.

Authority control is an old concept and was well-established before online catalogs existed. Most of the authority control concepts are rooted in manual processes and procedures. Automating authority control has had limited success; many synthetic rules require a contextual understanding that, while possible for humans to understand, has been difficult to automate. For example, the Library of Congress Subject Headings (LCSH) heading **Burns and scalds** can be subdivided by **Patients** because **Burns and scalds** is a medical condition and **Patients** can be used to subdivide medical conditions. But this rule presents a challenge to automating the process since the authority record for **Burns and scalds** does not explicitly indicate that it is a medical condition. While there have been great strides in areas such as artificial intelligence, fully automatic authority control has yet to be achieved. Today, most authority control is maintained and applied offline as a batch process by library system vendors.

NEED FOR AUTHORITY CONTROL

"Authority control is expensive; however, no control is even more so."[1] Without authority control, the quality of the catalog will deteriorate as erroneous headings creep in. As an example, a partial list of the errors found in online catalogs for the LCSH subdivision **History and criticism** is shown in Figure 15.1. Although a wide variety of errors can be seen in the figure, most of them resulted from simple typographical errors, misspellings, and inappropriate abbreviations. In full headings, incorrect subdivision practice, the use of unestablished headings, unestablished subdivisions, or obsolete headings also results in erroneous headings.

4istory and criticism	History and cirticism	History and crititcism
Hhistory and criticism	History and cisticism	History and crititicsm
Hiastory and criticism	History and citicism	History and critivcism
Hiatory and criticism	History and Creiticism	History and critricism
Hiatory nd criticism	History and cricism	History and crticism
Hictory and criticism	History and cricitism	History and crtiticism
Hietory and criticism	History and cricitisms	History andcriticism
Hiistory and criticism	History and criicism	History andd criticism
Hintory and criticism	History and criiticism	History ang criticism
Hisktory and criticism	History and cririicism	History anmd criticism
Hisoty and criticism	History and crisicism	History annd criticism
Hisrory and criticism	History and crit icism	History ans criticism
Hisroty and criticism	History and Crit.	History cand criticism
Hist & crit.	History and crit.	History criticism
Hist. & crit.	History and Critcism	History criticism, etc.
Hist. & criticism	History and critcism	History land criticism
Hist. and crit.	History and criticiam	History nad criticism
Hist. and criticism	History and criticicm	History nd criticism
Hist.& crit.	History and criticim	History qand criticism
Historical and criticism	History and criticims	History qnd ciriticism
Histories and criticism	History and criticis	History, criticism, etc.
History and criticism	History and criticis m	History. and criticism
History & Criticism	History and criticisim	Historyand criticism
History & criticism	HIstory and criticism	Histotry and criticism
History & Criticism	History And Criticism	Histoty and criticism
History & criticism	History and Criticism	Histoy and criticism
History [and] criticism	history and Criticism	Histpry and criticism
History an criticism	history and criticism	Histrory and criticism
History anad criticism	History and Criticizm	Histtory and criticism
History anc criticism	History and criticizm	Histy and criticism
History and criticism	History and criticsim	Hitory and criticism
History and 2 criticism	History and criticsism	Hitory and crticism
History and ccriticism	History and criticsm	Hixtory and criticism
History and ciricism	History and critiicism	Hoitory and criticism
History and ciritcism	History and critiism	Hostory and criticism
History and ciriticism	History and critiscm	Hstory and criticism
History and ciriticsim	History and critisism	istory and criticism
History and ciriticsm	History and critisizm	
History and ciritism	History and critism	

Figure 15.1. Variant Entries for **History and criticism**

The impact of erroneous headings varies with the type of error and search engine used for retrieval. Stylistic errors—capitalization and punctuation—rarely pose serious problems although they can clutter displays. Other types of errors, including misspellings and typographical errors, can render the records unretrievable. Without authority control, the number of erroneous headings will grow continuously to the point that the function of a catalog or database is significantly compromised.

VALIDATION

FAST was specifically designed to support automated authority control. Except for the chronological facet, FAST is fully enumerative; every valid heading is established, and an authority record is created for every heading. It is therefore very easy to determine if a given string is a valid FAST heading: if the string exactly matches an established heading, it is valid; otherwise it is erroneous. For computers, determining whether a particular string is included in a list or table of headings is a simple and quick process.

Since chronological headings are not routinely established, different procedures must be used to determine the validity of chronological strings. The only general restriction on chronological headings is that when a date range is used, the second date must be later than the first. Dates generally consist of only a year or range of years. As described in Chapter 7, except for geologic periods, which are established, there are only five distinct patterns used for chronological headings:

1. A single date:

   1940 (July 4)
   2001

2. An open date:

   Since 1970
   Since 1987

3. An ending date:

   To 1500
   To 1939

4. A date range:

   210–10 B.C.
   221 B.C.–220 A.D.
   1939–1945
   1989 (December 1)–1990 (January 20)
   1900–1999

In addition to the year, a date can include a month or a month and day as a qualifier. The only case where A.D. is used is when a date range starts with a B.C. date but ends with an A.D. date. For date ranges that are entirely B.C., B.C. is added only to the ending date.

The validation of dates assigned to metadata records involves a two-step process:

1. The chronological strings are checked against the authority file; if the string matches an established heading, the string is a valid chronological heading.
2. If the string does not match an established heading, the string is checked to ensure that it corresponds to one of the four patterns just described; if the string is a correctly formatted chronological heading representing either a single date or a date range, the string is a valid chronological heading.

The procedure for validating headings is simple, straightforward, and reliable. FAST headings can be automatically validated in real time as they are assigned rather than depending on a combination of manual validation and batch processing. The cost of authority control is dramatically reduced through automatic validation, and the quality of the database is correspondingly enhanced by preventing the use of erroneous headings.

CORRECTION

While validation is an essential part of authority control, it is certainly not the only part and arguably not even the most important part. The automatic correction of erroneous headings is also essential. While automatic correction of all errors is an unrealistic goal, it is possible to correct, or at least suggest corrections, for most common errors.

Stylistic

Stylistic errors are defined as those found in headings whose normalized form is the same as that of the established heading. A few examples of stylistic variants of the established heading **History and criticism** include:

> history and criticism
> History [and] criticism
> HIstory and criticism
> History And Criticism
> History and Criticism

By indexing the normalized form of established headings, a correct heading can be readily identified and substituted for the erroneous heading. Automatic stylistic corrections are extremely reliable and can safely be made without manual review.

Tagging and Subfield Coding

Tagging and subfield coding errors are similar to stylistic errors. They can be defined as those headings whose text is identical to that of the established heading but that differ in either their tagging or subfield coding. Two examples of headings with tagging or subfielding errors include:

> **600 Pecos Bill (Legendary character)**
> *[Legendary characters are topical and should be tagged as 650]*
> **651 Lake Michigan $x Grand Traverse Bay**
> *[Geographic subdivisions should be coded as $z, not $x]*

Tagging and subfielding errors can be easily corrected since, like stylistic errors, they share the same normalized form as the correct heading. These types of automatic corrections are also extremely reliable and can be safely made without manual review.

Cross-References

The FAST authority file contains numerous cross-references, and they can be very helpful in correcting erroneous headings. Cross-references, except AUF references, by definition are not valid headings but are linked to the correct heading. Most cross-references look like valid headings, and it is a relatively common mistake to assign the cross-reference instead of the established heading. The following examples show the conversion from the cross-reference to the established heading:

Higher education → **Education, Higher**

Obama, Barry → **Obama, Barack**

Alabama $zLake Weiss → **Alabama $zWeiss Lake**

Bougainville Conflict (Papua New Guinea : 1988–)
 → **Bougainville Crisis (Papua New Guinea : 1988–)**

If the cross-references are unique, it is a straightforward process to replace an unauthorized heading assigned in a bibliographic record with its authorized equivalent. If the heading "Higher education" had been mistakenly assigned, the cross-reference can be used to replace it with the established form **Education, higher**. These corrections are reliable and can safely be made with little or no manual review.

Typographical Errors

As long as records are manually entered into databases, typographical errors will continue to occur. Simple typographical errors fall into one of four general groups:

Omission: A single character is dropped [*History an criticism*],

Addition: A single character is inserted [*History and criiticism*],

Substitution: One character is substituted for another character [*Hintory and criticism*],

Transposition: Two characters are transposed [*History and criticsim*].

Although there are many more complex types of errors, these four account for the majority of the typographical errors. Almost 60 percent of the variants of the subdivision **History and criticism** shown in Figure 15.1 resulted from simple typographical errors. The methodology for correcting such typographical errors is well understood. The methodology as applied to subject headings was described in 1980 by O'Neill and Aluri.[2] This methodology ensures that all headings with a single typographical error can be matched to their authorized equivalents. However, particularly for short headings, the methodology does not guarantee either a correct or a unique match. By changing only the "E," "Eats" can be matched to **Cats**, **Bats**, **Rats**, and **Hats**. For longer headings, false matches still can occur but are far less common. As a result, it is advisable to manually review the algorithmically identified corrections.

Obsolete Headings

As discussed in Chapter 14, authority records for obsolete headings are retained in the FAST authority file. These obsolete authority records can be used to update or correct assigned headings similar to the way cross-references are used to correct headings. An obsolete status of "x" indicates that there is a one-to-one replacement for the obsolete heading. These replacements are very reliable and can safely be made without manual review. Instead of "x," some obsolete authority records are assigned the status of "s," indicating that the heading is obsolete but replacement is not a simple one-to-one. The links in authority records with status "s" should be viewed only as potential replacements that should be manually reviewed.

CONCLUSION

The correction methodologies discussed in this chapter are capable of correcting or suggesting corrections for the majority of errors commonly encountered with subject headings. They require minimal computing resources, so they can be used to correct erroneous headings before they are added to the database. However, they do not represent an exhaustive list of the methodologies available. A detailed review of potentially beneficial methodology is beyond the scope of this book, but with the advances in computer hardware and the development of new and improved algorithms, the cost of authority control should continue to decrease.

While the preceding discussion has focused on ensuring that all assigned headings are valid, the very same process can be used to improve searching. Queries can be validated and corrected as a routine part of the search process.

NOTES

1. Doris Hargrett Clack, *Authority Control: Principles, Applications, and Instructions* (Chicago: American Library Association, 1990), p. 9.

2. Edward T. O'Neill and Rao Aluri, *Research Report on a Method for Correcting Typographical Errors in Subject Headings in OCLC Record*, Research Report Number OCLC/OPR/RR-80/3 (Columbus, OH: OCLC, 1980).

16

FACETING LCSH INTO FAST

INTRODUCTION

The purpose of this chapter is to provide a general overview of the faceting process—it is not intended to provide sufficient detail to implement the process. Faceting is complex and often messy, frequently requiring that special procedures be developed for very small classes of headings. What is presented here is a high-level view, frequently simplified to focus on the broad view while omitting some of the details. Unlike most aspects of FAST—assignment, searching, and authority control, which are expected to be applied at the local level—the faceting process is expected to remain a centralized process at OCLC.

A hybrid approach is used to facet Library of Congress Subject Headings (LCSH). Initially it was believed that faceting could be done entirely algorithmically, but so many special cases were encountered that a purely algorithmic approach was found to be impractical. A major software development with extensive programming would have been required to correctly facet a single subject heading. As a result, a hybrid approach was adopted in which most of the faceting is performed algorithmically but with predefined mappings used in special cases.

IDENTIFICATION AND RECODING
OF FORM SUBDIVISIONS

Form subdivisions have been part of LCSH since its inception. However, when the MARC format was developed, no separate subfield code to identify form subdivisions was defined. Form and topical subdivisions were both included within a general subdivision category. In 1995, the USMARC Advisory Group approved a proposal defining subfield $v for form subdivisions, and in 1999 the Library of Congress began identifying form subdivisions with the new code. However, there are still millions of older bibliographic records lacking the explicit form subdivision coding. To correctly facet LCSH headings, the form subdivisions lacking explicit form subfield coding must be identified and recoded.

In identifying form subdivisions, the first question to be asked is how to determine whether a particular subdivision in a subject string represents a topic or form. Although many terms clearly belong to one or the other category, many others are ambiguous. While subdivisions such as —**Education** or —**Quality control** can only be topical, others are not so obvious. For example, subdivisions such as —**Texts** and —**Translations into French, [German, etc.]**, may be used as either a topical or form subdivision, depending on the context. A common approach is to determine whether the subdivision in question represents what the resource *is* (i.e., form), or what it is *about* (i.e., topic). Even subdivisions such as —**Periodicals** are sometimes used as topical subdivisions. For example, in the heading **Academic achievement $xPeriodicals $vIndexes** *[an index to a journal on academic achievement]*, the subdivision —**Periodicals** is topical; but in the heading **Universities and colleges $xFinance $vPeriodicals** *[a journal on higher education finance]*, it is a form since it represents a publication issued in serial form.

In some cases, multiple form subdivisions may be used within the same heading. Examples include:

—**Biography—Dictionaries** *[v-v]*
—**Biography—Sermons** *[v-v]*
—**Dictionaries—Polyglot** *[v-x]*
—**Maps—Facsimiles** *[v-v]*
—**Specifications—Iowa** *[v-z]*

In a few cases such as —**Specifications—Iowa,** a form subdivision can be further subdivided geographically, while others like —**Dictionaries—Polyglot** can be further subdivided topically.

Distinguishing between form and topical subdivisions is not a simple task. OCLC's WorldCat, as well as most local systems, contains millions of unique subject headings, and the majority lack explicitly coded form subdivisions. Identifying forms is difficult because many subdivisions can be either topical (general) subdivisions or form subdivisions depending on the context of the heading. The identification of form headings necessitated the development of an automated procedure. After extended review and analysis, the approach adopted for identification is first to deal with the special forms—that is, form subdivisions with special or unique application rules—and then to use a table-driven procedure to identify the remaining forms. The algorithm is described in detail by O'Neill and colleagues.[1]

The following subdivisions, all denoting forms or genres, are governed by special rules when used as the last subdivision in a heading string:

—**Periodicals**
—**Juvenile**
—**Juvenile literature**
—**Juvenile films**
—**Juvenile sound recordings**
—**Databases**
—**Early works to 1800**
—**Facsimiles**

If one of these form subdivisions is present, it is removed from the heading and the remainder is treated as if the forms were never part of the heading. For the purpose of identifying form subdivisions, the heading:

Land value taxation $zIreland $xTables $xEarly works to 1800

is reduced to:

Land value taxation $zIreland $xTables.

After removing any special forms, the remaining forms in the heading can be identified using the table-driven procedure.

A table of form subdivisions was created by supplementing the list of forms identified in *Free-Floating Subdivisions*[2] with other forms identified through various sources. After the special processing just described, all headings were then checked to determine if they have terminating subdivision(s) matching those in the list of form subdivisions. This expanded list of form subdivisions was used to identify form subdivisions that had been coded as $x (general) subdivisions in LCSH and, for FAST, their preferred subdivision coding.

Since the procedures require that there can be no more than three form subdivisions after removing the special forms, the list is searched in three steps. The first step is to search for the last three general subdivisions if there are three or more subdivisions present. If one matches an entry in the list, the heading is recoded using the preferred coding. If no match is found, the last two general subdivisions are searched. If still no match is found, a final search is made for the last subdivision. For example, in the heading:

American literature $xAfrican American authors $xHistory and
Criticism $xTheory, etc.

the last three general subdivisions, —**African American authors**—**History and criticism**—**Theory, etc.**, would be checked against the table. When no match was found, the last two subdivisions —**History and criticism**—**Theory, etc.** would be checked. If, again, no match was found, the final subdivision —**Theory, etc.** would be checked. If all matches failed, the conclusion would be that all of the subdivisions were topical and that the original coding would be assumed to be correct.

With complex processes of this type, developing an error-free process is an unrealistic goal. While not perfect, this algorithm produces very consistent results. The algorithm proved to be highly reliable with an error rate estimated to be less than 0.1 percent, significantly less than the observed error rate for manual coding. Perhaps the greatest advantages of the algorithmic approach are its high accuracy rate and its ability to efficiently handle a large number of operations.

The identification and recoding of form subdivisions can be done selectively. The recoding can be applied to all headings, applied only to headings from records created before 1999 (the date the Library of Congress began using the $v code), or not applied at all. As a general rule, it is not applied to any heading that already includes a $v subfield based on the assumption that those headings are coded correctly.

ALGORITHMIC FACETING OF LCSH TO FAST

Conceptually, except for the identification of the form subdivisions, the faceting of LCSH headings is simple and straightforward; the LCSH strings include enough detailed information in their tagging and subfielding to enable the matching of subfields with FAST facets. However, in practice, it is more complex.

Faceting of Forms

As mentioned earlier, the form headings are the first to be faceted. If the Library of Congress heading ends with any of the eight special form subdivisions, those subdivisions are faceted out to create form headings. For example, the faceting of the LCSH heading *$aHybrid corn $zOntario $vStatistics $vPeriodicals* would start by faceting—*Periodicals*, leaving the remainder of the LCSH heading as: *$aHybrid corn $zOntario $vStatistics*.

The next step in the faceting of forms is extracting the first form subdivision along with all following subdivisions. In this example, that would complete the form faceting and would have created two FAST form headings, **Statistics** and **Periodicals**, while leaving the remaining LCSH string *$aHybrid corn $zOntario* for further faceting.

In the LCSH heading *$aManuscripts $vBibliography $vCatalogs*, the two form subdivisions would be faceted together to create the single FAST form heading **Bibliography—Catalogs.** If an $x (general) subdivision followed the initial form subdivision, it would also be faceted as form subdivision. For example, in the LCSH heading *$aDrugs $vDictionaries $xChinese,* the two subdivisions would be faceted as the FAST form heading **Dictionaries—Chinese,** even though "Chinese" is coded as a general subdivision in the original LCSH heading. Because it refers to a type of dictionary, it is faceted as a FAST form heading. In other words, FAST defines forms more broadly than does LCSH. Several LCSH general subdivisions, including *History* are faceted into FAST form headings.

Faceting of Titles

When titles of works are used as the subject, they are all treated as part of the title facet regardless of whether the works are of known authorship or unknown authorship. This practice contrasts with the LC/NAF authority file, where titles of known authorship are grouped with their authors. In FAST, the title rather than the author becomes the primary element in the heading, and the author, when known, is used as a qualifier.

Titles of Anonymous Works

LC/NAF headings tagged as 630 for anonymous works are generally faceted with few, if any, revisions in the form of $a (Uniform title) and $p (Name of part or section). For example, the following headings:

> **$aBible. $pN.T. $pMark**
> **$aDead Sea scrolls**
> **$aTalmud**

are faceted *as is* to FAST. In some cases, the uniform title heading contains other significant fields that are not faceted as part of the uniform title. For example, the heading *$aTreaty of Versailles $d(1919)* contains the date of the treaty signing in the $d subfield. To avoid the loss of the date information, the $d subfield is recoded as a $y (Chronological) subdivision and left for further faceting as *$y1919* and eventually converted to a separate FAST chronological heading: **1919.** Any $x (General) or $z (Geographic) subdivisions would also be retained for further faceting.

Titles for Works of Known Authorship

For titles in LC/NAF headings tagged as 600, 610, or 611, the title becomes the primary element and the author is used as a qualifier. The subfields used for the qualifier are shown in Table 16.1. Some faceting examples for works of known authorship include the following:

> 600 *$aTwain, Mark, $d1835–1910. $tAdventures of Tom Sawyer*
> → **Adventures of Tom Sawyer (Twain, Mark)**
> 600 *$aShakespeare, William, $d1564–1616. $tKing Lear*
> → **King Lear (Shakespeare, William)**
> 600 *$aHemingway, Ernest, $d1899–1961. $tOld man and the sea*
> → **Old man and the sea (Hemingway, Ernest)**
> 600 *Gregory $bI, $cPope, $d ca. 540–604. $t Moralia in Job*
> → **Moralia in Job (Gregory I, Pope)**
> 610 *$aFrance. $tConstitution (1791)*
> → **Constitution (France : 1791)**

Faceting of Events

Many of the headings for events are processed as exceptions and will be discussed in the section on reference records. All conference and meeting headings (tagged as 611) are algorithmically faceted as event headings. For example, the LCSH heading *$aIndianapolis Speedway Race* is unchanged by the faceting. However, some conference and meeting headings contain elements associated with other facets. The LCSH heading *$aStauferland-Expedition $d(1967)* contains chronological information in the $d subfield. Since only the $a subdivision is faceted to a FAST event heading as **Stauferland-Expedition,** to avoid the loss of the date information, this $d subfield is recoded and left with the remaining LCSH string *$y1967* for subsequent faceting of the chronological information.

Table 16.1
Subfields Used as Title Qualifiers

Tag	Qualifiers Subfields
600	$a Personal name
	$b Numeration
	$c Person's title
610	$a Corporate name (Plus the 410 $a for treaties with multiple countries)
	$b Subordinate name
611	$a Meeting or jurisdiction name

Faceting of Geographic Names

In LCSH, geographic names can appear either as main headings or as subdivisions, such as:

> $aRoads $zCalifornia $zSan Francisco Bay Area $vMaps
> $aSan Francisco (Calif.) $xDescription and travel.

When the geographic name is used as a subdivision, FAST has adopted the indirect style, as explained in Chapter 5. This resulted in two different faceting approaches—one used to facet the geographic name from the main heading and the other to facet the geographic name from subdivisions.

Main Headings

From headings tagged 651 (geographic), only the main heading ($a subfield) is faceted. For example, from the LCSH heading *$aBoston (Mass.) $xDescription and travel,* "Boston (Mass.)" would be faceted out as the geographic name. Since this name is entered directly with "Mass." as a qualifier, the name must be reordered and subdivided to create **Mass. $zBoston.** Since FAST does not abbreviate geographic names, all abbreviations are spelled out to form the FAST geographic heading **Massachusetts—Boston**.

Geographic names with multiterm qualifiers require that these complex qualifiers be replaced with a single qualifier representing the smallest geographic unit that fully contains the place. The heading *$aFlaming Gorge National Recreation Area (Wyo. and Utah)* would be faceted into FAST as: **United States—Flaming Gorge National Recreation Area** rather than **Wyoming and Utah—Flaming Gorge National Recreation Area**. The geographic name from the heading *$aBerkel River (Germany and Netherlands)* is faceted to create the FAST heading **Europe—Berkel River.**

LCSH headings containing three levels of geographic names are also algorithmically faceted and transformed into indirect order FAST headings. The LCSH heading *$aCamelback East Village (Phoenix, Ariz.)* would be faceted as **Arizona—Phoenix—Camelback East Village.**

A distinction is made between geographic qualifiers and qualifiers that identify the type of place (lake, county, state, etc.). For headings with dual qualifiers such as *$aCornwall (England : Duchy),* the type qualifier ("Duchy") is retained, and the heading is faceted as **England—Cornwall (Duchy)** to distinguish it from the county with the same name.

Subdivisions

The faceting of geographic subdivisions is less complex than that of main headings since the subdivisions are already in indirect order and abbreviations are not widely used. In many cases, the subdivisions can be faceted as is. The geographic name in the LCSH heading *$aMusic $zFrance $zParis* is faceted simply as **France—Paris.**

Occasionally, the first-level LCSH geographic names may be different when appearing as subdivisions from those used as main headings. The LCSH heading for Sydney is *Sydney (N.S.W.)* with the abbreviated name of the state as the qualifier. When used as a subdivision, it appears as *$zAustralia $zSydney (N.S.W.).* In these cases, the initial geographic subdivision is replaced with the qualifier (spelled out if abbreviated), and the original qualifier is dropped. As a result, both of these would be faceted to **New South Wales—Sydney**. Other changes may also be required to ensure a consistent form of the FAST headings regardless of whether they were faceted from a main LCSH heading or from subdivisions.

Faceting of Personal Names

The faceting of personal names is generally straightforward. The $a (Personal name), $b (Numeration), $c (Titles), $d (Dates), and $q (Fuller form of the name) subfields are faceted to create the FAST heading. The LCSH heading *$aGrace, $cPrincess of Monaco, $d1929-1982* is faceted as **$aGrace, $cPrincess of Monaco, $d1929–1982.** Any subdivisions remaining in the LCSH heading are retained for further faceting.

Faceting of Corporate Names

The faceting of corporate names follows a very similar pattern to that of personal names. The $a (Corporate name) and $b (Subordinate unit) subfields are faceted to create the FAST heading. The corporate name in the Library of Congress heading *$aHawaii. $bDept. of Taxation $xAuditing* is faceted as **$aHawaii. $bDept. of Taxation**, leaving *$xAuditing* in the original heading for further faceting as a topical heading.

Faceting of Chronologicals

Since FAST only uses the date information from the period subdivisions, the faceting of chronological subdivisions consists of parsing the subdivisions to extract the date or date range as appropriate. Some examples of faceting on LCSH periods include:

—$y1970 → **1970**
—$y17th century → **1600–1699**
—$y1963–1969 → **1963–1969**
—$y1949– → **Since 1949**
—$yEarly modern, 1500–1700 → **1500–1700**

Faceting of Topicals

At this point in the faceting process, the only subfields remaining from the original LCSH heading are (1) topical main headings ($a subfield) from a 650 heading and (2) general subdivisions ($x). All other subdivisions would have been previously faceted. The remaining headings from topical headings (those with an $a subfield) are faceted as is into the topical facet. for example:

$aMolecular biology $xResearch
$aWomen $xPsychology
$aInternational business enterprises $xManagement
$aRetirees $xMedical care $xCosts.

After recoding the first subdivision as the main ($a) subfield, the remaining heading consists of only one or more general subdivisions, and these are also faceted as is into the topical facet. Some examples of such headings include:

$xKings and rulers
$xBiography
$xAntiquities
$xCommerce $xEnvironmental aspects.

Biography is an example of a subdivision that can be either form ($v) or general ($x). However, since any forms subdivisions would have been faceted out early in the process, any remaining subdivisions are assumed to be general subdivisions at this stage of the faceting.

REFERENCE RECORDS

While the algorithmic process just described can correctly facet most LCSH headings, it fails on many of the atypical LCSH headings. Rather than attempting to extend the algorithm to handle these exceptions, a hybrid system is employed that, in addition to the algorithm, uses a table that specifies how the heading should be faceted in these special cases. To ensure compatibility and to permit editing using existing tools, the MARC 21 authority format is used to store this special faceting information in *reference records*. The 1XX headings in the reference records are LCSH headings—not FAST headings. The FAST headings are only in the 7XX fields in reference records. Therefore reference records are not considered FAST authorities and are not distributed as part of the FAST authority file. Since these reference records are not being distributed, local extensions have been made to the authority format in order to facilitate the requirements for the reference records.

The reference records have many of the same fields that are common in authority records, but their use may be different. The 0xx fields are used the same as they are in other FAST authority records except that byte 9 (Kind of record) in the 008 field is coded as "b" to identify it as a reference record.

An example of a reference record for the heading **Earth—Crust—Graphic methods** is shown here:

```
001    fst01416742

003    OCoLC

005    20080124104508.0

008    070607nnebnnnnbbbn |n ana d

040    $aOCoLC $beng cOCoLC $ffast

151    $aEarth $xCrust $xGraphic methods

260    $i1. This LCSH heading requires special faceting. The
       corresponding set of FAST headings are identified in the
       7xx fields. This faceting should be applied after the
       normal faceting of forms.

750 7  $aCrust of the Earth $xGraphic methods $0fst01352655
       $2fast

751 7  $aEarth $0fst01243607 $2fast
```

This record indicates that the LCSH heading *$aEarth $xCrust $xGraphic methods* should be faceted into two FAST headings: the topical heading **Crust of the Earth—Graphic methods** and the geographic heading **Earth**. Without the reference record, the heading would have been algorithmically faceted to the topical heading **Crust—Graphic methods** and the geographic heading **Earth**.

The explanatory note specifies when in the process this faceting should be applied. The note in field 260 contains two elements, a note number ($il) and a textual description. The description is identical in every field with the same note number and in that sense is redundant. The number is used primarily for machine processing, while the text is provided to support manual interpretation. In this case, the note specifies that this faceting should be applied after the faceting of the form subdivisions, if any, has been completed.

Another use of the reference record is to override the default faceting of form headings. Before the adoption of the $v subfield code, *$xParts*, although coded as a topical subdivison ($x), was generally used as a form subdivision in music headings such as *$aWoodwind quartets (Crumhorns (4)), Arranged $xParts*. Therefore, if the recoding of form subdivisions is performed, by default *$xParts* would be assumed to be a form heading, which would be correct in this case. However, the subdivision *$xParts* is also used as a general subdivision for equipment parts. The following reference record is used to ensure that *$xParts* is recognized as topical when used to subdivide *Crawler tractors*:

001		fst01694843
003		OCoLC
005		20080307112700.0
008		080307nnebnnnnbbbn | n ana d
040		$aOCoLC $benq $cOCoLC $ffast
150		$aCrawler tractors $xParts
260		$i4. This main-subdivision combination is considered topical and is not faceted further.
750	7	$aCrawler tractors $xParts $0fst00882300 $2fast
750	0	$aCrawler tractors $xParts $0(DLC)sh 85033789

This reference record also includes a 750 field containing a link to the LCSH authority record.

Reference records are routinely used to facet event headings that often involve complex faceting, such as the following reference record:

001		fst01414333
003		OCoLC
005		20081104125805.0
008		080723nnebnznnbbbn | n ana d
040		$aOCoLC $beng $cOCoLC $ffast
151	0	$aArmenia $xHistory $yRevolution, 1917-1920
260		$i2. This heading is treated as an event in FAST and requires special faceting. The main heading and all

```
          included subfields should be extracted with the
          main heading. The corresponding set of FAST headings
          are identified in the 7xx fields.
711   7   $aRevolution (Armenia : 1917-1920) $0fst01404278
          $2fast

748   7   $a1917-1920 $2fast

751   7   $aAsia $zArmenia $0fst01206470 $2fast

755   7   $aHistory $0fst01411628 $2fast

751   0   $aArmenia $xHistory $yRevolution, 1917-1920 $0(DLC)
          sh 85007275
```

This record is used to facet the Armenian revolution. In this instance, a single LCSH heading is faceted into the four FAST headings, an event, a period, a place, and a form. Some additional examples of LCSH to FAST faceting are shown in Table 16.2.

The hybrid approach to faceting has proven to be very effective. The vast majority of LCSH headings can be algorithmically faceted, while the reference records provide a convenient and effective way of handling the exceptions. This hybrid approach also resulted in more stable software since reference records could be used to handle the exceptions without requiring any modifications to the software.

VALIDATION

Faceting can be done for either a single heading or for a set of headings such as those typically found in a bibliographic record. The faceting is a three-step process: (1) the faceting of the LCSH heading(s) to create the resulting set of FAST headings, (2) the removal of duplicate FAST headings and merging of chronological headings, and (3) the validation of the FAST headings. The validation step is basically the authority control process described in the previous chapter.

To illustrate the process, the following set of LCSH headings from the same bibliographic records was faceted as a group:

650 $aActions and defenses $zRussia (Federation)

650 $aComplaints (Civil procedure) $zRussia (Federation)

650 $aAppellate procedure $zRussia (Federation)

650 $aActions and defenses $zRussia (Federation) $vCases

650 $aComplaints (Civil procedure) $zRussia (Federation) $vCases

650 $aAppellate procedure $zRussia (Federation) $vCases

The faceting produces the following FAST headings:

650 $aActions and defenses

651 $aRussia (Federation)

650 $aComplaints (Civil procedure)

651 $aRussia (Federation)

650 $aAppellate procedure

Table 16.2
Examples of LCSH to FAST Faceting

	LCSH Heading		*Faceted FAST Headings*
Tag	*Heading*	*Tag*	*Heading(s)*
650	$aReading comprehension $xStudy and teaching	650	Reading comprehension—Study and teaching
650	$aPhotography, Artistic $vExhibitions	650 655	Photography, Artistic Exhibition catalogs
650	$aTourism $zColombia	650 651	Tourism Colombia
651	$aIndia $xArmed Forces $xAppropriations and expenditures	651 650	India Armed Forces—Appropriations and expenditures
651	$aChina $xHistory $yRevolution, 1911–1912	611 651 655	Revolution (China : 1911–1912) China History
600	$aDwiggins, W. A. $q(William Addison), $d1880–1956	600	Dwiggins, W. A. (William Addison), 1880–1956
600	$aWright, Teresa, $d1918–2005 $xPerformances	600 650	Wright, Teresa, 1918–2005 Performances
610	New Zealand. $bParliament. bHouse of Representatives. $bSelect Committee on the Electoral Law $vPeriodicals	610 655	New Zealand. Parliament. House of Representatives. Select Committee on the Electoral Law Periodicals
650	$aQuiltmakers $zArizona $vBiography.	650 651 655	Quiltmakers—Biography Arizona Biography
651	$aSouth Africa $xPolitics and government $y1978–1989	651 650 648	South Africa Politics and government 1978-1989
630	Haggadah	630	Haggadah
611	$aSan Joaquin County Fair $xHistory	611 650	San Joaquin County Fair History
611	$aIndianapolis Speedway Race $vJuvenile literature	611 655	Indianapolis Speedway Race Juvenile works
600	$aTwain, Mark, $d1835–1910. $tAdventures of Tom Sawyer	630	Adventures of Tom Sawyer (Twain, Mark)
650	$aPolitical violence $zNorthern Ireland $zBelfast $xHistory $y20th century	650 651 648 655	Political violence Northern Ireland—Belfast 1900–1999 History
611	$aPennsylvania. $tLobbying Disclosure Act	630	Lobbying Disclosure Act of 1995 (United States)

651 $aRussia (Federation)

650 $aActions and defenses

651 $aRussia (Federation)

655 $aCase studies

650 $aComplaints (Civil procedure)

651 $aRussia (Federation)

655 $aCase studies

650 $aAppellate procedure

651 $aRussia (Federation)

655 $aCase studies.

After the duplicate headings are deleted, the result is a set of five FAST headings:

650 $aActions and defenses

650 $aComplaints (Civil procedure)

650 $aAppellate procedure

651 $aRussia (Federation)

655 $aCase studies.

In LCSH, it is common to have multiple subject headings with different period subdivisions, for example:

$aSouth Africa $xPolitics and government $y1836–1909

$aSouth Africa $xPolitics and government $y1909–1948

The faceting of these LCSH headings would result in two chronological periods, 1836–1909 and 1909–1948. Since FAST, unlike LCSH, is not limited to pre-defined periods, as part of the process of eliminating duplicates, multiple chronological headings are combined to create a single heading covering the entire period—in this case, **1836–1948**.

The final step is the validation of the faceted FAST heading. Each of the preceding five headings would be checked against the FAST authority file. Since each of those five headings corresponds to a FAST authority record, each would be considered valid.

The four possible results of the validation are that the faceted heading:

1. Exactly matches an established FAST heading; the faceted heading is validated.

2. Is a stylistic variant of an established FAST heading; the faceted heading is replaced by the established heading from the authority file.

3. Matches a cross-reference; the faceted heading is replaced by the established heading from the authority file.

4. Does not match either an established heading or a cross-reference; the heading is assumed to be invalid and is removed from the list of faceted headings.

The final result of the faceting is a set of valid FAST headings.

CONCLUSION

The faceting process is an efficient and flexible means of adding FAST subject headings to bibliographic records that already contain LCSH headings. The algorithmically converted set of headings is nearly equal in quality to those originally assigned by experienced indexers. Since the faceting is fully automated, it is a very inexpensive process.

NOTES

1. Edward T. O'Neill, Lois Mai Chan, Eric Childress, Rebecca Dean, Lynn M. El-Hoshy, and Diane Vizine-Goetz, "Form Subdivisions: Their Identification and Use in LCSH," *Library Resource and Technical Services* 45, no. 4 (2001): 187–97.

2. Library of Congress, Cataloging Policy and Support Office, *Free-Floating Subdivisions: An Alphabetical Index,* 12th ed. (Washington, DC: Cataloging Distribution Service, Library of Congress, 2000).

APPENDIX A: FAST AUTHORITY RECORDS STRUCTURE

For each established FAST heading, an authority record is created. The authority record contains the authorized heading, *see from* and *see also from* references, and links to the Library of Congress Subject Headings (LCSH) authority record(s) from which the FAST heading and authority record are derived. As explained in Chapter 2, FAST authority records are encoded according to *MARC 21 Format for Authority Data*.[1] In addition to information relating to the established heading, the record also includes record control information. Several examples of various type of FAST authority records are shown here:

LIBRARY SCIENCE—ABSTRACTING AND INDEXING

```
LDR     00424cz  2200145n  4500

001     fst00997917

003     OCoLC

005     20080715102403.0

008     041024nn anznnbabn          || ana    d

016  7  $afst00997917 $2OCoLC

040     $aOCoLC $beng $cOCoLC $ffast

150     $aLibrary science $xAbstracting and indexing

688     $aLC (2008) Subject Usage: 3

688     $aWC (2008) Subject Usage: 13

750  0  $aLibrary science $0(DLC)sh 85076723
```

PACIFIC OCEAN—SAN FRANCISCO BAY

LDR	01201cz 2200253n 4500	
001	fst01242396	
003	OCoLC	
005	20091009130205.0	
008	060620nn anznnbabn || ana d	
016	7	$afst01242396 $2OCoLC
034		$dW1221649 $eW1221649 $fN0374230 $gN0374230 $2GeoNames
040		$aOCoLC $beng $cOCoLC $ffast
043		$ap
151		$aPacific Ocean $zSan Francisco Bay
451		$aCalifornia $zBoca del Puerto de San Francisco
451		$aCalifornia $zEstero de S. Francisco
451		$aCalifornia $zEstero de San Francisco
550		$aBays $0(OCoLC)fst00829042
670		$aGeoNames [algorithmically matched] $bbay; 37°42'30"N 122°16'49"W
670		$aGNIS, July 27, 1999 $b(variants: Drake's Bay, La Boca Del Puerto De San Francisco. Description: a bay on the California coast connected with the Pacific Ocean by the Golden Gate. History notes: The name San Francisco was applied to Drake's Bay in 1595. Subsequently the name was shifted to the present San Francisco Bay.)
688		$aLC (2008) Subject Usage: 127
688		$aWC (2008) Subject Usage: 3,609
751	0	$aSan Francisco Bay (Calif.) $0(DLC)sh 85117095
751	7	$aSan Francisco Bay $0(GeoNames)5391961 $2geonames

KILGOUR, FREDERICK G.

LDR	00406cz 2200145n 4500
001	fst00152831
003	OCoLC
005	20080131185832.0
008	040924nn anznnbabn || ana d

```
016   7 $afst00152831 $2OCoLC

040     $aOCoLC $beng $cOCoLC $ffast

100   1 $aKilgour, Frederick G.

688     $aLC (2008) Subject Usage: 1

688     $aWC (2008) Subject Usage: 9

700  10 $aKilgour, Frederick G. $0(DLC)n 85080079
```

Leader; Record status (Byte 5)

a - Increase in encoding level

c - Corrected or revised

d - Deleted

n - New

o - Obsolete

s - Deleted; heading split into two or more headings

x - Deleted; heading replaced by another heading

Control Number and Control Number Identifier (001/003)

All FAST authority records have a control number (in field 001) with a three-character prefix of "fst" followed by an eight-digit control number. The control number identifier (in field 003) is always "OCoLC." An example is:

```
001     fst01219723

003     OCoLC
```

Date and time of latest transaction (005)

The date and time of the latest transaction is required for each FAST authority record. The contents of this field contain either the date and time the record was initially added to the authority file or the date and time of last modification of the authority record. Following the MARC 21 Format, a string of 16 characters is used to specify the date and time, recorded according to the representation of dates and times (ISO 8601) in the pattern: yyyymmddhhmmss.f. The Date requires 8 numeric characters in the pattern yyyymmdd (4 for the year, 2 for the month, and 2 for the day). The Time requires 8 numeric characters in the pattern hhmmss.f (2 for the hour, 2 for the minute, and 2 for the second plus the decimal point and the tenth of a second). The time is entered to the closest second so the decimal portion of the date and time entry will be ".0." The 24-hour clock (00–23) is used. An example is:

```
005 20080204094445.0

    yyyymmddhhmmss.s
```

The authority record for this entry was last modified at 45.0 seconds after 9:44a on February 4, 2008.

Fixed-Length Data Elements (008)

Date entered on file (008/Bytes 00–05): For FAST authority records, this is the date on which a record was initially added to the authority file. Initially, this date will match the latest transaction date in the 005 field. However, the date entered on file never changes while the date and time of latest transaction will be updated every time the authority record is modified.

Direct or indirect geographic subdivision (008/Byte 06): Only three of the authorized values are used for FAST authority records:

Blank - Not subdivided geographically

i - Subdivided geographically-indirect

n - Not applicable

The value of "n" (not applicable) is used in all authority records except in those for the geographic facet. For geographic names, all two- and three-level names except for cities and a limited number of other names can be further subdivided. With few exceptions, such as **Ohio River Valley**, all single-level geographic names that are identified in Table A-2 in Appendix C are assigned the code of blank.

Romanization scheme (008/Byte 07): All authority records created specifically for FAST are coded as "n" (not applicable). Records derived from LC authorities retain the value from the source record.

Language of catalog (008/Byte 08): All authority records are coded as blank (no information provided).

Kind of record (008/Byte 09): Fast authority records are coded as "a" (established heading). FAST also includes untraced reference records (coded as "b"). The reference records have very limited application and are not included in the distribution version of the authority file.

Descriptive cataloging rules (008/Byte 10): All authority records are coded as "n" (not applicable).

Subject heading system/thesaurus (008/Byte 11): All authority records are coded as "z" (other). The MARC code of "fast" is contained in subfield $f (subject heading/thesaurus conventions) in field 040 to identify FAST as the source of the heading.

Type of series (008/Byte 12): All authority records are coded as "n" (not applicable).

Numbered or unnumbered series (008/Byte 13): All authority records created specifically for FAST are coded as "n" (not applicable). Records derived from Library of Congress authorities retain the value from the source record.

Heading use—main or added entry (008/Byte 14): All authority records are coded as "b" (not applicable).

Heading use—subject added entry (008/Byte 15): All authority records are coded as "a" (appropriate).

Heading use—series added entry (008/Byte 16): All authority records are coded as "b" (not appropriate).

Type of subject subdivision (008/Byte 17): All authority records are coded as "n" (no attempt to code).

Type of government agency (008/Byte 28): All authority records created specifically for FAST are coded as "|" (no attempt to code). Records derived from Library of Congress authorities retain the value from the source record.

Reference evaluation (008/Byte 29): All authority records are coded as "|" (no attempt to code).

Record update in process (008/Byte 31): All authority records are coded as "a" (record can be used).

Undifferentiated personal name (008/Byte 32): All records retain the value from the LC/NAF authority record from which they were derived.

Level of establishment (008/Byte 33): All authority records are coded as either:

a - Fully established
c - Provisional

Modified record (008/Byte 38): All authority records are coded as blank (not modified).

Cataloging source (008/Byte 39): All authority records are coded as "d" (other).

All other bytes in the Fixed-Length Data Elements (008) are undefined and have value of blank.

Cataloging Source (040)

All FAST authority records contain the following 040 field:

```
040 $aOCoLC $beng $cOCoLC $ffast
```

This field specifies (a) OCLC as the cataloging source; (b) English as the language of cataloging; (c) OCLC as the organization that entered the record into machine readable form; and (d) that it is a FAST heading.

Geographic Area Code (043)

Authority records for most geographic names include the Geographic Area Code (GAC). The GAC list is maintained by the Library of Congress, and the complete list is available on its web site.[2]

Library of Congress Call Number (050)

In FAST records derived directly from Library of Congress authority records, if the Library of Congress authority record includes the Library of Congress Call

Number, the call number is also included in the corresponding FAST authority record.

Established Heading (lxx)

The following fields are used for FAST headings:

    100 - Personal Name

    110 - Corporate Name

    111 - Event Name (Meeting Name)

    130 - Uniform Title

    148 - Chronological Term

    150 - Topical Term

    151 - Geographic Name

    155 - Genre/Form Term

Except for uniform titles where the entire heading with the author/contributor as a qualifier forms the $a subfield, the subfields and subfield coding follow MARC 21 standard practice.

Cross-Reference (See from Tracing, 4xx)

The following fields contain UF (used for) references:

    400 - Personal Name

    410 - Corporate Name

    411 - Event Name (Meeting Name)

    430 - Uniform Title

    448 - Chronological Term

    450 - Topical Term

    451 - Geographic Name

    455 - Genre/Form Term

The subfields and subfield coding generally follow MARC standard practice. However, in FAST authority records, the use of the "w" subfield is an exception to the standard practice. In FAST authority records, a $w subfield with the value of "ni" is used for *also use for* (AUF) references to indicate that this reference is also an established heading.[3] The need for and the use of the $w subfield in FAST authority records is discussed in more detail in Chapter 10, "Cross-References."

See Also Reference (See Also from Tracing, 5xx)

The following fields are used for *see also* references:

    500 - Personal Name

    510 - Corporate Name

    511 - Event Name (Meeting Name)

    530 - Uniform Title

548 - Chronological Term

550 - Topical Term

551 - Geographic Name

555 - Genre/Form Term

The subfields and subfield coding follow MARC standards.

Application History Note (688)

In FAST, the application history note is used to provide usage information, for example, the authority record for **Education, Higher** contains the notes:

688 $aLC (2008) Subject Usage: 7,003 (11,826)

688 $aWC (2008) Subject Usage: 53,882 (84,011)

Only the $a subfield is authorized for use in FAST authority records. It is used to indicate how frequently the heading has been assigned in both the Library of Congress's database and in OCLC's WorldCat database. Since, with rare exceptions, all Library of Congress records are included in WorldCat, the usage by the Library of Congress is included with the WorldCat usage. In both cases, the usage is based on the frequency of the headings after mapping the LCSH headings to FAST headings. These counts are updated periodically, and the date of the most recent update is included in the entry.

Two counts are included for the usage. The nonparenthetical usage is the frequency that the full heading has been assigned. The parenthetical usage includes not only the use of a heading as established in the 1xx field but also the count of the number of times it was assigned with additional subdivisions. For example, only the assignments of **Education, Higher** are counted for the first count, but assignments of the following headings would also be included in the second usage count:

Education, Higher—Accounting

Education, Higher—Accreditation

Education, Higher—Administration

Education, Higher—Administration—Decision making

Education, Higher—Aims and objectives

Established Heading Linking Entry (7xx)

The following fields are used for linking entries:

700 - Personal Name Heading

710 - Corporate Name Heading

711 - Event Name (Meeting Name) Heading

730 - Uniform Title Heading

748 - Chronological Term Heading

750 - Topical Term Heading

751 - Geographic Name Heading

755 - Genre/Form Term Heading

780 - General Subdivision
781 - Geographic Subdivision
782 - Chronological Subdivision
785 - Form Subdivision

The 7xx Heading Linking Entry fields provide a machine link within a system between equivalent headings whether they are structured in the same or different form, whether they are from the same or different authority files or printed thesauri, or whether they exist as separate authority records. The inclusion of a linking entry field in an established heading or established heading and subdivision record for a name, name/title, uniform title, topical term, form term, or extended subject heading or in an established heading record for an authorized subject subdivision may be used to relate such headings as:

1. Equivalent names in a multilingual thesaurus

   Example: Library and Archives Canada English heading *Francis, of Assisi, Saint, 1182–1226* and Library and Archives Canada French heading *François, d'Assise, saint, 1182–1226*

2. Equivalent topical term headings in different authority systems

   Example: Library of Congress Subject Headings (LCSH) headings **Medical referral** and **Medical consultation** and Medical Subject Headings (MeSH) heading *Referral and Consultation*

3. Topical term heading (field 150) and the same or similar term used as a subject subdivision (field 78x)

   Example: Established term **History** and the subject subdivision **History**

   Example: Established term *Twentieth century* and the subject subdivision *20th century*

4. Geographic name heading (field 151) and the indirect form of that name used as a geographic subject subdivision (field 781)

   Example: Established LCSH heading **Rome (N.Y.)** and the subject subdivision *New York (State)-Rome*

5. Genre/form term heading (field 155) and the same or similar term used as a form subject subdivision (field 785)

   Example: Established heading *Periodicals* and the subject subdivision *Periodicals*

The 7xx field tag identifies whether the heading linking entry field contains an established heading (fields 700–755) or an authorized subdivision heading (fields 780–785). The second indicator or the subfield $2 identifies the authority system to which the heading in field 7xx belongs. Subfield $0 (record control number) contains the system control number of the related record when a separate MARC authority record exists for the 7xx heading.

NOTES

1. Library of Congress, Network Development and MARC Standards Office, *MARC 21 Format for Authority Data: Including Guidelines for Content Designation*, prepared by Network Development and MARC Standards Office, Library of Congress, in coop-

eration with Standards and Support, National Library of Canada (Washington: Library of Congress, Cataloging Distribution Service; Ottawa: National Library of Canada, 1999–), http://www.loc.gov/marc/authority/ecadhome.html (accessed April 14, 2010).

2. Library of Congress, Network Development and MARC Standards Office, *MARC Code List for Geographic areas Areas,* http://www.loc.gov/marc/geoareas/gacshome.html (accessed April 13, 2010).

3. The code of "i" for byte 1 has not been approved by MARBI (MAchine-Readable Bibliographic Information) for use in MARC 21 authority records.

APPENDIX B: GEOLOGIC PERIODS

Table A-1 lists the geologic periods used for FAST and their associated dates. Each of the named geologic periods is established as a topical heading and the corresponding period is established as a chronological heading.

Table A-1
Geologic Periods Used for FAST and Their Associated Dates

Name of Geologic Period	Time of Period
Archaean Geologic Period	From 2500 to 5000 million years ago
Cambrian Geologic Period	From 500 to 570 million years ago
Carboniferous Geologic Period	From 280 to 345 million years ago
Cenozoic Geologic Period	From 65 million years ago
Cretaceous Geologic Period	From 65 to 140 million years ago
Devonian Geologic Period	From 345 to 405 million years ago
Eocene Geologic Epoch	From 40 to 55 million years ago
Holocene Geologic Period	From 10 thousand years ago
Huronian Geologic Period	From 1600 to 2600 million years ago
Jurassic Geologic Period	From 140 to 190 million years ago
Laurentian Geologic Period	From 2500 to 5000 million years ago
Mesozoic Geologic Period	From 65 to 230 million years ago
Miocene Geologic Epoch	From 10 to 25 million years ago
Mississippian Geologic Period	From 310 to 345 million years ago
Neogene Geologic Period	From 2 to 25 million years ago
Oligocene Geologic Epoch	From 25 to 40 million years ago

Table A-1 (*continued*)

Name of Geologic Period	Time of Period
Ordovician Geologic Period	From 425 to 500 million years ago
Paleocene Geologic Epoch	From 55 to 65 million years ago
Paleogene Geologic Period	From 25 to 65 million years ago
Paleozoic Geologic Period	From 230 to 570 million years ago
Pennsylvanian Geologic Period	From 280 to 310 million years ago
Permian Geologic Period	From 230 to 280 million years ago
Permo-Carboniferous Geologic Period	From 230 to 345 million years ago
Pleistocene Geologic Epoch	From 10 thousand to 2 million years ago
Pliocene Geologic Epoch	From 2 to 10 million years ago
Precambrian Geologic Period	From 570 to 5000 million years ago
Proterozoic Geologic Period	From 570 to 2500 million years ago
Quaternary Geologic Period	From 2 million years ago
Silurian Geologic Period	From 405 to 425 million years ago
Tertiary Geologic Period	From 2 to 65 million years ago
Triassic Geologic Period	From 190 to 230 million years ago

APPENDIX C: GEOGRAPHIC NAMES

There are three key tables that are associated with geographic names. The first of these is Table A-2, which lists all the first-level geographic names. The first column of the table is the FAST authority record number (ARN), the second column is the geographic area code (GAC), and the third column is the name. There are two distinct types of first-level geographic names: those that can be subdivided and those that can't. The names that can be subdivided are shown in bold font. There are a few cases where names that normally are not subdivisible can be subdivided in limited special cases, and these are identified in the notes.

Table A-2.
First Level Geographic Names

FAST ARN	GAC	Name (Bold Names Can Be Subdivided)
fst01205406	a-af	**Afghanistan**
fst01239509	f	**Africa**
fst01239510	fc	Africa, Central
fst01239511	fe	Africa, East
fst01696894	f	Africa, Eastern
fst01692674	f	Africa, English-speaking
fst01692677	f	Africa, French-speaking
fst01692604	fq	Africa, French-speaking Equatorial
fst01692605	f	Africa, French-speaking Western
fst01239515	ff	Africa, North
fst01239516	fh	Africa, Northeast

Table A-2 (*continued*)

FAST ARN	GAC	Name (Bold Names Can Be Subdivided)
fst01692606	f	Africa, Northwest
fst01692607	f	Africa, Portuguese-speaking
fst01239519	fs	Africa, Southern
fst01692716	f	Africa, Spanish-speaking
fst01239520	fb	Africa, Sub-Saharan
fst01239521	fw	Africa, West
fst01204694	n-us-al	**Alabama**
fst01204480	n-us-ak	**Alaska**
fst01692689	n-us-ak	Alaska, Southeast
fst01226682	e-aa	**Albania**
fst01204828	n-cn-ab	**Alberta**
fst01692697	n-cn-ab	Alberta, Northern
fst01205459	f-ae	**Algeria**
fst01239717	ea	Alps
fst01284159	ea	Alps Region
fst01692609	ea	Alps, Eastern
fst01342096	ea	Alps, Eastern, Region
fst01692610	ea	Alps, Western
fst01239763	sa	Amazon River
fst01239764	sa	Amazon River Region
fst01239765	sa	Amazon River Valley
fst01264744	sa	Amazon River Watershed
fst01239786	xd	America
fst01207148	poas	**American Samoa**
fst01310062	aa	Amur River
fst01342097	aa	Amur River Region
fst01311227	aa	Amur River Valley
fst01311016	aa	Amur River Watershed
fst01239883	sn	Andes
fst01241744	sn	Andes Region
fst01209980	e-an	**Andorra**
fst01208401	f-ao	**Angola**
fst01211573	nwxa	**Anguilla**
fst01239990	t	**Antarctic Ocean**
fst01239992	t	**Antarctica**
fst01225425	nwaq	**Antigua and Barbuda**

Table A-2 (*continued*)

FAST ARN	GAC	Name (Bold Names Can Be Subdivided)
fst01240091	n-usa	Appalachian Mountains
fst01240092	n-usa	Appalachian Region
fst01240128	ma	Arab countries
fst01692642	aw	Arabia, Southern
fst01240131	ar	Arabian Peninsula
fst01240132	au	**Arabian Sea**
fst01251218	xa	Arabian-Nubian Shield
fst01240224	r	**Arctic Ocean**
fst01240227	r	Arctic regions
fst01205614	s-ag	**Argentina**
fst01692666	s-ag	Argentina, Northeast
fst01692662	s-ag	Argentina, Northwest
fst01204820	n-us-az	**Arizona**
fst01204809	n-us-ar	**Arkansas**
fst01262063	a-ai	**Armenia (Republic)**
fst01205425	nwaw	**Aruba**
fst01208257	lsai	**Ascension Island**
fst01255825	u-ac	**Ashmore and Cartier Islands**
fst01240495	a	**Asia**
fst01240497	ac	Asia, Central
fst01240722	l	**Atlantic Ocean**
fst01723575	l	Atlantic Ocean Region
fst01240731	fa	Atlas Mountains
fst01342245	fa	Atlas Mountains Region
fst01240888	u	Australasia
fst01204543	u-at	**Australia**
fst01692667	u-at	Australia, Southeastern
fst01210641	u-at-ac	**Australian Capital Territory**
fst01204901	e-au	**Austria**
fst01260665	a-aj	**Azerbaijan**
fst01202649	lnaz	**Azores**
fst01205834	nwbf	**Bahamas**
fst01206601	a-ba	**Bahrain**
fst01241484	ed	Balkan Peninsula
fst01241546	eb	Baltic states
fst01213724	a-bg	**Bangladesh**

Table A-2 (*continued*)

FAST ARN	GAC	Name (Bold Names Can Be Subdivided)
fst01205547	nwbb	**Barbados**
fst01242377	ab	**Bay of Bengal**
fst01260637	e-bw	**Belarus**
fst01210278	e-be	**Belgium**
fst01206799	ncbh	**Belize**
fst01242373	el	Benelux countries
fst01206464	f-dm	**Benin**
fst01206531	lnbm	**Bermuda Islands**
fst01207216	a-bt	**Bhutan**
fst01242937	mb	**Black Sea**
fst01342390	mb	Black Sea Region
fst01205549	s-bo	**Bolivia**
fst01205320	nwbn	**Bonaire**
fst01243192	a-bn	**Borneo**
fst01212749	e-bn	**Bosnia and Hercegovina**
fst01205793	f-bs	**Botswana**
fst01246341	lsbv	**Bouvet Island**
fst01206830	s-bl	**Brazil**
fst01692630	s-bl	Brazil, North
fst01692631	s-bl	Brazil, Northeast
fst01692632	s-bl	Brazil, South
fst01692633	s-bl	Brazil, Southeast
fst01205265	n-cn-bc	**British Columbia**
fst01206732	i-bi	**British Indian Ocean Territory**
fst01218688	nwvb	**British Virgin Islands**
fst01216469	a-bx	**Brunei**
fst01212489	e-bu	**Bulgaria**
fst01342589	e-bu	Bulgaria Region
fst01229910	f-uv	**Burkina Faso**
fst01207835	a-br	**Burma**
fst01212359	f-bd	**Burundi**
fst01209292	mm	Byzantine Empire
fst01204928	n-us-ca	**California**
fst01692637	n-us-ca	California, Northern
fst01692638	n-us-ca	California, Southern
fst01207659	a-cb	**Cambodia**

Table A-2 (*continued*)

FAST ARN	GAC	Name (Bold Names Can Be Subdivided)
fst01212703	f-cm	**Cameroon**
fst01204310	n-cn	**Canada**
fst01692639	n-cn	Canada, Eastern
fst01692640	n-cn	Canada, Northern
fst01692641	n-cn	Canada, Western
fst01207252	nccz	**Canal Zone**
fst01222944	lnca	**Canary Islands**
fst01219323	f-iv	**Côte d'Ivoire**
fst01216993	lncv	**Cape Verde**
fst01244080	cc	**Caribbean Area**
fst01692660	cc	Caribbean Area, English-speaking
fst01244087	cc	**Caribbean Sea**
fst01244124	poci	**Caroline Islands**
fst01244227	ak	**Caspian Sea**
fst01343043	ak	Caspian Sea Region
fst01244425	e-urk	Caucasus
fst01343044	e-urk	Caucasus Region
fst01692709	e-ru	Caucasus, Northern
fst01209614	nwcj	**Cayman Islands**
fst01203762	f-cx	**Central African Republic**
fst01244535	nc	**Central America**
fst01208478	f-cd	**Chad**
fst01205362	s-cl	**Chile**
fst01206073	a-cc	**China**
fst01692654	a-cc	China, Northwest
fst01692655	a-cc	China, Southeast
fst01692656	a-cc	China, Southwest
fst01229370	i-xa	**Christmas Island**
fst01221980	i-xb	**Cocos (Keeling) Islands**
fst01239915	q	Cold regions
fst01205916	s-ck	**Colombia**
fst01210251	n-us-co	**Colorado**
fst01240090	b	Commonwealth countries
fst01240119	x	Communist countries
fst01208084	i-cq	**Comoros**
fst01208750	f-cf	**Congo (Brazzaville)**

Table A-2 (*continued*)

FAST ARN	GAC	Name (Bold Names Can Be Subdivided)
fst01208723	f-cg	**Congo (Democratic Republic)**
fst01240412	fg	Congo River
fst01343266	fg	Congo River Region
fst01273969	fg	Congo River Valley
fst01264815	fg	Congo River Watershed
fst01205688	n-us-ct	**Connecticut**
fst01207819	pocw	**Cook Islands**
fst01255823	u-cs	**Coral Sea Islands**
fst01205604	nccr	**Costa Rica**
fst01212674	e-ci	**Croatia**
fst01205805	nwcu	**Cuba**
fst01205241	nwco	**Curaçao**
fst01205213	a-cy	**Cyprus**
fst01692676	a-cy	Cyprus, Northern
fst01256743	e-xr	**Czech Republic**
fst01212490	c-cs	Czechoslovakia
fst01242328	eo	Danube River
fst01343449	eo	Danube River Region
fst01242332	eo	Danube River Valley
fst01264981	eo	Danube River Watershed
fst01427054	zd	**Deep Space**
fst01204929	n-us-de	**Delaware**
fst01204558	e-dk	**Denmark**
fst01294462	dd	Developed countries
fst01242969	d	Developing countries
fst01203974	f-ft	**Djibouti**
fst01202945	nwdq	**Dominica**
fst01206148	nwdr	**Dominican Republic**
fst01243607	x	Earth
fst01249209	n-usr	East (U.S.)
fst01243628	ae	East Asia
fst01243634	an	**East China Sea**
fst01343483	an	East China Sea Region
fst01733528	a-em	**Timor-Leste**
fst01243649	poea	**Easter Island**
fst01243653	xa	Eastern Hemisphere

Table A-2 (*continued*)

FAST ARN	GAC	Name (Bold Names Can Be Subdivided)
fst01205578	s-ec	**Ecuador**
fst01208755	f-ua	**Egypt**
fst01205530	nces	**El Salvador**
fst01219920	e-uk-en	**England**
fst01692693	e-uk-en	England, Eastern
fst01692645	e-uk-en	England, Northern
fst01692675	e-uk-en	England, Southern
fst01261775	x	English-speaking countries
fst01296648	w	Equator
fst01219325	f-eg	**Equatorial Guinea**
fst01266183	f-ea	**Eritrea**
fst01223630	e-er	**Estonia**
fst01205830	f-et	**Ethiopia**
fst01245058	me	Eurasia
fst01245064	e	**Europe**
fst01306854	e	Europe, Catalan-speaking regions
fst01244544	ec	Europe, Central
fst01245079	cc	Europe, Eastern
fst01692714	e	Europe, French-speaking
fst01692653	e	Europe, German-speaking
fst01692715	e	Europe, Italian-speaking
fst01245081	en	Europe, Northern
fst01245082	es	Europe, Southern
fst01272478	ew	Europe, Western
fst01204843	lnfa	**Faroe Islands**
fst01343836	lnfa	Faroe Islands Region
fst01208479	pofj	**Fiji**
fst01205503	e-fi	**Finland**
fst01692684	e-fi	Finland, Northern
fst01205150	n-us-fl	**Florida**
fst01298680	x	Former communist countries
fst01204289	e-fr	**France**
fst01692661	e-fr	France, Northern
fst01692692	e-fr	France, Southeast
fst01692608	e-fr	France, Southern
fst01692657	e-fr	France, Southwest

Table A-2 (*continued*)

FAST ARN	GAC	Name (*Bold Names Can Be Subdivided*)
fst01692679	e-fr	France, Western
fst01206832	s-fg	**French Guiana**
fst01260647	x	French overseas departments
fst01202933	pofp	**French Polynesia**
fst01253054	x	French-speaking countries
fst01205420	f-go	**Gabon**
fst01219610	pogg	**Galapagos Islands**
fst01692704	e-un	Galicia, Eastern
fst01202705	f-gm	**Gambia**
fst01240021	awgz	**Gaza Strip**
fst01204622	n-us-ga	**Georgia**
fst01221658	a-gs	**Georgia (Republic)**
fst01210272	e-gx	**Germany**
fst01210274	e-ge	Germany (East)
fst01210273	e-gw	Germany (West)
fst01692617	e-gx	Germany, Northern
fst01692618	e-gx	Germany, Southern
fst01208741	f-gh	**Ghana**
fst01215269	e-gi	**Gibraltar**
fst01715447	x	Gondwana (Continent)
fst01204623	e-uk	**Great Britain**
fst01345597	e-uk-ui	**Great Britain Miscellaneous Island Dependencies**
fst01240563	nl	Great Lakes
fst01258523	nl	Great Lakes Region
fst01265083	nl	Great Lakes Watershed
fst01240567	np	Great Plains
fst01240568	fr	Great Rift Valley
fst01208380	e-gr	**Greece**
fst01205290	n-gl	**Greenland**
fst01209745	nwgd	**Grenada**
fst01276312	x	Group of Seven countries
fst01292124	x	Group of Ten countries
fst01210394	nwgp	**Guadeloupe**
fst01202671	pogu	**Guam**
fst01205154	ncgt	**Guatemala**

Table A-2 (*continued*)

FAST ARN	GAC	Name (Bold Names Can Be Subdivided)
fst01206005	f-gv	**Guinea**
fst01208732	f-pg	**Guinea-Bissau**
fst01239980	nm	**Gulf of Mexico**
fst01347261	nm	Gulf of Mexico Region
fst01239974	af	**Gulf of Thailand**
fst01208722	s-gy	**Guyana**
fst01205135	nwht	**Haiti**
fst01208724	n-us-hi	**Hawaii**
fst01255824	i-hm	**Heard and McDonald Islands**
fst01242048	ah	Himalaya Mountains
fst01257195	ah	Himalaya Mountains Region
fst01242151	nwhi	**Hispaniola**
fst01206188	ncho	**Honduras**
fst01242900	n-cnh	**Hudson Bay**
fst01345671	n-cnh	Hudson Bay Region
fst01205132	e-hu	**Hungary**
fst01210572	e-ic	**Iceland**
fst01211709	n-us-id	**Idaho**
fst01205143	n-us-il	**Illinois**
fst01210276	a-ii	**India**
fst01692634	a-ii	India, Northeastern
fst01692635	a-ii	India, South
fst01243379	i	**Indian Ocean**
fst01243380	i	Indian Ocean Region
fst01204604	n-us-in	**Indiana**
fst01243485	xa	Indo-Australian Region
fst01243492	ai	**Indochina**
fst01209242	a-io	**Indonesia**
fst01243491	xa	Indo-Pacific Region
fst01205835	n-us-ia	**Iowa**
fst01204889	a-ir	**Iran**
fst01205757	a-iq	**Iraq**
fst01205427	e-ie	**Ireland**
fst01244130	x	Islamic countries
fst01244134	mm	Islamic Empire
fst01204236	a-is	**Israel**

Table A-2 (*continued*)

FAST ARN	GAC	Name (Bold Names Can Be Subdivided)
fst01204565	e-it	**Italy**
fst01692643	e-it	Italy, Northern
fst01692644	e-it	Italy, Southern
fst01211575	nwjm	**Jamaica**
fst01241438	lnjn	**Jan Mayen Island**
fst01204082	a-ja	**Japan**
fst01257257	poji	**Johnston Island**
fst01205669	a-jo	**Jordan**
fst01244812	zju	**Jupiter (Planet)**
fst01204323	n-us-ks	**Kansas**
fst01260664	a-kz	**Kazakhstan**
fst01204494	n-us-ky	**Kentucky**
fst01692695	n-us-ky	Kentucky, Northern
fst01208718	f-ke	**Kenya**
fst01245176	poki	**Kermadec Islands**
fst01212694	pokb	**Kiribati**
fst01206434	a-kr	Korea*
fst01214151	a-kn	**Korea (North)**
fst01206791	a-ko	**Korea (South)**
fst01695919	e-kv	**Kosovo (Republic)**
fst01208566	a-ku	**Kuwait**
fst01260659	a-kg	**Kyrgyzstan**
fst01348184	n	Lake Champlain Region
fst01244723	nl	**Lake Erie**
fst01348188	n	Lake Erie Region
fst01333782	nl	**Lake Huron**
fst01348192	n	Lake Huron Region
fst01239989	nl	**Lake Michigan**
fst01350983	nl	Lake Michigan Region
fst01265451	nl	Lake Michigan Watershed
fst01333795	nl	**Lake Ontario**
fst01348207	n	Lake Saint Clair Region
fst01245743	nl	Lake States
fst01245983	nl	**Lake Superior**
fst01348212	n	Lake Superior Region
fst01210322	a-ls	**Laos**

Table A-2 (*continued*)

FAST ARN	GAC	Name (Bold Names Can Be Subdivided)
fst01245945	cl	Latin America*
fst01210821	e-lv	**Latvia**
fst01715476	x	Laurentia (Continent)
fst01206063	a-le	**Lebanon**
fst01211571	nwli	Leeward Islands (Federation)
fst01240648	nwli	**Leeward Islands (West Indies)**
fst01208477	f-lo	**Lesotho**
fst01240020	nwla	**Lesser Antilles**
fst01205331	f-lb	**Liberia**
fst01205534	f-ly	**Libya**
fst01211042	e-lh	**Liechtenstein**
fst01259617	poln	**Line Islands**
fst01227863	e-li	**Lithuania**
fst01207035	n-us-la	**Louisiana**
fst01211813	e-lu	**Luxembourg**
fst01212818	e-xn	**Macedonia (Republic)**
fst01209332	f-mg	**Madagascar**
fst01202648	lnma	**Madeira Islands**
fst01204270	n-us-me	**Maine**
fst01209421	f-mw	**Malawi**
fst01219926	am	Malaya
fst01204590	a-my	**Malaysia**
fst01692624	a my	Malaysia, East
fst01216917	i-xc	**Maldives**
fst01204327	f-ml	**Mali**
fst01207170	e-mm	**Malta**
fst01205787	n-cn-mb	**Manitoba**
fst01233588	poxd	**Mariana Islands**
fst01243014	n-cnm	Maritime Provinces
fst01243063	zma	**Mars (Planet)**
fst01215147	poxe	**Marshall Islands**
fst01207564	nwmq	**Martinique**
fst01204739	n-us-md	**Maryland**
fst01692627	n-us-md	Maryland, Southern
fst01692628	n-us-md	Maryland, Western
fst01204307	n-us-ma	**Massachusetts**

Table A-2 (*continued*)

FAST ARN	GAC	Name (Bold Names Can Be Subdivided)
fst01205364	f-mu	**Mauritania**
fst01205325	i-mf	**Mauritius**
fst01216982	i-my	**Mayotte**
fst01239752	mm	Mediterranean Region†
fst01239753	mm	**Mediterranean Sea**
fst01239781	ag	Mekong River
fst01310764	ag	Mekong River Delta
fst01347260	ag	Mekong River Region
fst01273208	ag	Mekong River Valley
fst01264901	ag	Mekong River Watershed
fst01239785	pome	**Melanesia**
fst01239838	zme	**Mercury (Planet)**
fst01211700	n-mx	**Mexico**
fst01692664	n-mx	Mexico, North
fst01692663	n-mx	Mexico, Southeast
fst01208387	n-us-mi	**Michigan**
fst01240014	pott	**Micronesia**
fst01225345	pomi	**Micronesia (Federated States)**
fst01240044	n-usl	Middle Atlantic States
fst01241586	aw	**Middle East**
fst01347439	aw	Middle East Region
fst01240052	n-usc	Middle West
fst01240060	poxf	**Midway Islands**
fst01204560	n-us-mn	**Minnesota**
fst01207034	n-us-ms	**Mississippi**
fst01240238	n-usm	Mississippi River
fst01347506	n-usm	Mississippi River Region
fst01240240	n-usm	Mississippi River Valley
fst01265281	n-usm	Mississippi River Watershed
fst01204724	n-us-mo	**Missouri**
fst01240244	n-uss	Missouri River
fst01347525	n-uss	Missouri River Region
fst01274695	n-uss	Missouri River Valley
fst01264793	n-uss	Missouri River Watershed
fst01256791	e-mv	**Moldova**
fst01215184	e-mc	**Monaco**

Table A-2 (*continued*)

FAST ARN	GAC	Name (Bold Names Can Be Subdivided)
fst01208752	a-mp	**Mongolia**
fst01207555	n-us-mt	**Montana**
fst01692600	e-mo	**Montenegro**
fst01211569	nwmj	**Montserrat**
fst01240375	zmo	**Moon**
fst01205592	f-mr	**Morocco**
fst01214418	f-mz	**Mozambique**
fst01204890	f-sx	**Namibia**
fst01220266	ponu	**Nauru**
fst01208998	n-us-nb	**Nebraska**
fst01206102	a-np	**Nepal**
fst01241750	zne	**Neptune (Planet)**
fst01204034	e-ne	**Netherlands**
fst01204578	nwna	**Netherlands Antilles**
fst01205660	n-us-nv	**Nevada**
fst01212846	n-cn-nk	**New Brunswick**
fst01212756	ponl	**New Caledonia**
fst01241913	n-usn	New England
fst01241921	a-nw	**New Guinea**
fst01204318	n-us-nh	**New Hampshire**
fst01208379	n-us-nj	**New Jersey**
fst01204269	n-us-nm	**New Mexico**
fst01204788	u-at-ne	**New South Wales**
fst01203034	xd	New Spain
fst01210280	n-us-ny	**New York (State)**
fst01692701	n-us-ny	New York, Western
fst01204542	u-nz	**New Zealand**
fst01348096	u-nz	New Zealand Region
fst01296050	n-cn-nf	**Newfoundland and Labrador**
fst01228307	ncnq	**Nicaragua**
fst01205480	f-ng	**Niger**
fst01242127	fi	Niger River
fst01348161	fi	Niger River Region
fst01274780	fi	Niger River Valley
fst01265041	fi	Niger River Watershed
fst01205229	f-nr	**Nigeria**

Table A-2 (*continued*)

FAST ARN	GAC	Name (Bold Names Can Be Subdivided)
fst01692621	f-nr	Nigeria, Eastern
fst01692622	f-nr	Nigeria, Northern
fst01692678	f-nr	Nigeria, Southern
fst01692698	f-nr	Nigeria, Southwest
fst01692686	f-nr	Nigeria, Western
fst01242174	fl	Nile River
fst01348181	fl	Nile River Region
fst01274166	fl	Nile River Valley
fst01265050	fl	Nile River Watershed
fst01227610	poxh	**Niue**
fst01242475	n	**North America**
fst01692685	n	North America, French-speaking
fst01242477	ln	North Atlantic Ocean
fst01242478	ln	North Atlantic Region
fst01204304	n-us-nc	**North Carolina**
fst01205582	n-us-nd	**North Dakota**
fst01242497	pn	North Pacific Ocean
fst01304217	pn	North Pacific Region
fst01242521	n-use	Northeastern States
fst01274794	u-atn	Northern Australia
fst01245894	xb	Northern Hemisphere
fst01205215	e-uk-ni	**Northern Ireland**
fst01212709	u-at-no	**Northern Territory**
fst01229661	n-cn-nt	**Northwest Territories**
fst01204556	e-no	**Norway**
fst01692665	e-no	Norway, Northern
fst01206030	n-cn-ns	**Nova Scotia**
fst01287524	n-cn-nu	**Nunavut**
fst01242982	po	**Oceania**
fst01348408	po	Oceania Region
fst01277092	x	OECD countries
fst01205075	n-us-oh	**Ohio**
fst01243053	n-uso	Ohio River
fst01348409	n-uso	Ohio River Region
fst01243054	n-uso	Ohio River Valley
fst01265156	n-uso	Ohio River Watershed

Table A-2 (*continued*)

FAST ARN	GAC	Name (Bold Names Can Be Subdivided)
fst01205031	n-us-ok	**Oklahoma**
fst01212768	a-mk	**Oman**
fst01204832	n-cn-on	**Ontario**
fst01692688	n-cn-on	Ontario, Eastern
fst01692668	n-cn-on	Ontario, Northern
fst01692629	n-cn-on	Ontario, Southern
fst01692687	n-cn-on	Ontario, Southwestern
fst01204579	n-us-or	**Oregon**
fst01692690	n-us-or	Oregon, Eastern
fst01692691	n-us-or	Oregon, Western
fst01243437	zo	**Outer space**
fst01243504	p	Pacific Area
fst01225346	poup	**Pacific Islands (Trust Territory)**
fst01242543	n	Pacific Northwest
fst01243528	p	**Pacific Ocean**
fst01210275	a-pk	**Pakistan**
fst01215428	popl	**Palau**
fst01205585	ncpn	**Panama**
fst01715449	x	Pangaea (Supercontinent)
fst01212610	a-pp	**Papua New Guinea**
fst01243719	aopf	**Paracel Islands**
fst01205550	s-py	**Paraguay**
fst01692636	s-py	Paraguay, Eastern
fst01204598	n-us-pa	**Pennsylvania**
fst01244348	ap	**Persian Gulf**
fst01205190	s-pe	**Peru**
fst01205261	a-ph	**Philippines**
fst01207817	popc	**Pitcairn Island**
fst01710146	zpl	**Pluto (Dwarf planet)**
fst01206891	e-pl	**Poland**
fst01245645	x	Polar regions
fst01245821	pops	**Polynesia**
fst01208476	e-po	**Portugal**
fst01280614	x	Portuguese-speaking countries
fst01246004	n-cnp	Prairie Provinces
fst01241720	x	Prime Meridian

Table A-2 (*continued*)

FAST ARN	*GAC*	*Name (Bold Names Can Be Subdivided)*
fst01204804	n-cn-pi	**Prince Edward Island**
fst01692702	e	Prussia, East
fst01692703	e-pl	Prussia, West
fst01205432	nwpr	**Puerto Rico**
fst01239972	ep	Pyrenees
fst01205755	a-qa	**Qatar**
fst01207316	n-cn-qu	**Québec**
fst01204261	u-at-qn	**Queensland**
fst01205795	i-re	**Réunion**
fst01240414	mr	**Red Sea**
fst01349458	mr	Red Sea Region
fst01241013	er	Rhine River
fst01349460	er	Rhine River Region
fst01241015	er	Rhine River Valley
fst01265458	er	Rhine River Watershed
fst01204599	n-us-ri	**Rhode Island**
fst01241420	nr	Rocky Mountains
fst01349475	nr	Rocky Mountains Region
fst01205085	e-rm	**Romania**
fst01204885	x	Rome (Empire)
fst01207312	e-ur	Russia
fst01262050	e-ru	**Russia (Federation)**
fst01692646	e-ru	Russia, Northern
fst01692673	e-ru	Russia, Northwestern
fst01692670	e-ru	Russia, Southern
fst01692672	e-ru	Russia, Western
fst01212358	f-rw	**Rwanda**
fst01241948	nwsd	**Saba**
fst01242088	fd	Sahara
fst01230111	lsxj	**Saint Helena**
fst01349740	lsxj	Saint Helena Region
fst01211574	nwxi	**Saint Kitts and Nevis**
fst01204826	nwxk	**Saint Lucia**
fst01242135	nwst	**Saint Martin**
fst01223918	n-xl	**Saint Pierre and Miquelon**
fst01221750	nwxm	**Saint Vincent and the Grenadines**

Table A-2 (*continued*)

FAST ARN	*GAC*	*Name (Bold Names Can Be Subdivided)*
fst01281578	pows	**Samoa**
fst01242368	posh	**Samoan Islands**
fst01215789	e-sm	**San Marino**
fst01202978	f-sf	**Sao Tome and Principe**
fst01204834	n-cn-sn	**Saskatchewan**
fst01242721	zsa	**Saturn (Planet)**
fst01210372	a-su	**Saudi Arabia**
fst01242804	ev	Scandinavia
fst01206715	e-uk-st	**Scotland**
fst01204328	f-sg	**Senegal**
fst01692602	e-rb	**Serbia**
fst01299831	e-yu	Serbia and Montenegro
fst01205626	i-se	**Seychelles**
fst01692712	a-br	Shan States, Northern
fst01692713	a-br	Shan States, Southern
fst01692706	e-ru	Siberia, Eastern
fst01692707	e-ru	Siberia, Northeastern
fst01692711	e-ru	Siberia, Northwestern
fst01692708	e-ru	Siberia, Western
fst01210248	f-sl	**Sierra Leone**
fst01205288	a-si	**Singapore**
fst01264472	nweu	**Sint Eustatius**
fst01203007	e-xo	**Slovakia**
fst01212712	e-xv	**Slovenia**
fst01244288	zs	**Solar system**
fst01204144	pobp	**Solomon Islands**
fst01205351	f-so	**Somalia**
fst01204616	f-sa	**South Africa**
fst01244515	s	**South America**
fst01244520	az	South Asia
fst01244523	ls	South Atlantic Ocean
fst01350015	ls	South Atlantic Ocean Region
fst01206258	u-at-sa	**South Australia**
fst01204600	n-us-sc	**South Carolina**
fst01244526	ao	**South China Sea**
fst01350075	ao	South China Sea Region

Table A-2 (*continued*)

FAST ARN	GAC	Name (Bold Names Can Be Subdivided)
fst01204322	n-us-sd	**South Dakota**
fst01260107	lsxs	**South Georgia and South Sandwich Islands**
fst01226141	lsfk	**South Orkney Islands**
fst01244531	ps	South Pacific Ocean
fst01240499	as	Southeast Asia
fst01245895	xc	Southern Hemisphere
fst01244550	n-usu	Southern States
fst01244556	n-ust	Southwest, New
fst01210281	e-ur	Soviet Union‡
fst01692647	e-ur	Soviet Union, Northwestern
fst01692648	e-ur	Soviet Union, Southern
fst01692649	e-ur	Soviet Union, Western
fst01204303	e-sp	**Spain**
fst01692650	e-sp	Spain, Northern
fst01692651	e-sp	Spain, Southern
fst01244945	aoxp	**Spratly Islands**
fst01208730	a-ce	**Sri Lanka**
fst01204591	f-sj	**Sudan**
fst01244244	fn	Sudan Region
fst01245970	zsu	**Sun**
fst01204607	s-sr	**Suriname**
fst01207362	lnsb	**Svalbard**
fst01214603	f-sq	**Swaziland**
fst01204537	e-sw	**Sweden**
fst01205401	e-sz	**Switzerland**
fst01692658	e-sz	Switzerland, French-speaking
fst01692652	e-sz	Switzerland, German-speaking
fst01692619	e-sz	Switzerland, Italian-speaking
fst01208757	a-sy	**Syria**
fst01207854	a-ch	**Taiwan**
fst01260661	a-ta	**Tajikistan**
fst01210143	f-tz	**Tanzania**
fst01206536	u-at-tm	**Tasmania**
fst01205353	n-us-tn	**Tennessee**

Table A-2 (*continued*)

FAST ARN	*GAC*	*Name (Bold Names Can Be Subdivided)*
fst01692611	n-us-tn	Tennessee, East
fst01692612	n-us-tn	Tennessee, West
fst01220948	i-fs	**Terres australes et antarctiques françaises**
fst01210336	n-us-tx	**Texas**
fst01692613	n-us-tx	Texas, East
fst01692671	n-us-tx	Texas, South
fst01205310	a-th	**Thailand**
fst01692680	a-th	Thailand, Eastern
fst01692614	a-th	Thailand, Northeastern
fst01692615	a-th	Thailand, Northern
fst01692616	a-th	Thailand, Southern
fst01692705	a-tu	Thrace, Eastern
fst01692710	e-gr	Thrace, Western
fst01240111	at	Tien Shan
fst01208739	f-tg	**Togo**
fst01263375	potl	**Tokelau**
fst01209803	poto	**Tonga**
fst01211577	nwtr	**Trinidad and Tobago**
fst01273920	lstd	**Tristan da Cunha**
fst01240674	w	Tropics
fst01205477	f-ti	**Tunisia**
fst01208963	a-tu	**Turkey**
fst01692659	a-tu	Turkey, Eastern
fst01260658	a-tk	**Turkmenistan**
fst01215557	nwtc	**Turks and Caicos Islands**
fst01212693	potv	**Tuvalu**
fst01210282	f-ug	**Uganda**
fst01211738	e-un	**Ukraine**
fst01692681	e-un	Ukraine, Southern
fst01692620	e-un	Ukraine, Western
fst01205954	a-ts	**United Arab Emirates**
fst01208756	mm	United Arab Republic
fst01204155	n-us	**United States**
fst01241583	zur	**Uranus (Planet)**

Table A-2 (*continued*)

FAST ARN	GAC	Name (Bold Names Can Be Subdivided)
fst01202667	s-uy	**Uruguay**
fst01204563	n-us-ut	**Utah**
fst01260657	a-uz	**Uzbekistan**
fst01293325	x	Valdivia Group countries
fst01214612	ponn	**Vanuatu**
fst01208574	e-vc	**Vatican City**
fst01204166	s-ve	**Venezuela**
fst01692623	s-ve	Venezuela, Northeast
fst01242235	zve	**Venus (Planet)**
fst01204305	n-us-vt	**Vermont**
fst01205049	u-at-vi	**Victoria**
fst01204778	a-vt	**Vietnam**
fst01274298	a-vt	Vietnam (Republic)
fst01692682	a-vt	Vietnam, Northern
fst01692683	a-vt	Vietnam, Southern
fst01210255	nwvi	**Virgin Islands of the United States**
fst01204597	n-us-va	**Virginia**
fst01692694	n-us-va	Virginia, Northern
fst01692669	n-us-va	Virginia, Southwest
fst01259615	powk	**Wake Island**
fst01207649	e-uk-wl	**Wales**
fst01692625	e-uk-wl	Wales, North
fst01692626	e-uk-wl	Wales, South
fst01692696	e-uk-wl	Wales, West
fst01236920	powf	**Wallis and Futuna Islands**
fst01204505	n-us-dc	**Washington (D.C.)**
fst01243122	n-us-dc	Washington (D.C.) Metropolitan Area
fst01243124	n-us-dc	Washington (D.C.) Region
fst01243125	n-us-dc	Washington (D.C.) Suburban Area
fst01204703	n-us-wa	**Washington (State)**
fst01692699	n-us-wa	Washington, Eastern
fst01692700	n-us-wa	Washington, Western
fst01243255	n-usp	West (U.S.)
fst01243256	awba	**West Bank**
fst01243265	nw	**West Indies**

Table A-2 (*continued*)

FAST ARN	GAC	Name (Bold Names Can Be Subdivided)
fst01205316	n-us-wv	**West Virginia**
fst01206031	u-at-we	**Western Australia**
fst01302083	x	Western countries
fst01245897	xd	Western Hemisphere
fst01216405	f-ss	**Western Sahara**
fst01243427	nwwi	**Windward Islands**
fst01204595	n-us-wi	**Wisconsin**
fst01204583	n-us-wy	**Wyoming**
fst01243834	ay	**Yellow Sea**
fst01351585	ay	Yellow Sea Region
fst01309629	a-ye	**Yemen (Republic)**
fst01279262	e-yu	Yugoslavia
fst01207074	n-cn-yk	**Yukon Territory**
fst01243944	fz	Zambezi River
fst01351594	fz	Zambezi River Region
fst01275754	fz	Zambezi River Valley
fst01266344	fz	Zambezi River Watershed
fst01209422	f-za	**Zambia**
fst01209419	f-rh	**Zimbabwe**
fst01213323	a-yc	Aden

✦ This heading is subdividable for features such as coast lines, mountain ranges and demilitarized zones.

† This heading is subdividable for features such as islands, ancient cities and empires, and the Algeria Italy Natural Gas Pipeline.

‡ This heading is subdividable for works discussing collectively the independent countries that emerged from the dissolution of the former Soviet Union (former Soviet republics).

Table A-3 shows all the qualifiers used to qualify a geographic name by feature type. These qualifiers are used for disambiguation when the same name is used for different geographic features such as a city and a lake. For example, in Nunavut, Canada, there is a village named Baker Lake as well as a lake with the same name. To distinguish between the two Baker Lakes, (Lake) is added as a qualifier to form the heading **Nunavut—Baker Lake (Lake)**. The fact that a FAST geographic heading is qualified does not necessarily imply that without the qualifier there would be a conflict. As a general role, FAST headings will retain Library of Congress Subject Headings (LCSH) qualifiers even when it is not necessary to resolve a conflict.

Table A-3
Geographic Qualifiers.

FAST Qualifier	Description	Scope
Administrative region	Administrative division of various countries	
Air base	Military air base	
Airfield	Location where a variety of aviation operations take place	
Alcaldía Mayor	Municipality	Honduras and Mexico
Amphoe	District	Thailand
Amt	Township or county	Denmark, Germany, Switzerland
Amtsbezirk	District	Switzerland
Amusement park	Theme park created solely for entertainment purposes	
Ancient kingdom	Monarchical state that no longer exists	
Arrondissement	Municipality, county, district, city-section	
Āwraja	Province	Ethiopia
Bailliage	Area of jurisdiction of a bailiff	France
Barony	Administrative division generally below a county	Ireland, England, France, Scotland
Basketball camp		
Bay	Area of water mostly surrounded by land	
Beach	Geologic feature that occurs along the shore of a body of water	
Bürgergemeinde	Commune of citizens	Switzerland
Bezirk	District	Austria, Germany, Switzerland
Block	Subdistrict	Bangladesh and India
Bluff	Hill or cliff, often next to a body of water	
Borough	Township or section of a populated place	
Brook	Similar to creek	
Bucak	Subdistrict	Turkey
Camp	Often a historic military location	
Campground	Area designated for outdoor recreational activity	
Canal	An artificial channel of water	
Canton	District, township, or semi-sovereign state (Switzerland)	

Table A-3 (*continued*)

FAST Qualifier	Description	Scope
Canyon	Deep valley between cliffs	
Cape	A geographic feature similar to a peninsula	
Capitania-mór	District	Mozambique
Captaincy	State or province	Spanish and Portuguese Colonial Empires
Cave	Underground geographic feature	
Cemetery	An area for the burial of human remains	
Census division	Equivalent to county	Canada
Cercle	District, province, region	
Channel	Physical confines of a river or ocean strait	
Chiefdom	Society led by a chief	
City	Populated place	
Cliff	A vertical or near-vertical rock face	
Coast	Where an area of land meets a body of water	
Collective settlement	Populated place, usually based on utopian ideals	
Colonial jurisdiction	Administrative division of colonial governments	
Colony	Possession of a colonial empire	
Comarca	Region	
Commune	Township or municipality	
Comuna	ADM3 below county in Romania	
Concejo	Municipality	Spain
Concelho	County, municipality, district	
Condado	Parish	Spain
Contea	County	Medieval Italy
Contrada	District or ward within a city	Italy
Corregimiento	Country or district subdivision	
Coulee	Valley, gulch, ravine, and so forth	
County	District or municipality	
Creek	A small stream	
Dam	A natural or man-made feature that acts as a barrier to a body of water	
Daerah Istimewa	Special region	Indonesia
Deme	Municipality or community	Greece

Table A-3 (*continued*)

FAST Qualifier	Description	Scope
Department	State or province	
Desert	Region that is characterized as receiving little to no precipitation	
Diocese	Territory governed by a bishop	
District	County, township, or municipality	
District municipality	District	Canada
Division	An administrative division used in various countries	
Duchy	Territory ruled by a duke or duchess	
Ecclesiastical principality	State governed by a prince or princess	
Electorate	State, province, territory (ancient)	
Emirate	Territory ruled by a Muslim monarch	
Empire	Political entity composed of different states and territories under the control of a single ruler	
Eparchy	Province or district	Greece and Cyprus
Estate	Often used contemporaneously with farm	
Extinct city	Populated place, often from antiquity, that no longer exists	
Farm	Often used contemporaneously with estate	
Farmstead	Equivalent to farm	
Federation	Political entity made up of a group of semi-sovereign states	
Fjord	An inlet created by glacial activity	
Forest	Area characterized by a large concentration of trees	
Fort	Military, often denotes a historical place	
Fortress	Military, often denotes a historical place	
Fu	Prefecture	Tokyo, Japan
Fürstentum	Principality	
Généralité	Prefecture	*Ancien Regime,* France
Gemeente	Municipality	Netherlands
Gemeinde	Municipality or district	Germany and Austria
Gericht	Jurisdiction	Germany
Gerichtsbezirk	District or county	Austria and Germany

Table A-3 (*continued*)

FAST *Qualifier*	*Description*	*Scope*
Glacial lake	Lake formed from a melted glacier	
Glacier	Large, slow-moving concentration of ice	
Gmina	Municipality	Poland
Gobernación	Administrative division of the Spanish Empire below viceroyalty	
Graafschap	County or shire	Netherlands and Germany
Grafschaft	County	Germany
Grand duchy	Territory led by a monarch	
Grossgemeinde	Municipality	Germany
Guberniya	Governorate or province	Imperial Russia
Harbor	Body of water generally characterized as being safe for ships to dock within	
Hauptamt	District	Germany
Herad	Rural district or township	Denmark and Norway
Herred	Rural district or township	Denmark and Norway
Herrschaft	Feifdom of a lord	Feudal Germany, Switzerland, Austria
Hill	Similar to a mountain, though generally not as steep	
Hills		
Hundred	County subdivision	
İlçe	District	Turkey
Indian Territory	Territory given to Native American tribes for their exclusive use	United States and Canada
Inlet	Narrow body of water flowing between two separate land masses	
Intendancy	State, department, province, district	Colombia, Mexico, Peru
International Settlement	Foreign-controlled area in Shanghai until 1949	Formerly used in Shanghai, China
Island	An area of land completely surrounded by water	
Islands		
Judet	County	Romania
Judicial district	Area of judicial jurisdiction	
Kabupaten	Regency	Indonesia
Kampung	Village	Indonesia, Malaysia
Kaza	District	Turkey
Kecamatan	Subdistrict	Indonesia

Table A-3 (*continued*)

FAST Qualifier	Description	Scope
Ketjamatan	Suburban area	Indonesia
Kingdom	Territory ruled by a monarch	
Kirchengemeinde	Parish	Germany
Kirchspiel	Parish	Germany
Kommun	Parish or community	Sweden and Finland
Kommune	Parish or community	Norway and Denmark
Kotamadya	ADM2-level city	Indonesia
Kraj	Region	Czech Republic, Slovakia
Krajevna skupnost	Community	Slovenia
Kreis	District	Germany
Kunta	Municipality	Finland
Lagoon	Shallow body of water separated from an adjacent sea or ocean	
Lake	An inland body of water	
Lakes		
Land	State or province	Austria
Land district	Similar to region	
Landesbezirk	District	Germany
Landgerichts-bezirk	District	Germany
Landgrafschaft	State	Holy Roman Empire
Landgraviate	Territory of the Holy Roman Empire	
Landkreis	District, specifically rural districts	Germany
Landvogtei	Municipal confederation or township	Old Swiss Confederacy and Germany
Liva	Subprovince	Turkey
Local government area	District (ADM2)	Nigeria
Local government district	Similar to rural municipality	Manitoba, Canada
Magisterial district	Minor civil division	
Maakunta	Region	Finland
Mandalam	County	India
Marquisate	Principality or state	Italy
Margraviate	Principality or state	
Markaz	Region	Egypt
Marsh	Wetland characterized by frequent flooding	

Table A-3 (*continued*)

FAST Qualifier	Description	Scope
Meierij	Obsolete administrative unit	Netherlands
Mesa	Geographic feature characterized by steep cliffs on the side and a level top	
Military area	Area used for military purposes	
Mine	Place where resources are extracted from the ground	
Mountain	Landform that rises above the surrounding area, higher in elevation than a hill	
Mountains		
Mountain community	Equivalent to other ADM3s in Italy	Italy
Mountain pass	The point between two areas of higher elevation	
Municipal district	City, town, or village	
Municipality	Administrative division that includes a populated place or combination of populated places	
Munizipalge- meinde	Municipality	Switzerland
Natural bridge	Rock formation with an arch shape	
Neighborhood	A section of a populated place	
Nevado	Volcano	
Nome	Prefecture	Greece and Ancient Egypt
Oasis	Area of vegetation amid a desert climate	
Občina	Municipality	Slovenia
Oberamt	District	Germany
Oberlandesger- ichtsbezirk	District	Germany
Oblast	Province or region	Eastern Europe
Obshtina	Municipality	Bulgaria
Oilfield	Area of heavily concentrated oil wells	
Okres	District	Slovakia and Czech Republic
Okruha	Province or region	Ukraine
Općina	Municipality	Croatia

Table A-3 (*continued*)

FAST Qualifier	Description	Scope
Opština	District	Used, formerly, in Bosnia and Hercegovina
Pagasts	Equivalent to rural municipality	Latvia
Parish	Administrative area of a civil government, or area governed by a church	
Park	Place designated as a recreational area	
Partido	Municipality	Argentina (unique to Buenos Aires Province)
Partido judicial	Judicial district	Spain
Peninsula	Area of land surrounded by water on three sides	
Pfarramt	Ecclesiastical parish	Germany
Pillar	Geologic formation, often found undersea	
Plain	Flat area of land	
Planned community	Community carefully planned and developed from its inception	
Plantation	Similar to an estate or farm, but generally larger	
Plateau	Area of land characterized by flat terrain and high altitude	
Plaza	Urban public space	
Politischer bezirk	Political district	Austria
Powiat	County, district, or prefecture	Poland
Proposed homeland	Area advocated for by various political parties and factions	South Africa
Provisional government	Generally an interim government established in the wake of the collapse of the previous governmental structure	
Prefecture	Generally equivalent to province, state, or department	
Preserve	Nature reserve	
Presidency	Administrative division of British India	India
Princely state	State ruled by a prince under the auspices of a colonial government	
Principality	State ruled by a prince or princess	
Province	State, department (generally an ADM1)	
Provincial district	Province	New Zealand
Qi	County	Inner Mongolia Autonomous Region of China

Table A-3 (*continued*)

FAST *Qualifier*	*Description*	*Scope*
Quận	District, county	Vietnam
Quarter	Generally a section of a populated place	
Railroad bridge	Bridge used exclusively for train traffic	
Raionul	District	Moldova
Ranch	Area set aside for raising various types of livestock	
Rapids	Section of a river where water velocity and turbulence increase	
Refugee camp	Camp created to temporarily house refugees	
Regierungsbezirk	Roughly equivalent to province	Germany
Region	Geographic term used to describe areas of land or sea, or used as a designation for an administrative unit designation for an administrative unit	
Regional county municipality	Census division unique to Quebec, Canada	
Regional district	ADM2 in Canada (exclusive to British Columbia)	
Regional municipality	District or county	Canada
Reichsgau	State	Exclusive to Areas Annexed by Nazi Germany
Reino	Kingdom, province	Spain
Religious community	Community of people who share a particular religious belief	
Republic	Form of government where head of state is not a monarch	
Reserve	Generally refers to nature reserve or Indian reserve	
Reservoir	Often used to describe an artificial lake	
Residency	Administrative division used in the Dutch East Indies	Indonesia
Ridge	Geologic formation characterized by increasing elevation over a significant distance	
River	Natural body of water that often flows into a sea, ocean, lake, or larger body of water	
Rock	Geologic formation	
Rrethi	District	Albania

Table A-3 (*continued*)

FAST *Qualifier*	*Description*	*Scope*
Rural district	Former administrative division under counties in England, Ireland, and Wales	
Rural municipality	County or township	Canada
Rural sanitary district	Now referred to as rural districts	England
Sancak	ADM1 of Ottoman Empire	Ottoman Empire/ Turkey
Savanna	Similar to a plain but characterized by a significant number of woodland elements	
Section	Generally a section of a populated place	
Seigneurie	Synonym of Seigniory	
Seigniory	Semi-feudal system used in French American colonies	
Sénéchaussée	Royal judicial district	*Ancien Regime,* France
Shahristan	Province	Iran
Sheriffdom	Judicial district	Scotland and Canada
Shire	County (Ireland, England) or municipality, township (Australia)	
Slope	Geographic Feature	
Special administrative region	Autonomous subnational area	China
Springs	Natural source of water	
Srez	District	Serbia
Srŏk	District	Cambodia
Stadtkreis	Urban district	Germany
Standesherrschaft	Roughly equivalent to duchy	Germany
State	Province, department (generally an ADM1)	
Street	Area designated for pedestrian or vehicular traffic	
Subdistrict	Administrative division of various levels depending on country	
Subdivision	ADM3 below districts	Bangladesh and India
Subprefecture	District, county, township	Central African Republic, Rwanda, Cote d'Ivoire
Subregion	District	Congo (Democratic Republic)

Table A-3 (*continued*)

FAST *Qualifier*	*Description*	*Scope*
Sultanate	Area of land ruled by a sultan (a Muslim ruler)	
Tahsil	County	India and Pakistan
Taluk	County	India and Pakistan
Taluka	County	India and Pakistan
Tehsil	County	India and Pakistan
Territory	Administrative division with, generally, less autonomy than an ADM1	
Thana	Police station or precinct	Bangladesh
Theme	Primary administrative division of the Byzantine Empire	
Town	Populated place	
Townland	Administrative division below a county in Ireland	
Township	Also a municipality	
Trading post	Place where the trading of goods takes place	
Trail	Path generally used for walking and hiking	
Union territory	State governed directly by the federal government	India
Upazila	Subdivision	Bangladesh
Urban commune	Community situated in an urban area	
Valley	Geologic feature	
Verbandsge-meinde	Roughly equivalent to township	Rhineland-Palatinate in Germany
Verwaltungs-bezirk	District or county	Austria
Viceroyalty	Form of government used, generally, in Spanish colonial possessions	
Vicomté	Synonym for viscounty	
Vilâyet	Province or governorate	
Village	Populated place	
Viscounty	Territory controlled be a viscount	Feudal Europe
Vogtei	Municipal confederation or township	Germany
Voivodeship	Province	Poland
Volcano	An opening in a planet's surface allowing magma, lava, and so forth to rise to the surface	

Table A-3 (*continued*)

FAST Qualifier	Description	Scope
Volost	District	Belarus, Russian Federation, Ukraine
Wadi	Valley	
Waterfall	Area where flowing water drops in elevation rapidly	
Waterfalls		
Wilaya	Province, governorate, or district	
Zent	Court with autonomous jurisdiction	Germany
Zone	Administrative division of various levels depending on country (ADM1–ADM3)	
Županija	County	Croatia

Table A-4 lists the feature types used in the 670 fields of the FAST authority records. The abbreviated form of these feature types are also the values used to search the FAST database for geographic feature. The full name for the feature type is given in the first column and its abbreviated or brief form is given in the second column. The description is provided in the third column.

Although the qualifiers shown in Table A-3 and the feature types in Table A-4 are similar, they are derived from different sources: the qualifiers are derived from LCSH, while the feature types are those used by GeoNames. Some entries, such as "Valley," appear in both tables, while others appear in only one of the tables.

The two tables also are used very differently. The qualifiers are used to validate geographic headings. Geographic names can be qualified by a place or by a type to differentiate names, and the syntax of the type and place qualifiers are identical. Any qualifier listed in Table A-3 is assumed to be a feature type, while the qualifiers not listed in the table are assumed to be a place. However, qualifiers are not a reliable way to identify all occurrences of authority records for that type of feature, since a qualifier is added only to an authorized heading when a conflict or potential conflicts exist rather than to all headings belonging to that feature type.

By contrast, the feature types listed in Table A-4 are added to all geographic authority records where the feature type can be identified. All of the feature types used by GeoNames are included in the table even though some of the feature types—"Hospital," "School," and so forth—are not considered to be geographic features in LCSH or FAST.

Table A-4
Geographic Feature Types

Geographic Feature Types	Abbreviated Feature Types	Description
First-order administrative division	ADM1	A primary administrative division of a country, such as a state, province, or region.
Second-order administrative division	ADM2	A subdivision of a first-order administrative division, such as a county.
Third-order administrative division	ADM3	A subdivision of a second-order administrative division, often a township.
Unspecified administrative division—civil	Civil	A political division formed for administrative purposes (borough, county, incorporated place, *municipio*, parish, town, township) with legally defined boundaries. See also **Census** and **Populated place** classes. Used only when the ADM level is not known.
Country or political entity	PCL	Country or similar political entity that may or may not be independent.
Airport	Airport	Man-made facility maintained for the use of aircraft (airfield, airstrip, landing field, landing strip).
Ancient	Ancient	Extinct cities or countries.
Arch	Arch	Natural archlike opening in a rock mass (bridge, natural bridge, sea arch).
Region or area	Region	A general area associated with a city or natural feature, or any one of several spatially extensive natural features not included in other categories (badlands, barren, delta, fan, garden).
Arroyo	Arroyo	Watercourse or channel through which water may occasionally flow (coulee, draw, gully, wash).
Bar	Bar	Natural accumulation of sand, gravel, or alluvium forming an underwater or exposed embankment (ledge, reef, sandbar, shoal, spit).
Basin	Basin	Natural depression or relatively low area enclosed by higher land (amphitheater, cirque, pit, sink).
Bay	Bay	Indentation of a coastline or shoreline enclosing a part of a body of water; a body of water partly surrounded by land (arm, bight, cove, estuary, gulf, inlet, sound).
Beach	Beach	The sloping shore along a body of water that is washed by waves or tides and is usually covered by sand or gravel (coast, shore, strand).
Bench	Bench	Area of relatively level land on the flank of an elevation such as a hill, ridge, or mountain where the slope of the land rises on one side and descends on the opposite side (level).

Table A-4 (*continued*)

Geographic Feature Types	Abbreviated Feature Types	Description
Bend	Bend	Curve in the course of a stream and (or) the land within the curve; a curve in a linear body of water (bottom, loop, meander).
Bridge	Bridge	Man-made structure carrying a trail, road, or other transportation system across a body of water or depression (causeway, overpass, trestle).
Building	Building	A man-made structure with walls and a roof for protection of people and (or) materials, but not including church, hospital, or school.
Canal	Canal	Manmade waterway used by watercraft or for drainage, irrigation, mining, or water power (ditch, lateal).
Cape	Cape	Projection of land extending into a body of water (lea, neck, peninsula, point).
Cave	Cave	Natural underground passageway or chamber, or a hollowed out cavity in the side of a cliff (cavern, grotto).
Cemetery	Cemetery	A place or area for burying the dead (burial, burying ground, grave, memorial garden).
Census	Census	A statistical area delineated locally specifically for the tabulation of Census Bureau data (census designated place, census county division, unorganized territory, various types of American Indian/Alaska Native statistical areas). See also **Populated place** class.
Channel	Channel	Linear deep part of a body of water through which the main volume of water flows and is frequently used as a route for watercraft (passage, reach, strait, thoroughfare, throughfare).
Church	Church	Building used for religious worship (chapel, mosque, synagogue, tabernacle, temple).
Cliff	Cliff	Very steep or vertical slope (bluff, crag, head, headland, nose, palisades, precipice, promontory, rim, rimrock).
Crater	Crater	Circular-shaped depression at the summit of a volcanic cone or one on the surface of the land caused by the impact of a meteorite; a man-made depression caused by an explosion (caldera, lua).
Crossing	Crossing	A place where two or more routes of transportation form a junction or intersection (overpass, underpass).
Dam	Dam	Water barrier or embankment built across the course of a stream or into a body of water to control and (or) impound the flow of water (breakwater, dike, jetty).
Falls	Falls	Perpendicular or very steep fall of water in the course of a stream (cascade, cataract, waterfall).
Flat	Flat	Relatively level area within a region of greater relief (clearing, glade, playa).

Table A-4 (*continued*)

Geographic Feature Types	Abbreviated Feature Types	Description
Forest	Forest	Bounded area of woods, forest, or grassland under the administration of a political agency (see **Woods**) (national forest, national grasslands, state forest).
Gap	Gap	Low point or opening between hills or mountains or in a ridge or mountain range (col, notch, pass, saddle, water gap, wind gap).
Geyser	Geyser	A type of hot spring with intermittent eruptions of jets of hot water and steam.
Glacier	Glacier	Body or stream of ice moving outward and downslope from an area of accumulation; an area of relatively permanent snow or ice on the top or side of a mountain or mountainous area (icefield, ice patch, snow patch).
Gut	Gut	Relatively small coastal waterway connecting larger bodies of water or other waterways (creek, inlet, slough).
Harbor	Harbor	Sheltered area of water where ships or other watercraft can anchor or dock (hono, port, roads, roadstead).
Hospital	Hospital	Building where the sick or injured may receive medical or surgical attention (infirmary).
Island	Island	Area of dry or relatively dry land surrounded by water or low wetland (archipelago, atoll, cay, hammock, hummock, isla, isle, key, moku, rock).
Isthmus	Isthmus	Narrow section of land in a body of water connecting two larger land areas.
Lake	Lake	Natural body of inland water (backwater, lac, lagoon, *laguna*, pond, pool, resaca, waterhole).
Lava	Lava	Formations resulting from the consolidation of molten rock on the surface of the Earth (kepula, lava flow).
Levee	Levee	Natural or manmade embankment flanking a stream (bank, berm).
Locale	Locale	Place at which there is or was human activity; it does not include populated places, mines, and dams (battlefield, crossroad, camp, farm, landing, railroad siding, ranch, ruins, site, station, windmill).
Military	Military	Place or facility used for various aspects of or relating to military activity.
Mine	Mine	Place or area from which commercial minerals are or were removed from the earth; not including oilfield (pit, quarry, shaft).
Oilfield	Oilfield	Area where petroleum is or was removed from the earth.
Park	Park	Place or area set aside for recreation or preservation of a cultural or natural resource and under some form of government administration; not including national or state forests or reserves (national historical landmark, national park, state park, wilderness area).

Table A-4 (*continued*)

Geographic Feature Types	Abbreviated Feature Types	Description
Pillar	Pillar	Vertical, standing, often spire-shaped, natural rock formation (chimney, monument, pinnacle, *pohaku,* rock tower).
Plain	Plain	A region of general uniform slope, comparatively level and of considerable extent (grassland, highland, *kula,* plateau, upland).
Populated place	ppl	Place or area with clustered or scattered buildings and a permanent human population (city, settlement, town, village). See also **Census.**
Section of populated place	pplx	A section or subdivision of a populated place.
Post office	post office	An official facility of a postal service used for processing and distributing mail and other postal material.
Range	Range	Chain of hills or mountains; a somewhat linear, complex mountainous or hilly area (cordillera, sierra).
Rapids	Rapids	Fast-flowing section of a stream, often shallow and with exposed rock or boulders (riffle, ripple).
Reserve	Reserve	A tract of land set aside for a specific use (does not include forests, civil divisions, parks).
Reservoir	Reservoir	Artificially impounded body of water (lake, tank).
Ridge	Ridge	Elevation with a narrow, elongated crest which can be part of a hill or mountain (crest, *cuesta,* escarpment, hogback, *lae,* rim, spur).
School	School	Building or group of buildings used as an institution for study, teaching, and learning (academy, college, high school, university).
Sea or ocean	Sea	Large body of salt water (gulf, ocean).
Archaeological site	Site	Archaeological or historical site.
Slope	Slope	A gently inclined part of the Earth's surface (grade, pitch).
Spring	Spring	Place where underground water flows naturally to the surface of the Earth (geyser, seep).
Stream	Stream	Linear body of water flowing on the Earth's surface (anabranch, *awawa,* bayou, branch, brook, creek, distributary, fork, kill, pup, rio, river, run, slough).
Summit or mountain	Summit	Prominent elevation rising above the surrounding level of the Earth's surface; does not include pillars, ridges, or ranges (*ahu,* berg, bald, butte, *cerro, colina,* cone, *cumbre,* dome, head, hill, horn, knob, knoll, *mauna,* mesa, *mesita,* mound, mount, mountain, peak, *puu,* rock, sugarloaf, table, volcano).

Table A-4 (*continued*)

Geographic Feature Types	Abbreviated Feature Types	Description
Swamp	Swamp	Poorly drained wetland, fresh or saltwater, wooded or grassy, possibly covered with open water (bog, *cienega, marais,* marsh, *pocosin*).
Tower	Tower	A man-made structure, higher than its diameter, generally used for observation, storage, or electronic transmission.
Trail	Trail	Route for passage from one point to another; does not include roads or highways (jeep trail, path, ski trail).
Tunnel	Tunnel	Linear underground passageway open at both ends.
Other	Other	A feature class that cannot be chosen at this time.
Unknown	Unknown	This class is assigned to legacy data only. It will not be assigned to new or edited records.
Undersea	Undersea	Any undersea geological feature.
Valley	Valley	Linear depression in the Earth's surface that generally slopes from one end to the other (*barranca,* canyon, chasm, cove, draw, glen, gorge, gulch, gulf, hollow, ravine).
Well	Well	Man-made shaft or hole in the Earth's surface used to obtain fluid or gaseous materials.
Woods	Woods	Small area covered with a dense growth of trees; does not include an area of trees under the administration of a political agency (see **Forest**).
Watershed	Watershed	Area drained by a river or stream.
Road	Road	Roads or streets, and similar features such as squares, plazas, and so forth.
Coast	Coast	Shore of a sea or ocean.
Farm	Farm	Include ranch or similar place of agricultural production.
Geology	Geology	The subsurface of the Earth.
Space	Space	Any feature not on the Earth.

APPENDIX D: MUSICAL INSTRUMENTS

When an LCSH heading includes a list of musical instruments, both the form of the instrument name and the order of the instruments in the list is specified. FAST requires this same order. In Table A-5, each instrument is assigned a four-digit sequence number. The first digit identifies the general instrument class:

1. Keyboard
2. Winds
3. Plucked
4. Percussion and electronic
5. Strings
6. Unspecified and continuo

The last three digits represent the order of the instrument within the group; the particular value is somewhat arbitrary. Gaps were left in the numbering so that as additional instruments are identified, they can easily be inserted into the sequence. This table includes the common instruments, but not every possible instrument. This table is used to validate the instrument lists in FAST headings. There are two requirements for validation: (1) each instrument must match a name in the list and (2) the names must be in ascending order by sequence number. The singular and plural names are assigned the same sequence number to prevent both the singular and plural forms of the name from appearing in the same instrument list.

Table A-5
Musical Instruments

Sequence Number	Established Instrument Name	Sequence Number	Established Instrument Name
4010	Accordion	4080	Bells
4010	Accordions	2150	Birbynės
2010	Alphorn	3050	Biwa
2020	Alto flute	3050	Biwas
2030	Alto horn	2160	Bugle
2040	Alto saxophone	2160	Bugles
2040	Alto saxophones	4090	Calliope
2050	Alto trombone	4110	Carillon
1010	Archiphone	4115	Castanets
5090	Arpeggione	4120	Celesta
2070	Bagpipes	4125	Chimes
3010	Balalaika	3060	Chitarrone
3010	Balalaikas	3070	Cimbalom
4030	Bandoneon	3070	Cimbaloms
3020	Bandora	3080	Cittern
3030	Banjo	2170	Clarinet
3030	Banjos	2170	Clarinets
2060	Bānsurĭ	1020	Clavichord
2080	Baritone	1020	Clavichords
2080	Baritones	3090	Colascione
4050	Barrel organ	4130	Computer
5100	Baryton	4140	Concertina
2090	Bass clarinet	6020	Continuo
2090	Bass clarinets	2180	Contrabassoon
4060	Bass drum	2180	Contrabassoons
2100	Bass flute	2190	Cornet
3040	Bass guitar	2190	Cornets
2110	Bass trombone	2200	Cornett
2120	Basset clarinet	2200	Cornetts
2130	Basset horn	2210	Crumhorn
2130	Basset horns	2210	Crumhorns
2140	Bassoon	4150	Cymbals
2140	Bassoons	2220	Czakan
4070	Bayan	2230	Didjeridu
4070	Bayans	3100	Dobro

Table A-5 (*continued*)

Sequence Number	Established Instrument Name	Sequence Number	Established Instrument Name
2550	Di Zi	3150	Gottuvadyam
5120	Double bass	3160	Guitar
5120	Double basses	3160	Guitars
4160	Drum	4220	Handbell
2240	Dulcian	4220	Handbells
3110	Dulcimer	5012	Hardanger fiddle
3120	Dutār	5012	Hardanger fiddles
3130	Electric bass	4230	Harmonica
3140	Electric guitar	4230	Harmonicas
3140	Electric guitars	3170	Harp
1030	Electronic harpsichord	3170	Harps
1030	Electronic harpsichords	1070	Harpsichord
		1070	Harpsichords
1040	Electronic keyboard	3180	Hawaiian guitar
1050	Electronic organ	2310	Heckelphone
1050	Electronic organs	2320	Horn
1060	Electronic piano	2320	Horns
4170	Electronics	4260	Hurdy-gurdy
4190	Electronium	4270	Jawbone
2250	English horn	4280	Jew's harp
2250	English horns	3190	Kankles
5140	Er hu	3200	Kayagæum
2260	Euphonium	1080	Keyboard instrument
2260	Euphoniums	1080	Keyboard instruments
2270	Fifes	5150	Keyed fiddle
2280	Flageolet	3210	Koto
2290	Flügelhorn	3210	Kotos
2290	Flügelhorns	3220	Lute
2300	Flute	3220	Lutes
2300	Flutes	5110	Lyra viol
4200	Ghatam	3230	Mandoloncello
4205	Glass harmonica	3240	Mandola
4210	Glockenspiel	3250	Mandolin
4215	Gong		

Table A-5 (*continued*)

Sequence Number	Established Instrument Name	Sequence Number	Established Instrument Name
3250	Mandolins	2450	Ryūteki
4285	Maracas	2460	Sackbut
4290	Marimba	2460	Sackbuts
4290	Marimbas	3300	Santūr
4300	Melodica	3310	Sarod
4332	Mridanga	2470	Saxhorn
2330	Nāy	2470	Saxhorns
2350	Oboe	2480	Saxophone
2340	Oboe d'amore	2480	Saxophones
2350	Oboes	2490	Serpent
2340	Oboi d'amore	2490	Serpents
2360	Ocarina	2500	Shakuhachi
2360	Ocarinas	2500	Shakuhachis
4330	Ondes Martenot	3320	Shamisen
2370	Ophicleide	2520	Shawm
1090	Organ	2530	Shehnai
1090	Organs	3330	Sheng
3260	Oud	2535	Shō
2380	P'iri	3340	Sitar
2390	Panpipes	3340	Sitars
5040	Pardessus de viole	4340	Snare drum
2400	Penny whistle	4340	Snare drums
4335	Percussion	2540	Sousaphone
1100	Piano	2540	Sousaphones
1100	Pianos	3350	Surbahar
2410	Piccolo	4350	Synthesizer
2410	Piccolos	4350	Synthesizers
2420	Pipes	4360	Tabla
3270	Poi poa	4360	Tablas
2430	Post horn	4362	Tambourin
3280	Psaltery	4365	Tambourine
3290	Qānūn	3360	Tambura
2440	Recorder	4368	Tam-tam
2440	Recorders	3370	Theorbo
1110	Reed organ	3370	Theorbos

Table A-5 (*continued*)

Sequence Number	Established Instrument Name	Sequence Number	Established Instrument Name
4370	Theremin	5080	Viol
4380	Timpani	5030	Viola
4390	Trautonium	5070	Viola da gamba
4400	Triangle	5020	Viola d'amore
2560	Trombone	5030	Violas
2560	Trombones	5070	Viole da gamba
2570	Trumpet	5015	Violetta d'amore
2570	Trumpets	5010	Violin
2580	Tuba	5010	Violins
2580	Tubas	5060	Violoncello
4410	Tubular bells	5050	Violoncello piccolo
6010	Unspecified instrument	5060	Violoncellos
6010	Unspecified instruments	5130	Violone
		5080	Viols
4420	Vibraphone	4430	Whistles
4420	Vibraphones	4410	Xylophone
3380	Vihuela	4450	Xylorimba
		3390	Yang qin
		3400	Zithers

GLOSSARY

Associative reference. See **Related term reference**.

*****Authority file.** A file containing individual **authority records** for established **name headings** or **subject headings** and **subdivisions**.

*****Authority record.** A record that contains the established form of a **name heading,** a **subject heading,** or a **subdivision,** a list of cross-references made to the heading or subdivision from alternative or related forms, and a list of sources that justify the established and alternative forms. See also **Name authority record**; **Subject authority record**.

*****Broader term reference (BT).** A reference from one **subject heading** to another subject heading that is at a higher level in a hierarchy and is therefore a more inclusive term. See also **Hierarchical reference**; **Narrower term reference**.

BT. See **Broader term reference**.

Controlled vocabulary. A controlled vocabulary is a list of terms designed to be used to indicate document content. Such a vocabulary contains no synonyms except as pointers (called lead-in terms) to preferred terms, for example, "Laissez-faire *use* Free enterprise." Good controlled vocabulary lists include an extensive cross-reference structure, leading searchers to broader and narrower terms and to terms related to their search terms non-hierarchically.

Cross-reference. A direction from one term or heading to another in the catalog. See also **Explanatory reference**; **Hierarchical reference**; **Related term reference**; **Use reference (USE)**.

Depth indexing. See **In-depth indexing**.

Enumeration. Listing precombined subject headings or index terms for compound or complex subjects in a subject headings list or thesaurus. See also **Precoordination**; **Synthesis**.

Equivalence reference. See **Use reference**.

Exhaustive indexing. The practice of assigning indexing terms or subject headings to represent all significant concepts or aspects of a subject. See also **In-depth indexing**; **Summarization**.

Explanatory reference. A reference providing explanatory statements with regard to the heading involved. It is used when a simple reference does not give adequate information or guidance to the user.

Facet. Any of the various terms or classes into which a given category in a controlled vocabulary or classification scheme may be divided (e.g., division of the class "literature" into language, genre, time period, theme, etc.). Each facet contains terms based on a single characteristic of division (e.g., poetry, drama, fiction, prose, etc. in the genre facet).

Facet analysis. The division of a subject into its component parts (**facets**). Each array of facets consists of parts based on the same characteristic (e.g., language facet, space facet, time facet).

First-level geographic heading. See **Geographic heading**.

*Form. The physical, bibliographical, artistic, or literary nature of a work.

*Form heading. A type of **subject heading** that expresses what a work *is* (in contrast to what it is *about*), such as "Dictionaries," "Law reports, digests, etc.," "Large type books," and so forth.

Full-text systems. Systems that search all words in a given document. Much of Internet-accessible material is in full text—in other words, all the words in a given document are there to be read. GoogleBooks, for instance, contains the full text of a high fraction of the collections of many major libraries. When queries come in, Google searches for term matches on full text, but its reported listings are **surrogates**.

Geographic heading. A name heading representing a place or an entity closely associated with a place (e.g., a park, a forest, a tunnel, etc.). A geographic heading may contain up to three levels, beginning with the largest area that represents or contains the place in question. The first-level heading normally consists of the name of a country or a larger area. The second-level heading represents a geographic entity that lies within, or is part of, a first-level geographic entity. The third-level heading, the lowest level, represents the geographic entity in question; examples include: city sections, neighborhoods, highway interchanges, sites within a city, geographic features within a city, and so forth. See also **Jurisdictional name heading**; **Nonjurisdictional name heading**.

*Geographic qualifier. The name of a larger geographic entity added in parentheses after the name of a more specific locality or other entity to designate its location, as in the subject headings "Whitney, Mount (Calif.)"; "Gobi Desert (Mongolia and China)"; "Colorado River (Colo.-Mexico)"; and "Empire State Building (New York, N.Y.)."

Geographic subdivision. A type of **subdivision** that, in FAST, consists of the name of a place within a larger place represented by the main heading or subdivision preceding it. A geographic heading may contain one or two geographic subdivisions. Also called **local subdivision**. See also **Geographic heading**.

Hierarchical reference. A **cross-reference** connecting headings on different levels of a hierarchy. See also **Broader term reference**; **Narrower term reference**; **Related term reference**.

In-depth indexing. The practice of assigning indexing terms or subject headings to represent individual parts of a publication. See also **Exhaustive indexing**; **Summarization**.

*Individual biography. A biography of one person.

*Inverted heading. A heading that consists of a noun modified by an adjective, formulated to place the noun in the initial position followed by a comma and the adjective.

Jurisdictional name heading. A **geographic heading** representing a political or ecclesiastical jurisdiction. Entities that belong to this category include countries, principalities, territories, states, provinces, counties, administrative districts, cities, archdioceses, and dioceses. Jurisdictional name headings are established in accordance with *Anglo-American Cataloguing Rules,* second edition revised (AACR2R).

Keywords. Natural-language terms used in searching full-text resources. Keyword searching is distinguished from controlled-vocabulary searching, especially in studies of search effectiveness.

*Library of Congress Subject Headings. The printed list of headings produced from the **subject authority file** maintained by the Library of Congress and published annually. The term is frequently abbreviated as LCSH and is sometimes used interchangeably with the term *subject authority file.*

Literary warrant. The use of an actual collection of material or body of literature as the basis for developing an indexing or classification system. In the case of LCSH, the literary warrant is the Library of Congress collection.

Local subdivision. See **Geographic subdivision.**

*Name authority file. A file containing individual **name authority records.** As used in this book, this term refers specifically to the name authority file created and maintained by the Library of Congress with contributions from participating libraries.

*Name authority record. An **authority record** for a **name heading.**

*Name heading. A heading that is a personal name, corporate name, meeting name, or geographic name.

*Narrower term reference (NT). A reference to a **subject heading** at a lower level in a hierarchy than the term referred from. Narrower term references do not appear in **subject authority records,** but are generated by automated systems as the reciprocals of **broader term references**.

Nonjurisdictional name heading. A geographic heading representing an entity other than a jurisdiction. Typical nonjurisdictional name headings include those for rivers, mountains, parks, roads, and so forth.

OPACs. The acronym for Online Public Access Catalogs, the term used for modern library catalogs.

Postcoordination. The representation of a complex subject by assigning separate single-concept terms at the indexing stage and the retrieval of that subject through combining the separate terms at the search or retrieval stage. Also called a coordinate system. See also **Precoordination.**

Precoordination. The representation of a complex subject by means of combining separate elements of the subject in the subject headings list or thesaurus or at the indexing stage. See also **Postcoordination.**

Qualifier. A term (enclosed in parentheses) placed after a heading to distinguish between two different meanings of an identical term or to clarify the meaning of the heading, as in the subject headings "Plates (Engineering)"; "Plates (Tableware)"; "BASIC (Computer program language)"; "Adonis (Greek deity)" or clarifying the meaning of the heading— for example, "Jive *(Dance)*"; "Juno *(Roman deity)*"; "New York *(State)*."

Reference. See **Cross-reference.**

*Related term reference. A reference from one **subject heading** to another subject heading that is in a different hierarchy.

RT. See **Related term reference.**

Second-level geographic heading. See **Geographic heading.**

*See also reference. See **Related term reference.**

*See reference. See **Use reference.**

*Subdivision. The portion of a subject heading string that is used to identify a specific aspect of the main **subject heading,** such as form, subtopic, time period, or place.

*Subheading. The portion of a corporate body name heading that is subordinate to the main heading. In printed or in nontagged displays, subheadings are conventionally separated from main headings by a period and two spaces. In the heading "United States. Congress. House," for example, "Congress" and "House" are subheadings.

Subject analysis. The process of identifying the intellectual content of a work. The results may be displayed in a catalog or bibliography by means of notational symbols, as in a classification system, or through verbal terms such as subject headings or descriptors.

***Subject authority file**. A file containing individual **authority records** for **subject headings** and **subdivisions**.

***Subject authority record**. An **authority record** for a **subject heading**.

***Subject heading.** A heading that designates what a work *is* or what it is *about.*

Summarization. The practice of assigning indexing terms or subject headings to represent the overall content of a document rather than its individual parts. See also **Exhaustive indexing**; **In-depth indexing**.

Surrogates. Brief representations of information resources, showing such information as author, title, publisher, and so on, as well as various subject indicators.

Syntax. The rules controlling how the individual words or phrases are combined to form a complete heading.

Synthesis. The representation of a subject by combining individual terms that are listed separately in a subject headings list or thesaurus. See also **Precoordination**.

Thesaurus. A list of controlled indexing terms used in a particular indexing system.

Third-level geographic heading. See **Geographic heading**.

***Topical heading**. A heading that expresses what a work is about.

Type-of-jurisdiction qualifier. A term (enclosed in parentheses), indicating type of jurisdiction, added to a geographic name in order to distinguish between places of the same name—for example, "Washington (*State*)." Also called political qualifier.

UF. See **Use reference**.

Uniform heading. The representation of a given subject by one heading in one form only.

Uniform title. The title by which a work is identified for cataloging purposes. It is established according to *Anglo-American Cataloguing Rules,* second edition revised (AACR2R) and is used in both descriptive and subject cataloging.

Unique heading. The use of a heading to represent one subject or one concept only.

***Use reference (USE)**. A reference from a term that is not valid for use as a subject heading to an equivalent term that is the valid heading.

NOTE

Items marked with an asterisk (*) are based on Library of Congress, Cataloging Policy and Support Office, *Subject Headings Manual* (Washington, DC: Library of Congress, 2008).

BIBLIOGRAPHY

Anderson, James D., and Melissa A. Hofmann. "A Fully Faceted Syntax for Library of Congress Subject Headings." *Cataloging and Classification Quarterly* 43, no. 1 (2006): 7–38.

Anglo-American Cataloguing Rules. 2nd ed., 2002 revision, with 2005 update. Prepared under the direction of the Joint Steering Committee for Revision of AACR, a committee of: the American Library Association, the Australian Committee on Cataloguing, the British Library, the Canadian Committee on Cataloguing, Chartered Institute of Library and Information Professionals, the Library of Congress. Chicago: American Library Association, 2005.

Art and Architecture Thesaurus Online. The J. Paul Getty Trust. http://www.getty.edu/research/conducting_research/vocabularies/aat/ (accessed April 13, 2010).

Association for Library Collections and Technical Services, Cataloging and Classification Section, Subject Analysis Committee, Subcommittee on Metadata and Subject Analysis. *Subject Data in the Metadata Record: Recommendations and Rationale: A Report from the ALCTS/CCS/SAC/Subcommittee on Metadata and Subject Analysis,* 1999, http://www.ala.org/ala/mgrps/divs/alcts/mgrps/ccs/cmtes/subjectanalysis/metadataandsubje/subjectdata.cfm (accessed April 14, 2010).

Attig, John. "The USMARC Formats—Underlying Principles." *Information Technology and Libraries* 1, no. 2 (1982).

Batty, David. "WWW—Wealth, Weariness or Waste: Controlled Vocabulary and Thesauri in Support of Online Information Access." *D-Lib Magazine* (November 1998), http://www.dlib.org/dlib/november98/11batty.html (accessed April 9, 2010).

Berman, Barbara L. "Form Headings in Subject Cataloging." *Library Resources and Technical Services* 33 (2): 134–39.

Chan, Lois Mai. *Library of Congress Subject Headings: Principles and Application.* 4th ed. Westport, CT: Libraries Unlimited, 2005.

Chan, Lois Mai, Eric Childress, Rebecca Dean, Edward T. O'Neill, and Diane Vizine-Goetz. "A Faceted Approach to Subject Data in the Dublin Core Metadata Record." *Journal of Internet Cataloging* 4, no. 1–2 (2001): 35–47.

Clack, Doris Hargrett. *Authority Control: Principles, Applications, and Instructions.* Chicago: American Library Association, 1990.

Crawford, Walt. *MARC for Library Use: Understanding Integrated USMARC.* Boston: G. K. Hall & Co., 1989.

Cutter, Charles Ammi. *Rules for a Dictionary Catalog.* 4th ed. London: The Library Association, 1953.

Drabenstott, Karen M., Schelle Simcox, and Marie Williams. "Do Librarians Understand the Subject Headings in Library Catalogs?" *Reference and User Services Quarterly* 38, no. 4 (1999): 369–87.

Dublin Core Metadata Initiative. *Dublin Core Metadata Element Set, Version 1.1.* 2008. http://dublincore.org/documents/dces/ (accessed April 12, 2010).

Dykstra, Mary. "Can Subject Headings Be Saved?" *Library Journal* 113 (1988): 55–58.

Ebenezer, Catherine. "Trends in Integrated Library Systems." *VINE* 32, no. 4 (2003): 19.

"Extensible Markup Language (XML)." http://www.w3.org/XML/ (accessed April 13, 2010).

Geographic Names Information System (GNS). http://geonames.usgs.gov/ (accessed April 14, 2010)

Getty Thesaurus of Geographic Names (TGN). Los Angeles, CA: J. Paul Getty Trust, 1999. http://www.getty.edu/research/tools/vocabulary/tgn/index.html (accessed April 14, 2010).

Harold, Elliotte Rusty, and W. Scott Means. *XML in a Nutshell.* 3rd ed. Sebastopol, CA: O'Reilly, 2004.

Haykin, David Judson. *Subject Headings: A Practical Guide.* Washington, DC: Government Printing Office, 1951.

Hickey, Thomas B., Jenny Toves, and Edward T. O'Neill. "NACO Normalization." *Library Resources and Technical Services* 50, no. 3 (2001): 166–72.

Hillmann, Diane. "Using Dublin Core." 2007. http://dublincore.org/documents/2005/11/07/usageguide/ (accessed April 13, 2010).

"The History of Yahoo!—How It All Started . . ." http://docs.yahoo.com/info/misc/history.html (accessed April 13, 2010).

Hopkinson, Alan, ed. *UNIMARC Manual: Bibliographic Format.* 3rd ed. Munich, Germany: K. G. Saur, 2008.

Hulme, E. Wyndham. "Principles of Book Classification." *Library Association Record* 13 (1911): 445–47.

International Federation of Library Associations, Study Group on the Functional Requirements of Bibliographic Records. *Functional Requirements of Bibliographic Records: Final Report.* Munich, Germany: K. G. Saur, 1998.

Library of Congress. *Library of Congress Subject Headings.* 8th ed. Washington, DC: Library of Congress, 1975–.

Library of Congress. *MARC 21 Format for Authority Data.* http://www.loc.gov/marc/authority/ecadhome.html (accessed April 14, 2010).

Library of Congress, Cataloging Policy and Support Office. *Free-floating Subdivisions: An Alphabetical Index.* Washington, DC: Cataloging Distribution Service, Library of Congress, 1989–.

Library of Congress, Cataloging Policy and Support Office. *Subject Headings Manual.* Washington, DC: Library of Congress, Cataloging Distribution Service, 2008.

Library of Congress, MARC Development Office. *Information on the MARC System.* 4th ed. Washington, DC: Library of Congress, 1974.

Library of Congress, Network Development and MARC Standards Office. *MARC Standards.* http://www.loc.gov/marc/ (accessed April 13, 2010).

Library of Congress, Subject Cataloging Division. *Subject Headings Used in the Dictionary Catalogues of the Library of Congress.* Washington, DC: Government Printing Office, Library Branch, 1910–1914.

Library of Congress Rule Interpretations. Washington, DC: Cataloging Distribution Service, Library of Congress, 1989–.

List of Subject Headings for Use in Dictionary Catalogs. 3rd rev. ed. Prepared by a Committee of the American Library Association. Chicago: American Library Association, 1911.

MARC Code List for Geographic Areas (GAC). http://www.loc.gov/marc/geoareas/gacs home.html (accessed April 13, 2010).

MARC Code List for Geographic Areas (GAC). 2006 edition (last updated April 7, 2008). http://www.loc.gov/marc/geoareas (accessed April 14, 2010).

MARC 21 Concise Formats. Prepared by Network Development and MARC Standards Office, Library of Congress. Washington, DC: Cataloging Distribution Service, Library of Congress, 2000–.

MARC 21 Format for Authority Data. Network Development and MARC Standards Office, Library of Congress. 1999–. http://www.loc.gov/marc/authority/ecadhome.html (accessed April 14, 2010).

MARC 21 Format for Bibliographic Data. Network Development and MARC Standards Office, Library of Congress. 1999–. http://www.loc.gov/marc/bibliographic/ecbd home.html (accessed April 13, 2010).

"MARCXML: MARC 21 XML Schema." http://www.loc.gov/standards/marcxml/ (accessed April 13, 2010).

Miller, Joseph, and Joan Goodsell, eds. *Sears List of Subject Headings.* 19th ed. New York: H. W. Wilson Company, 2007.

MODS Metadata Object Description Schema. http://www.loc.gov/standards/mods/ (accessed April 13, 2010).

NACO. *Authority File Comparison Rules, 9/16/98, Revised February 9, 2001.* http://www. loc.gov/catdir/pcc/naco/normrule.html (accessed April 13, 2010).

National Information Standards Organization. *Guidelines for the Construction, Format, and Management of Monolingual Thesauri.* Bethesda, MD: NISO Press, 1994.

National Information Standards Organization (U.S.). *Understanding Metadata.* 3.

National Library of Medicine. *Medical Subject Headings.* 1st–48th ed. Bethesda, MD: U. S. Department of Health and Human Services, Public Health Service, National Institutes of Health, National Library of Medicine, 1960–2007. http://www.nlm. nih.gov/mesh/ (accessed April 14, 2010).

O'Neill, Edward T., and Rao Aluri. 1980. *Research Report on a Method for Correcting Typographical Errors in Subject Headings in OCLC Record.* Research Report number OCLC/OPR/RR-80/3. Columbus, OH: OCLC.

O'Neill, Edward T., Lois Mai Chan, Eric Childress, Rebecca Dean, Lynn M. El-Hoshy, and Diane Vizine-Goetz. 2001. "Form Subdivisions: Their Identification and Use in LCSH." *Library Resources & Technical Services* 45 (4): 187–97.

Online Computer Library Center. *Normalization Service.* 2009. http://www.oclc.org/ research/activities/naco/default.htm (accessed April 13, 2010).

Ranganathan, S. R. *Elements of Library Classification.* 3rd ed. Bombay, India: Asia Publishing House, 1962.

Subject Subdivisions Conference. *The Future of Subdivisions in the Library of Congress Subject Headings System: Report from the Subject Subdivisions Conference.* Ed. Martha O'Hara Conway. Washington, DC: Cataloging Distribution Service, Library of Congress, 1992.

Svenonius, Elaine. "Design of Controlled Vocabularies." In *Encyclopedia of Library and Information Science,* ed. Allen Kent, vol. 45, supplement 10. New York: Marcel Dekker, 1990.

Svenonius, Elaine. *The Intellectual Foundation of Information Organization.* Cambridge, MA: MIT Press, 2000.

Taube, Mortimer. "Specificity in Subject Headings and Coordinate Indexing." *Library Trends* 1, no. 2 (1952): 219–23.

Taylor, Arlene G. "Authority Control: Where It's Been and Where It's Going." Paper presented at conference Authority Control: Why It Matters, sponsored by the NELINET

Cataloging and Technical Services Advisory Committee, November 1, 1999, at College of the Holy Cross, Worcester, MA. http://www.nelinet.net/edserv/conf/cataloging/cts/1999/taylor.htm (accessed March 1, 2007).

Taylor, Arlene G., and Daniel N. Joudrey. *The Organization of Information*. 3rd ed. Westport, CT: Libraries Unlimited, 2009.

Thesaurus of ERIC Descriptors. Washington, DC: U.S. Department of Education, Institute of Education Sciences. http://www.eric.ed.gov/ (accessed April 9, 2010).

Tuleya, Lisa Gallagher, ed. *Thesaurus of Psychological Index Terms*. 11th ed. Washington, DC: American Psychological Association, 2007.

Willer, Mirna, ed. *UNIMARC Manual: Authorities Format*. Munich, Germany: K. G. Saur, 2009.

Wilson, Patrick, and Nick Robinson. "Form Subdivisions and Genre." *Library Resources and Technical Services* 34, no. 1 (1990): 36–43.

W3C. *SKOS Simple Knowledge Organization System*. http://www.w3.org/2004/02/skos/ (accessed April 14, 2010).

W3C. *SKOS Simple Knowledge Organization System Reference*. http://www.w3.org/TR/2009/REC-skos-reference-20090818/ (accessed April 14, 2010).

"XML Schema." http://www.w3.org/2001/XMLSchema.html (accessed April 13, 2010).

Yee, Martha M. "Two Genre and Form Lists for Moving Image and Broadcast Materials: A Comparison." *Cataloging and Classification Quarterly* 31, no. 3–4 (2001): 237–95.

INDEX

AACR2R. *See Anglo-American Cataloguing Rules*

abbreviations, 131–132; in geographic names, 81, 223–224

abstracting and indexing (A&I), 4

adjectival phrase headings, in multiple-word headings, 69–70

advanced searching, 155–159, 155*f*, 156*f*, 157*f*, 158*f*, 159*f*; phrase searching in, 152–154, 152*f*, 153*f*, 154*f*

A&I (abstracting and indexing), 4

ALA (American Library Association), 18, 28

ALCTS (Association of Library Collections and Technical Services), 53–55

The Alfred Whital Stern Collection of Lincolniana, MARC record on, 172–173

algorithm, 180, 224–225, 265, 268; errors *v.*, 269

algorithmic faceting (LCSH into FAST), 269; chronologicals faceting in, 273; corporate names faceting in, 273; events faceting in, 271; forms faceting in, 270; geographic names faceting in, 272–273; personal names faceting in, 273; titles faceting in, 270–271; topicals faceting in, 273–274

also used for (AUF) references, 129, 134–135, 258

American Library Association (ALA), 18, 28

American Library Association Committee on Technical Services, 21

American Memory: The Alfred Whital Stern Collection of Lincolniana in, 171–173,

172*f*; in Dublin Core, 169–170; in MARC, 168–169, 171, 172–173; mission/history of, 167–168; in qualified Dublin Core records, 170–171

Ameritech Corporation, 167–168

Anglo-American Cataloguing Rules (2nd edition, revised) (AACR2R), 77–78, 107, 114, 119, 121, 138, 177, 222, 229–230

anonymous works: title headings for, 121; titles faceting for, 270–271; titles of, 230–231

ARN (authority record number), 148, 149

assigned headings, 22; enumeration of, 217–218; topical headings and, 217–218

assigning FAST headings: identifying topics concepts/facets, 172; selecting form/genre headings in, 172–179; subject relations in, 179

Association of Library Collections and Technical Services (ALCTS), 53–55

associative relationships: for class of persons and their fields, 138; for discipline/object studied links, 138; for overlapping meanings, 138; RT references and, 130, 137–138

asterisk, 149

AUF (also used for) references, 129, 134–135, 258

authority control, 6, 22–23; correction of, 264–266; definition of, 261; errors in, 262; need for, 262, 262*f*; validation of, 262–263 authority data: digital representation and, 44–48; in FAST authority records, 235; for MARC 21, 45–46; metadata encoding and, 44–48; print representation and, 44

authority files, 6, 11, 46. *See also specific authority files*

authority record number (ARN), 148

authority record structure, 236

authority records, 6; LCCN for, 236–237, 236*f*. *See also specific types of authority records*

authorized terms, 8, 235

automation, of authority control, 261

bibliographic data, 4; digital representation and, 26–44; metadata encoding and, 25–44; print representation and, 25–26

bibliographic record, 33

bibliographic records coding: Dublin Core and, 162–164; MARC records and, 162

bound terms, 18

broader term (BT) references, 8, 129, 235; in hierarchical relationships, 130, 135–137

BT (broader term) references, 8, 129, 130, 135–137, 235

capitalization, 226, 254, 255, 255*t*

card catalogs, 15, 16*f*; card sets of, 26, 27*f*; print representation, 26; schemas and, 16–17; synthetic languages and, 17

catchword, 18

Chan, Lois Mai, 55

chronological headings, 99, 109; B.C./A.D., 100; cross references for, 232; with dates only, 101–102; in FAST authority records, 248–249; FAST headings derivation for, 232; forms of, 99–101; geologic periods, 101; historical periods, 101; patterns for, 263; selection of, 176–177; strings in, 263; validation of, 262–263

chronologicals faceting, 273

chronology, in event headings, 109

city sections, 86–87, 224

class: class member relationship, 136; of persons and their fields, 138

classical mythology, 74–75

classification, 7

classification schema, 22–23

coding, 25–44, 48–49, 53, 218–219, 264, 267–269; in Dublin Core, 162–164; in MARC 21, 162

COM catalogs (computer output microform (COM) catalogs), 26

common usage, 57

complex subjects representation, 10–11

complex-topic headings, 174

compound phrase headings, 71

compound/complex relationship, 136–137

computer output microform catalogs (COM catalogs), 26

concept, 161–162; as topical headings type, 73

conflicts: cross references and, 257; facets for, 256; LCSH *v.* FAST and, 256; military conflicts, 105–106; normalization of, 256; among personal name headings, 256; qualifiers for, 256; among topical headings, 256

Connexion, 29

control fields, in MARC record structure, 32

controlled vocabulary, 4; for metadata records, 54; principles of, 7–9; specific entry in, 9; terminology in, 9; unique headings *v.* uniform headings, 8

controlled vocabulary access, 5–6

controlled vocabulary searches, keyword searches *v.*, 6–7

controlled vocabulary systems: FAST and, 21; in information organization, 17–21; LCSH and, 19–20, 19*t*; MeSH and, 20–21

corporate bodies proper names subject headings, 122, 273; for corporate name changes, 118–119; forms of, 114–116; for governments, 116; language in, 114–115; for main corporate bodies, 116–117; for subordinate bodies, 117–118

corporate bodies works, 231–232

corporate headings: in FAST authority records, 250–251; qualifiers for, 115–116

correction: of authority control, 264–266; of cross references, 264–265; of obsolete headings, 265–266; stylistic, 264; tagging and subfield coding, 264; of typographical errors, 265

Council on Library Resources, 27

cross references, 9–10, 129; for changes in geographic names, 141–142; for changes in jurisdictional names, 142; for chronological headings, 232; conflicts and, 257; for corporate names, 140; correction of, 264–265; for dynasties, 139–140; equivalence relationship and,

130–135; for family names, 139; for
fictitious and mythological characters,
139; for geographic names, 140–142;
hierarchical relationships and, 135–137;
for houses of duke/counts/earls, 140;
for individuals names, 138–139; LCSH
authority file for, 220; for miscellaneous
names, 142; for named events, 143; for
nonjurisdictional names, 141; for
personal names, 257; for proper name
headings, 138–144; for titles, 144
Cutter, Charles A., 56–57

data fields: in MARC record structure, 32.
See also specific types of data
DCMI (Dublin Core Metadata Initiative), 40
DCMI Type Vocabulary (DCMITYPE), 163
DCMI Type Vocabulary (DCTI), 41
DCMITYPE (DCMI Type Vocabulary), 163
DCTI (DCMI Type Vocabulary), 41
descriptors, 4, 8, 17, 235
diacritics, 148, 219, 255
Digital Object Identifier (DOI), 42
digital representation: authority data and,
44–48; bibliographic data and, 26–44;
Dublin Core, 39–44; MARC 21 and,
44–46; MARC bibliographic formats in,
28–36; other MARC authority formats
and, 46; SKOS, 46–48; XML, 36–39
discipline/object studied links, 138
DOI (Digital Object Identifier), 42
Dublin Core, 21; *American Memory* in,
169–170; bibliographic records coding and,
162–164; contributor in, 41; coverage in,
42, 163; digital representation and, 39–44;
elements of, 40–43; format in, 41–42;
language in, 42; qualified Dublin Core
v., 43–44, 180; relation in, 42; resource
identifier in, 42; rights in, 42–43; SKOS *v.*,
47; subject in, 41, 53–54, 163; tags in, 43;
type in, 41, 163–164; for Web, 40–44.
See also qualified Dublin Core records
Dublin Core Data Element Set, 162–163
Dublin Core Metadata Initiative (DCMI), 40
Dublin Core metadata records, 21

element refinement, in qualified Dublin
Core, 43
El-Hoshy, Lynn, 55
encoding scheme, in qualified Dublin Core,
43–44
entry vocabulary, 57
enumeration, 14, 60; of assigned headings,
217–218; synthesis *v.*, 56

enumerative languages, synthetic languages *v.*,
11–13
equivalence relationships, 129;
abbreviations/acronyms/initials, etc.,
and, 131–132; alternative forms and,
133; ambiguous relationships and, 134;
different entry elements and, 133;
different language terms and, 132;
narrow terms not used as headings and,
134; popular and scientific terms and,
133; synonymous terms and, 130–131;
variant spellings and, 131
errors, 264–266; algorithm *v.*, 269; in
authority control, 262; inconsistency as, 161
established headings, 235
events, 226; national *v.* local, 228
event headings: capitalization in, 226;
chronology and geography in, 109; in
FAST authority records, 251–253; forms
of, 103–105; LCSH and, 226–229; LCSH
conferences/meetings names derivations
of, 229; LCSH *v.* FAST for, 226–229;
for meetings, 106–107; for military
conflicts, 105–106; for miscellaneous
events, 108; period subdivision
derivations of, 227–229; qualifiers for,
104–105, 107–108, 226, 228–229;
reference records and, 275–276; for
sporting events, 107–108; topical
headings derivations of, 226–227; types
of, 105–108
exhaustivity, summarization *v.* in-depth
cataloging/indexing and, 164–166, 166*f*
Extensible Markup Language (XML),
36–39

facets, 172–173, 221; for conflicts, 256;
heading order *v.*, 149–150
Faceted Application of Subject
Terminology. *See* FAST
faceting, 275; FAST headings and, 59–60;
of forms, 270; as indexing languages
characteristic, 13–14; precoordination *v.*,
15; of titles, 270–271. *See also*
algorithmic faceting
faceting LCSH into FAST, 279; form
subdivisions identification/recoding,
267–269; reference records and,
274–276; validation and, 276–278,
277*t*. *See also* algorithmic faceting
facet-specific indexes, 156
FAST (Faceted Application of Subject
Terminology): controlled vocabulary
systems and, 21; headings sources in,

56; history of, 55–56; LCSH v., 21, 34, 55–56, 80, 82, 123, 129–130, 217, 223; OCLC and, 21, 55, 267; principles of, 56–59; semantics in, 56–59

FAST Authority File, 147

FAST authority file, FAST authority records v., 245–246

FAST authority records: additional examples of, 246–254; authority data in, 235; authority records in, 235–236, 236f; chronological headings in, 248–249; conflicts in, 256–257; corporate headings in, 250–251; creation of, 236–246, 236f; event headings in, 251–253; FAST authority file v., 245–246; Fixed-Length Data Elements in, 237, 238t; form headings in, 254; genre headings in, 254; geographic headings in, 247–248; Library of Congress authority record v., 237, 238–245; minimal, examples of, 239, 240, 241, 242, 243, 254; multiple-step creation of, 237; normalization in, 254–255, 255t; obsolete authority records and, 257–259; personal name headings in, 249–250; temporary number for, 237; title headings in, 253–254; topical headings in, 246–247; upgraded, examples of, 239, 240, 241, 242–243, 244, 245; validation in, 246, 257

FAST database, 147, 147f, 149–150

FAST Forms, 147

FAST headings: faceting and, 59–60; syntax of, 59–62

FAST headings application, 161, 172–179, 216; bibliographic records coding for, 162–164; cataloging/indexing exhaustivity and, 164–166, 166f

FAST headings application examples: example 1: *People and Predators: from Conflict to Coexistence*, 180–183, 180 (photo); example 2: *Daily Life in Colonial New England*, 183–186, 183 (photo); example 3: *Style and the Nineteenth-century British Critic: Sincere Mannerisms*, 186–189, 186 (photo); example 4: *Fife and Tayside*, 189–191, 189 (photo); example 5: *Ann Frank: Reflections on Her Life and Legacy*, 191–195, 191 (photo); example 6: *2005 Hydrographic Survey of South San Francisco Bay, California* [Web site], 195–197, 195f; example 7: *Shakespeare in the Victorian Periodicals*, 198–200, 198 (photo); example 8: *Portrait of*

an Unknown Woman, 200–203, 200 (photo); example 9: *The Pretender*, 203–205, 203 (photo); example 10: *First Emperor of China* [DVD], 206–209, 206 (photo); example 11: *Japan: Economic Political and Social Issues*, 209–211, 209 (photo); example 12: *Detours* [Audio CD], 211–213, 211 (photo)

FAST headings derivation: for chronological headings, 232; for corporate body names, 230; of event headings, 226–229; for form headings, 232–233; geographic headings and, 222–225; for person and family names, 229–230; for titles, 230–232; of topical headings, 217–221

FAST headings structure, 62–64

FAST introduction, 53–54, 64; history of, 55–56

fictitious/legendary/mythological characters, 73–75, 139

field text, 32–34

fields, 33–36, 35f, 138; of indexes, 148. *See also* subfields

Fixed-Length Data Elements, 237, 238t

forms, 67–70, 73, 133, 270; of chronological headings, 99–101; of corporate bodies proper names subject headings, 114–116; normalized, 254–255, 255t

form and genre headings, 172–179; for art, 126; for audiovisual materials, 126; for cartography, 127; examples of, 125–128; form v. topical heading in, 123–124; forms of, 124–125; for law, 126; for literature, 127; for main heading, 124; for music, 127–128; principles of, 123–124; for religion, 128; subdivision in, 124–125

form headings, 125–126, 254, 275; FAST headings derivation for, 232–233

form headings default faceting, 275

form subdivisions: determination for, 268–269; identification/recoding, 267–269; position in, 268; topical subdivisions v., 268–269

FRBR (Functional Requirements for Bibliographic Records), 13, 226

Free-Floating Subdivisions, 269

free-floating terms, 222

full-text databases, 4

Functional Requirements for Bibliographic Records (FRBR), 13, 226

GAC (Geographic Area Codes), 84, 148, 157, 222, 237

generic term, 75

genre headings, 73, 125–126, 172–179, 233, 254

Geographic Area Codes (GAC), 84, 148, 157, 222, 237

geographic authority records, 222; LCSH *v.* FAST, 223; nonjurisdictional names in, 223; without subdivisions, 223

geographic headings, 175–176, 247–248; abbreviations and, 81; archaeological sites in, 91–92; bodies of water in, 92–94, 225; China in, 222; city sections in, 224; disputed territories in, 94; extinct cities/ancient kingdoms in, 90–91; extraterrestrial bodies in, 95–96; grammatical form of, 81; indirect order in, 84; islands/land with bodies of water in, 93–94; jurisdictional headings as, 77–78; language of, 80–81; language-based territories in, 94; latitude/longitude/feature type, 96–97; LCSH *v.* FAST for, 222–225; levels of, 84–90; man-made structures (large), 95; mapping failures in, 224–225; name changes and, 78–80; nonjurisdictional headings as, 78; outer space in, 96; parks/reserves, etc., 94–95; qualifiers and, 81 83, 224–225; sources of, 222; types of, 77–78; validation of, 225

geographic headings levels: areas associated with cities in, 89; bridges and tunnels in, 90; city sections/neighborhoods in, 86–87; entities within cities in, 89–90; first-level of, 84–85; London boroughs in, 87–88; New York City boroughs in, 87; second-level of, 85–86; third-level of, 86–90

geographic indexes, 156, 157*f*; *Add Coordinate Page* link for, 159, 159*f*; GAC as, 157; geographic coordinates and, 157–159, 158*f*; geographic feature as, 157; Google Maps, 159; MapIt link and, 158*f*, 159

geographic names, 64, 81, 140–142, 163, 223–224; faceting of, 272–273

geography, in event headings, 109

geologic periods, 75–76, 101

GeoNames (geonames.org), 96–97

Getty Thesaurus of Geographic Names (TGN), 64, 163

heading order, facets *v.*, 149–150

headings, 34, 267–279; keywords in, 150–151, 150*f*, 151*f*; normalized forms of, 254–255, 255*t*; sources of, in FAST, 56; synonyms *v.*, 58; syntax of, 59–62; topical headings *v.*, 67. *See also specific types of headings*

Hickey, Thomas B., 255

hierarchical relationships, 130, 135–137

historical periods, 101

history, 55–56, 167–168

Hulme, E. Wyndham, 57

identification, 42, 173, 267–269

IFLA, 36

imaginary places/organizations, 75

index view, 159–160, 160*f*

indexes, 4, 6, 164–166, 166*f*; facet-specific indexes, 156; geographic indexes, 156–159, 157*f*, 158*f*, 159*f*; keyword indexes, 147–149; phrase indexes, 147–149

indexing languages characteristics, 11–15

indexing overview: in FAST database, 147–149; keyword indexes in, 147–149; normalization in, 148; other indexes in, 147–149; phrase indexes in, 147–149

indicators, in data fields, 32–34

individual authority records, 151

information organization, 3; cards to computers in, 15–17; characteristics of indexing languages in, 11–15; complex subjects representation in, 10–11; controlled vocabulary principles in, 7–9; controlled vocabulary systems in, 17–21; selecting indexing/classification schema in, 22–23; subject access to information, 4–7; terminological control/term relationships in, 9–10

Intellectual Property Rights (IPR), 42–43

International Organization for Standardization (ISO), 9

International Standard Book Number (ISBN), 42

Internet, 3–4, 53–55

Internet Media Types (MIME), 42

inverted headings, 76

IPR (Intellectual Property Rights), 42–43

ISBN (International Standard Book Number), 42

ISO (International Organization for Standardization), 9

Joudrey, Daniel N., 18, 26

keyword indexes, 147–149
keyword searching, 5–7, 154, 154*f*, 155*f*, 156*f*; facet-specific indexes and, 156; multiple words in, 155
keywords, in headings, 150–151, 150*f*, 151*f*
known authorship works, 271

language, 14–15, 36, 38–39, 42, 119–120, 132, 162; in corporate bodies headings, 114–115; in geographic headings, 80–81; synthetic language, 11–13, 17
LCCH subdivision authority record, 245
LCCN (Library of Congress Control Number), 159, 227, 236–237, 236*f*
LC/NAF authority file, 114, 217, 222, 229; titles and, 230–232
LC/NAF authority record, 238–240, 242, 243–245, 270
LCSH (Library of Congress Subject Headings), 6, 18; ALCTS on, 53–55; controlled vocabulary systems and, 19–20, 19*t*; description of, 19–20, 19*t*; disadvantages of, 54–55; event headings and, 226–229; FAST *v.*, 21, 34, 55–56, 80, 82, 123, 129–130, 217, 223; free-floating terms in, 222; headings in, 12–13, 14; SKOS and, 47–48; subject strings *v.* OPACs, 54; as synthetic language, 11–12
LCSH authority file, 220–221, 226, 245
LCSH authority record, 240, 241, 244–245
LCSH *v.* FAST, 21, 34, 55–56, 80, 82, 123, 129–130, 217; capitalization for, 226; conflicts and, 256; for event headings, 226–229; for form headings, 232–233; for geographic headings, 222–225; for titles, 230. *See also* faceting LCSH into FAST
LDR (leader), 29–31, 31*f*, 36
leader (LDR), 29–31, 31*f*, 36
lead-in terms, 130
level of establishment, 148
Library of Congress (LOC), 12, 17–18, 26, 167–168, 222, 267
Library of Congress authority record, 237, 238–245
Library of Congress Control Number (LCCN), 159, 227, 236–237, 236*f*
Library of Congress Subject Headings. *See* LCSH

Library of Congress Subject Headings (31st edition), 44, 45*f*
literary warrant, 57
LOC. *See* Library of Congress
logical operators, 5

MAchine-Readable Cataloging. *See* MARC
main headings, 62–63, 124, 220–221
mapping failures, 224–225
MARBI, 28
MARC (MAchine-Readable Cataloging), 17, 27, 230; *American Memory* in, 168–169, 171, 172–173; authority record structure and, 236; FAST *v.*, 34; form subdivisions and, 267; normalization and, 255
MARC 21, 21, 28–29, 162, 236; digital representation and, 44–46; reference records and, 274; UNIMARC *v.*, 36
MARC 21 Format for Authority Data, 44–46, 235
MARC 21 Format for Bibliographic Data, 29
MARC 21 records: example 1: *People and Predators: from Conflict to Coexistence*, 181–182; example 2: *Daily Life in Colonial New England*, 184–185; example 3: *Style and the Nineteenth-century British Critic: Sincere Mannerisms*, 187–188; example 4: *Fife and Tayside*, 191; example 5: *Ann Frank: Reflections on Her Life and Legacy*, 194–195; example 6: *2005 Hydrographic Survey of South San Francisco Bay, California* [Web site], 196–197; example 7: *Shakespeare in the Victorian Periodicals*, 200; example 8: *Portrait of an Unknown Woman*, 203; example 9: *The Pretender*, 206; example 10: *First Emperor of China* [DVD], 208–209; example 11: *Japan: Economic Political and Social Issues*, 211–212; example 12: *Detours* [Audio CD], 214
MARC bibliographic formats: in digital representation, 28–36; MARC 21, 28–29; MARC record structure, 29–36; UNIMARC, 36
The MARC II Format: A Communications Format for Bibliographic Data, 28
MARC record structure, 33–35; control fields in, 32; data fields in, 32; directory in, 31, 32*f*; LDR in, 29–31, 31*f*, 36; variable fields in, 32

MARC records, 162; *on The Alfred Whital Stern Collection of Lincolniana*, 172
MARCXML, 38, 162
Medical Subject Headings (MeSH), 20–21, 43, 170
MeSH (Medical Subject Headings), 20–21, 43, 170
metadata encoding, 49, 53; authority data and, 44–48; bibliographic data and, 25–44. *See also* digital representation; print representation
Metadata Object Description Schema (MODS), 38–39
metadata records, 54
MIME (Internet Media Types), 42
MODS (Metadata Object Description Schema), 38–39
multiple headings, 219–220
multiple links, 245
multiple subject headings, 278
multiple words, in keyword searching, 155
multiple-concept headings, 71–72, 174
multiple-facet topics, 177–179
multiple-topic headings, 173–174
multiple-word headings, 69–70
music headings, 127–128, 221

NACO (North Authority Cooperative Program normalization rules), 148, 219
NACO Authority File Comparison Rules, 255
names. *See specific types of names*
Name Authority File, 106–107
name changes: corporate name changes, 118–119; geographic headings and, 78–80; linear name changes, 79; mergers, 79; splits, 79–80
name headings, 176
named animals, as topical headings type, 75
narrower term (NT) references, 8, 129, 235
National Center for Supercomputing Applications (NCSA), 40
National Digital Library Program, 167–168
National Information Standards Organization (NISO), 9, 40
National Library of Medicine (NLM), 20–21
NCSA (National Center for Supercomputing Applications), 40
NISO (National Information Standards Organization), 9, 40
NISO *Guidelines for the Construction, Format, and Management of Monolingual Thesauri*, 18

NLM (National Library of Medicine), 20–21
nonrepeatability (NR), 33
normalization, 255*t*, 257–258; of conflicts, 256; definition of, 254; in FAST authority records, 254–255, 255*f*; in indexing overview, 148; MARC and, 255; multiple headings and, 219–220; subfield delimiter and, 219; in topical headings, 219–220
North Authority Cooperative Program (NACO) normalization rules, 148, 219
NR (nonrepeatability), 33
NT (narrower term) references, 8, 129, 235

object, as topical headings type, 73
object studied links, 138
obsolete authority records: changed normalized forms and, 258; FAST authority records and, 257–259; new authority records *v.*, 258–259; record status of, 258–259; UF in, 258; unchanged normalized forms and, 257
obsolete headings, correction of, 265–266
OCLC (Online Public Access Library Catalogs), 17, 29, 56, 140, 217, 268; FAST and, 21, 55, 267; for FAST database, 147
O'Neill, Edward T., 55, 218, 255, 268
online databases, 4, 17
Online Public Access Catalogs. *See* OPACs
Online Public Access Library Catalogs. *See* OCLC
OPACs (Online Public Access Catalogs), 4, 28, 147; codes and, 35; LCSH subject strings and, 54
overlapping meanings, 138

period subdivision: event headings derivations from, 227–229. *See also specific periods*
Permanent UNIMARC Committee (PUC), 36
personal authorship works, 231
personal name headings: conflicts among, 256; in FAST authority records, 249–250
personal names, 257, 273
persons proper names subject headings: for dynasties, royal houses, etc., 113–114; for families, 112–113; for individual persons, 111–112; principles of, 111
phrase indexes, 147–149

phrase searching, 152–154, 152*f*, 153*f*, 154*f*

postcoordination: precoordination *v.*, 14–15, 17, 60; syntax headings and, 60, 62

pound sign, 149

precoordination, 20; faceting *v.*, 15; postcoordination *v.*, 14–15, 17, 60; syntax headings and, 60–62

preferred terms, 8, 235

prepositional phrase headings: in multiple-concept headings, 72; in multiple-word headings, 70

principle of specificity, 173

print files, distribution and, 12–13

print representation: authority data and, 44; bibliographic data and, 25–26; book catalogs, 25–26; card catalogs, 26

proper names subject headings: for corporate bodies, 114–119; for persons, 111–114; for titles, 119–122. *See also* corporate bodies proper names subject headings; persons proper names subject headings

publishers' descriptions, summarization *v.*, 164–165

PUC (Permanent UNIMARC Committee), 36

qualified Dublin Core records, 43–44, 180; *American Memory* in, 170–171; example 1: *People and Predators: from Conflict to Coexistence*, 182–183; example 2: *Daily Life in Colonial New England*, 185–186; example 3: *Style and the Nineteenth-century British Critic: Sincere Mannerisms*, 188–189; example 4: *Fife and Tayside*, 190–191; example 5: *Ann Frank: Reflections on Her Life and Legacy*, 194–195; example 6: *2005 Hydrographic Survey of South San Francisco Bay, California* [Web site], 196–197; example 7: *Shakespeare in the Victorian Periodicals*, 200; example 8: *Portrait of an Unknown Woman*, 200–203; example 9: *The Pretender*, 203–205; example 10: *First Emperor of China* [DVD], 206–208; example 11: *Japan: Economic Political and Social Issues*, 209–211; example 12: *Detours* [Audio CD], 211–213

qualifiers, 58–59; for conflicts, 256; for corporate headings, 115–116; date qualifiers, 104, 109; for event headings, 104–105, 107–108, 226, 228–229; event type qualifiers, 104, 107–108; for extinct cities, 90–91; in FAST headings

structure, 63–64; in fictitious characters, 73–74; geographic headings and, 81–83, 224–225; in geographic names faceting, 272–273; for miscellaneous events, 108; place qualifiers, 82, 104–105, 109, 228; for subordinate bodies, 117–118; in titles, 120–121, 230–232, 271, 271*t*; type qualifiers, 82; for works from corporate bodies/conferences/meetings, etc., 122

question mark, 149

R (repeatability), 8, 33

recoding, 267–269; of forms, 218–219

reference records: event headings and, 275–276; faceting LCSH into FAST and, 274–276; form headings default faceting and, 275; MARC 21 and, 274

related term (RT), 8, 129, 235; in associative relationships, 130, 137–138; in classical mythology, 74–75

relation, in Dublin Core, 42

repeatability (R), 8, 33

resource identifier, in Dublin Core, 42

RT (related term) references, 8, 74–75, 129, 130, 137–138

schemas, 38–39; assignment ease and, 22; card catalogs and, 16–17; classification schema, 22–23; compatibility and, 22; maintenance cost and, 22–23; retrieval effectiveness and, 22; selecting, 22–23

searching, 3–4; advanced searching, 152–159, 152*f*, 153*f*, 154*f*, 155*f*, 156*f*, 157*f*, 158*f*, 159*f*; FAST authority record number indexes, 159; (LCCN) for LCSH source heading indexes, 159; geographic indexes, 156–159, 157*f*, 158*f*, 159*f*; index view in, 159–160, 160*f*; keyword searching, 5–7, 154–156, 154*f*, 155*f*, 156*f*; keywords in headings, 150–151, 150*f*, 151*f*; phrase searching, 152–154, 152*f*, 153*f*, 154*f*; record status indexes, 159

Sears, Minnie Earl, 19

Sears List of Subject Headings, 19, 53–54

see reference (USE reference), 129, 130–132, 235

selecting form/genre headings, in assigning FAST headings, 172–179

semantics (FAST): common/current usage for, 56–57; literary warrant and, 57; uniform heading and, 57–58; unique heading and, 58–59

Simple Knowledge Organization System (SKOS), 46–48, 54
single-concept headings, 68–70
single-topic headings, 173
single-word headings, 68–69
SKOS (Simple Knowledge Organization System), 46, 54; Dublin Core *v.*, 47; LCSH and, 47–48
specificity, principle of, 173
strings, 12, 54; in chronological headings, 263; validity of, 262–263
stylistic correction, 264
Subcommittee on Metadata and Subject Analysis, 53
subdivisions, 11; corporate bodies names and, 230; facets and, 221; in FAST headings structure, 63; in form and genre headings, 124–125; form subdivisions, 267–269; free-floating subdivision, 221; geographic authority records without, 223; in geographic names faceting, 272–273; for multiple subject headings, 278; in multiple-concept headings, 72; in recoding of forms, 218; in topical headings, 221; topical subdivisions, 268–269; validation of, 221. *See also specific types of subdivisions*
subfield delimiter, 33; normalization and, 219
subfields, 160, 160*f*, 255; coding of, 264; in field text, 32–34; in titles, 231, 271, 271*t*
subject: definition of, 161–162; in Dublin Core, 41, 53–54, 163
subject access to information, 4; classification for, 7; keyword searching, 5–7
subject cataloging, 6
subject heading list, 8, 235; development of, 18–19
subject heading strings, 12
subject headings, 4, 8, 235; thesauri *v.*, 17–18
Subject Headings Manual, 20
subject indexing, 6
subject relations: in assigning FAST headings, 179; assignment and, 179
summarization, in-depth cataloging/ indexing *v.*, 164–166, 166*f*
surrogates, 4
Svenonius, Elaine, 11, 12, 13, 15, 67
synonyms, 235; headings *v.*, 58
syntax, 10, 67; of FAST headings, 59–62
syntax headings: enumeration *v.* synthesis, 60; faceting and, 59–60; postcoordination and, 60, 62;

precoordination and, 60–62; precoordination *v.* postcoordination, 60
synthesis, enumeration *v.*, 60
synthetic language(s): card catalogs and, 17; enumerative languages *v.*, 11–13; LCSH as, 11–12

tagging, subfield coding and, 264
tags: in data fields, 32–33; in Dublin Core, 43; in MODS, 39
Taylor, Arlene G., 18, 26
term relationships, terminological control and, 9–10
terminological control, term relationships and, 9–10
terminology, in controlled vocabulary, 9
TGN (Getty Thesaurus of Geographic Names), 64, 163
thesauri, 8, 64, 163, 235; subject headings *v.*, 17–18
time periods, 227
titles : of anonymous authorship works, 121, 230–231, 270–271; of corporate bodies works, 231–232; cross references for, 144; faceting of, 270–271; FAST headings derivation for, 230–232; heading types for, 121–122; LC/NAF authority file and, 230–232; LCSH *v.* FAST for, 230; in MARC, 230; of personal authorship works, 231; proper names subject headings for, 119 122; qualifiers in, 120–121, 230–232, 271, 271*t*; subfields in, 231, 271, 271*t*; uniform title, 119; WorldCat and, 232
title headings: for anonymous works, 121; in FAST authority records, 253–254; selection of, 177
title qualifiers, subfields as, 271, 271*t*
topical headings: assigned headings and, 217–218; conflicts among, 256; event headings derivations from, 226–227; in FAST authority records, 246–247; FAST headings derivation of, 217–221; form *v.*, in form and genre headings, 123–124; functions of, 67; headings *v.*, 67; LCSH authority file in, 220–221, 226; normalization in, 219–220; recoding of forms in, 218–219; selection of, 173–174; subdivisions in, 221; validation of, 218–221
topical headings forms, 67; multiple-word headings in, 69–70; single-concept headings, 68–70
topical headings types: concepts/objects as,

73; fictitious/legendary/mythological characters as, 73–75; forms/genre as subjects in, 73; geologic periods as, 75–76; imaginary places/organizations as, 75; inverted headings as, 76; named animals as, 75; object as, 73; other proper named entities as, 76
topical subdivisions, form subdivisions identification/recoding *v.*, 268–269
topicals faceting, 273–274
topics, 161–162
Toves, Jenny, 255
type, in Dublin Core, 41, 163–164
typographical errors, correction of, 265

UF (used for) references: in cross references, 129–134, 138–144; in obsolete authority records, 258
uniform headings, 8; semantics and, 57–58
Uniform Resource Identifier (URI), 42
uniform title, 119
UNIMARC, 28; MARC 21 *v.*, 36
unique headings, 8, 58–59
URI (Uniform Resource Identifier), 42
USE references, 130–132, 237; definition of, 129
used for (UF) references: in cross references, 129–134, 138–144; in obsolete authority records, 258

USMARC, 28, 36
USMARC Advisory Group, 267

validation: of authority control, 262–263; of chronological headings, 262–263; faceting LCSH into FAST and, 276–278, 277*t*; in FAST authority records, 246, 257; of geographic headings, 225; LCSH authority file and, 220–221; results of, 278; subdivisions and, 221; of topical headings, 218–221
validity, of strings, 262–263
variable fields, in MARC record structure, 32

W3C Semantic Web Deployment Working Group, 44
Web, Dublin Core for, 40–44
wildcard characters, 149
World Wide Web, 53–55
WorldCat, 56, 57, 106–107, 268; for corporate body names, 230; headings derivation from, 217; for person/family names, 229; titles and, 232

XML (Extensible Markup Language), 36; MARCXML, 38, 162; MODS, 38–39

ABOUT THE AUTHORS

LOIS MAI CHAN is Professor of Library and Information Science at the University of Kentucky.

EDWARD T. O'NEILL did his undergraduate work at Albion College and his doctoral work at Purdue University in Industrial Engineering. His research focused on the application of operations research techniques to libraries. In 1978–1979, he spent a sabbatical year as OCLC's first Visiting Distinguished Scholar. He was appointed as Dean of the Matthew A. Baxter School of Library and Information Science at Case Western Reserve University in 1980 where he stayed until returning to OCLC in 1983 as research scientist. His research interests include authority control, subject analysis, database quality, collection management, and bibliographic relationships. He is active in IFLA and is a member of the IFLA Standing Committee of the Classification and Indexing Section.